'A delightful book. Flanders takes nothing at surface value; alongside a scholar's appetite for research she has a novelist's delight in inferring the human reason why things happen . . . *A Circle of Sisters* surely marks a significant moment both in the onward march of group biography and in the understanding of the Victorian woman' Lynne Truss, *Sunday Times*

'A *Circle of Sisters* gives an extraordinarily vivid sense of what it was like to be alive a century ago' Rachel Barnes, *Guardian*

'This family would make a fine subject for any competent biographer, but Judith Flanders is far more than competent. Having read her, you could imagine meeting all these women and knowing immediately which was which and what to talk to them about . . . Within her enthralling and often amusing narrative are innumerable snapshots of other characters whose lives touched on those of the sisters: Rossetti, for instance, and William Morris, Gladstone and George Eliot, all of them caught unbuttoned and unposed, and all the more intriguing and convincing for that. And the details of Victorian life are marvellous . . . she brings Victorian England alive' Sue Gaisford, *Independent*

'A most impressive debut: a scholarly, entertaining, constantly interesting biography' William Trevor

'This is a terrific book – a biography of four remarkable sisters, all at a go, and also a pageant-like exhibition of Victorian artistic and middle-class life, public and domestic. The astonishing skill of its complex narrative, and the sustaining wealth of allusion and social comment, makes it seem almost incidental that one of the sisters should have been the mother of the Prime Minister and another the mother of Rudyard Kipling' Jan Morris

'*A Circle of Sisters* is a revelation. The Macdonald sisters, each interesting in herself, but also an astonishing foursome, blow away all the tired platitudes about "Victorian women"' Roy Porter

'The Macdonald sisters were four remarkable women from a humble background, who rose to eminence and helped weave the web of power and influence in Victorian England. Judith Flanders recreates their inner and outer worlds with wit, sympathy and insight' Hilary Mantel

'A scintillating debut. The author gives fascinating insights into the lives of this brilliant group, holding her huge cast of characters firmly controlled and vividly realized in a finely maintained structure – no small feat – as she weaves her complex web of relationships, beliefs, values and social mores. An engrossing chronicle. I turned the last pages of this real tour de force, with its ingenious mix of turbulent private lives and fascinating background material, with real regret, and its aroma has haunted me for days' Penelope Hughes-Hallett

'Provides compelling insights into the extraordinary lives of the four Macdonald sisters . . . Accessibly but informatively written, this is an intriguing journey of an obscure family of women on their way to a life of splendour and influence' *Time Out*

'*A Circle of Sisters* wears its learning lightly, weaving the supporting evidence into the fabric of this curious tale of four sisters who fortuitously made rather good marriages . . . This is a book with fascinating range and admirable control – definitely recommended' Penelope Lively, *Daily Mail*

ABOUT THE AUTHOR

Judith Flanders is a writer and journalist. *A Circle of Sisters* is her first book. She is currently working on her next book, on domestic life in the nineteenth century. She lives in London.

A Circle of Sisters

*Alice Kipling, Georgiana Burne-Jones,
Agnes Poynter and Louisa Baldwin*

JUDITH FLANDERS

PENGUIN BOOKS

PENGUIN BOOKS

Published by the Penguin Group
Penguin Books Ltd, 80 Strand, London WC2R 0RL, England
Penguin Putnam Inc., 375 Hudson Street, New York, New York 10014, USA
Penguin Books Australia Ltd, 250 Camberwell Road, Camberwell, Victoria 3124, Australia
Penguin Books Canada Ltd, 10 Alcorn Avenue, Toronto, Ontario, Canada M4V 3B2
Penguin Books India (P) Ltd, 11 Community Centre, Panchsheel Park, New Delhi – 110 017, India
Penguin Books (NZ) Ltd, Cnr Rosedale and Airborne Roads, Albany, Auckland, New Zealand
Penguin Books (South Africa) (Pty) Ltd, 24 Sturdee Avenue, Rosebank 2196, South Africa

Penguin Books Ltd, Registered Offices: 80 Strand, London WC2R 0RL, England

www.penguin.com

First published by Viking 2001
Published in Penguin Books 2002
13

Set in Monotype Bembo
Printed in England by Clays Ltd, St Ives plc

ISBN-13: 978–0–14–028489–8

www.greenpenguin.co.uk

Mixed Sources
Product group from well-managed
forests and other controlled sources
www.fsc.org Cert no. SA-COC-1592
© 1996 Forest Stewardship Council
FSC

Penguin Books is committed to a sustainable future
for our business, our readers and our planet.
The book in your hands is made from paper
certified by the Forest Stewardship Council.

For F.M.T.

Contents

List of Illustrations

Inset 1

George and Hannah Macdonald, *c.* 1865 (*Reproduced by courtesy of the Librarian and Director, the John Rylands Library: University of Manchester; by courtesy of Helen Macdonald*)

Harry, Caroline, Fred and Edith Macdonald (*By courtesy of Helen Macdonald*)

Alice, Georgiana, Agnes and Louisa Macdonald (*By courtesy of Helen Macdonald*)

Edward Burne-Jones, *King's Daughters*, 1858 (*The Trustees of the Bowood Collection*)

Alice and Lockwood Kipling, *c.* 1864–5; Rudyard Kipling, *c.* 1871 (*Reproduced by permission of the National Trust*)

Dante Gabriel Rossetti, *Georgie Burne-Jones*, 1860; Georgiana Burne-Jones, woodcut; Edward Burne-Jones, early 1860s (*Private collection; the Trustees of the Victoria & Albert Museum; The Maas Collection*)

Edward Burne-Jones, *Georgie at the piano*, early 1860s (© *Christie's Images/ Christopher Wood*)

The Burne-Jones and Morris families, *c.* 1874 (*By courtesy of the National Portrait Gallery, London*)

Edward Poynter, *Agnes Poynter*, 1866; Edward Poynter, 1883 (*By courtesy of Helen Macdonald; National Portrait Gallery, London*)

Edward Poynter, *Louisa Baldwin*, 1868; Stanley Baldwin, 1876; Alfred Baldwin in later life (© *reserved; Hulton Getty; Worcestershire Record Office*)

Inset 2

Text illustrations

Every effort has been made to contact all copyright holders. The publishers will be glad to correct in future editions any error or omission brought to their attention.

Acknowledgements

I would like to thank the following for their help in writing this book: Juliet Annan, Meryl Macdonald Bendle, John Christian, Robert Cohen, John Dee, Peter Funnell, Robin Gibson, Charlotte Greig, Tonie and Valmai Holt, Alison Inglis, Gráinne Kelly, Sharad Keskar, Andrew Kidd (who came up with the title), Jeffery Lewins, Lisa Lewis, Andrew Lycett, Helen Macdonald, Sara Marafini, Fiona Markham, Jan Marsh, Douglas Matthews, David Miller, John Radcliffe, Charles Saumarez-Smith, John Singleton, John Slater, Fergal Tobin, Anya Waddington and Christopher Walker. Bob Davenport, by his sympathetic and intelligent editing, made every paragraph read more smoothly.

I am indebted to the following individuals, institutions and libraries: the Bodleian Library; Brompton Cemetery; the British Library; the Hon. Simon Howard, Castle Howard, for permission to quote from the papers of the 9th Earl and Countess of Carlisle, with special thanks to Alison Brisby and Chris Ridgway; the Carl A. Kroch Library, Cornell University; Edinburgh University; Eton College; the Fitzwilliam Museum; the Harry Ransom Humanities Research Center, University of Texas at Austin, in particular Steve Lawson; the Houghton Library, Harvard University; the Huntington Library; the John Rylands Library, Manchester University; the Kipling Society; the Library of Congress; the London Library; McGill University Library; the National Gallery; the National Portrait Gallery; the National Trust for Places of Historic Interest or Natural Beauty, for permission to quote from the works of Rudyard Kipling; the Pitt-Rivers Museum, in particular Elizabeth Edwards; the Probate Office; the Public Record Office of Northern Ireland; Queen's University, Belfast; the Royal Academy; the Royal Institute of British Architects; the Tate Gallery; the University of Birmingham; the University of British Columbia; University College London; the University of Sussex, especially Elizabeth Inglis; A. P. Watt; the Worcester Public Record Office. I am also indebted to the two individuals who allowed me access to their collections who wish to remain anonymous.

Finally, my thanks to Ravi Mirchandani, who gave me the best advice I received. When I first began to think about this book he said, 'Great subject. Don't talk about it. Write it.'

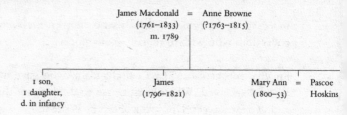

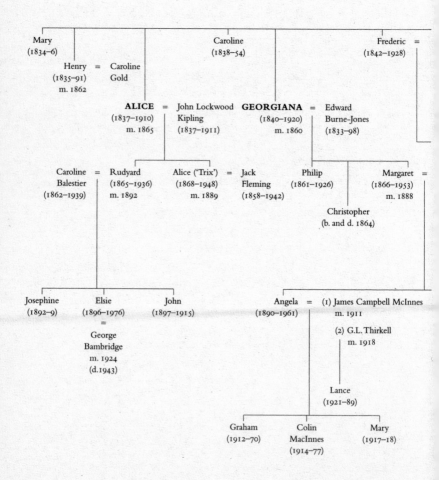

James Macdonald = Anne Browne
(1761–1833)   (?1763–1815)
m. 1789

1 son,   James   Mary Ann = Pascoe
1 daughter,   (1796–1821)   (1800–53)   Hoskins
d. in infancy

Mary   Caroline   Frederic =
(1834–6)   (1838–54)   (1842–1928)

    Henry = Caroline
    (1835–91) Gold
    m. 1862

        ALICE = John Lockwood   GEORGIANA = Edward
        (1837–1910) Kipling   (1840–1920)   Burne-Jones
        m. 1865   (1837–1911)   m. 1860   (1833–98)

Caroline = Rudyard   Alice ('Trix') = Jack   Philip   Margaret =
Balestier (1865–1936) (1868–1948)   Fleming   (1861–1926)   (1866–1953)
(1862–1939) m. 1892   m. 1889   (1858–1942)   m. 1888

                                              Christopher
                                              (b. and d. 1864)

Josephine Elsie   John   Angela = (1) James Campbell McInnes
(1892–9)   (1896–1976) (1897–1915)   (1890–1961)   m. 1911
           =
           George   (2) G.L. Thirkell
           Bambridge   m. 1918
           m. 1924
           (d.1943)
                                                    Lance
                                                    (1921–89)

                        Graham   Colin   Mary
                        (1912–70)   MacInnes   (1917–18)
                                    (1914–77)

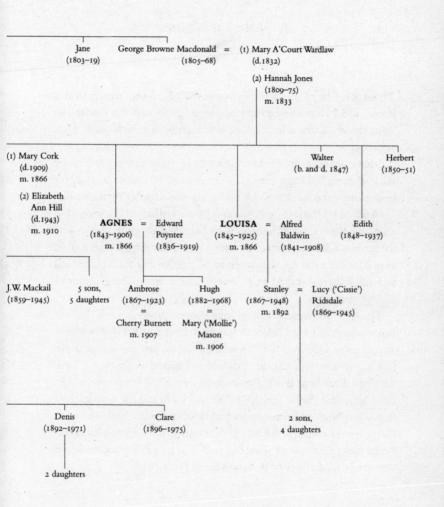

Jane
(1803–19)

George Browne Macdonald
(1805–68)

= (1) Mary A'Court Wardlaw
(d.1832)

(2) Hannah Jones
(1809–75)
m. 1833

(1) Mary Cork
(d.1909)
m. 1866

(2) Elizabeth
Ann Hill
(d.1943)
m. 1910

Walter
(b. and d. 1847)

Herbert
(1850–51)

AGNES
(1843–1906)
m. 1866

= Edward
Poynter
(1836–1919)

LOUISA
(1845–1925)
m. 1866

= Alfred
Baldwin
(1841–1908)

Edith
(1848–1937)

J.W. Mackail
(1859–1945)

5 sons,
5 daughters

Ambrose
(1867–1923)
=
Cherry Burnett
m. 1907

Hugh
(1882–1968)
=
Mary ('Mollie')
Mason
m. 1906

Stanley
(1867–1948)
m. 1892

= Lucy ('Cissie')
Ridsdale
(1869–1945)

Denis
(1892–1971)

Clare
(1896–1975)

2 sons,
4 daughters

2 daughters

The Macdonald Family

A Note on Names

There are a large number of people with the same names in this book, and I have tried to rationalize usage so that the reader can immediately know which James Macdonald, or which 'Jack', I am referring to.

I have called most of the characters by their first names, or by what they called each other. Louie instead of Louisa was almost invariable. John Lockwood Kipling was called John by his family, Lockwood by the rest of the world; I have settled on Lockwood so that later there is no confusion with his grandson John. Agnes was sometimes called Agnes, sometimes Aggie. I have stuck with Agnes, as to a modern ear Aggie is taken to be a nickname for Agatha (and was indeed reproduced so in one of the standard biographies of Baldwin).

Those with the same names have proved more difficult. Burne-Jones was called Ned Jones in youth, Edward Burne-Jones thereafter. I have followed the chronology for his last name, but as his brother-in-law was also an Edward – Edward Poynter – I have usually called them Burne-Jones and Poynter. Where these would have appeared silly – 'Burne-Jones and Georgie' for example – I have used Ned for Burne-Jones and Edward for Poynter. Margaret Burne-Jones and Trix Kipling both married men named John and called Jack; I have used their last names as much as possible, as no one ever called either of them anything but Jack.

Introduction

I first came across the Macdonald sisters when reading a biography of Rudyard Kipling. Around him as a little boy in Southsea were his mother's sisters: one the wife of Burne-Jones, another the mother of Stanley Baldwin, a third the wife of the director of the National Gallery, Edward Poynter. Looking further, I saw that all the many biographies of the men in the family – of Kipling, of Burne-Jones, of Baldwin – mention that the sisters were the wives or mothers of famous men as an interesting fact, but not an important one. There have been two biographies of the sisters, one by Stanley Baldwin's son Windham Baldwin in 1960, and one by Ina Taylor, in 1987, but neither was received in the way the 'male' biographies were. This made me think more about biography, and what its function is. Can it really be that our families have so little influence on our lives that they can safely be tucked away in Chapter 1, and thereafter disregarded?

It seemed to me that families are one of the two most important influences in our lives – families and domestic life. Yet it is only in the last decade that biographies treat both in anything other than a subsidiary fashion. They are women's topics, not important enough in the big male world for full-scale treatment, and until recently they have been traditionally displaced into the 'women's read', which is fiction. While families and domestic life are what we all share, so much of history was being written off with a brief 'They were just like us.' Was this the case? Is this why there is such a lack of interest in families and family life? Because they (we?) are all the same? An exploration of the creation and dissolution of a family at a different period, a look at how families lived in the mid- and high-Victorian periods, seemed a way into the mindset of a different time, and could be used as a proving ground: how were these people different from our own families? How were they the same?

★

The Macdonalds were fascinating people at a fascinating moment of time. They were there at the death of the nineteenth century – Burne-Jones, although later embraced by the Symbolists, was old-fashioned even at the height of his career, painting mythological pictures and illustrations of courtly legends while Manet was producing *Olympe*. The next generation, in particular Baldwin and Kipling, was at the forefront of the new wave, and helped create the way we perceive the twentieth century – Kipling, in his life so reactionary, was a daring modernist in his work; Baldwin was the first British politician to embrace twentieth-century techniques of campaigning such as radio and film.

Parallel to the men's story was another one which fascinated me. This was the story of domestic life. I was interested in seeing how families lived; what the ingredients were that went into making up lives. The Macdonalds gave me a wide range to cover. They started as a family that was middle class by the skin of its teeth, with little prestige and less money. The women married within their social circle, and yet by the end they were managing town houses and country houses, out in a world that as children they could barely imagine. These women were not the meek little stay-at-homes of fiction. Georgie Burne-Jones ran for local-government office the very first time women could be elected; Louisa Baldwin wrote novels; Alice Kipling published poetry. Yet their homes were the focus of their lives.

The range of possibilities for women varied both with the society each woman found herself in and with the woman herself. Before the Married Women's Property Act of 1870 – when an engaged woman could not dispose of her property without her fiancé's consent; when on marriage all her property, personal and real, passed to her husband; when she could not make a will without permission, nor enter into a contract, nor go to law, nor keep her own earnings or her own inherited money – what hope had any woman of a separate intellectual existence? After all, she had, in law, no separate physical existence: she could not sue her husband, because legally they were the same person. A modern scholar notes that 'Under married law women were classed with criminals, lunatics and minors – legally incompetent and irresponsible.'[1]

John Stuart Mill thought women's suffrage one of the most

important questions of the day; in 1866 he would petition Parliament for its consideration, and in 1869 he published his *On the Subjection of Women*. But Coventry Patmore's *The Angel in the House*, published between 1854 and 1863, was more popular, with its blend of premature death, sticky sentiment and frigid women whose life's purpose was to serve men. Tennyson followed this same pattern, creating a raft of passive, patient heroines who waited to be acted upon, rather than acting themselves. His Mariana, waiting for her man, can stand in for all of them: '"My life is dreary/He cometh not," she said.' The poet William Allingham, who was briefly engaged to Alice Macdonald, had noted that he 'could not put up with a wife without Genius', but her genius was to be 'in appreciating'.[2] (It is perhaps not surprising that his engagement to Alice was short-lived.)

In 1865 Ruskin published his essay 'Of Queens' Gardens', in which he laid out his considered views on the separate roles of men and women. He judged that woman's 'intellect is not for invention or creation, but for sweet ordering, arrangement, and decision . . . Her great function is Praise.' Woman must be 'wise, not for self-development, but for self-renunciation'. 'All such knowledge should be given her as may enable her to understand, and even to aid, the work of men: and yet it should be given, not as knowledge, – not as if it were, or could be, for her an object to know; but only to feel, and to judge.' 'Speaking broadly, a man ought to know any language or science he learns, thoroughly – while a woman ought to know the same language, or science, only so far as may enable her to sympathise in her husband's pleasures, and in those of his best friends.'[3] Women, in other words, were supposed to be self-denying to a pathological degree; they were supposed to be that interesting psychological paradox, fragile pillars of strength.

Given the weight of public opinion, it is not surprising that the Macdonald sisters in many ways ended by fulfilling the roles allotted to women, although at some cost. Their experiences varied widely, and illustrated the possibilities that women saw (if only unconsciously) opening before them. Georgie Burne-Jones stopped her own work and instead 'echoed' her husband's art, painting his designs on to tiles and embroidering yet more designs on to fabric. Alice Kipling saw herself as integral to her husband's career – she knew that he would get along faster, and further, with her on board. Louisa Baldwin's and Agnes Poynter's husbands needed no help and, perhaps because of this, Louisa and Agnes retreated to the sickroom. They were, in many ways, absentee wives and mothers; they accrued power to themselves by their fragility. They were vortexes around which family life whirled. No one could fail to be aware of them, but it was awareness of an absence, not a presence. They are, similarly, absent presences in this book. I felt it was important to show not just that they were 'missing', but the group dynamic, and it was one that operated on the premiss that they were not there.

As a result, Alice and, in particular, Georgie, and their families, come to the foreground of the story. In the main, I think that this was actually the way the families functioned – Alice and Georgie managed and organized; Louisa and Agnes were managed and organized.* Inevitably, this emphasis also is a function of what material has survived. The Burne-Jones family carefully hoarded material, as did several of Burne-Jones's women friends. Most of this has found its way into public collections. The Kipling family, by contrast, were great destroyers, and, although more than 6,000 letters by Rudyard Kipling survive, his letters to Alice and Lockwood, his parents, were for the most part destroyed on their deaths. What does remain is, however, extremely enlightening, as are his parents' letters.

The Poynter family was dispersed soon after the deaths of Agnes and Edward Poynter. Letter-hoarding could not have been paramount in their sons' minds. Much of the material that has survived is by Edward Poynter, and relates solely to his working life. That in itself I found noteworthy. Burne-Jones, Lockwood and Rudyard

---

* This shadowy existence for Louisa in particular is exacerbated by the fact that Earl and Countess Baldwin refused me permission to see their family archive, even though this archive is maintained and administered by the Worcester Public Record Office at the taxpayers' expense. Lady Baldwin has been thinking of writing a book of her own on the subject of the sisters, and is therefore guarding the material from outside researchers. Fortunately, much of it has been seen by biographers of Kipling and Baldwin, and, through conversations and correspondence with many of them, I don't feel that any of the main outlines of the story are lost to me, although some corroborating detail remains to be filled in when restrictions on the archive are eventually lifted.

all wrote letters that merged business and domestic affairs as a matter of routine; Poynter was the only one to segregate his professional from his family life. In the 150 letters he wrote to George Howard, Earl of Carlisle, there are just two references to his wife – one saying that she is ill, and so Carlisle can't be asked to dinner; one that 'we' have returned from holiday. That this scanty gleaning is the sum total from a decade's correspondence is surely revealing. Carlisle's wife, Rosalind, was on visiting terms with Agnes; Poynter had known Carlisle for more than thirty years. There seemed to be no reason for Poynter not to mention his wife, unless it was that he rarely thought of her himself.

One question that I became aware of as I progressed was, What, precisely, does a family consist of? Parents and children seemed the obvious answer. But when does a person stop being part of one family, and start to become part of another? To my surprise, it was very obvious when it happened, even if the participants would not have been able to recognize the point at the time. The Macdonald siblings and their parents, Hannah and George, made up a family unit. When the girls married and had children, although their interests broadened, they didn't, for the most part, 'join' their husbands' families; they remained part of the Macdonald family. When their own children grew up and married, however, the overarching structure that had supported their lives dissolved. They stopped being the Macdonald family, and instead became part of the Burne-Jones, Kipling, Poynter and Baldwin families. It appeared that the women controlled 'family-dom' until their pro-creative and child-rearing days were over, when they then became unimportant. It was not that they stopped doing things – many of their most important contributions came after their children had left home. It was more as if both they and others suddenly felt that, now they had performed their biological function, they had somehow become invisible. Consequently the last third of the book felt very much as if all the material was flying apart rather than cohering. I think that this is appropriate – the family was flying apart, and this literary sense is a reflection of the very real forces at work in its members' stories. There was a circular rhythm in place that mimicked the rhythm of family life, as they went from a family (as children) to individuals (adolescents and young married life) to a family (with young children) to individuals (after the children left home).

The dynamism of family life mirrored the times. From the birth of Alice soon after Queen Victoria came to the throne, to their dispersal at the end of the long Edwardian summer, the Macdonalds were a prime example of the fluidity and social mobility that characterized the age. British society has always been permeable to money, but in the nineteenth century it became permeable to talent to an extent that had rarely occurred before. Alfred Baldwin, Louisa's husband, reached the upper echelons of society in the old-fashioned way – he made so much money that he was invited to join the club. Poynter and Burne-Jones were accepted by the aristocracy in a new way. Previously when an artist was taken up by a patron it was he alone who was fêted, not his family. By the mid nineteenth century the rigidity of that code was softened enough for wives and children to take part in the rise: Georgie Burne-Jones went with her husband to Hawarden to visit the Gladstones; the Earl and Countess of Carlisle had them to stay at Naworth Castle and invited them both to dinner with Princess Louise, Queen Victoria's artist daughter; their children played with the children of their aristocratic friends and patrons. Even so, all parties were aware of the differences in their social standing, and, while the Baldwins effortlessly joined the upper classes, the Burne-Joneses always remained slightly in awe of their social 'superiors'.

The routes they had taken had marked them. Even in the next generation, Kipling, for one, despite his outward appearance as a country squire, never really felt he belonged. By the time *their* children, in turn, reached adulthood, the aspirant world of their grandparents was barely a memory: Elsie Kipling and her husband bought a forty-four-bedroom house in Cambridgeshire and lived like their landed neighbours; Phil Burne-Jones was in every way the stylish man about town, living off his patrimony just as his friends lived off theirs. That his was his father's art, theirs land or industry, was a detail that if anything Phil thought elevated him above the common herd. In effect, they had become part of the twentieth century rather than the nineteenth: what you were was now beginning to be more important than where you had come from.

I began to research the Macdonald sisters because they represented an extraordinary family. What I found as I continued was that, remarkable as they were, the relationships they developed, the feuds, the fondness, the friendships, were ultimately so ordinary. The Macdonalds were both of their own time and yet our contemporaries. In the personal and social journeys they made they were creatures of an exceptional moment in history, a social drama set in a privileged time and place, while in the ordinary dynamics of their relationships with each other they were us.

I
Childhood

1. Inheritance

Four women connect four men by a slender but steely thread. One man is an earl, and three times prime minister; the second a Nobel prizewinner who turned down a knighthood, the Poet Laureateship and the Order of Merit; the third is a baronet and leading Pre-Raphaelite painter; and the fourth is also a baronet, who has been both director of the National Gallery and president of the Royal Academy. The thread is the Macdonald sisters – four women who were the mothers of Stanley Baldwin and Rudyard Kipling and the wives of Edward Burne-Jones and Edward Poynter.

Louisa Baldwin, Alice Kipling, Georgiana Burne-Jones and Agnes Poynter were not the children of privilege. Their father had been a Methodist preacher, middle class by virtue of his calling, to be sure, but without either the income to support a family in comfortable middle-class style or the approbation of society which membership in the more socially acceptable Church of England would have brought.

Their great-grandfather, John Macdonald, had left Skye between 1745 and 1760, after the second Jacobite uprising. The family were later to claim descent from Flora Macdonald of Skye, and for many decades brandished their Celtic heritage. At best Flora may have been a fifth cousin by marriage to John Macdonald. He decided to put the turmoil that was eighteenth-century Scotland behind him, and family legend says that he planned to go to Canada, as so many emigrants of the time did. He may have changed his mind; he may have run out of money; the legend may have been wrong. Whatever the case, he settled only a short hop away from his homeland, in northern Ireland.

By 1761 John was a smallholder, living in Ballinamallard, near Enniskillen, and his son James was born that year. At some point John Macdonald or his wife had heard the preacher John Wesley, whose evangelical mission had first brought him to Ireland in 1747, and whose success there enabled him to plant the seeds of a constituency that was to flourish and grow throughout the next century. In 1784, when James Macdonald was twenty-three, Wesley decided to ordain some of his most promising followers, in order to establish the succession after his death. James Macdonald was one of those ordained directly by Wesley, and he immediately began the wandering life of a Methodist minister, sent to ten different postings in Ireland in the next ten years.★

His grandson Fred gives a picture of a serious young man, conscious of his lack of formal education and determined to make up for it:

By great self-denial and strict economy of time, amidst constant journeyings on foot and on horseback through the wide circuits to which he was appointed, without teachers or companions in learning, his pursuit of knowledge was such as would have done credit to a student with all the opportunities and appliances at his command. He became a good Latin scholar and learnt enough Greek and Hebrew to read the Scriptures in the original tongues ... He acquired an excellent knowledge of French and could read Italian and Spanish.[1]

He was a powerhouse, with an unquenchable drive for work. Later in his life he complained to his son that in the following six weeks he had to preach 'on the week-days but about ten times', and that he could do with more work; also, 'If I could plan a literary work I could not find a more favourable time for executing it.'[2]

In 1789, aged twenty-eight, the Revd James Macdonald married Anne Browne. She came from a farming family, and had lost her grandfather and two uncles in the 'French War' when they were press-ganged into the Navy and never returned. The Macdonalds' first child, a daughter, was born in Newry in 1791; before her fourth birthday she was dead. Their second child, a son, fared no better, also dying when he was three. In 1795 James and Anne sailed to England, leaving behind their two infants' graves. With the minister's new appointment in Chester, all connection with

★ His itinerary from 1784 to 1794 was Ballyconnell, Charlemont, Longford, Londonderry, Castlebar, Newry, Belfast, Dublin, Lisburn, then back to Newry again.

Ireland ceased. A new son, James Jr, to go with this new life, was born in Chester in May 1796. This time the child thrived.

Like all Methodist ministers, James was moved regularly to a new station, sometimes as often as every year, and three more children were born as the family progressed around the industrial heartland that was to be James's focus for the next decade: Mary Ann in Liverpool in 1800; Jane in Halifax in 1803; George Browne (after his mother's family, and perhaps in memory of his lost great-grandfather because he was born just three weeks before the Battle of Trafalgar) in Stockport in 1805.

James Macdonald was clearly a formidable man, with a strong sense of right and wrong. His sense of humour may have been equally well developed. His grandson remembers a family story that tells of his

dislike of evil-speaking [which] was a marked feature of his character . . . in one instance where an absent person was spoken of by one and another in severe terms, after endeavouring to give another turn to the conversation, he silenced the company by saying, 'This must indeed be a bad man; let us pray for him,' kneeling down then and there . . . He heard no more evil-speaking from those who were present.[3]

James Macdonald and the Methodists were part of a great evangelical revival which occurred towards the end of the eighteenth century, a movement informed by the new urban, industrial world that was being created. The response of many was to turn to an active form of religion: one that stressed the religious in everyday life, with the emphasis on deeds rather than theology, the Bible rather than priestly function, and living a daily life that was permeated with a love of God and righteousness – all the ingredients of what is now perceived as High Victorianism.

Within this religious upsurge Methodists occupied an odd niche. They were still part of the Church of England, until the end of the nineteenth century, but at the same time they were separated from it by an urgency and immediacy in their religious affairs that was not shared by their Anglican brethren. The sober, self-improving cast of their lives, together with active participation in church life, meant that most socializing was done inside the Church rather than out: chapel services, weekly class meetings, tea meetings, bazaars, choir groups, temperance-society meetings and fund-raising for the Missionary Society – all took up the small time not given to work and home.

The focus of James's hopes and ambitions was his eldest son, a precociously intelligent boy. Young James 'became almost the constant companion of his father, reading and studying with him, and such was the progress that he made in his various studies, and in knowledge generally, that his father would, before he was fifteen years old, consult him with advantage on most subjects of which he was writing'.[4] In 1811 the minister had been sent to London, where he was the assistant editor of the *Methodist Magazine*. Young James worked in the Methodist Book-Room and studied in his spare time. George, the youngest, was sent to Woodhouse Grove, the Methodist boarding school in Yorkshire, at the age of ten, in 1815. While he was clearly a good, diligent boy, he did not shine in his father's eyes as James did. The Revd James Macdonald confided to young James that after George had been a year at school he was 'pleased with his progress', but when he heard that George had written a prize essay it was natural to him to ask James, 'Did you give him any assistance?' George was not expected to flourish on his own, apart from his brilliant brother, but by the age of fourteen he had shown his mettle: the school committee offered to keep him on for an extra year, on condition that he became an assistant master, his family paying £12 for the privilege.

James Macdonald's income at the time was £83 10s. per annum, which he said was enough for them to manage on: a pound a week for himself and the household expenses, 16 guineas a year for his wife, and 14 guineas a year for the servant's wages. The £12 could be scraped together for George, his father noting that 'The circumstances of your having to devote part of every day to teaching is to me *highly* satisfactory, as your being so employed will make you still better acquainted with the rudiments of Greek and Latin, and be an additional stimulus.'[5] There was, however, no money for university for either boy. Instead when young James turned twenty he took a job as an assistant master at a small school. He clearly had a winning way as well as intelligence: within a year the owner of the school offered to lend him the money to go to

Cambridge. After a conference with his father it was decided that his increased earning potential would mean that after university the money could be repaid. In October 1818 James entered Queens' College, Cambridge, leaving only the two girls at home.

His sister Jane was now showing the first signs of consumption, the killer of the time. In 1815 her mother, Anne, had died in her early fifties. It is not clear what it was that killed her – it may have been consumption, which, unknown to the Victorians, was highly contagious and was also often caught from contaminated sources like tubercular milk, which all the family had in common. By 1819 Jane too was dead. Worse was to follow. In February 1821 James left Cambridge because of his health. His father was distraught. All 'his hopes and affections were centred in his son',[6] who was clearly going as Anne had gone, and as Jane had gone. George was brought back from school in Yorkshire, and James distributed his few possessions: his watch to Mary Ann, his Bible to George. By September he was dead, and it seemed as if his father's hopes had died with him.

George now became the focus for the kind of attention that James had thrived on. His father urged him to 'carry a Greek Testament with you wherever you go, that when you have a few minutes' leisure you may read some part of it';[7] also 'Be sure to apply yourself diligently to your learning. This is your indispensable duty. Never be a moment unemployed, or triflingly employed. Be serious, but not demure. Oh, George, be steadfast, immovable, as I trust you will, that you may be happy in time and in eternity.'[8]

Life for George was not only mentally and emotionally rigorous – it was physically so. Before the railways, stagecoaches were a luxury and, once the family were sent back to the north from London, there was one obvious way of seeing them without spending too much. When George was only fourteen, his father wrote:

I rejoice in the prospect of having you at home for a few weeks shortly ... Mr. Laycock and I are agreed that you and his James are to walk home. You are to come as far as Halifax the day you leave the Grove. Mr. Myles or Mr. Whiteside will procure you both lodging and food. You may walk the next forenoon to Heptonstall, and stop there all night, or take Mr. Laycock's pony to Todmorden after dinner. I should be ashamed to think that you would regard walking twelve, or fifteen, or even twenty miles for a day or two together as a hardship. You can rest yourselves for an hour or two at Mr. Elwell's of Shelf.[9]*

His life was rigorous, and he was closely watched by his father, who had already lost so much: 'I would have you be on your guard against rusticity of manners . . . Study ease and propriety in your conversation, and never talk carelessly. Keep at an equal distance from drawling on the one hand, and precipitancy on the other. Be thoroughly sincere and upright, and let your language be that of the heart.'[10]

By the age of eighteen he was back in London. The Revd Macdonald now had a ministry in Portsmouth, and watched him anxiously from afar: 'Being handsome, genial, sociable and fond of jokes and story-telling, he was tempting prey to the devil.'[11] To the horror of his father and sisters, for a few months he even allowed his membership of the Methodist Society to lapse. His natural ebullience of manner was, however, deceptive and his vocation was never really in doubt. At nineteen George was preaching the Hammersmith circuit in London – Brentford, Twickenham, Richmond, Isleworth, Mitcham, Harrow and Hounslow. By 1825 he was received as a minister on trial, and within a few months the Methodist Conference confirmed his appointment as a full minister. He was immediately sent to Devonport, where his father also had an appointment.

George was, even for the time, on the short side of average: five foot six, although his broad shoulders and deep chest made him appear bigger. His high spirits were un-Methodist-like to some, but according to his youngest daughter this hid a deeper nature, and, although he 'said of himself that trouble rolled off him like water off a duck's back, under his frank, open manner lay funds of reserve; of what he felt most deeply he found it difficult to speak'.[12] This was to be a recurring trait in all his children.

---

* Both the place names and the family situation remind one of another minister's family, later to live close by at Haworth Parsonage, particularly as while George was at Woodhouse Grove the headmaster's niece, Maria Branwell, had married the local curate, Patrick Brontë.

At sixty-four, James Macdonald was reaching the end of his professional life. His pride in and care for his cheerful, vigorous son, following so closely in his own footsteps as he was preparing to retire, were extreme and extremely touching. As always, much advice was offered, now almost entirely on the practice rather than the theology of religion:

Take time in preaching, and stand sufficiently erect, that your lungs may take in a sufficient quantity of air . . . Sound the consonants well; in doing this you cannot avoid sounding the vowels. Do not study intensely before going into the pulpit. It drinks up the animal spirits, a considerable portion of which it is necessary in order to preach comfortably. In short, go into the pulpit in a devotional spirit; but take care that you do not *tear a passion in rags*.[13]

In 1826 James Macdonald was made supernumerary* in Portsmouth, and two years later George was sent to Manchester – his first ministry on the northern circuit where he was to spend so much of his life. In 1831 his father had a slight stroke, affecting his speech and partially paralysing his right side. Perhaps so that he could be near his invalid father, George was sent to Bristol, the only circuit outside the industrial north that he was to hold for the next twenty-five years.

It was either at this time or during his earlier tour of the south-west that George met and married Mary A'Court Wardlaw. Apart from her name, virtually nothing is known of her, or of this marriage. The only thing that is certain is that by 1832 she was to die at her father's house in Dorset. She was followed just eighteen months later by her father-in-law, James. George did not leave his posting in Bristol until 1835, but within a year of Mary's death he had remarried. He had met Hannah Jones during his ministry in Manchester, and it was with her that he was to make his life.

---

* Methodist-speak for 'retired'.

2. 'So entirely domestic'
1835–1850

In 1835 George returned to the nearest thing he had to home. Despite his brief sojourn in the West Country, his childhood had been spent with his father on the northern circuit and he had gone to school near Bradford. Now, in Sheffield, he was back in familiar country.

In the early part of the century the north was fertile territory for the Methodists: both rich and middle class, the newly urbanized areas found in evangelical religion a sense of community that had been lost with the population movement from country to town. With this impetus, the evangelicals reached their apogee in that period of transition from agriculture to industry, and the middle classes were at the forefront of this rise. In the north and Midlands, Nonconformists made up more than 50 per cent of total church attendances in Bradford, Leeds, Oldham, Wolverhampton and Sheffield, and between 40 and 50 per cent in Birmingham, Manchester, Salford and Newcastle. After the Roman Catholics, Anglicans were in the minority in all the main manufacturing districts.* Industrial growth and the vast influx of people made the north a place of possibility, of change. With the creation of a greatly expanded middle class, the Nonconformist Churches saw potential for new recruits wherever they looked.

Hannah Jones was the daughter of John and Mary Jones of Manchester, the very kind of people who were now embracing an evangelical way of life. John Jones was a wholesale grocer who had prospered in the economic boom of the early part of the century and, together with his wife, had brought up four girls and two boys in substantial comfort. Being a wholesaler was rather grander then than now. The warehouses of Manchester were regarded by many as 'more impressive' than the mills, representing 'the essentials

---

* Although the Methodists were officially still part of the Established Church, in a social context it is helpful to think of them as Nonconformists.

of Manchester's trade, the very reason for her existence'. The Manchester Exchange, extended in 1838, was a sign of growing mercantile prosperity; in 1836, one scandalized writer reports, warehouse space was being rented for 14 shillings per square yard.[1]

The four daughters of John Jones received a more than usually advanced education for girls of the time, which included some Latin, Italian and theory of music. The main emphasis, however, was on the more ordinary girlish accomplishments. As well as the standards – she wrote verse; she was 'musical' – Hannah took great pride in her leatherwork, fashionable in the early part of the century. The family attended chapel regularly together, and at some point in the late 1820s Hannah met the cheerful new minister. She was a good contrast to his ebullience. Although she was not pretty – her mouth was too small, her hair too thin – she had a quiet, dignified manner, a general air of calm control. Perhaps this was the attraction after the upheavals George had suffered in the previous year: the loss of his first wife, his dying father. Whatever the case, in 1833, two days before her twenty-fourth birthday, at the Collegiate Church, Manchester (later to become Manchester Cathedral), George Browne Macdonald and Hannah Jones were married.

Hannah may have been taking on more than she knew. The life of a minister's family was not easy. Although George was not like the itinerant preachers, proselytizing in fields, his calling ensured that he was often away from home for several days each week. In addition, the family moved to a new town every three years, with George's new ministries. And, of course, there was not much money. A house was provided rent-free by the Conference, but in the early days George's annual income was only about £150. (In 1841, one of the few years for which we have a precise record, George's salary was £163 16s., his outgoings £162 5s. 1d.) At the beginning this was plenty, but as child succeeded child the houses seemed to get smaller and smaller, as did their resources, while the work involved in keeping house and ensuring that eight children were properly clothed, fed and educated seemed to grow ever greater.

And the houses filled with children in rapid order. Ten months after her marriage Hannah gave birth to her first child, named Mary Rawlinson Macdonald after Hannah's mother. She seemed a sturdy enough infant, blonde and plump. Yet shortly after her second birthday she began to go blind, and she was dead before she was three. This was particularly hard, as Hannah was by now nursing her second child and first son, Harry. For the following fourteen years, one child following hard on the heels of the last was to be the pattern: every eighteen months a new baby appeared, to be nursed for a year, then weaned as Hannah became pregnant with the next. The children's birthplaces map an itinerary of their father's appointments, as the growing household trailed along behind him, in much the same way that James Macdonald's children had followed him. After Harry, Alice was born in Sheffield in 1837; then Caroline and Georgiana in Birmingham in 1838 and 1840; Frederic and Agnes in Leeds in 1842 and 1843; Louisa in Wakefield in 1845; and Edith in Huddersfield in 1848. There were two more small coffins: Walter died in 1847 a month after his birth, and Herbert struggled on for only a short time more, dying in 1851.

While infant deaths were not unexpected, they were none the less traumatic. Hannah wrote to one of her sisters that, when Herbert's death was broken to the children, Louie, then aged five, said:

'Have we only 8 children now?' On being answered she wept: 'I'm crying because we only have 8 children.' My thoughts are incessantly reverting to my last darling. I have a feeling of desolation in my heart. O how I wish you could have seen him, his beauty was most touching to behold, stamped with the marble hue of death . . . I miss him from my arm and sadly I miss him from the bosom that sustained him, in which the well spring of life is not dried up . . . You will perhaps be ready to wonder that I should be so greatly afflicted. I almost wonder myself. My life is so entirely domestic, so completely merged in those of my husband and children that the loss of one out of my circle, though it be the least and latest, makes a fearful blank in my heart.[2]

These deaths were hard to assimilate, particularly as Hannah had successfully reared eight healthy children in the seven years following Mary's death. Current religious belief told parents that a child's death was a dispensation of providence, taking the child into a better world. It certainly felt so to the parents who could only sit and watch their children die. Hannah wrote to a friend that death was the only prospect of relief for her suffering baby Walter. Grieving parents were told they should see a child's death as a challenge to their faith and humility before God. If they mourned their lost child, they were refusing God's lesson of submission, and harbouring the sin of pride. This was not easy; the loss of children reverberated through the whole family. Louie was particularly delicate and nervous. Once, when feverish, she was found warming her hands in front of a door, thinking it a fire, saying, 'I am going to a little child's funeral.'[3] Louie was not unusual; children's funerals loomed large, and it was not at all uncommon for small children to play 'Funerals' instead of 'Mummies and Daddies'.[4]

Despite the loss of the babies, the eight surviving children made their houses seem full to overflowing: as well as the immediate family of ten, there were a nursemaid for the current infant and a servant (soon to become two, a cook and a housemaid), and for some months George even shared his study with one of Hannah's brothers. It was common for married couples to take in unmarried or widowed relations, and after Hannah and George's marriage Mary Ann, George's sister, lived with them for some years after their father's death, until she herself married. As they moved from town to town, servants had to be persuaded to stay on (or new ones had to be found), George's library of more than 1,000 books had to be packed up (and unpacked at the other end), and furniture had to be crated, uncrated, rearranged, new curtains made, carpets altered to fit. Most of this had to be done in George's absence, as he criss-crossed the district on preaching engagements. Given Hannah's phenomenal rate of childbearing, most of it had to be done while pregnant – for example, she packed up, moved herself and the children from Sheffield to Birmingham, unpacked, settled, found a school for Harry and started him there, all a mere seven weeks before giving birth to Caroline.

As Hannah acknowledged in her letter to her sister, her life was almost 'entirely domestic'. It was hardly surprising. Housekeeping took up an enormous amount of time. Even with the help of two servants, it was a heroic undertaking simply to keep a house clean. An average household burned a ton of coal every six weeks. Apart from the labour involved in carrying coal around the house, the dirt thrown out by the fires was immense. Until the 1890s, coal rather than gas ranges were used in the kitchen for cooking and heating water, and it was only in the 1880s that 'close' ranges were sold widely. Hannah's cook would have had an open-hearth range. The chimney in the kitchen needed to be swept every six weeks,★ and in addition once or twice a week the cook needed to sweep it as far as she could reach, otherwise soot would fall down into the food beneath. In the sort of houses Hannah and George were given, running water (cold) would be restricted to the scullery and was probably available for only a limited number of hours each day. Gas lighting was just beginning to filter down to the houses of the middle classes, and oil and paraffin lamps were filthy and time-consuming to fill and maintain. It could take a day to clean one room thoroughly, given that detergents had yet to be dreamed of. Then there were all sorts of jobs that with the arrival of modern sanitation were to disappear. For example, young housewives were warned that uncovered cisterns 'must be cleaned out at least every quarter; if covered, once a year suffices, unless the presence of a dead cat be suspected'.[6] Add to this list the laundry, which, before organic chemistry came to the aid of the housewife, took three or four days out of every fortnight, and a very restricted life outside the house was all that was possible. Although the normal routine for a practising Methodist was chapel twice a day on Sundays and 'class' at least once a week, in the early days of Hannah's married life she very often did not go to class for months on end and missed chapel on Sundays two weeks out of four. For a minister's wife this was shocking, and she was 'misunderstood sometimes in declining to undertake religious or philanthropic duties expected from a minister's wife'. Over eighty years later, Edith still felt that justification was necessary.[7]

It was lucky for Hannah that George's superiors kept him on the same circuit for much of his time, thus enabling her to stay within visiting distance of her family. For ten years after her marriage she periodically returned to Manchester to visit them. These visits continued until the death of her mother in 1843 and her father two

★ This was important, as 'every fire-engine is charged for, £5', warned Mrs Haweis, the author of *The Art of Housekeeping: A Bridal Garland*, and many other works of a similar nature.[5]

years later. With his death came the final dispersal of her 'first' family, a process that had been started by the marriages of her sisters some ten years before. The Manchester house was sold, the remaining possessions knocked down at auction. It appears that by the time of John Jones's death most of his money had disappeared, although quite how is not clear. Family myth suggested avaricious and feckless sons-in-law; the more likely explanation was that with increasing age he simply found it harder to keep up in business; the boom times were over for him. In 1852 one of Hannah's brothers emigrated to Australia, that enticing prospect for those looking for a fortune.

Hannah clung tenaciously to the family that remained behind. She was particularly close to one of her sisters, naming her second daughter Alice after her. Visits were essential, for, as if her life were not hard enough, she, along with several of her siblings, had inherited from her mother a strong depressive streak. Her youngest daughter, Edith, who lived with her until her death, diplomatically suggested that hers was a 'sensitive' temperament, in which 'every pain of body or of mind had its full weight'. Edith is very careful to separate her mother from two other siblings, who 'seemed framed neither to be happy nor to make happy',[8] but it would appear that this same tendency to melancholy was strong in Hannah too. Fred, her second son, remarked that her letters to him at school 'suggest that touch of sadness that was never far away from even her brightest moments. Her health was delicate and her spirit sensitive, and she felt the strain of a life that was not in all its details congenial to her.'[9] The letters he quotes have more than a 'touch' of sadness – it is hard to imagine an appropriate response from a fourteen-year-old to the following from his mother: 'My mind has been bordering upon distraction with the multiplicity of my cares. This removing is a growing (I was going to say evil) burden, and I think sometimes I shall sink under it – unless, indeed I never find time to do so.'[10]

Fred suggests that her religious faith carried her through these trials, but it is not clear what was supposed to carry him through the loneliness of his exile at school combined with worry about his mother and family. Edie, on the contrary, felt that religion did not save her mother from sinking under the weight of her depression, but instead was responsible for much of her hopelessness:

Religion silently moulded her whole nature, but I do not think it was a great source of happiness to her. The early Methodist training which had been hers encouraged introspection, which was not a healthy influence in her sensitive disposition. Looking within, she did not find the confident spiritual experiences which she was led to expect in a 'believer', and this saddened her. There was a melancholy tinge in the teaching which she gave to her children, which was unfortunate.[11]

This inheritance, combined with the facts of her life, makes it hardly surprising that much of Hannah's life was spent in despair. The novelist Mrs Gaskell – another Dissenting minister's wife – said that the loss of her baby would 'never heal on earth, although hardly any one knows how it has changed me'.[12] This certainly was true of Hannah. She observed the anniversaries of the deaths of her three children every year, although she made no outward show of it. George's absences hurt her deeply. She was a devout woman and recognized that he was doing God's work, but when he was away her letters took on a querulous tone that was otherwise absent.* During the Chartist uprisings in the late 1830s she worried about the safety of her family when her husband was away and sometimes kept the children in all day for fear of riots. In addition, it is perfectly clear that she loathed the forced march that was her life, the perpetual house-moving, the need to make new friends every three years and – worse – say goodbye to the old ones. 'I think I have something of the limpet in my constitution, if I may judge by the violence done to my feelings when I am torn from my rock.'[14] She had few intimate friends, relying on old

---

* The constant travel demanded of preachers by the Methodists was a source of distress to many wives. Robert Newton, one of the greatest preachers of the day and four times president of the Methodist Conference, said that the only unhappy words that had ever been spoken in his marriage were when he had been away for a long time, returned for a night, and was then to go away again the next morning. 'Mrs Newton, according to her usual practice, rose to see him comfortably provided for before his departure; and at the hour of five o'clock, as she was pouring out a cup of coffee for him, burst into tears, and said, "This is melancholy work." He said, "I left home that morning with a sad heart." It grieved him to find that his mode of life was a cause of sorrow to one who stood in so near and tender a relation to himself; but that which she for the time being felt to be "melancholy" was a source of joy and everlasting benefit to thousands.'[13]

friendships for life; her nomadic routine made each separation hard to bear.

Fred saw the results of such itinerancy in himself and his siblings:

One result . . . is that the . . . sons and daughters grow up with the least possible amount of local feeling and attachment. They do not remain in one place long enough for these to be developed. Associations both local and personal are snapped off short, and they have to begin again elsewhere with others who may or may not be of a better kind, but in any case there is change and not continuity in life's setting . . . The minister himself has little difficulty in taking up the threads of this work in a new circuit . . . but it is otherwise with his children . . .[15]

He does not seem to have recognized that the same effects might be felt by his mother. Her letters are full of plaints: the anniversary of a child's death is a day of woe; her life is filled with pain and depression almost more than she can bear; she is 'distracted' with fatigue and worries. In a letter of about 1843 she complains that 'The children have colds . . . I am so wearied of sickness and nursing in addition to my many domestic cares, that I sometimes feel almost stupefied, and fearful of sinning against God, by a sort of reckless indifference as to what may befall me.'[16]

And nursing was a major component of her life, as it was for every Victorian woman – wife, mother, sister, daughter. Along with painting watercolours and playing the piano, it was considered to be one of the things women were particularly fitted for. Hannah's offspring, like all children, were regularly at risk from various childhood dangers, through which she nursed them: chickenpox, colds, whooping cough, fevers, inflammations, sprains, falls and, that now obsolete worry, accidents involving open fires.* In addition, they had to be protected from more serious infections – removed from the vicinity of smallpox, diphtheria or scarlet fever, with cholera also a constant anxiety, as was brain fever (meningitis).

* A random sampling of causes of house fires from the logbook of the Metropolitan Fire Brigade for 1879 shows the dangers. It contains, one after the other: 'airing linen', 'children playing with lucifers', 'hot ashes', 'swinging [that is, loose] gas bracket'.

Before routine dentistry, a large number of ailments can with hind-sight all be attributed to bad teeth: as well as abscesses and fevers, neuralgia, migraines, and headaches can often be traced to the one source.

Medical intervention could be more traumatic than the illness. Painkillers were almost entirely opium-based. Given their side-effects, and the meat-heavy Victorian diet, it is therefore not surprising that constipation was a great nineteenth-century obses-sion. According to the manuals of the day, laxatives were a cure for almost everything: cases of troublesome teething should be treated with laxatives, teething rings and hot baths; for chicken-pox, more laxatives and hot baths; for croup, laxatives and hot baths, plus a blister down the throat. Even diarrhoea was treated with laxatives: infants with diarrhoea should be treated with a mixture of morphine powders and laxatives every four hours. Whooping cough, according to Mrs Beeton, was a 'purely spasmodic disease, and is only infectious through the faculty of imitation', like yawning. The patient should be made to vomit 'continuously' and be given laudanum,* hot baths – and laxatives. A 'moral regimen . . . should never be omitted'. This involved distracting the patients when they were coughing, or even using 'measures of intimidation', to stop the 'imitative' coughing.[17] It is a tribute to the skills of the family nurses that any children at all survived such regimes.

The eight Macdonald children not only survived; they flourished. Despite Hannah's woes, her children's memories are of growing up loved and cared for, surrounded by affection and friends. Unlike the children of the upper classes, who were con-signed to separate parts of the house and the care of others, or those of the lower classes, who not only had parents who worked twelve-hour days, but often had to go out to work themselves, the home life of the middle classes in the mid-Victorian age was very much as we picture it from fiction and coloured Christmas cards. The Macdonald children were high-spirited and gregarious, making friends easily. By the 1850s cheap 'Bristol toys' were available –

---

* Laudanum, that great comforter of the nineteenth century, was essentially opium diluted in brandy or other spirits.

wooden carts, horses, omnibuses, all at a penny each. Picnics, tea parties, visits to the children of congregants, all were undertaken regularly, as were charades and other forms of play-acting. The whole family went on expeditions, to Chatsworth, to King's Norton, to Newstead Abbey. The children played the piano and sang. Above all they enjoyed playing with each other: when Georgie is to visit one of her mother's sisters, Hannah fears 'she will greatly miss dear Carry, for they seem to find inexhaustible pleasure in contradicting each other, Caroline doing her part with the mildest coolest perseverance imaginable, and Georgie with all the vehemence, spluttering and wagging her head and finger, that you can conceive of. And with all this they seem particularly attached to each other . . .'[18]

One of the main sources of amusement, and friendship, was visits to other branches of the family, which were greeted with rapturous approbation by the children. Hannah took the girls to Birmingham, or Manchester, or Leeds, to see her married sisters and have a little visiting time herself; or, when she could manage it, she left them at home and went on her own. She and George also went to see Harry at his boarding school, although this could rarely be done more than once a year. When possible, the children were sent, as Hannah had been as a child, to the countryside for a 'change of air' in the summer. It was more difficult for the minister with a large family to find the money for this than it had been for the wholesale merchant. So Hannah usually took three or four of the older girls to a farmhouse where they were lodged with locals, returning home after settling them in. In a week or so she brought a couple of the younger children out and took home some of the older ones. They could rarely afford to stay for more than a fortnight. At the end of that time Hannah would take the remaining children for a day's outing as she went to collect the others. These excursions were made infinitely simpler with the coming of the railways. In the 1830s George had travelled by stagecoach; by the mid-1840s there were 2,200 miles of line across the country,[19] and rail travel was regarded as the norm, to the point where it was never mentioned.

George had a passionate love of books, and they were readily accessible to the children. Wesley had himself thought that 'the work of grace would die out in one generation if the Methodists were not a reading people'.[20] Contrary to the practice in most Victorian households, hardly anything was censored or withheld from the children. They read indiscriminately – as well as Methodist tracts and the *Methodist Magazine*, they all recalled in later life the treasures in their father's library: everything from *The Pilgrim's Progress* to Robin Hood ballads, Grimms' fairy tales to the *Edinburgh Review* and the occasional *Blackwood's Magazine*. Only Shakespeare, in keeping with the general feelings of the time, was forbidden as a little too near the knuckle. (One Methodist contemporary foamed, 'Barefaced obscenities, low vulgarity, and nauseous vice so frequently figure and pollute his pages that we cannot but lament the luckless hour in which he became a writer for the stage.' And another altered 'Under the greenwood tree who loves to lie with me' to 'Under the greenwood tree who loves to work with me', 'thus removing the possible double entendre and exalting the virtue of industry'.)[21] George regularly acquired new books, although the bulk of them were on divinity and not of great interest to the children. Books were the one thing that this very unmaterialistic man longed for, spending nearly as much on his library as he did on Harry's education.

Like most early-Victorian women, bookish or not, Hannah saw to the children's education, secular and religious, teaching them all at home when they were small. It was she who took them to chapel and to Sunday school to begin their religious educations when they were about three. Once the boys got older they began to go to schools, first locally, then further away. Harry was started at a small day school just a week after his fourth birthday, although he didn't stay there very long – after half a year Hannah decided to keep him at home a bit longer, although it is not clear whether this was a reflection on the quality of the school or on how Harry adapted to it. A few months after that he started at another school and settled down happily enough. This was fortunate, as his parents had all their hopes pinned on their first son. From his birth, half a crown a week was set aside for his future education – a large sacrifice when seen as nearly 5 per cent of their total income. At eight he was sent off to a Methodist boarding school, Wesley College, in Sheffield, where he stayed until 1850, when he was fourteen. As with most schools of the time, life at Wesley College was fairly rigorous: up at six o'clock; lessons from 6.30 to 7.30, then half an hour of football before breakfast and the real start of the day.

George, as his father had done before him, wrote regularly to his eldest son, exhorting him to achieve, grounding him in the classics when he was at home, and throughout his school career ensuring he was intimately bound up in Harry's education and moral growth. Harry initially repaid this intensive nurturing. Although he was not as quick of speech, nor as witty, as his sisters, he was a clever boy who had no trouble with any of his lessons that he put his mind to. He was, according to Fred, 'the apple of his father's eye, the son of his right hand. For biblical language seems necessary to describe the affection, hope and pride with which my father regarded his eldest son.'[22] Hannah too saw her relationship with Harry as out of the ordinary, closer than with her other, later-born, children, and felt that, 'next to the fear of God I think it "will save him from a thousand snares" to have so fond and intimate friendship with his Mother'.[23]

There was no doubt in any of the family's minds that, as eldest boy, Harry had privileges that the others did not. He was brought breakfast in bed by his sisters when he was home for the holidays (although this may partly have been to make up for the six o'clock start to his days at school). This was very much the norm at the time,★ and Harry fitted right into the mould. Fred suffered from it the most:

He set great store by authority that had moral or mystic foundations, and of such a kind, in his view, was that of an eldest son and an elder brother. His quasi-feudal supremacy over us derived additional strength . . . from the fact that . . . he was away at school the greater part of his time, returning for the holidays in a blaze of superiority . . . He was very good to me in the matter of my lessons, and would take great pains to put me on the right track and do things in the right way – more pains, I thought, than they deserved. I had a small boy's indifference to accuracy where Latin Grammar was concerned, and the stress he laid upon it seemed to me excessive to the point of superstition.

★ Even a generation later, Molly Hughes, a stockbroker's daughter from London, remembered that in relation to her brothers 'I came last in all distribution of food at table, treats of sweets, and so on. I was expected to wait on the boys, run messages, fetch things left upstairs . . .'[24]

But there were matters on which the rigour of his principles galled me even more. He had . . . 'a passion for cleanliness' that I did not wholly share. As regards the washing of hands, I did not hold with the Pharisees, but I took the larger view. Knowing this, he would make me 'show hands' before sitting down to meals . . .

Then he had strict views as to the time for a little boy to go to bed, and when my gentle mother was disposed to relax the rule in my favour, he would urge the letter of the law . . .

It was not ill-nature, or any grudging of happiness to his juniors that made my brother act as he did, but a perhaps exaggerated sense of law and order, together with a feeling of responsibility for the right working of the universe.[25]

This is generous of Fred, but Harry, it is abundantly clear, was both a bully and a prig. The times helped create him, of course, as did his family circumstances – eldest surviving child with only one other brother, and he seven years younger. Fred had therefore not been present when Harry had learned he was cock of the walk and could cajole his doting mother into almost anything. Harry always got the best that was going. Harry had money set aside for his education; Fred did not. Harry was sent to the best school his parents could afford; Fred went to the local day school. Harry was in his father's confidence; the girls were – well, girls.

Being girls, their education was limited in scope. They were, for the most part, taught what she knew by their affectionate mother at home, at least initially. There were later intermittent periods of day schools or shared governesses with other children. None lasted for long, and they were always easily interrupted – by the chance of a visit, by family emergencies. The girls received what was in essentials very much the traditional education of the time: reading, a little (probably very little) arithmetic, a smattering of French or Italian, plus the usual accomplishments: poetry, drawing, music.*

---

* Molly Hughes again: 'after her stint at reading [the Bible] she had to parse every word in one of the verses, and then while her mother pursued her hobby of water-colour painting Molly continued reading, sewing, writing or learning by heart. Instruction was given in French and Latin while English history was gleaned "from a little book in small print that dealt with the characters of the kings at some length". Geography was studied sketchily from a large atlas and a

George had no interest in any of the arts, and so was even more distanced from this aspect of their education than he might otherwise have been, though the girls all evinced great aptitude there.

Louie showed her literary flair particularly young, writing a poem which, Fred kindly reported, 'promised well. There was no preliminary dallying with the subject, no idle invocation of the Muse, but a plunge into the heart of things: "And down the shady path that devil walked."' Unfortunately for Louie's inspiration, that was where the poem both began and ended.[27] She made a better showing in prose. When she was about six, before she could write, she dictated 'The History of the Piebald Family' to one of her sisters. She had seen what Fred later described as

a motherly old horse, or rather, grey mare, that grazed in a neighbouring paddock. She invested her straightaway with the character of a widow and mother of a family. The respectable old cart-horse, her husband, was dead, leaving her to bring up a family of colts. Some of these were steady and good, worked for their living, and from time to time brought her presents of oats and hay. But the darling of her widowed heart was her youngest, a frisky, mischievous imp of a colt, who didn't like work, and didn't like school, and did all sorts of foolish things, in spite of which his fond mother loved him dearly, and said he would know better by and by.

Her story continued:

And after a while, Mrs. Piebald, that was her name, was taken ill and had not long to live. And her family of colts was very sorry. And they sent for the doctor's horse to give her medicine, and then for the minister's horse to pray with her; and after telling them all to be very good, never to run away or to kick anybody, she died. And they all cried very much, and wiped their eyes with their hoofs as well as they could. And her darling little colt went to live in a gentleman's stable, and grew up to be a beautiful carriage horse. So that is all about the Piebald family.[28]

---

small geography book, of which she could recall only the opening sentence, "The earth is an oblate spheroid" . . . Dr Brewer's Guide to Science, written in the form of a catechism, was used for science lessons . . . Her mother . . . took little interest in arithmetic . . .'[26]

Louie's story has several interesting aspects. Rossetti was later to
refer to her as a 'grimly kid', and, as well as this one, many of the
surviving stories about her in childhood show an inordinate relish
for death and destruction of all sorts. In addition, although she and
her sisters were not orphaned, it is telling that, in a household
where her father was absent for anything up to three months a year,
she wrote a story about a widow trying to cope alone. Finally, her
application and determination can be noted already in her desire to
move on to the important act of creation before the boring bits
(writing, reading) had quite been mastered.

Apart from this premature foray into the world of literature, all
the girls took well to the accomplishments of the day: Alice and
Carrie wrote verse (rather more elaborate than Louie's first
attempt), Agnes played the piano, Georgie and Louie drew nicely.
In addition, it was part of every girl's education to do ladylike work
around the house. In the days before domestic appliances, mending,
making clothes, dusting and baking (not the heavy cooking) were
part of their daily lives. This, in typical Victorian fashion, was
turned into a moral as well as a physical good:

Every girl ought to know the elements of domestic economy, whether
she looks after a house for herself or supervises servants. Apart from any
other reason: All Waste is sinful. It is abominable ingratitude to God. It
is heartless robbery of the poor. It is base and knavish dishonesty to the
master and mistress. It is worse than downright *picking and stealing* or
vulgar thieving, because they can be punished by the policeman, the
lock-up, and the house of correction; whereas waste cannot.[29]

George took little or no part in the girls' day-to-day lessons, not
even their religious education: preaching engagements took him
away from home during the week, and on Sundays he held services
in his own chapel. His influence was mostly felt by moral example:
he rose before six every day to pray and study. (He so loved the
early morning that he often woke up his family to watch the dawn.)
He was restless himself, and disapproved of idleness. If he was not
fully occupied – or thought his family not fully occupied – he
would hold a brief prayer session sooner than let this continue. He
warned them against speaking evil of others, although not always

quite in the way he intended. His family long remembered the time he rebuked them for discussing a particularly ugly woman passing on the street: 'It is true she is a female of revolting exterior, but . . .'[30] What the mitigating circumstance was was never heard, as the children chorused that this was exactly what they meant.

Religion and righteous living permeated their lives, although never in a dour or forbidding way – the hellfire and brimstone of evangelical salvation were not for George Macdonald. 'He used to say, "If my children are good Christians I do not care whether they are Methodists or not"', and he often quoted his own father: 'I am not so much a Methodist as to forget that I am a Christian.'[31] For all that, the religious was closely woven into their existence. Hannah wrote to her mother when Harry was three:

He was so very troublesome this morning in several instances, that I at length rebuked him very sharply for his inattention to my commands; he raised his head & eyes from the mischief he happened to have in hand, & with a sort of coaxing, deprecatory look, he shook his head and said: 'I must pray for you.' I told him to pray for himself at the same time, & there the matter ended, for I could not keep my countenance and look at his any longer.[32]

This sort of charming episode, half ecclesiastic, half the sort of story any fond mother would tell, came not only from Harry. When Fred was three, presaging his later career, he 'preached' a sermon in the nursery, which Hannah took down:

There was once a little boy, and he was very wicked, and he went to hell. And Satan burnt him, and the little boy begged him to let him go, and Satan wouldn't. So the little boy told Satan that if he would let him alone, and not burn him any more, he would sweep hell's chimneys for nothing. So when the little boy had begged very hard, he let him and he was Satan's sweep. One day when he was sweeping and wishing to get away, there came a great wind and blew him up hell's chimney right out at the top.[33]

And Louie once came to breakfast to report, 'I have had a bad dream. I dreamt I was Antichrist, and had my ears boxed with sheet-lightning for impudence.'[34]

Part of the way religion manifested itself was the commitment to charity that George maintained his whole life. Wesley constantly urged his followers to give away their money – otherwise they would be 'guilty of robbing God and the poor, corrupting their own souls, wronging the widow and the fatherless and of making themselves "accountable for all the want, affliction and distress which they may, but do not, remove"'.[35] He thought that charitable giving should be extreme – 'sacrificial', he called it. George took these precepts to heart. He had little; his family was large; and yet every year without fail some 10 per cent of his income was given away to those who had even less. His account book was headed with a line from Proverbs: 'Honour the Lord with thy substance, and with the first fruits of all thine increase.' In one early year his household expenses were £72, with £7 given away to charity; another year his expenses were £67, charitable giving was £7 7s. As well as money given regularly to the Missionary Society, or the Bible Society, spontaneous gifts of sixpences and shillings went to 'A poor man', 'A poor Christian brother', 'A poor sailor boy'. In 1839, to mark the centenary of Methodism, a special fund was set up by the Conference, which ultimately raised over £220,000.[36] George contributed 10 guineas in 1839, with another 10 pledged for the following year. Hannah, of course, had no money of her own, so, apart from the odd penny slipped to poor women she saw on the streets, she contributed her share by making clothes for orphans, or by working for chapel bazaars, for which she produced drawings, or made clothes to be sold.

Charity, however, does not seem to have involved kindness or gentleness. There was a caustic streak in Hannah when she was displeased, and none of her children were known for their soft ways. Like all mothers, she had constantly to stop her children from quarrelling. Unlike most, she suggested a rather startling alternative: 'If you want to be rude to anyone let it be to a stranger. Perhaps you will never meet again.'[37] (Not, at least, if the stranger had anything to say about it.) The girls took to this with vigour:

Of every sort of eccentricity or absurdity that came within our range they had a keen perception, and could ring changes on it with a ready skill, good-natured enough for the most part, but a little keen in the case of pretentious people and the pompously dull, who seemed to deserve all they got in the way of criticism or caricature.[38]

One indication of Hannah's lack of concern for those not intimately bound to her was her inability to keep cooks and maids for any length of time. From her letters a fairly complete list of servants can be made, and it would appear that between 1828 and 1868, she went through fifteen. Where both the arrival and departure dates are known, the average time they spent working for her was ten and a half months. Only two stayed more than a year; if these are taken out of the reckoning then the average stay of each servant was a mere six and a half months. Given that the period from 1837 to 1842 has been referred to as economically 'the grimmest period in the history of the 19th century',[39] it says a great deal about the difficult atmosphere in the house, or of the treatment they received, that very few chose to stay for long.

Most of the time the girls were funny, and so a great deal was excused. But often 'funny' could turn into 'savage' in an eye-blink. Alice, who was particularly quick, used her wit 'as a weapon of whose keenness of point there could be no doubt, and foolish or mischievous people were made to feel it'.[40] A hard return for mere foolishness. Georgie, who was known for her kindness and caring for others, could also be rather sharper than perhaps her friends would have enjoyed if they heard, as for instance when she commented that the invalid son of a poor family was 'wearing medals bestowed upon him for abstaining from vices of which he was incapable'.[41]

Fred blamed this intolerance on the fact that their lives were a 'moving tent':

the life that it contained was all the more close-knit for the shifting scenes amid which it was pitched ... A highly developed family-life is not perhaps without its dangers. It may lead to insufficient sympathy with persons and things outside itself, and may strengthen mental habits and tendencies that do not need to be strengthened, but rather toned and modified by freer intercourse with others. In their love and admiration for each other the members of a family may come to think more highly of their common gifts and qualities than is altogether good for them, and to undervalue some other qualities which it would not be amiss for them to cultivate.[42]

Given that he is writing about his own family, a not altogether whole-hearted endorsement.

3. 'A moving tent'
1850–1853

In 1850 George was sent to Birmingham, his second appointment there. The family was pleased to be going back to familiar places, old friends and, not the least of it, a good local school for Harry. He was now fourteen, and he left Wesley College in Sheffield with great pleasure. King Edward VI School was not only the most prestigious school in Birmingham: moving there also meant that he could live at home, and be cosseted by his doting mamma. Fred, at eight, as always received the smaller portion, and was sent to a little local school. In later life he stoutly defended the place, protesting that Mr Howell, its owner and single master, had 'something of a reputation as a schoolmaster', and 'a constituency of his own'; but even he had to admit that 'King Edward's School overshadowed all others in the town',[1] not only in educational attainment, but also in its new buildings, recently designed by Barry and Pugin, who would next move on to rebuild the Houses of Parliament.

At Edward VI Harry fell in with a group of like-minded boys, all on the 'classical' rather than the 'commercial' side – that is, they expected to go to university rather than leave at sixteen to go into business. Ned Jones, Cormell Price, Richard Watson Dixon and William Fulford were already firm friends. Harry may have been brought into the group by Wilfred Heeley, who, as well as being a stalwart of Ned Jones's group, was also the son of Methodist congregants who were close to George and, particularly, Hannah. The boys were from more or less the same background – the mildly prosperous middle class, professional people in a small way – and they spent their spare time together, visiting back and forth. Harry took them in turn to meet his family, where they were a great success:

They were sufficiently our seniors for us to think them wise and clever, yet not too much our seniors for free and genial intercourse. My sisters were bright, quick-witted girls, very responsive to intellectual and moral stimulus, and capable of ready enthusiasm for anything that appeared

better or more beautiful than they had known before. They received
with frank enjoyment the friendship of their brother's friends; and these
were only too pleased to have the companionship of girls who sang
delightfully, had a blessed gift of humour, and were willing to be talked
to and read to on all manner of subjects. So a good deal of new life came
whirling through our doors with these our visitors, rejoicing in their
youth and finding it bliss to be alive.[2]

They were the first independent friends the girls had – friends
made because of their own mutual interests, not their parents'. The
girls' circle widened beyond chapel events – the missionary teas,
the sewing circles, the Sunday-school picnics. They now knew
people who were interested in the greater world, and particularly
in the world of the arts that they so much admired, which had
hitherto been for them an exclusively 'girlish' sphere. Fulford 'fed
us with Longfellow first of all, as the food suitable for our years,
and so brought us gradually into a condition more or less fit for the
revelation before introducing us to the works of his prime hero
Tennyson . . . He loved music, also, and taught us the names and
some of the works of Beethoven and Mendelssohn.'[3] Heeley too
entertained the girls. Born in 1833, he seemed much older than
they – a manageable four years older than Alice, to the younger
children he was virtually a grown-up. Even so,

a certain shyness and big-boy clumsiness made him occasionally the
victim of the little girls to whom he was so indulgent. He could at all
times express himself best in writing, and, as he found we enjoyed it, used
to amuse himself and us with writing notes at school and sending them
by our brother as postman to one or the other of the sisters . . . What he
said and wrote lit up a new world for us, who, as girls, in those days had
small chances of education.[4]

For two years they were all together, forming close friendships.
Alice, with her razor wits, was rather taken with literary William
Fulford, while Caroline became close to the lamb-like Wilfred
Heeley. Georgie, quieter, often unaware of others as she moved in
her own little world, remembered her first glimpse of Ned Jones
more than half a century later:

Edward was then in his nineteenth year, and of his full height; to me he looked a grown man because he wore a coat, but I believe there was in fact an early maturity about him. His aspect made the deepest impression on me. Rather tall and very thin, though not especially slender, straightly built and with wide shoulders. Extremely pale he was, with the paleness that belongs to fair-haired people, and looked delicate, but not ill. His hair was perfectly straight, and of a colourless kind. His eyes were light grey (if their colour could be defined in words), and the space that their setting took up under his brow was extraordinary . . . From the eyes themselves, power simply radiated, and as he talked and listened, if anything moved him, not only his eyes but his whole face seemed lit up from within. I learned afterwards that he had an immovable conviction that he was hopelessly plain.[5]

The sole child of a picture framer of straitened means, Jones had won a scholarship to Edward VI and only late in the day had moved from the commercial to the classical side. He was unused to social gatherings, and to children in general, and when he first visited the Macdonalds he frightened three-year-old Edith to tears by making faces at her. He was a serious boy. He had elevated ideals, and planned to study for the ministry. Altogether he could be an uncomfortable guest:

someone mentioned the name of a certain girl and said of her that she was a 'flirt'. At the word his face lit up suddenly, and without raising his voice at all he said with the utmost distinctness and volubility: 'A flirt's a beast, a bad beast, a vile beast, a wicked beast, a repulsive beast, an owl, a ghoul, a bat, a vampire.' As we sat amazed at the rush of words the usual placid expression returned to his mouth . . . The 'chatter' of women had evidently struck him very much, for he denounced it in one of the visits mentioned, muttering to himself under his breath: 'Hear the ladies when they talk; tittle tattle, tittle tattle/Like their pattens when they walk, pittle pattle, pittle pattle.'[6]

This virtuous demeanour hid a wilder streak. Georgie understood it from the beginning: Jones could be 'ominous in silence whilst some swiftly conceived Puck-like scheme of mischief took shape, carrying all before it, compelling the least likely to join in it, always ending in the laugh that we remember, the cloud-scattering laugh!'[7] 'Sometimes he would laugh till he slid down from his chair to the floor and rolled there, holding himself together.'[8] Crom Price said that the earliest thing he remembered about Jones 'was his laugh – I knew him by that before I knew him any other way'.[9]

Their pastimes were wide-ranging: not only Tennyson and Beethoven, but also a new craze. Spiritualism had arrived from America in the 1840s, and during the next twenty years was to spread rapidly across England. Two seemingly opposing forces drove this. One was that church attendance had slumped radically, even if those who did attend were more fervent than ever before. While the decline in organized religion was pronounced, the habit of belief itself had not perished, and into that vacuum swept spiritualism. If you were not now going to see your loved ones in heaven, communicating with the dead became a serious concern to many in these days of early and frequent death. The second motivating force is more curious today. In the 1840s and 1850s there were many clergymen interested in mesmerism (the precursor to hypnotism). Samuel Wilberforce, Bishop of Oxford, was fascinated; William Davey, a Wesleyan, was a well-known mesmerist who travelled the country 'treating' subjects with mesmerism's 'healing' powers. The faith involved was seen as a counter to the dangerous currents of science; it 'suspended the physical instincts and allowed one's pure, untrammelled conscience to work'.[10] Science believed in outside forces that were not seen but could be understood to be present, such as gravity. Those opposed to the great strides science was making became a receptive audience for another kind of unseen power, and the 'other' world was a reality for many.

With the ground thus prepared, table-turning, table-rapping and other séance-like preoccupations took root rapidly when they arrived in Britain. As with mesmerism, the clergy did not automatically condemn; they were not sure that the origins of these activities might not be divine. Table-turning moved quickly from professional demonstrations to become an amateur pastime, something to try out at home of an evening. By the summer of 1853 the Birmingham set had taken to it with enthusiasm, and according to Georgie they practised it regularly, with what are still to me astonishing results. The power, whatever it might be, was discovered whilst our parents were from home, and duly reported to them on their return as treasure-trove. Our father said something like, 'Well, well, my children, if ever it does it again, call me'; so one day, when he was safely within the double doors of his study, we set to work. We had no theory about it, and were only curious each time to see what would happen. The table, a large round one, did not fail us now, but seemed to awaken just as usual, turning at first with slow heaviness and then gradually quickening its pace till it spun quite easily and set us running to keep up with it. 'Call Papa!' was the word, and a scout flew to the study. He was with us at once, not even waiting to lay down his long Broseley pipe. Incredulity gave way to excitement at the first glance, but to convince us of our self-deception, he cried out, 'Don't stop, children,' and leapt lightly between us, pipe in hand, upon the middle of the table, thinking to stop it in a second. His weight, however, made no difference – the table turned as swiftly and easily as before, and we ran round and round with it, laughing at our amazed father.

And not only tables did we turn, but other objects also, especially a very communicative tea-urn with which we established a code of rapping. Our removal [from Birmingham] put an end to these *séances*, but none of us ever understood the things we saw at them.[11]

Georgie, at least, wrote it off as a childhood experience; Alice took it far more seriously, and it became a major part of her later life.

There were wilder aspects to their play, too. One of Louie's grandsons tells a story which he does not appear to find peculiar. He says, 'There was a debate as to whether, if necessary, one could eat a mouse. Wilfred Heeley said that he would willingly eat one, so Alice issued him an invitation, and cooked a good mouse-pie, baked in a patty-pan. He never came to taste it, but Georgie ate some.'[12] If true, this is an extraordinary story. Surely both they and all later auditors of the story would have made more of it? No, there is just the one mention – Alice made and Georgie ate a mouse pie. One can certainly see the discussion taking place; probably even the dare too. But baking a mouse pie? This would involve catching a mouse (not impossible, probably not even difficult, in Victorian houses, constantly waging war against vermin). Then, one assumes, to make a 'good' pie the mouse would have to be skinned and gutted before being cooked. Even in a time when people's food sources were much closer to them than supermarket shelves are to shoppers today, can one really see this happening? This appears to be an instance of a family tall story which with retelling moved from being a comic tale to being gospel truth. All families have myths which, to a greater or lesser extent, they know are not true factually, even if they may be emotionally true. The mouse-pie story fits this mould – Alice the audacious, in a moment of mirth offering a dare; Georgie the determined, who will grit her teeth and see through anything that has to be done.

The Macdonalds, with their strong artistic streak, often preferred emotional and artistic truth over mundane facts. There are a number of family stories that have this smell about them. Another, also related by Louie's grandson, tells of Mary Macdonald, Hannah's first child: Hannah 'once observed her struggling upstairs, puffing and chanting: "As he heard the great bell of St Genevieve chime, He strode up the back stairs three steps at a time"; which is a couplet (very slightly adapted) from the *Ingoldsby Legends*'.[13] He adds a rider querying how this 'grim and adulterous poem' could have been known to a baby a year before its first publication, but concludes that this question 'is not the main point'. On the contrary, it is very much the main point: the main point is that the story is not – *cannot be* – true. It is a conflation of what two separate children did, or a half-memory, a merging together of the two possibilities to create a greater, more interesting, story – one where the family is well read and well educated down to the youngest member of the nursery.

Louie's grandson is not the sole disseminator of such stories. All the family did it. Edie said that her father was a natural orator, and once had a curious meeting. One evening after the service an actor stopped him to say how much he had enjoyed George's preaching, and he offered him a gold pencil case. It was David Garrick. That is the story as Edie tells it. Louie's grandson is not gullible; he points out that Garrick died in 1779, more than twenty-five years before George was born. He fails to understand, however, that this is a family myth; that literal truth is not the point. He thinks that Edie has simply made a mistake and has muddled one famous actor with another – he suggests Edmund Kean instead. Kean did not die until

1833, and in 1824 and 1825 George was preaching around the western reaches of London. But what are the chances of a nineteen- or twenty-year-old boy, yet to be ordained, preaching in small chapels in rural villages outside London, being heard by the most famous actor of his day, much less making that kind of impression? It is, of course, possible; it is also extremely unlikely. It is far more likely that Edie later heard her father praised as an orator (and he certainly was highly regarded as a preacher), heard him compared to Garrick, and unconsciously rearranged her memories to create a truth that was more 'true' than the facts.

In 1852 the group of friends, the Birmingham set, was partly broken up by the departure of Jones, Dixon, Heeley and Fulford to Oxford. Harry and Crom Price were younger and had another year to complete at school. Letters would, in the meantime, have to keep them in touch. Jones was looking forward to the Oxford of New- man and Pusey, full of ideals and the desire to create a better world through faith. The only lack would be Harry: 'I would have given almost anything to have had Macdonald up here. No fellow has ever had more influence on me: at least on certain parts of the "Me", and no fellow's influence has been more advantageous.'[14]

Still, Ned was thrilled to be leaving modern Birmingham behind him for what he thought would be the glories of medieval Oxford. Birmingham, for all its new wealth, was not the City Beautiful. Even the local councillors had difficulty in finding good things to say about it. In a statement put out ten years earlier, they had described a place where 'The streets are a scandal to the name – a nuisance in wet, and a greater nuisance in dry weather; the footpaths in the centre of the town would disgrace a rural village: both footway and horseway, in the remote streets and the outskirts, are but alterna- tion of kennel [gutter] and mire: the lighting is little better than darkness visible.'[15] The city came late to civic reform – in the 1850s there was no town medical officer, nor a public baths, nor a library; schemes which had previously been accepted, such as sewage and street lighting, were now cancelled as too expensive. The death rate rose rapidly in the late 1840s and early 1850s. Alcoholism among the working classes was a chronic scandal. Crom Price remembered 'one Saturday night walking five miles into the Black

Country, and in the last three miles I counted more than thirty
lying dead drunk on the ground, more than half of them women'.[16]

The Macdonalds, the following year, would also be leaving
Birmingham, at the end of George's current three-year stint.
Although there would be the same weary work – packing, organizing, moving – to do yet again on their seventh remove in twenty
years, this time there was a new excitement in store. George's next
appointment was not for any of the usual round – Huddersfield,
Wakefield, Sheffield. This time they were going to London – the
capital, the largest city in Europe, the home of the only-just-finished
Great Exhibition. Hannah's favourite sister and her husband, Alice
and Edward Pullein, were now living in London, in Great Coram
Street, in the heart of what is now Bloomsbury, and in the early
summer Alice had already been to stay with them for a fortnight.

In their final year in Birmingham, there were major decisions to
be made. The most important was, What should happen to Harry's
education? He was settled at Edward VI and he was doing well. It
was unlikely that they could find an affordable school of equivalent
standing near them in London. And so it was agreed that Harry
should stay behind. In June he moved into lodgings in the house of
congregants of George. The other children presented less difficulty:
Fred was eleven, and a local day school could be found anywhere;
Alice, Carrie and Georgie had intermittently been going to Miss
Howell's, a little school nearby, when they were not needed at
home; the smaller ones continued to be taught by Hannah. Certainly disrupting their education was not going to worry anybody.

The main anxiety was Carrie. Early in March 1852 she had had
pleurisy. It did not seem serious and, apart from a persistent cough,
she quickly recovered. By the summer, however, Hannah was
worried: Carrie was still coughing. The doctor advised bed rest,
and she was soon well enough to go to school again. By October
she was back in bed, and this time nothing helped; she got weaker
and weaker over the next few months, although tonics, cod-liver
oil, iron and cough medicine were all tried. Around this time it
was decided to have her portrait painted, no matter how tiring the
sittings – an indication of how the family saw the illness progressing.
In December Hannah wrote to a friend that Carrie now was never
well enough to come downstairs – though, because she was still in

the house, still clinging to life, her absence from the family circle seemed to pass unnoticed. The unspoken question Would Carrie ever come downstairs again? was always in the air for Hannah. The others, truly, seemed 'scarcely to be aware': when Edie wrote her little book of family memoirs, in 1923, she didn't even bother to give Carrie's birth date.

Hannah undertook all the nursing herself, as was expected of her. Not a lot could be done, apart from keeping the patient warm and comfortable. The main preoccupation was to ensure that she ate enough. There were entire books dedicated to invalid (or 'maigre') cookery, which were usually based on the premiss that food with little taste is more digestible to a 'lowered' constitution than anything flavourful.* Bread was the basis for many 'strengthening' foods, including 'bread jelly': pour boiling water over toast, boil the liquid until it turns to a jelly, strain, and (if desired) add sugar, lemon peel, wine or milk. 'This jelly is said to be so strengthening that one spoonful contains more nourishment than a tea-cupful of any other jelly.'[18] Mrs Beeton recommended toast and water, which was simply boiling water poured over toast, allowed to go cold, and then strained. She saved her highest recommendation for toast sandwiches: 'Place a very thin piece of cold toast between 2 slices of thin bread-and-butter in the form of a sandwich . . . [it] will be found very tempting to the appetite of an invalid.'[19] Luckily for the invalid, Mrs Beeton conceded that mutton, chicken, rabbit, calves' feet or head, game, fish and boiled puddings were also easily digested.

The great unnamed fear all this time was consumption, a vicious killer. Over 50,000 deaths a year could be attributed to it, and only 20 per cent of those diagnosed as having the disease had any chance of survival. The symptoms were frighteningly general: listlessness, lack of appetite, weight loss, pallor (especially combined with flushed cheeks), night sweats, coughs and colds, a raspy throat, wheezing, shortness of breath.[20] The only sure sign was unfortunately also one of the last – when the patient began to cough up

---

* Although even for the healthy the question of flavour was a vexed one. *The English Housekeeper* solemnly warned cooks to 'Take care not to over season, or let soup have any predominating flavour. This is a great fault, and a common one.'[17]

blood. Infection and contagion were not yet ideas in common currency in disease theory: only that year the Committee for Scientific Enquiry had rejected the suggestion that cholera was water-borne; Ignaz Semmelweiss was still being ridiculed for his notion that doctors should wash their hands between doing post mortems and examining live patients; and it was to be another twenty-five years before Koch's isolation of the tubercle bacterium was recognized. Until then, a varying range of causes were blamed: everything from unaired sheets to 'improper clothing', which by lowering body heat could give the disease a grip. The Revd Faunthorpe, author of that vade mecum *Household Science: Readings in Necessary Knowledge for Girls and Young Women*, had no doubts on this subject (or indeed on any other): 'Severe colds, which may terminate fatally, are sometimes caught through wearing damp garments, or sleeping in unaired sheets. Nearly every person we meet knows some sad story of lameness, consumption, or early death from some other disease, as the result of sleeping in damp sheets. Putting damp sheets on a bed, is little short of murder.'[21] Other suggested causes ranged from air that had been rebreathed too often (Florence Nightingale was a supporter of this latter idea) to 'the dread triad of sexual indulgence, masturbation and celibacy'. ('We need look no further than the Catholic nunneries in France where not more than one in ten entrants survive their period of novitiate.')[22]

Great strides had been made in the previous decade – in the 1840s, the stethoscope, the thermometer and the percussive technique for listening to the chest had all been developed[23] – but there was still uncertainty of diagnosis. This meant that hope always existed, even where none appeared warranted. Treatment was as wide ranging as the causes were thought to be. *The Family Oracle of Health* recommended a version of asses' milk for those who couldn't get the real thing.* The application of blisters, to provide a 'counter-irritation', was common. Other drugs used included quinine, hydrocyanic acid and even creosote. Iodine was recommended for tubercular lesions – either applied topically or given orally as a

---

* It begins, 'Bruise eighteen garden snails with one ounce of hartshorn shaving . . .'[24]

liquid or in mercury pills. Dr John Savory of the Edinburgh Royal Infirmary noted that, in the last formulation, and in the doses recommended, it usually caused 'serious derangements of the nervous system', but 'beneficial effects outweighed the disadvantages'[25] (a nineteenth-century variant of 'The operation was successful but the patient died'?). Tonics and cod-liver oil, to build up the patients' strength, at least had the benefit of not sending them mad, even if they died.

Although by December 1852 the doctors had definitively said that Carrie's lungs were diseased, the family carried on as normally as possible. Alice went in March to stay with her aunt in Manchester for two months. In May they swapped over, Hannah, Carrie and Edie now travelling to Manchester. Hannah and Edie stayed with Aunt Howell briefly; Carrie visited for two months before she could think of enduring the trip back to Birmingham. Soon she would have to make a much longer trip south.

The family set off for London in September 1853, and Ned Jones came back from Oxford to see them off. Despite the allure of the capital, Georgie for one felt only regret: 'As the train passed slowly through the tunnel of the Great Western Railway at the beginning of our journey . . . I grieved in the darkness because I was leaving the place where he lived.'[26] However, the family settled quickly into their first London house, at 39 Sloane Square. George had been given the Seventh London circuit, centred on the Sloane Square Chapel in Chelsea, which, while having 'nothing very heroic or high-pitched in [its] spiritual life . . . was honest and wholesome'.[27] The large congregation was welcoming – within two days of moving, invitations to tea and dinner had already been received and accepted – but the house itself was too small for twelve people: ten family members (one now an almost complete invalid) and two servants. Hannah's first job after getting them all settled was to begin the search for another place to live.

Chelsea was still a villagey outpost of the big city; Fred remembered it as

if not exactly rural, [it] had not quite lost its rural memories when we went to live there. Cheyne Walk had still an eighteenth-century look, and old mansions . . . preserved still earlier traditions. No one had as yet thought of rebuilding Sloane Square, and Lower Sloane Street had shabby little cottages on either side with dissolute-looking gardens before them . . . The Queen and Prince Albert used frequently to drive through Sloane Square on their way to or from Buckingham Palace and Kew, and it was my frequent joy to take off my cap to them as they passed.

Thomas Carlyle lived just down the road, at Cheyne Walk, although until the Chelsea Embankment was built in 1874 the area was subject to periodic flooding, and therefore not considered very desirable.* There were no wood (much less asphalt) pavements, 'and the omnibus, which elderly and old-fashioned people still spoke of as "the stage", rattled over cobble stones'.[29]

At the age of eleven Fred was comfortably settled in a local school near Eaton Square. He was without the heavy hand of his brother, and the joys of a big city were spread out before him. He went everywhere and saw everything: the new Houses of Parliament were nearly finished, and Fred managed to find a way to the top of 'Westminster Clock Tower' as it was called. 'Big Ben had recently been put in position, and I crawled under the rim and stood upright within the great bell while it struck four, losing my hearing thereby for a while . . .'[30] It was clearly well worth it for the glory of the deed.

Really the only anxiety was the school holidays, when Harry would return. Three weeks after they arrived in Sloane Square, Harry wrote to Fred:

I am glad so very convenient a school has turned up for you. Do yourself credit in both the amount of work you do, and in the manner of doing it. Accuracy will be no end of use to you . . . If your knowledge can be relied on, you will find people will be glad to make use of it in this careless, ramshackle world.

Three months later he fired off another missive:

* Carlyle was well known to the omnibus drivers, who hailed him by name. It may have been self-preservation on their part: Carlyle dodged 'the carriages, sometimes, at risk . . . he usually insists on crossing when he has made up his mind to it, carrying his stick so as to poke it into a horse's nose at need.'[28]

Your handwriting is much improved, I see . . . When I come home you will be put through your drill, that I may see what progress you have made. If it's satisfactory we shall both be pleased; if not, why – . . . What time do you go to bed? I expect we shall have to make a revolution in this . . .

Fred, ever mild, wrote in retrospect: 'Perhaps they [the letters] will explain the fact that my love and admiration for him were just a little tempered with fear.'[31]

It was surely all the more irritating when just now Harry himself had been attracting unwelcome attention at school. He and Crom had started a school magazine, which they wrote out laboriously in longhand. After a few issues it was suppressed by the headmaster. Ned Jones wrote indignantly to Harry from Oxford:

I have written also to Crom, and expressed my sympathy with him on the suppressions of the Hebdomadal, – sympathy which I would offer you too as co-editor. Whatever heresy the article in question may have inculcated, it was unfair and undignified to take such proceedings – unfair because it involved in that suppression much that might have become beneficial, and undignified because it hinted at a fear that 'absurdity and conceit' would subvert obedience: the argument is either very lame, or the discipline of the school at a very low ebb.[32]

At this distance we cannot know what Harry was up to, nor what caused the suppression, but the words 'absurdity' and 'conceit' were being bandied about by those in authority in connection with him – a worrying sign for someone hoping to get a scholarship place at university within the year. But he didn't let it worry him, even if others showed signs of anxiety. George wrote to him for his eighteenth birthday, 'You will wear now, in my imagination, the *toga virilis* . . . The blessing of your father and mother be on your head. You are, I believe, fully impressed with the importance of improving this year to the utmost. It is the last of your school-boy life . . .' Harry's reply, just at this stage, cannot have reassured: '*Toga virilis* may come when it likes; but I will be a boy as long as I can. It seems jollier to me to be boy than man, just now; months and years will bring submission . . .'[33] The boy who recommended to his brother the virtues of hard work, application and high moral seriousness felt that for himself a Peter Pan attitude was perfectly acceptable.

George reverted to his theme as the months went on:

We never forget you at family prayer. You are with us then. And seldom do I bow my knees in secret without imploring a blessing on you. The temptations and dangers of life now begin to thicken around you ... Could you not in some thoughtful and studious hour write out a short prayer to be used daily before your private studies?

Harry's reply is in hindsight a masterpiece of ambiguity: 'Thanks for reminding me of what one is always tempted to forget, that with God lies the power of improving us, and that all attempts of our own merely will be failures.'[34] It can be read as dutiful submission to God, or it can seen to be a fatalistic throwing up of the hands – why make an effort if only God can improve us? It is probable that Harry intended and George understood the former interpretation; in light of later events, the latter one is also worth bearing in mind.

It was not only Harry's family who were worried. His friends were also noticing a difference from the serious boy they had left in Birmingham. Jones wrote to Price, 'Macdonald one of the lapsed!! Good Evans, as Dixon says – can it be? Poor fellow, I pity him from the innermost recesses of my heart. Don't let him influence *you*, Crom – remember I have set my heart on our founding a brotherhood.'[35]

In February 1854 the new house Hannah had found for the family was ready, and they left Sloane Square for 33 Walpole Street, around the corner, near the Royal Hospital and the old Ranelagh Pleasure Gardens. During the confusion of the move, Carrie had been sent to some 'kind friends', who looked after her tenderly; but only one outcome was now possible. By March Hannah acknowledged to a friend that 'Dr Radcliffe has told us today that our dear Carrie is so much worse that our case is hopeless and the end may be very soon. God help me.' Carrie was moved into Hannah's room, and Hannah was determined that nothing but death would part her from her daughter now. Only one event that month could draw Hannah's attention from her failing child: Harry had won his hoped-for scholarship, and with enormous pride Hannah informed her friends that he was due to leave for Corpus Christi, Oxford, in a few weeks.

Apart from this distraction, Hannah and George's one hope was that Carrie would be able to make a 'good death' and would not suffer too much. A good death gave the sufferer time for moral reflection, to enable her to make amends for any transgressions. Wasting illnesses such as consumption were appalling physically, but morally they were conducive to good deaths because there was no delirium, nothing clouding the mind, and the patient's lingering also gave the family time to gather; last thoughts could be exchanged, prayers said. For these reasons, death by consumption was sometimes called 'the death of the chosen'.[36] When it was decided that an illness was terminal, the patient was told, as 'no human being should meet his Judge unprepared'.[37] At that point, medicines were given to palliate the worst of the symptoms, so that the patient could prepare for the end with as few distractions as possible. Brandy or port wine was used to stimulate the heart and aid digestion; ether mixed with laudanum was an anti-spasmodic used to help breathing.[38] Opium was given to suppress pain. It was only fairly good at that, but its sedative powers were supreme – fear vanished, and the dying could seem even happy under its influence.

Literature and painting in the nineteenth century glorified death by consumption. Its victims were often young (always a plus in art), and the hectic flush, the gradual wasting, could be seen as conferring a glamorous end. In addition 'what was soon to become known as the *spes phthisica*, "the hope of tuberculosis", an irrational optimism' which was often present in the dying,[39] made the going out appear gentle. Edgar Allan Poe said, 'I would love to perish of that disease. How glorious! To depart in the heyday of the young life, the heart full of passion, the imagination all fire.'[40] Later he described the actual death: 'Suddenly she stopped, clutched her throat and a wave of crimson blood ran down her breast . . . It rendered her even more ethereal!'[41] This last description was of his own wife, and Poe was fooling himself. Death by consumption was a laboured, filthy business, agonizing for sufferer and watcher alike. Hannah sat by her daughter, doing all the nursing alone, emptying cups as Carrie spat a mixture of blood and phlegm out of her lungs in a desperate attempt to breathe. Coughing could turn to paroxysm in an instant. Convulsions were common. The patient wasted away day by day. With luck, exhaustion or secondary infections took the patient before she literally drowned in her own blood.

In early April George's health broke down and he became unable to preach – the first time he was to crack under outside pressure. The doctor diagnosed exhaustion, and prescribed bed rest and a change of air, those stalwarts of the nineteenth century. After a few weeks in bed George went to convalesce in Brighton, with Alice to look after him. It was cold and windy, and did not do him much good, but he stuck it out. By the end of the month it was clear that there was not much time left for Carrie. George and Alice were sent for, although Harry was left at Oxford for the moment. Hannah's strength, mental and physical, was giving way under the strain of twenty-four-hour care and two invalids, and early in May Alice Pullein arrived from Great Coram Street to stay until the end and share the load with her sister. Carrie was conscious part of the time, and asked her mother to pray for her. On 15 May she died, five months before her sixteenth birthday.

On 20 May Carrie was buried. Early-Victorian funerals had been elaborate, and elaborately expensive; reaction was setting in, and funerals were now offered from £3. Even this included 'a carriage with one horse, a lined elm coffin, and the use of a pall, bearers, coachman and attendant, complete with black hatbands and gloves'.[42] (Flowers and wreaths were not to become routine until the 1870s, when the increasing simplicity of the ceremony seemed to call for something extra.) Brompton Cemetery was chosen: it was nearby, and it had a special area for Dissenters, consecrated by their own ministers. A private grave was purchased, and it was dug to a depth of fourteen feet, which indicates that George and Hannah expected it to accommodate another family member at a later date.* A tombstone was ordered, reading 'In Sure and Certain Hope of the Resurrection Unto Eternal Life'.

---

*In the event, it was not used, and, according to the Brompton Cemetery records, the 'extra' space was most probably sold. In February 1892 Maria Malyon, aged sixty-eight, of 26 Simpson Street, Battersea, was buried above Carrie.

4. London: 'enchanted ground'
1853–1858

After Carrie's death, for a short time life moved smoothly, at least superficially. Still, they had all been marked by the loss. Hannah years later copied part of a letter that Louie, aged nine, had sent to her when she and George had gone on a brief holiday to recuperate from that terrible time: 'tell my dear Papa that I hope that god will send him home safe and sound. But if god chuss for him to die and to pass from deth unto life like poor dear Carry did pray let us have her life writen do.'[1] Immediately after Carrie's death Alice and Edward Pullein took care of the girls and Fred while George and Hannah went to visit Harry at Oxford, both to see him in his new surroundings and also to allow George to recover his health entirely. By the summer he was back in the pulpit, and life resumed its usual round of visits, chapel, and chapel-related social events.

George and Hannah had, on their arrival in London, become friendly with a Methodist family who lived in Stourport, Worcestershire, but who spent much of their time in the capital. George Pearce Baldwin had been a small-scale iron-founder together with his brother Enoch. George's wife, Sarah, was the daughter of the Revd Jacob Stanley, who in 1845 had been president of the Methodist Conference. They had six surviving children, three older boys and three younger girls, who were roughly the same ages as Alice and Georgie, as well as three children from George Baldwin's first marriage, who were now grown. The Macdonalds became fast friends with the entire Baldwin clan, entertaining them and being entertained. Early in 1856 George and Hannah made their first visit to stay with them in Stourport.

The Baldwins also took the Macdonald children to concerts, mostly at Exeter Hall, in the Strand. Apart from chapel choirs, this was the first experience they had of music outside the home. Music was a growing force in English public life, initially introduced with the idea that listening to 'good' music would promote the Christian virtues – tolerance, temperance, love of family and of country.[2]

Although the Methodists were at first chary – there had been heated debate earlier in the century as to whether organs in chapel would corrupt the congregation – they were finally won over. All over the country, and in all denominations, congregational singing led to choirs, which led to choral societies, then orchestras. It is difficult today – when Mozart is played to children in the womb; when great hunks of orchestral music are known to everyone who watches television, listens to radio, visits a shopping centre, even rides in a lift – to imagine what it must have been like to hear an orchestra for the first time, the sheer glory and grandeur of so many instruments all making a noise at once. At the beginning, in keeping with their background, the Macdonalds mostly went to hear sacred music – oratorios (*Elijah* and *Messiah*), requiems – but after a couple of years they became more daring, and piano recitals began to creep in, and concerts at the very secular Hanover Square Rooms. The Oxford friends were widening the girls' horizons; and the girls were also widening their own.

Harry had settled into university life well, although the pre-eminence he had enjoyed among the group in Birmingham was fading. Jones had met William Morris – a fellow student for the ministry – in his first term. At first he had described Morris as 'the precise counterpart of Macdonald – full of enthusiasm for things holy and beautiful and true and what is rarest, of the most exquisite perception and judgement'.[3] Soon Morris was taking Harry's place entirely, as they discovered the world of the Pre-Raphaelites together. It quickly became a habit for Morris to read aloud while Jones worked – one that would continue for the rest of their lives.

Morris ran in one morning bringing the newly published book [Ruskin's *Edinburgh Lectures*] with him: so everything was put aside until he had read it all through to me. And there we first saw about the Pre-Raphaelites, and there I first saw the name Rossetti. So for many a day after that we talked of little else but paintings which we had never seen.[4]

Harry too was interested, sending copies of Ruskin's essays back to his sisters, but he was never completely at home in the 'artistic' world. Jones saw that; and saw too that Morris shared the moral quest that at this time he himself still saw as his future. 'One by one, for one cause or another, I dropped apart from my contemporaries there, and by a fortnight's end it seemed settled that Morris and I only would be companions.'⁵ By the time the group decided to start the *Oxford and Cambridge Magazine*, along the lines of the earlier Pre-Raphaelite magazine *The Germ*, Jones noted that 'Macdonald is at present only a complement. When we have filled our staff to completion he will retire, and two giants come in his place.'⁶★

But the bond was not yet broken, and in London the Birmingham set (now largely merged with the various additions made in Oxford) was beginning to reassemble. Harry was back from Oxford regularly. Fulford was preparing for ordination, and he and Wilfred Heeley had taken lodgings in London. Heeley had been brought even closer to the family by Carrie's illness and death; he had been particularly her friend, and through her last illness had written to her regularly, to keep her amused and distracted.

In the summer of 1855 Jones went on a trip to France with William Morris. After sixteen-hour days sightseeing, the evening before their return 'it was resolved while walking on the quay at Havre at night that we would begin a life of art, and put off our decision no longer – he should be an architect and I a painter . . . That was the most memorable night of my life.'⁷ It is a mark of their increasing distance that Harry, who was doing well at Oxford, receiving a first at moderations in April, expected Jones to stay at Oxford 'and work on oil painting. If he can get a fellowship it will be delightful for him.'⁸ But Jones had no interest in fellowships. By Easter 1856 he had left Oxford without a degree and moved to London, taking lodgings at Sloane Terrace, opposite the Methodist chapel. There he was happy to work and starve, painting, finding his feet and – most importantly – meeting his idol Dante Gabriel Rossetti, who encouraged him in his plans.

Rossetti thought Jones and Morris 'wonders of their kind. Jones is doing designs which quite put one to shame, so full are they of everything – *Aurora Leighs* of art. He will take the lead in no time.'⁹

★ It is interesting that Georgie felt able to reprint this letter in her biography of Burne-Jones. Did it not occur to her that, even though Harry was by now dead, it was not particularly tactful – or kind – to highlight the failings of one who had achieved so much less than her husband? Or did she just not care?

Rossetti took him to meet his friends. These included the painter G. F. Watts, who lived for decades at Little Holland House, the home of the Prinseps, who enjoyed sharing in the artistic life and were trophy-hunters of no mean order. There Jones was introduced to Tennyson, Browning, Gladstone, Thackeray, Carlyle and other lions of the day. He may also have met George Howard, heir to the Earl of Carlisle, who was often with the Prinseps. Howard hoped to be an artist, and he and his wife, Rosalind, were later to become great friends of the Burne-Joneses. Jones also attended the Working Men's College, where Ruskin lectured. Jones had sent him a copy of the *Oxford and Cambridge Magazine*, which Ruskin had acknowledged with interest. Now Ruskin met the man who had been his disciple since his *Edinburgh Lectures*, and whose work, in turn, he admired.

For the time being poverty kept Jones away from most of his Oxford friends' haunts; he wrote rather ingenuously to Crom Price in the summer that 'the Macdonalds are the only people I ever see (not that they ever come here, understand). Fred turns in to break-fast now and again – he is a jolly little fellow, and makes one die outright at his quaint stories . . . Harry prefers the company of ladies, so I seldom see him.'[10] Jones went to the Macdonalds for tea and spent evenings with them, drawing with the older girls and teasing Edie.

All the time, he and Georgie were growing closer together. Georgie had by now grown to her full height – which wasn't saying much: even among her small sisters she was tiny, possibly just reaching five foot in her boots. She had beautiful brown hair, with bronze lights in it, and wonderful dark-blue eyes. Alongside the tall, fair Jones, she looked like a small, neat doll. Without saying anything, they both understood their importance to each other, and each was aware of the other's presence. Georgie remembered long after that 'Sometimes, after service, as the congregation filed out, the eyes of a girl amongst the slowly moving crowd were lifted and saw for a minute his face watching at a window.'[11] She had begun to study drawing at the Government School of Design, although later she was to belittle both her talent and her application, saying she went only because she 'had a certain deftness of hand . . . I did not learn anything vital.'[12] Jones often met her on her way

back, bringing flowers and walking with her. In early June 1856 he
went to speak to the Revd Macdonald; then

my mother called me into her room and told me that Edward had been
to see my father and herself; and then she went on with what seemed to
me to have been written from the beginning of the world, and ended by
saying that they left the answer they should give him entirely to my
decision. There was no difficulty in seeing what that was, and we knelt
down together and asked the blessing of God upon it. I was not quite
sixteen then. Looking back I feel the deepest respect for my parents
because they never discussed with me the 'prospects' of my marriage; my
father asked Edward no questions about his 'position', but, so far as my
judgment goes, acted as a minister of the Christian religion should
do, seeking nothing but character and leaving the question of fortune
altogether on one side.[13]

Jones went up to Birmingham to tell his father, and brought him
back to London to meet Georgie. The engagement was expected
to be a long one – it would clearly be years before 'Mr Edward', as
the younger children now called him, could hope to support a
wife. But Jones had long been part of the family circle. When
Georgie was away on visits to her aunts he continued to visit, being
petted by Hannah and in turn petting the younger children – he
was particularly fond of eleven-year-old Louie, teaching her to
draw and amusing her with comic drawings. Two months after the
engagement he wrote to her:

Ah, Louie, my little pupil, best and dearest, I was so very glad you wrote
to me, it would not have been quite my birthday without some memorial
of you: even upon other days I can't get along so very well without you,
and yesterday I should have been less happy certainly . . .
  It is so strange, dear, that this time last year I did not know you.* I
spent the day with Topsy† and Fulford, and I remember we laughed and
enjoyed ourselves . . . and all the time I never dreamed that the circling

---

* This is not, of course, actually true. But the emotion behind it is.
† The Oxford set's nickname for Morris, a reference to his tendency to stoutness
– like Topsy in *Uncle Tom's Cabin*, a huge best-seller the year Harry went to
Oxford, he just 'grow'd'.

A Circle of Sisters

of another year would alter all my destinies so much: now I love you all more than life.[14]

Georgie was not the only one who was moving away from childhood. At some point Fulford had become engaged to Alice – it may have been as early as 1852, when she was just sixteen. At that time Hannah had written cryptically to a friend that something 'unexpected' had been brought to her for approval by Alice. This could, of course, refer to almost anything, but it is a fact that later Georgie referred to an engagement between them. It appears to have been an on-again off-again thing. In May 1856 the subject may once more have been brought up, and it remained current for a while; but when Fulford was ordained that autumn he disappeared from all their correspondence. He then reappeared the following year; then by the end of 1858 he became estranged from not only the Macdonalds, but also the rest of the Oxford set.

The engagement could have been a youthful attachment that was soon grown out of, or perhaps it was a way of staying close to a family he loved. He was engaged not so much to Alice as to the whole family: 'we all especially appreciated the fact that [the engagement] did not make him neglect the rest of us, but that he still fetched the little ones for walks, or to take tea with him in a comforting way'.[15] At any rate, the engagement was destined not to survive. Alice was gaining a reputation as a flirt. Edie later drily noted that 'Alice never seemed to go on a visit without becoming engaged to some wild cad of the desert.'[16] It was not surprising. She was taller than her sisters, pale, with dark hair and either grey or blue eyes, depending on which source you follow.* All sources agree that, whatever their colour, their glance was devastating:

The Irish blood which is pretty certainly in our family seemed to take effect in Alice; she had the ready wit and power of repartee, the sentiment, and I may say the unexpectedness which one associates with that race. It was impossible to predict how she would act at any given point. There was a certain fascination in this, and fascinating she certainly was. Needless

---

* Edie said they were grey, with dark lashes; Editha Plowden, later to be a good friend to Alice both in India and back in England, called them 'bright Irish-blue'.

to say she had many admirers, and it must be confessed was a flirt. On one occasion her father warned her against being a flirt; with an air of innocent surprise she said, 'Ph-l-u-r-t, phlurt: what is that?'[17]

With all these engagements (or half-engagements), now everything was change once again. The Crimean War, which had begun in January 1854, had reached its end. The family had taken part in the days of 'public solemnity, humiliation and prayer for the national sins and calamities' decreed by the government in both 1854 and 1855; Sebastopol had finally fallen in September 1855, and in May 1856 they went to Green Park to see a fireworks display marking the end of the war. Fred, out and about as usual, watched the troops return:

When the shattered remnant of the Brigade of Guards returned from the Crimea, and half London was in the streets to give them welcome, I kept up with the gallant fellows all the way from Waterloo Bridge to Buckingham Palace, the tears running down my face as I pushed along through all obstacles, cheering with such voice as I had.[18]

Perhaps Fred was too much on the streets: at any rate it was decided that he should spend a year at school in Jersey. This was a tacit acknowledgement that George would not be able to afford to send both sons to university: even if Fred managed to obtain a scholarship, living expenses would stretch the family income too far. Apart from the academic fees, there was the cost of a room, furniture, heating, laundry and servants (about £30 a term), plus kitchen and buttery bills. Fred was therefore to acquire a second language instead – this, it was hoped, would help him in the business world. In July 1856, with Harry to supervise him, he set off. Louie felt bereft – with Harry at Oxford and Fred in Jersey, they would have to borrow a brother to look at. Georgie, beginning to take on the character for which she was later known – faithful, steady, always dependable – wrote to Fred with astonishing fidelity for a sixteen-year-old; he thought of her as his 'spiritual directress, writing me a pastoral letter every week. She knew my weaknesses . . . and where a gentle warning or word of encouragement would be timely.'[19]

Morris had arrived in London in the early summer of 1856, and quickly moved Jones out of his sordid furnished lodgings near the Macdonalds; within a few months they had moved again on the advice of Rossetti to old lodgings of his own, in Red Lion Square. These were unfurnished, which meant they were less expensive and had the added bonus that they could be done up to meet the occupants' own tastes. Rossetti was not quite sure about Morris's plans for the rooms, although he came to admire the place almost despite himself: '[He] is rather doing the magnificent there, and is having some intensely mediaeval furniture made – tables and chairs like incubi and succubi.'[20] Fred later described the rooms in burnished colours:

[They] were enchanted ground to me, a kind of paradise where I seemed to breathe another air, and converse with other beings than those to be found in the world outside . . . [The studio] was generally in a state of noble confusion – massive furniture of Morris's design, old pieces of metal-work, easels, canvases mounted on wooden frames, armour, lay-figures, pieces of tapestry and drapery, half-finished pictures, sketchbooks, bits of Flemish or Italian earthenware, and here and there a hat, or coat, or pair of boots. Near the fire-place was something like a clearing – an open space, as it were, in the forest or jungle – with a table and chairs for joyous meals, and for general converse when work was done.[21]

The move suited Georgie very well, as her father had reached the end of his time in Chelsea and had been posted to Marylebone, to the Hinde Street Chapel and a small house around the corner in Beaumont Street, only half an hour's walk away from Red Lion Square. The Macdonalds were now leaving behind the semi-rural village that Chelsea still was for the centre of a seething metropolis. Although they had been in big cities before, the size of London was unparalleled, with 2½ million people. Weekday traffic was terrible, particularly during the afternoons; the carriages carrying shoppers jockeyed for space with those carrying morning callers ('morning' calls were always paid after lunch). Carriages took up far more space than modern cars; there were no policemen on point duty, no traffic lights, no one-way streets, and it could take three-quarters of an hour to drive from Savile Row to the Royal

Academy, a quarter of a mile away. The noise too was tremendous: horses' hoofs; newsboys shouting the headlines; itinerant vendors; Punch and Judy men; Italian street bands; 'the cat-meat purveyor's drum; the chair-mender's whistle; barrel organs, fire brigades'.[22] Overpowering smells all fought each other – the sulphur of the fog, horse dung, effluent from drains during excavations, the reek from cesspits. Add to this woollen clothes that were difficult if not impossible to wash, and it is surprising that only the women carried eau de Cologne and smelling salts.

Hannah was not well pleased by the move. In fact she was even more resistant to moving than she normally was. She poured out her feelings to Fred:

It makes my heart sad to think that the house which has been the scenes of so many sorrows and so many blessings must become the home of a stranger who can have no sympathy with any of the events which have cheered or troubled us.

Since the death of your dear sister my room has been sacred in my eyes as the last spot upon earth which her presence brightened . . . Oh! How often I have knelt by the side of the bed since then, sometimes agonising in prayer for entire submission to a loss that still wrings my heart, sometimes thanking God that He had so gently taken her from the evil that is in the world. It adds bitterness to my feelings in leaving this house that no future one can have any association with her.[23]

In addition, the house in Beaumont Street was in terrible condition:

If you can imagine a house in a state of utter confusion and disorder, many degrees transcending anything you ever saw, you may perhaps form some conception of things here. Whitewashing, papering, joinering, blacksmith's work and glazier's repairs, mingle with washing, sweeping, rubbing, scrubbing, arranging and disarranging, and form a whole so discordant that order and decorum seem to have taken flight in terror . . . This is a very old house, and it has evidently suffered an amount of neglect sufficient to break the heart of anything but an old house. I do not despair, however, of making the poor old thing look something younger and more cheerful before I have done with it.[24]

'I do not despair' was something of an exaggeration, possibly added at the last minute so that Fred did not worry. To her friends she was more open: the first sight of the house made her 'more sick and sad than I can tell'; 'I cannot realize the idea of living in this gloomy abode'; the house was 'oppressive', 'dark and dirty', and 'I feel so many disappointments here'. It was 'the most painful remove of my life'; and 'if I knew where to run to I think I should desert'. The most heart-piercing letter says, 'I feel a restless distress, a feeling of wanting to go home' – but the sad truth was that, for the next three years, this *was* home.

By October 1856, things were more settled and gas had been installed. This indicates that, however horrible Hannah thought the house, the basic hygienic requirements were in place. This was important not simply from fastidiousness, but for essential health. In 1815 for the first time cesspits and household drains had been allowed to be connected to the main sewage system. This was made a standard requirement for new buildings in 1848. Unfortunately this promoted rather than alleviated disease, as the raw sewage was then dumped, untreated, straight into the Thames, the main drinking-water supply for London. In addition, hundreds of thousands of houses continued to rely on cesspits for waste. These were on the whole not designed to hold liquid waste, which was absorbed by the surrounding land, and from there went either into the tributary streams of the Thames or into the groundwater and thence into the local wells. Emptying a cesspool cost about 1s. a time, and so was often neglected. A surveyor reported, 'I found whole areas of the cellars . . . were full of nightsoil to the depth of three feet, which had been permitted for years to accumulate from the overflow of the cesspools.'[25] In 1854 a third cholera epidemic had killed 10,738 people in London; more than 30,000 had been killed by the disease in the previous twenty years. The Great Stink of 1858 was to become notorious: hot weather and stagnant water combined to make the Thames more putrid than can be imagined. Parliament, on the edge of the river, could sit only if its windows were hung with sheets dipped in chloride of lime. The great clean-up, with plans for outfall sewers and sewage-treatment plants, began that summer. A decade later, in 1866, cholera ravaged the East End of London, not yet connected to these new sewers, and this finally brought home the water-borne nature of the disease. Still, it was another twenty years before, in 1887, the discharge of sewage into the river was finally forbidden. Even then, in 1889 housekeeping manuals could advise, 'all washing, cooking, floor-washing, plate and dishwashing water goes down the sink. There will probably be another outlet for slops. If not, they must go down the sink.'[26] In light of this, Hannah's concern with the condition of her house was sensible rather than neurotic.

In addition, London was not particularly safe. Soon after the move to Marylebone, Agnes and Hannah were robbed when out shopping one day, and lost nearly £2. Another time, Edie remembered, they heard a man calling for help late one night. George ran out and saw that some men were kicking a policeman, while passers-by just watched. He shouted at them to help, and, embarrassed, they did so, and probably saved the policeman's life.

Throughout the move, and the following excitement, the sisters kept up their busy visiting schedule. They went to stay with Alice Pullein regularly, often travelling to her by omnibus on their own; in addition, there was Aunt Howell in Manchester, and the Salts, old friends from their Birmingham days. Hannah, who never really shook off the depression caused by Carrie's death, was invited to Stourport by Miss Baldwin, but was too 'sick at heart' to go, although later this became a regular destination for her and George. She did manage to get away to the seaside in August of the following year. Alice may have been with her – she was certainly away on a visit somewhere, as Louie planned to write her, according to her mother, 'a letter full of kind geniel and wholesome advice'. In addition, from the middle of the summer, Jones had gone to join Rossetti and friends – including William Morris and Val Prinsep (son of the Prinseps of Little Holland House) – in Oxford, where they had taken on the job of producing murals for the Debating Hall of the Oxford Union. They had offered to do the work in exchange for lodgings and the price of their materials; Rossetti had estimated it would take them six weeks. As they knew nothing of murals or decorative wall-painting, it actually took closer to six months, and Jones was not back in London full-time until February 1858.

This was a loss to the Macdonalds; they had become used to

having Red Lion Square and its inmates as a focal point of their social life. Still, Jones wrote to Louie, and sent caricatures to Agnes, calling them 'The Topsy Cartoons'.* Not only did the whole family visit regularly when he was in London, but expeditions to the British Museum, never before part of their lives, now became a feature under his guidance, as did trips to the Royal Academy, visits to see collections of photographs and a picture of Rossetti's, and other similar treats. The whole family also became acquainted with Jones's friend Rossetti, although Lizzie Siddal, Rossetti's sometime fiancée and sometime model, was not part of their circle – models were not quite nice, and certainly not ones who lived on their own and spent time unchaperoned with male painters. Lizzie had never had a particularly conventional existence – the daughter of a cutler, she had been a milliner's assistant until she began modelling for the Pre-Raphaelites; she was then possibly (if inter-mittently) Rossetti's mistress until he finally married her some eight years after rumours about them first began to circulate.

For Louie's twelfth birthday in August 1857 Jones took her as a special treat to visit Rossetti on her own. Jones and Morris became extremely fond of her in particular, and 'she used to spend whole days with [Morris] and Edward in their studio, furnished by them with pencils and paint, working after her own fashion'.[27] (Part of their fondness for her was due to her well-known ghoulishness: she wrote to Harry, reported Hannah to friends, of a little boy who had had 'its brains dashed out at the top of this street', of going to Tottenham Court Road to see where some houses had fallen down and the owner had been smothered, and of other excitements of a similar nature.) Fred, who was now back home from Jersey and ready to start work in his Uncle Pullein's accountancy office,† particularly appreciated being able to spend time with Jones, away from his almost entirely female home life:

---

* Burne-Jones continued to make these comic drawings throughout his life. They often involved himself – a long, thin, oppressed-looking man – and Morris, exuberant, roly-poly, with buttons flying off in all directions under the strain his waistcoat was put to. There are examples on pp. 112 and 113.

† Edmund Pullein was in partnership with a Mr Harding (later knighted); they wound up joint-stock companies under the Courts of Chancery.

I was sometimes allowed to go home and spend the night with him . . .
In the dimly-lighted studio, full of shapeless objects and black shadows,
he would tell me the weirdest and ghastliest stories he knew, raked from
old French and Italian sources . . .

Sometimes we . . . play[ed] a game that we called 'The Mexican Duel'
. . . First we turned off all the lights, and during a moment or two of
truce secured such strategic positions as we thought best. Then, in perfect
silence, we set ourselves each to discover the other and pounce upon him
with a yell . . . Once, I remember, after half an hour or more of painful,
ineffectual effort to find him, I called out that I was tired of it and would
play no more. I got no answer. 'It's no use lying low, the game's over.'
As I got no answer I made my way to the door which led into the
bedroom . . . I undressed and crept into the bed that he shared with me
– and there he was! Having started me some half-hour previously on the
silent war-path, he had crept straight to his room and gone to bed, where
he nearly swallowed the pillow in suppressing his laughter at the success
of his joke.[28]

This does not sound like someone amusing his fiancée's small
brother out of duty.

A great deal of Jones's and his friends' energy was spent on
practical jokes. Everyone around them was sucked in. 'Red Lion
Mary' was the woman who looked after the rooms at Red Lion
Square. She kept them as clean as possible (although that was not
very clean – according to Georgie, 'hers was not a nature to
dash itself against impossibilities, so the subject was pretty much
ignored'). More importantly, she entered into the spirit of the
group with a vigour: she and Morris were often at odds, so once
when he asked her to wind his watch before he left to catch the
Oxford train, she set it an hour ahead. She wrote comic notes at
Jones's dictation. ('Mr Bogie Jones' compts: to Mr Price and begs
to inform him he expects to be down for Commemoration and
that he hopes to meet him, clean, well-shaved, and with a contrite
heart.') She modelled for Jones when he needed her to, she learned
how to embroider under Morris's tuition, and – essentially – the
'raffish' life they led, with models and other such undesirables
visiting, held no terrors for her: 'She could be trusted also like a
good woman to show kindness to another woman whose goodness

was in abeyance, and could understand the honest kindness of a young man to such a one.'[29]

Georgie writes of this calmly in retrospect. There were aspects of the artists' lives that at the time Jones and his friends were not able to share with the minister's family, no matter how liberal they might be. This was, after all, the girl who found the simple fact that Watts and his friends had made studies of an actress exciting enough for her, 'to whom theatres were things unknown'.[30] Gabriel (as Rossetti was known to his friends) took Morris and Jones to see '*poses plastiques*' shows in Leicester Square;★ these featured women in flesh-coloured garments (or, in really daring shows, women in states of partial undress) who posed in historical or literary tableaux which involved nudity or near-nudity. He also took them to the Argyll Rooms in Piccadilly, a dance hall where prostitutes met their clients.

Despite Rossetti's best efforts, there was something charming, almost naive, about Jones & Co.'s attitude to sex, and women in general. At Oxford, reported their new friend Algernon Swinburne,

One evening – when the Union was just finished – Jones and I had a great talk. Stanhope and Swan attacked and we defended, our idea of Heaven, viz. A rose-garden full of stunners.† Atrocities of an appalling nature were uttered on the other side. We became so fierce that two respectable members of the University – entering to see the pictures – stood mute and looked at us. We spoke just then of kisses in Paradise, and expounded our ideas on the celestial development of the necessity of life; and after listening five minutes to our language they literally fled the room! Conceive our mutual ecstasy of delight![31]

This is the behaviour of undergraduates the world over.

Rossetti clearly felt that Jones needed wider experience. One night he paid a prostitute five shillings to follow his unsuspecting friend, telling her, according to Jones many years later, that 'I was very shy and timid and wanted her to speak to me. I said no, my

---

★ At least, this is asserted by several writers on the subject, although in no case is a source for it cited.

† Rossetti's word for any beautiful woman was quickly picked up by all his followers.

dear, I'm just going home – I'm never haughty with those poor things, but it was no use, she wouldn't go, and there we marched, arm and arm down Regent Street.'[32] Other meetings with the inhabitants of the street were less comic. Ford Madox Brown, a great friend of Rossetti, recorded in his diary:

To Jones yesterday eve with an outfit Emma [Brown's wife] had purchased at his request for a poor miserable girl of 17 he had met in the street at 2 a.m. The coldest night this winter, scarce any clothes & starving in *spite of prostitution*, after only 5 weeks of London life. Jones gave her money & told her to call next morning which she did & telling her story & that she had parents willing to receive her back again in the country. Jones got her to ask Emma to buy her this outfit & has I believe sent her home this morning.[33]

Apart from this bohemian existence, Jones was increasing his acquaintance with the more respectable end of the art Establishment. Ruskin was extremely impressed with the work he was now doing, and soon became a regular visitor at Red Lion Square. (The resemblance between the two men had been remarked on before, but never so strongly as the first time he called: 'he was shewn straight into the room where Edward was with no more introduction than, "Your father, sir." ')[34] Jones was also moving into society with frequent visits to Little Holland House. The Prinseps had taken to him, and felt the need to make sure that all aspects of his life were up to their standards: in 1858, the summer of the Great Stink, he became ill, and Sarah Prinsep swooped down and carried him off to be nursed at her home, away from his insalubrious lodgings (and friends?). Jones was rumoured to be infatuated – with whom or what was not at the time quite clear. Ostensibly it was with Sophia Dalrymple, one of Sarah Prinsep's sisters, who was then living at Little Holland House. In retrospect it is more likely that what really attracted him was the upper-middle-class way of life, which he was experiencing for the first time. Much later, Georgie acknowledged this: '*I could not realise then as I do now* what this visit to Little Holland House must have been to him' (my italics):[35] it was the opening of a new social world rather than an artistic one, and one he came to care very much for. Sophia

Dalrymple was merely the first appearance of a pattern that was to be repeated over and over again until his death.

Harry might have understood, but Harry was at Oxford, and with troubles of his own. George had seen them coming. He warned, 'The temptation and dangers of life now begin to thicken around you. The good principles with which I believe your mind and heart to be stored are really valuable when they guide, regulate, and restrain practice . . . The real and highest mark to aim at is the glory of God.'[36] Harry's troubles were not, however, the sort that talk of God's glory could help. For one thing, Harry was in love – with Peggy Talboys, a local girl he had met sometime in the last year. The main problem, however, was lack of focus, lack of drive. Harry had had a crisis of faith early on in his Oxford career, and with that crisis had lost his ambition (or his father's – it is not easy to separate the two) to become a minister. In the following terms Harry had found nothing with which to replace this. He was not cut out for academia; he had no interest in business. The dispersed Birmingham set were all forging ahead: Fulford was already ordained, Dixon was well on the way; Price was planning to study medicine; Heeley to go out to India; Jones was painting in London; Morris was working for G. E. Street, an Oxford architect. Harry was adrift.

What happened next has to be pieced together from memories set down long after the event. Hannah had been to Oxford in February 1858 to see the finished murals in the Oxford Union, and everything had seemed fine then. In May, Harry was due to sit his finals. His anxious family, who had sacrificed financially during the previous twenty years for this event, waited with increasing nervousness to hear the results. A day went by; three. Finally a letter came which 'buried our hopes'. Whether through nerves or fear, Harry had failed to sit his exams at all. George tried to remain calm, but his sorrow and disappointment were overwhelming – two days after Harry's letter he fainted in chapel and had to be helped home. It was a month before a hangdog Harry (now referred to by Hannah as 'my son from Oxford' rather than her more usual 'my dear son') returned home. Even then he arrived a day after he had promised, making Hannah and George sit up late waiting for him. Alice and Georgie had gone to Oxford the week before, but now they were staying with Jones's friends rather than appearing as the sisters of Macdonald.

What had happened was quickly overtaken by what was to be done. The money George had put aside for Harry's education since birth was gone and beyond recovery. Harry needed to find a job, if he was not to have a profession, and it had to be one for which no expensive training was necessary. It does not appear that any suggestion of going to work for Uncle Pullein was made – maybe because the indignity of being the new boy in an office where his younger brother, so recently patronized, was an old hand was just too great; maybe because Uncle Pullein had made it clear he was not wanted. Finally, in July, Harry sat the Indian Civil Service exam. He had shown no inclination whatsoever for the civil service or diplomacy until now; nor had he ever discussed the colonies as a possibility – not even when Heeley had made his plans to go. In light of this lack of interest, combined with the tales of the Indian Mutiny the year before which were still filtering back to England, this seems a hysterical response – a 'You'll be sorry when I'm dead' sort of gesture.

Harry did moderately well in his exams – sixteenth out of sixty-seven – and he was given an interview with the Indian Civil Service board. He and his parents talked of India, and what the opportunities were. He also went back to Oxford, to visit his friends and bring Peggy Talboys back to London with him for a visit. There was more talk, and yet more. Then, with no warning, on 4 November Harry announced that he was not going to India and would instead be leaving in a week for New York: he would send for Peggy when he got work and could afford to marry. Everything now moved at lightning speed. Harry went back to Oxford to say goodbye to Peggy, and his mother followed to do his packing for him. Suddenly he was gone.

This was the first major crisis since Carrie's death, and in some ways a more difficult one. Once Carrie had been diagnosed with consumption, all hope was gone and it was only a matter of waiting for the end. With Harry, blame could actually be laid, and the word 'failure' could be thought, if not used. The family needed to explain this incident to others, and to themselves, and they approached it in various ways over the years. The eldest and youngest sisters took similar routes: they ignored their brother's existence as much as possible. Edie published a memoir of her family in 1923 in which she managed to include one solitary sentence about Harry, blandly saying that he moved to America when she was young and she saw him only once thereafter. Alice too blocked him out of her mind. When her son was preparing to go to America for the first time she 'recalled' that she had a brother in New York.[37]

Her daughter, who probably heard it from her, remembered the story rather differently: 'Of course Uncle Henry Macdonald passed brilliantly into the Indian Civil Service – but refused to take up his appointment when Miss Peggy Passingham [*sic*] – to whom he was engaged – jilted him.'[38] A brilliant career destroyed by a faithless woman. It makes a good story.

Georgie was similarly oblique and, although she knew the story at first hand, little more factual: according to her account, 'largely through sickness, [he failed] to win honours in scholarship'; Peggy refused to go to India with him, so he changed his plans and went to America, getting a job there through the Talboys, 'hoping she would wait until he had made enough money to send for her'.[39] In this version the exams were taken, and it was illness that prevented the brilliant results expected. Georgie says Peggy's family got him a job, even though the first steady job he appears to have held in New York was found only after nearly a year's search. It was as a proofreader for the *New York Times*, and it is hard to see why, if her family could have helped, they had waited that long.

Fred, in his memoirs, gave another version of events:

His intellect was a strong one, and he found little difficulty in mastering any task to which he really gave himself. But his mind was not well-served by his body. There lurked within his constitution a certain tendency to lethargy which would now and again assert itself to the detriment of his work, and involve him in self-reproach and dissatisfaction . . . He . . . was expected by all his friends to take the highest classical honours in his final Exam. Then the high-strung cord of his endeavours seemed to slacken. I know not why or how, he left the university without taking a degree, and, breaking entirely with his past life, went to America and entered into business.[40]

This is probably the nearest anyone in the family got to comprehending the disaster that had befallen Harry – he had a promising career ahead of him; he threw it away; none of them ever understood what happened. But it does appear that none of them worked terribly hard at understanding. After Harry left, Hannah wrote to him regularly, the sisters practically never. At Christmas 1858, only six weeks after he sailed, Hannah wrote that 'Poor Harry's absence was sorely felt *by some of us*' (my italics). A cold epitaph.

II

Marriage and Children

5. Travelling in New Worlds
1859–1862

Ned and Georgie had been engaged for nearly three years, and marriage was not getting any closer. In 1856, things had briefly seemed promising when William Graham, a Liberal MP for Glasgow, had bought a picture, but since then sales had been thin on the ground. Morris married in April 1859. His wife was Janey Burden, the daughter of an Oxford stable hand, and they had met when Morris was in Oxford working on the Union murals. It was easier for Morris to take the plunge – he had an independent income and was wealthy enough to build a house in the country for himself and his wife. Until it was finished they lived at Great Ormond Street, which meant they were within visiting distance. For Ned and Georgie things were not so straightforward, although their engagement held and it was clear that it was now permanent. In March 1859 Mrs Prinsep and another of her many sisters, Lady Somers, came to call on Hannah, Georgie recalled:

The two tall, handsome women brought with them a breath from a world that was strange to us, but its brilliance and kindness were familiar to our imagination, and love for Edward was our common meeting-ground. Nevertheless the visit was felt to be one of inspection as well as courtesy, and in spite of the gracefulness of the callers was something of an ordeal to pass through.[1]

That the family made the grade was clear when an invitation to dinner for Georgie and Alice arrived soon after.

Jones too was travelling in new worlds, if more literally. Under Ruskin's watchful eye, and with his encouragement, he was planning his first trip to Italy. As well as tutoring at the Working Men's College, he had also begun to design stained-glass windows, which gave him a regular, if small, income. He, Val Prinsep and Charley Faulkner (another member of the Oxford set) planned to leave in

September for four weeks, going via Paris and Marseille to Genoa, Livorno, Pisa, Florence, Venice and Milan.

Georgie had left the Government School of Design, and in the summer of 1859 had started, together with Louie, to work on wood engravings. Ford Madox Brown offered to give both of them lessons. He did not have the most equable of temperaments, and when he had first been introduced to Georgie, the year before, had been worried that she 'threatens to turn out an other genious'.* (This was a reference to Lizzie Siddal, whom Rossetti was engaged in turning into an artist.) On further acquaintance Brown took to Georgie (as he had to Lizzie also), and decided that 'Her designes in pen & ink show real intellect.'[2] Georgie never felt as strongly. The most she would commit herself to was that Brown 'allowed me to come and try whether I could handle a paint brush'.[3] Edie later thought that her sister's talents, which she rated quite highly, were swallowed up by 'being thrown among artists of genius [which] discouraged her from continuing to cultivate this gift'.[4] That may have been the case; she may also have been discouraged by the reactions of the 'artists of genius' around her, including her fiancé. Jones wrote to Brown, 'God bless you, old fellow, how good you are to my Stunner . . . There never was any one in all this blessed world half so unselfish as you.' If this weren't indication enough of his estimation of Georgie's ability, the next letter he wrote, when Emma Brown was ill, makes it crystalline: 'Wouldn't it be better to give up that little Academy for the present – it must jar on you.' Georgie apparently found nothing unattractive in this sentiment. She repeats the above in her biography of Burne-Jones, adding, 'These last words refer to Madox Brown's incredible kindness in allowing me to come and try to paint from a model in his studio.'[5]

The 'Academy' didn't last long. In September 1859 George was to be moved again, to his next ministry, and the bad news for the girls was that it meant a return to the north – this time to Manchester. Despite the short amount of time left in London –

---

*Brown grew up and received his education in France; his English spelling remained eccentric.

particularly distressing for Georgie, who would be separated from Ned – it was decided that, before yet another move was under way, Hannah was to go to the seaside, with Georgie, Agnes and Edie. Their servant had had rheumatic fever, and Agnes, as the oldest girl not occupied outside the house, had taken care of both the housework and the nursing of the servant before the latter went into hospital; she had also nursed Hannah, who was again ill. Agnes was 'done up', and the doctor who had looked after Carrie suggested that she needed rest, and Hannah a change of air – 'I certainly need something I have not got.' Deal, in Kent, was settled on, and in July they set off for nearly six weeks.

Fred was to stay in London, where he was working and studying, like his uncle before him, at the Methodist Book-Room; lodgings were found for him with a congregant. He had settled well into London life, even founding a club, the Chelsea Athenaeum, with some friends. Just a few months before the family was to leave, he gave his first 'public' lecture, which, at any rate as he remembered it in retrospect, was a quite remarkable affair:

I served out Sydney Smith, as it were, in bucketsful, and turned on Macaulay as with a hose. The effect was all I had hoped for, and when after dilating upon Macaulay the essayist, and Macaulay the orator, I recited 'Horatius' from beginning to end, the chairman beamed approval, and the applause was long and loud. It is true that 'Horatius' had little or nothing to do with my subject, and was of unconscionable length, but 'time was made for slaves', not orators, and moreover I already had it by heart and might never again have the opportunity of using it. So it was thrown in, a kind of bonus, something over and above the bargain – which surely no one could object to.[6]

It is to be hoped that George – the orator par excellence – was there to see his son's debut.

As usual the family dispersed for the move itself. Hannah went ahead to set the new house straight; Alice stayed in London with Aunt Pullein for two and a half months; Georgie went to Birmingham; Agnes, Edie and Louie were fostered out to friends. Before Hannah left London, she visited Carrie's grave for the first time since the funeral; leaving it behind was her sole regret – she had become no more fond of the house in Beaumont Street than when she had first seen it, and she was looking forward to a new and better place to live. Georgie and Alice, with lively social agendas, could not feel the same. The younger girls, after six years in London, had few memories of their lives before – Agnes, the oldest, had been only ten when they moved south, and she was now reaching maturity. Louie, who six years earlier had protested loudly that she didn't like London and wanted to return to Birmingham, was now just as vehemently against this move. But a minister's family had no choice: north they went.

It may have been around this time that Alice became engaged to William Allingham. Allingham was an Irishman, a customs officer by day and a poet and friend to the great and good by night; he had known Jones for at least the past year, probably meeting him through Rossetti. Today Allingham is most famous as a poet for 'The Fairies', which begins, 'Up the airy mountain,/Down the rushy glen,/We daren't go a-hunting,/For fear of little men.' His diaries, edited by his wife, were published posthumously, and the wonderful eye for detail with which he recorded his friendships with Tennyson, Carlyle, Rossetti and Patmore has ensured him a vicarious fame. The fact that his wife was his literary executor does mean, however, that all entanglements before his engagement to her have been airbrushed out of the picture. Information about his engagement to Alice has therefore to be inferred from a few scraps only.

There is no question that Alice was at some point engaged to him: she even set his poem 'The Sailor' to music. When precisely in her career as a serial fiancée this happened cannot be determined. In the late 1850s Allingham was custom-house officer in New Ross, Ireland; a few years later he moved to a post in Lymington, Hampshire. As he made regular trips to London each year from both postings neither location precludes an engagement. In 1859, when Alice stayed in London on her family's return to Manchester, Hannah wrote to a friend that Alice had sent some news that astonished her, but she failed to say what the news was. With Alice it was often an engagement, although of course it might have been an engagement to someone else, and the engagement to Allingham could have taken place any time in the next few years.★

It is perhaps not surprising that the engagement did not last. Allingham was a quiet, self-effacing man (which was what made him such a good diarist, and perhaps was also the reason so many famous men enjoyed his company). At one point he described himself as having 'a queerish stained face; thick black hair and eyebrows, small, slight body'. He admitted that 'my outside is not my strong side'.[8] His was not the kind of character to appeal to self-believing, self-propelling Alice, and the thing was quickly ended.

It was not only Alice and Georgie who were attracting attention: Agnes at sixteen, and even Louie at fourteen, were receiving admiring looks. Agnes was blossoming; her finely cut features, delicacy of colouring, and wonderfully deep blue eyes made her a magnetic attraction for men: one young man proposed after merely seeing her in chapel. In addition, her musical skills were considerable, and made her much in demand socially. Jones, as a quasi-member of the family, used her as a model, as he did all the sisters. Georgie remembered:

Sometimes he would ask one of us to sit or stand for him for a few minutes, and if it was my sister Agnes, there were sure to be passages of fun between them. For a joke had grown up that she, whose features were certainly the most symmetrical in the family, was the plain, homely daughter who needed a little encouragement from time to time to keep her from being quite overwhelmed by a sense of her own deficiencies; and the task of reconciling this view with a request that she would just

★ There are two tantalizing scraps in Rossetti's letters to Allingham. In 1861 a postscript says, 'I will give your love to Ned Jones and wife. They have a nice pretty elder sister of Mrs. Ned's in town. There might be a chance for you!! Only a little elder!!!' This might have been the beginning of a relationship between Allingham and Alice; equally, Rossetti might not have known of earlier meetings. The second reference is more obscure. In 1863 Rossetti wrote, 'Pardon one last necessary word on this subject. Will you let me know whether you have written to Miss M. or intend writing, as otherwise I do not know whether or not I must show her what you wrote me.' That this might have been about Alice – no other 'Miss M.' is mentioned in the letters of the time – is the most that can be said.[7]

let him draw her profile, or please take such and such an action for a minute, was only to be achieved by the use of many words. It was a happy moment for us all when he begged her one evening to be good enough to sit for the witch who tolls the bell in the second scene of 'The Waxen Image', and her willingness to do it completed the jest.[9]*

Louie was pretty in a quieter way, and she was accomplished both artistically and in prose. Rossetti became her champion, writing that 'only one, I think, and that one a youngster as yet' was likely to prove Georgie's equal.[10] Jones was equally smitten: 'I want to see you, dear, so much, and look at your work [her wood engravings] and calculate how long it is to come before we bring out a picture book together with little LMs and EJs in the corners and make people say that Albert [*sic*] Durer has come back again.' He added later, 'I am determined to labour in every direction to get good engraving again, and I shall need you beyond words.'[11]

In the meantime his engagement to Georgie continued without showing any sign of moving closer to resolution. Georgie was taken one day on a state visit to meet Jones's god, Ruskin, at the National Gallery, where, nine years after Turner's death, he was still working on the collection of paintings that Turner had bequeathed to the nation. Ruskin was delighted with her, calling her 'a little country violet with blue eyes and long eyelashes, and as good and sweet as she can be'.[12]† Despite his approval, and now that she, with her family, was in Manchester, marriage was no closer. Finally, and luckily for her, Jones's friends took a hand.

Ford Madox Brown and his second wife, Emma, with their children, lived in Kentish Town, north London. Although highly respected by the Pre-Raphaelites, Brown had never managed more than a hand-to-mouth existence, sometimes even hawking his

---

* It is fascinating that the most Georgie can bring herself to say of her ravishing sister is that her features were 'the most symmetrical in the family', whereas she had no trouble at all in retailing Harry's lack of success. Why were positive qualities so much harder to acknowledge than negative?

† This assessment may have had more to do with Ruskin's renowned ignorance of women rather than any character traits of Georgie – she was not yet the formidable woman she was to become, but no one who had anything to do with her for any length of time thought her primary characteristic her long eyelashes.

work from a pushcart. In 1858, when his baby son died, he had to ask one of his very few patrons for money for the burial.[13] Despite his straitened circumstances, in April 1860 he and his wife invited Georgie on a visit of several months so that she could spend time with Ned. She wrote of that time:

Before my visit came to an end Madox Brown had decided that Edward had better be married without further delay, and since his character as counsellor stood high and we had no arguments to oppose the suggestion, it was suddenly settled. I wrote to my mother to the effect that so much of me had already left her kind hands that I prayed her now to set the rest free, and she and my father consented, asking Edward no questions, but committing us both to the care of God.[14]

This set off a flurry of activity in Manchester. Ned and Georgie had become engaged on 9 June (the day Beatrice had first been seen by Dante, Ned's hero),* and they wanted to be married on 9 June as well. The wedding might not be a high-society match, but Hannah was going to produce the best trousseau she could in the limited time she had been given. Georgie and her sisters were roped in to help, and during the next six weeks the house was a snowstorm of fabric – bonnets were trimmed; frocks, petticoats and under-clothes made; stays and boots bought. It was not for another three years that Ebenezer Butterick developed the paper pattern for home dressmakers in America, and yet another ten years before this innovation was on sale in England. But Hannah and her girls were thoroughly adept at judging a style and size by eye, then transferring this guess to a calico toile – a cheap 'trial' version that was snipped and stitched before the final, more expensive, material was cut.

In the meantime, Jones was working out his financial position – not very difficult, unfortunately, as the grand total of his funds did not reach £30.† In addition, he had one outstanding commission, to T. E. Plint, a northern collector introduced by Rossetti. When

---

* Actually, it appears from their work that Dante was far more Rossetti's hero than Jones's – but at this point Ned had taken over wholesale all of Rossetti's heroes as well as his opinions and slang.

† The bare minimum for entry into the middle class was £100 a year for a small family.

that was completed, there would be a little more cash to come in. On 6 June 'came a note from the unfailing Mr. Plint: "The two pen-and-ink drawings [Jones had sent on spec] are to hand to-day. I enclose order for £25 which you may need just now." '[15]

With these riches in hand, Jones really had no further reason to postpone marriage, apart from the one he 'confessed' to later – that it terrified him. He warned, 'I shouldn't be surprised if I bolt off the day before and am never heard of again.'[16] He didn't. On 9 June 1860 Georgiana Macdonald married Edward Coley Burne Jones at the Collegiate Church, Manchester, the same place her parents had married in, with her father to give her away – the only daughter he was to perform this function for. As all her sisters were to do, she married in an Anglican church.

Rossetti had preceded Jones by a mere seventeen days: he and Lizzie Siddal finally married on 23 May, and immediately set off for Paris. The plan was for the four of them to meet there and spend a couple of weeks together. But Jones, starting as he was to go on, became ill on his wedding night in Chester:

a sharp check . . . but a gleam of satisfaction reached us when the doctor spoke of me to Edward as 'your good lady', and gave me directions about what was to be done for the patient, with no apparent suspicion that I had not often nursed him before. Trusting in this and in some half-used reels of sewing cotton ostentatiously left about . . . we felt confidence that no one would guess how ignominiously newly married we were.[17]

It was lucky that Georgie felt able to slip into the role of nurse, as it was one she never ceased to play thereafter. Jones's highly strung nature meant that every emotional disturbance showed itself in physical symptoms: 'We always likened his constitution to that of an infant, who is at death's door one day and in full activity the next.'[18] Medical science at this time generally held that one had a certain amount of 'nerve force' at one's disposal: if it was used up in over-exertion – either physical or mental – then physical debility would naturally follow. There was no moral stigma to nervous collapses – they were thought to be organic in nature, and not caused by lack of will or lack of moral fibre. (This latter interpretation would come to predominate later in the century.)

Jones's breakdowns were therefore understood as the outward manifestation of the extreme pressure he put on himself to produce.

Instead of Paris, the Joneses returned to London and Russell Place, where they had taken rooms. It was not an auspicious beginning to married life:

> Russell Place had not expected us so soon and was unprepared to receive us; there were no chairs in our dining room, nor any other furniture that had been ordered, except a table. But what did that matter? If there were no chairs there was a table . . . sitting upon which the bride received her first visitors . . . The boys at the Boys' Home in Euston Road [one of Ruskin's projects] had made the table from the design of Philip Webb and were busy with chairs and a sofa.[19]

Other friends contributed much-needed pieces as they could. Philip Webb, Morris's architect friend, designed a cabinet painted with 'Good and Bad Animals', and William Burges, also an architect, created another, with panels decorated by a new acquaintance, Edward Poynter, a young painter recently back from studying in Italy and France.★

Other wedding presents were equally useful – Watts sent Georgie a sewing machine, a novelty at the time, and ferociously expensive:† 'A little thing that makes dresses and buys the stuff and almost pays for it,' was how Jones explained it.[20] Jones's beloved Aunt Catherwood sent a piano. In addition, another painter friend, Simeon Solomon, directed students along to Jones, which was surely as good as any present. Jones must have been selling at least a small amount of work. The rooms in Russell Place, while not glamorous, were what most of their friends expected. Nearly everyone they knew lived in more or less the same way.

The one exception was William Morris. In the same month the Joneses married, he and Janey moved into the Red House, in Bexleyheath, designed by Philip Webb. Morris had been involved in every detail – not merely the main rooms, but also the kitchen, 'fitted with capital Range; Buttery Hatch, Large and Light Pantry

★ Both cabinets are now in the Victoria & Albert Museum.
† Patented by Isaac Singer in the USA in 1850, a new machine could take a householder earning £150 per annum nearly three years to pay off.

... Large Store Room, Scullery, Larder, Housemaid's Closet, Watercloset, Beer and Wine Cellars'.[21] During the planning and decoration, Morris realized how hard it was to find furnishings and fabrics to meet his requirements. He decided that, as others must have the same difficulty, he would start a company to make the items he wanted. Morris, Marshall, Faulkner & Co. was born at 8 Red Lion Square, and consisted of an office and a basement for the workrooms and the kiln, all only yards from Morris and Jones's old rooms. The directors were Morris himself, Peter Paul Marshall,★ Charles Faulkner (who left his Oxford fellowship in mathematics to keep the books), Ford Madox Brown, Philip Webb, Rossetti and Jones – the latter four, together with Morris, being the firm's designers. Initially the company specialized in ecclesiastical commissions, with their first prospectus boasting 'Fine Art Work-men in Painting, Carving, Furniture and the Metals'; they soon moved on to private commissions and non-ecclesiastical public spaces.†

It is difficult to say even approximately how much Jones was earning in these early days – in Georgie's recollection it was a tiny amount. But on this tiny income they managed to keep a maid, for which an annual income of £100 was considered the bare minimum.‡ George du Maurier was at this time paying 25s. per week for his lodgings (breakfast included), which were similar to the Joneses', and in the same district. He had rather more funds, and so paid an additional £25 per annum for his studio.[24] Jones painted at home, and kept his rent to roughly £65 a year. It was

★ Peter Paul Marshall (1830–1900), a friend of Ford Madox Brown, was by training a surveyor and sanitary engineer. No one could ever quite remember why he had been a founding member of the company, and he certainly took no part in its day-to-day running. By the time the company dissolved, in 1875, he was a confirmed alcoholic.[22]

† The date of the founding of the firm fits in quite neatly with the increasing professionalization of artists. In 1861, for the first time, painting was listed in the census as a profession. (Jones listed himself in a later census as 'Artist. Painter of Pictures'.)

‡ Ford Madox Brown and his family paid a workhouse skivvy £5 a year 'and every thing found her',[23] but Mrs Beeton in 1860 gives £100–£300 as the minimum household income for hiring a maid-of-all-work – to her way of thinking the lowest of the low.

recommended that rents should not take up more than an eighth of a household budget, but London rents had risen sharply in the early Victorian period, and people often found that they were paying up to 20 per cent of their income for accommodation. Is it possible that Jones was already earning the £325 these figures would imply? Although he had few commissions, those he did have brought a reasonable price. Within a few years of his marriage he was charging 180 guineas for a smallish (three foot by two foot) painting. In addition he was earning about £130 a year from Morris, Marshall, Faulkner & Co. (or the Firm, as it was generally known to the designers). This was for dozens of small jobs, many of them paying only 10–15s. each. They were time-consuming, but would bring his income well into the middle-class bracket. A year after her marriage, Rossetti wrote to Georgie asking for the loan of her coral necklace, to use in a picture. This does not appear to have come with her into the marriage, and so, despite the poor-but-happy image she and her husband both liked so much to remember in later years – perhaps because by then they were rich but unhappy – it seems that they were doing relatively well from the very beginning. Certainly by the mid-1860s Burne-Jones (as he now began to sign himself) was much in demand. He joined in all the pastimes of his fellow artists. Later he would take pride in not being much of a joiner; now, joining was all part of the game.

In the 1850s Napoleon III had increased French spending on the Navy and on coastal defences. Then France annexed Nice and Savoy. By the late 1850s the British government began to fear an invasion, and this fear quickly spread across the country. By mid-1860 there were about 100,000 men in volunteer regiments; by 1862 this figure had grown to 160,000.[25]* Burne-Jones and his friends joined the Artists' Army Corps or, more formally, the 38th Middlesex (Artists') Rifle Volunteer Corps. It was a rather Keystone Kops version of the Army – or at least that was how they later chose

---

* Tennyson even wrote a poem in their praise: 'Riflemen Form!', which was published in *The Times* in May 1859. It was not, to put it politely, one of his best: '. . . Better a rotten borough or so/Than a rotten fleet and a city in flames!/ Storm, Storm, riflemen form!/Ready, be ready against the storm!/Riflemen, Riflemen, Riflemen, form!/Form, be ready to do or die!/Form in Freedom's name and the Queen's!'

to remember it, particularly Morris, who moved politically leftward and became embarrassed by his earlier conventionality. Simeon Solomon, Rossetti, Watts, Leighton, Millais, Ford Madox Brown, Holman Hunt and Val Prinsep all joined. Rossetti was quickly drummed out for querying orders – on 'Eyes right!' at his first drill, his unmistakable tones were heard to ask, very politely, 'Why?' Solomon, 'upon being requested to swear on oath of allegiance . . . asked, "Would the sergeant be satisfied if I just said 'drat it', as I have a conscientious objection to stronger language?" '[26] Others didn't (or couldn't) pay the membership fee of a guinea a year; yet others could not find time to attend the eight one-hour drills a month. Hunt kept losing parts of his rifle. Leighton fell off his horse.[27]

Georgie was appalled at this foray into politics, and later refused to say more than, 'of this episode in his life I remember little except a very tired man in a grey uniform'.[28] She added, as if this excused a shameful act, that Burne-Jones had never attended regularly.

A second sally into public life was no more successful. The Hogarth Club was an attempt to set up an alternative to the Royal Academy. In the admittedly prejudiced version of Violet Hunt, an early biographer of the Pre-Raphaelite Brotherhood, who disliked both Burne-Jones and Rossetti, it was 'not small enough to be friendly and not large enough to be important, a room to which nobody sends things and Friday night meetings to which nobody cares to go. Funerals are performed in the shop below through which one passes.'[29] Clearly she was not in its favour, but when it was first formed, in 1856, the artists had high hopes for it. Ultimately, after many meetings and much organization – both of which Burne-Jones found he disliked – it held only one exhibition and then dissolved in 1861. It was important in that Burne-Jones at the very outset of his career decided that he had no interest in the public aspect of being an artist, and no interest in the administration of the art world; these were not for him, and he had no plans to change. In this he was backed up by Georgie, who saw his attitude not as withdrawal but as the sort of self-reliance that the Wesleyans had long advocated.

In June 1861 the Burne-Joneses moved from Russell Place to 62 Great Russell Street, just opposite the British Museum. These lodgings were in every way better: unlike Russell Place, Great

Russell Street had a regular supply of water; in addition, Burne-Jones for the first time had his own room to paint in, with somewhat better light. Georgie now had space to have her sisters visit her regularly and spend weeks or even months at a time with her in London. This particularly suited Alice, who had not been entirely content to be eclipsed by her younger, less brilliant sister when she married first. Alice had spent much of that year rushing round the country, on visits to friends in Bolton, in Broughton, in Chorley. London was an even better proposition.

For the first time, the Burne-Joneses felt they had a home. Despite the fact that there was probably no proper kitchen (Georgie remembered this as a great time of eating at 'pothouses' – Solferino's in Rupert Street, the Cavour in Leicester Square),★ bake-shops that took in householders' food to cook were still relatively common, and made entertaining possible. Books of the period suggest that 'It is convenient, occasionally, to send the dinner out to be cooked', and give instructions on how to prepare the food properly: 'Put [the pig] in a shallow baking dish, wrap the ears and tail in buttered paper; send a good sized piece of butter tied in muslin for the baker to rub over it frequently.'[31] Not having a kitchen could make daily life very inconvenient: the landlady would supply hot water for washing at set times only (although a kettle could always be boiled over the fire). However, lack of a kitchen was also in many ways a blessing. For most of the period, cooking ranges were primitive. In the 1850s the common range had the oven on one side, a boiler on the other, to heat water. (The boilers tended to explode, as, to get the water hot, they had to be too near

---

★ The names of the restaurants were a sign of how closely the British population was watching the war for Italian independence. From the windows of their rooms in Great Russell Street, in 1864, the Burne-Joneses watched the arrival of Garibaldi at the British Museum. The chief librarian and creator of the great Reading Room was Anthony Panizzi, an exiled Italian much involved in the struggle in his homeland. The Burne-Joneses saw the Italian hero arrive, 'followed and surrounded by a great cheering crowd that surged through the gates and up to the house [that is, the Museum]. There he stopped before entering, and as he turned on the top step and stood bareheaded for a moment, his red-shirted figure showed clear above the dark mass of the people.'[30] Such was the popular adulation of the time that objects in daily use were branded 'Garibaldi': and so the squashed-fly biscuit was born.

the heat source.) The alternative was a Dutch stove, a round brick structure which burned charcoal and had a trivet on top to support a pan. The stove was set on four legs, about a foot off the ground. It was not until the 1870s that coal-burning stoves were in common use. By the 1880s 'close' ranges meant that the cook no longer had to lean over an open fire, but these ranges too had a tendency to explode. Gas was not used for cooking until the 1890s, and was not very common even then.

None of this limited the Burne-Joneses. Suppers and little parties were frequent. Janey and Morris, Lizzie Siddal and Rossetti were frequent guests – Lizzie also came to use Georgie's sewing machine. Swinburne would run in and out of the rooms, bringing verses to read as they were finished, and a new group of friends formed: Edward Poynter, who had taken over their old rooms in Russell Place, George du Maurier and Thomas Armstrong had all been art students together in Paris.★

The most important reason for the move was that Georgie was by now five months pregnant. With homes and now children, Georgie and her friends were leaving their youth behind. Janey had had a child, Jenny, in January 1861; Lizzie's pregnancy had ended in April with a stillbirth, and she was not recovering well. Georgie described their first visit: 'We found her sitting in a low chair with the childless cradle on the floor beside her, and she looked like Gabriel's "Ophelia" when she cried with a kind of soft wildness as we came in, "Hush, Ned, you'll wake it!" '[32] Rossetti issued a *cri de cœur* to Burne-Jones: 'By the bye, Lizzie has been talking to me of parting with a certain small wardrobe to you. But don't let her, please. It looks such a bad omen for us.'[33] Georgie and Ned managed to refuse Lizzie's offer of her baby's clothes, while accepting her suggestion of a baby-nurse for their expected child,† but nothing

★ Du Maurier never fulfilled his artistic dreams, but settled down as one of *Punch*'s most regular cartoonists; Armstrong too gave up painting, and from 1881 to 1898 became the director of the art division of the Department of Science and Art, South Kensington Museum (later known as the Victoria & Albert Museum).

† Rossetti's mother had suggested this particular woman, and no doubt she was gratefully taken up. Although midwives needed a licence to practise, to obtain it they had only to be recommended by some 'matrons' and take an oath to forswear child substitution, abortion, sorcery and overcharging – not in itself a guarantee of competence.[34]

could really help Lizzie now. Rossetti was at this stage a teetotaller (or, as he phrased it, 'a temperate person'),★ but Lizzie had been using laudanum since at least 1857, and after the death of their child the dosages were ever increasing.

Georgie can have only been terrified by this, but she waited out her time quietly. It was usual for the baby-nurse to arrive some time before the actual birth. The mother-to-be was considered an invalid, and the nurse had to expect to 'have much to endure from [her] whims and caprice'.[35] Whether Georgie felt capricious or not, it was a comfort to have an experienced woman to talk to, for there was a large amount of quasi-scientific information floating around, all of it suggesting, as childcare books always have, that if you did not provide for your children in exactly the method prescribed you would irreparably damage them for life. Childcare was an important subject: throughout the Victorian period, nearly 35 per cent of the population was under fifteen. Mothers were told that they should 'on no account' sleep in the same room as their babies: children required such a large amount of oxygen that if they breathed the same air as an adult they would not be able to get enough.[36] (There is no indication of why the same was not true of babies who were awake.) In addition, infants do not like to be moved, and 'cannot be too little handled'. The best baby food was 'baked flour', which was simply flour cooked into a pale-brown mass and then powdered with a spoon.

In the third week of October Georgie went into labour. It is unlikely that any anaesthetic was used. Queen Victoria had been given anaesthetic for the birth of Prince Leopold in 1853, which had begun to reconcile people to the novelty, but in 1861 it was still necessary for articles vehemently protesting its safety to be published. Rendering someone unconscious was dangerous, and immoral – it was taking God's power into man's hands. In addition, there were qualms from the Church: had God not told Eve that, for her transgression, 'in sorrow thou shalt bring forth children'? Was it right to alter this?

Without a doctor, anaesthetic would not have been possible

★ A bond he shared with Georgie, who remained true to her Methodist background and never drank alcohol in any form to the end of her life.

anyway, and there is no indication that Georgie had anything except a midwife. (Doctors cost up to £2, while midwives charged between 2s. 6d. and 10s.) Whatever the case, labour must have been prolonged, because her mother managed to arrive from Manchester only twenty minutes after the birth of Philip Burne-Jones (always to be known as Phil), on 21 October 1861. (According to his sister years later, he was originally to have been named Gilbert, but Georgie heard the nurse saying to him, 'Oh Gilbird, Gilbird, I wish I was as innicent as you,' and this put her off. Instead, said Burne-Jones, 'He is named Philip "after nobody".')[37]

There were no complications – a week later Georgie was taking the baby to see Aunt Pullein; not three weeks after that Phil, his mother and her parents all went to Manchester for his christening, Ruskin and Rossetti standing as godparents. (This trip was despite the books: Mrs Beeton recommended that the mother should remain in a darkened room for ten days, and that the baby should not be exposed to strong light or much fresh air during its first month.)[38] While the birth was straightforward, the radical changes brought by a child found Georgie unprepared, both physically and mentally: unlike many women of her day, she seems not to have read any of the multitude of books now available. 'No one had told us any details connected with it essential for our guidance . . . I can remember . . . a day on which the small stranger within our gates was the most valiant member of the family.'[39] This may be an indication that Burne-Jones was at the birth. It would not have been uncommon at the time – Gladstone saw all his children born, and commented that his wife quietly suffered at least 'six times as much bodily pain as I have undergone in my whole life'.[40]

Four months after the birth Burne-Jones thought that 'Georgie is thriving on the kid and the kid on Georgie he is the fattest boy known our friends here do me the compliment to say.'[41] That was probably true. There was another truth as well, seen by Georgie:

The difference in our life made by the presence of a child was very great, for I had been used to be much with Edward – reading aloud to him while he worked, and in many ways sharing the life of the studio – and I remember the feeling of exile with which I now heard through its closed doors the well-known voices of friends together with Edward's familiar laugh, while I sat with my little son on my knee and dropped selfish tears upon him as the 'separator of companions and the terminator of delights'.[42]

Georgie was trying valiantly to keep some semblance of independent life, apart from her husband's. It was not easy. After the departure of the baby-nurse, who normally stayed only a month after the birth, she hired a nursemaid to look after Phil during the day. She initially showed the same kind of unworldliness that Burne-Jones had done when Rossetti had sent a tart after him. She found a woman named Norma, and

I think, looking back, that she must have been entangled in a kind of life she hated and wished to get out of, and the door which it occurred to us in our simplicity to open that she might do so was that of our nursery. It touches me now to remember how much she seemed to like the idea of coming to take care of our baby. At first the arrangement appeared quite easy to make, but afterwards difficulties arose, and I do believe that Norma withdrew from it for our sakes and not because she did not wish to come.[43]

Once a more conventional nurse was in place, Georgie went back to the wood engraving she had worked at off and on for years. The few scraps of her work that survive today certainly show ability, but the response she received cannot really be regarded as very encouraging. Rossetti recommended her to his friend Alexander Gilchrist, who was looking for someone to copy some engravings by Blake for his biography of the poet and artist: 'She is very diffident, but I believe in her capabilities fully, as she really draws heads with feeling, and could give the expression.' Then the killer phrase: 'besides, Jones would be there to give help without trouble to himself'.[44] Ruskin was even more depressing:

I am delighted to hear of the woodcutting. It will not, I believe, interfere with any motherly care or duty, and is far more useful and noble work than any other of which feminine fingers are capable, without too much disturbance of feminine thought and nature. I can't imagine anything prettier or more wifely than cutting one's husband's drawings on the woodblock: there is just the proper quantity of echo in it, and you may put the spirit and affection and fidelity into it which no other person could. Only never work hard at it. Keep your rooms tidy, and baby happy – and then after that as much woodwork as you've time and liking for.[45]

A woman should be first a mother, then a housekeeper, then an 'echo' of her husband. This was the standard response to any artistic or academic endeavour by women. Just over twenty years before, Robert Southey, the Poet Laureate, had written to the young Charlotte Brontë, 'Literature cannot be the business of a woman's life, and it ought not to be. The more she is engaged in her proper duties, the less leisure she will have for it, even as an accomplishment and a recreation.'[46] Little had changed since then. All Georgie's female friends, and later her sisters, hurled themselves against this brick wall of male expectation again and again, until finally they each stopped trying, choosing different routes out.* Even Lizzie Siddal, the most obviously talented of them all, ultimately failed (although in the twentieth century her reputation was post-humously established). First she was told that her illnesses were caused by the 'overtaxing' of her 'mental power': that is, she was a woman trying to do something that it was perfectly clear should be done only by men. Then, when she had achieved something, the general consensus was that 'one sees in her black-and-white design and beautiful little watercolours Gabriel always looking over her shoulder, and sometimes taking pencil or brush from her hand to complete the thing she had begun'.[47]

Finally the women accepted their lot. Du Maurier wrote to his mother:

* Madeline Smith was a slightly unusual example of what happened to women who moved outside the boundaries set for them. She was the daughter of a prosperous architect in Glasgow. In 1857 she was accused of murdering her lover, Émile l'Angelier. After her acquittal, she could clearly no longer go on living in Glasgow: an unmarried woman who admitted to having a lover was unacceptable, even if she hadn't killed him. She moved to London under an assumed name, and eventually got work with the Firm as an embroiderer. Then, once safely back in 'womanly' mode, she married Morris's foreman, George Wardle.

The other day I happened to mention to [Val Prinsep] that Pem [Emma, du Maurier's fiancée] had thought of engraving, and he went to Burne Jones, the proeraphaelite [*sic*], whose wife is an amateur engraver. Yesterday he took me there, such a stunning fellow Burne-Jones – what *dear* fellows artists are. He insisted on my bringing Pem to his wife to see all about it, and if she likes it begin with her. So I'm going to take Pem there this afternoon.

Georgie took her responsibility seriously, as she took most things. The following month 'Emma and I went and coached up all sorts of information; the result of which is the enclosed performance . . . we are going to take the block to Mrs. Jones this afternoon for approval and correction.'[48] Then Emma cut herself badly on one of the engraving tools, and that was the end of that.

It may be that these women had little of any originality to offer. But it is impossible today to see the death of Lizzie Siddal in any other way than as that of an artist – of a *person* – who was not allowed to flower, who was imprisoned by the expectations of society. Lizzie's laudanum habit may have been a symptom of the constrictions she suffered in her life; she may also have suffered from some form of anorexia – her illness, while never diagnosed, caused extreme thinness and made it next to impossible for her to eat. The death of her child was one blow too many. In February 1862, coming home late one night, Rossetti found her dying of an overdose.

Although death was ever present in Victorian life, this was different: it was not disease, nor childbirth; it was nothing organic. In addition, for Georgie and Ned, with their religious backgrounds, Lizzie's despair was not only terrible to comprehend, it was also a *sin*. Georgie in particular had loved Lizzie dearly, but in the months before her death she had perhaps not been able to give her as much attention as she otherwise would have. On Christmas Eve, after weeks of sore throats and coughs, Burne-Jones had taken his handkerchief away from his mouth and seen that he was coughing up blood. Even forty years after the event, Georgie's terror was palpable when she wrote that 'this was his death-warrant'.[49] However, the doctor rapidly assured her that this was bleeding from the throat, where there was an infection, not the dreaded consumption.

Georgie retells the story vividly, with all the graphic details that remained fresh in her mind. But there is one curious omission. She asks, 'Who does not know' of the mad dash for the doctor, the horror of the errand? She does not say just how well she knew it. There is no mention of Carrie's death from the same disease (or even of Carrie's life) – not even an acknowledgement that the doctor she went for was the same one who had cared for Carrie in her final days. The Macdonalds, throughout their lives, never spoke of things that were unpleasant. Was this how Georgie now classed Carrie, or at least her death?

6. The Industrious Apprentices
1862—1866

By the spring of 1862 Burne-Jones had recovered, although he still needed to take care. Ruskin began to talk of taking Ned and Georgie abroad. He was more and more impressed with Burne-Jones, and wanted to introduce him to the wider world. He had done this on a smaller scale the previous year, when he had taken the Burne-Joneses to the theatre, which he described to a friend in America:

I took them both to the theatre the other night. She had only been twice in her life, and had never seen a ballet – and unluckily there was one, and the deep astonished pain of the creature, not in prudery, but in suddenly seeing into an abyss of human life, both in suffering and in crime, of which she had had no previous conception, was quite tragic.[1]

It is safe to say, looking back on the rest of Georgie's life, that the ballet was not nearly as much of a shock to her as it was to Ruskin – either that, or she weathered this exposure to 'crime' remarkably well. However, Ruskin persisted in his need to enlighten even those already enlightened, and Italy was next on his list.

Burne-Jones had been on two trips to France and Italy; Georgie had never been out of England. It was agreed that Phil would go to his grandparents in Manchester – Alice could easily come to London to fetch him – and Ruskin and the Burne-Joneses set off in May. They travelled via Paris, so they could visit the Louvre; but they were permitted only three days there by Ruskin. Then it was south, via the Italian lakes, to Milan and Parma. In Milan Ruskin took them to *Rigoletto*, which Georgie loved so much he took her again the following night. At this Burne-Jones drew the line, starting a lifetime of separate theatre-going habits. From Parma they were allowed to leave Ruskin and head off to Venice on their own, which was something of a relief. Georgie blossomed, and

Ned – now more in her company than he had been since the birth of Phil – was impressed. He wrote to Ruskin that 'Georgie is growing an eye for a picture, she darts at a little indistinct thing hung away somewhere, and says timidly "Isn't that a very nice picture?" and it generally ends in being a Bellini or Bonifacio.'[2]

Georgie was beginning to take on very clear characteristics of her own; no longer Ruskin's 'country violet', she felt able to disagree with him straightforwardly. On their return from Italy in July she told him:

Ned and I agree in liking our pleasure hot and strong, thick and fast, we would rather eat our cake then merely have it any day. I cannot imagine feeling as you do, that you would rather go without your cake than feel hungry for it tomorrow. We have been pulling the plums out of *our* cake at a fearful rate for the last month, and on Saturday we came to a sudden end of the feast, but we are glad we did it.[3]

The Burne-Joneses were glad to be back: Georgie had been missing Phil, and Burne-Jones had been missing his work (from now on to be a chronic reason never to leave home). Ruskin heard from his father, who disapproved of the Burne-Joneses on principle, and strongly suspected Ruskin of having paid for their trip. (He had.) Ruskin rose to their defence:

into this intensity of a mistake you fall – because you look to manner – of which you are only a judge so far as it is connected to wealth – not with character . . . I cannot possibly bear the injustice you do my noble friends in thinking they do me harm . . . Try and correct yourself at least in this one mistake – ask Jones out to any quiet dinner . . . and try to forget that he is poor.[4]

Burne-Jones and his wife were duly asked to dinner, and passed with flying colours.

In September 1862 George Macdonald was moved to Wolverhampton, which proved to be his final appointment. Fred had been studying for the ministry for the past two years. He, like the others in his family, found it difficult to speak of things that were important to him, and when he had first decided he had a vocation and wanted to enter the ministry he had found it easier to talk to the man he lodged with in London than to his father. He had moved to Manchester in 1860, just before Georgie's marriage, and began to receive the kind of focused attention that Harry had been the recipient of previously. He flourished, receiving a prize of £15 for excellence in study, and he gave at least one lecture before his ordination. Then in September 1862, just as the Macdonalds were moving to Wolverhampton, Fred left his family to go to Burslem in Staffordshire, where he was to begin his life's work as a Methodist preacher, following in the steps of his father and grandfather. Hannah's only comment was 'God help the poor boy.'

Shortly after her second son was settled on his path in life, her first wrote to her from New York. It was becoming abundantly clear that Harry was not going to find his fortune in America any more than he would have done in England. He was putting down roots all the same – he wrote that he had married, which increased the probability that he would never come back to England. This passed almost without comment among the sisters – Harry and his mother wrote to each other at least twice a month, and had done ever since his departure; in the intervening five years so much had happened among his siblings that somehow they had ceased to think of him.

The unmarried sisters carried on with their daily round of chapel-related activities. Their main concern was that their father was ill for most of the time now. Early in 1862 he had been taken ill after preaching – so much so that he couldn't even reach home, and was taken directly to the doctor's, where he was kept for three days. He was prescribed opiates and rest, and a few weeks later, when he was stronger, he was sent to Deal to convalesce for a month. He began preaching again in the summer, but was never really strong again. By the end of the year Hannah was referring to him as 'my invalid husband'.

Their friends were supportive, bringing gifts of food and drink. The Baldwins in particular were very attentive, visiting Hannah and George, and taking the girls out to concerts and teas. Although they had started out as Hannah and George's friends, by now George Baldwin's brother Alfred was a frequent caller, on Louie in particular. She was, according to the prejudiced Violet Hunt, extremely flirtatious – Burne-Jones said he could tell 'even at a distance, if she was talking to a man or a woman, by the shape of her shoulders'.[5]* Louie was only eighteen, however, and could afford to move slowly. Alice, at twenty-six, was beginning, despite her many fiancés, to look like an old maid. This did not suit her at all. Fred was settling in Burslem, and, before Christmas of his first year there, Louie went for a visit. Alice thought that there would be more excitement in London, and in October went on a four-month visit to Georgie.

By the time she returned there was a crisis at home. George could no longer walk, and had to be carried up and down stairs by his daughters. He was diagnosed with 'spinal irritation', a catch-all that covered many physical and mental illnesses that otherwise had no explanation. (With the discovery earlier in the century of the spinal cord's reflex functions, and its control over motor and sensory functions, it was thought logical that many illnesses should be rooted there.)[6] If George had not been seriously ill before, it is unlikely that after this diagnosis he was going to get much better: spinal irritation was another way of saying inflammation of the spinal cord, and for any inflammations bleeding, purging and the application of blisters were all considered helpful, together with a 'low' (that is, liquid) diet. Opiates were useful: 'What can be more appropriate in this condition of anaemia and exhausted nerve power than a drug producing increased action of both the [blood] vessels and the nerves?'[7] (If his illness was viral meningitis, which sounds possible, not much more could have been done for him today.)

Alice stayed in Wolverhampton until April 1863. Then, as George was not improving, she went to Fred in Burslem for a month. She was rewarded for her patience with a picnic at Lake Rudyard. There, family legend has it, while eating a spring onion she first set eyes on John Kipling.†

* One wonders if this is true – no one else remarked upon it.

† At this stage he had not added his mother's maiden name as he was later to do – John Lockwood Kipling. Soon he would be known to his family as John, to all others as Lockwood. To avoid confusion, Lockwood will be used from the beginning.

Born in Pickering, in Yorkshire, on 6 July 1837,* he was one of six children of Joseph Kipling, a Methodist preacher, and of Frances Lockwood, the daughter of a local architect. He was sent to Woodhouse Grove, the same Methodist school that George had attended. Unlike George, he had no desire to enter the ministry. Despite an education that had consisted of Greek, Latin, French, English, arithmetic, algebra, trigonometry, mensuration, Euclid, scripture, conference catechism, evidences of Christianity and scriptural antiquities,[9] with drawing tacked on only at the end, on leaving school he went to work as a designer and modeller at the pottery firm of Pinder, Bourne & Co., in Burslem. (Pinder and his brother, a minister, had both gone to Woodhouse Grove.) While working there he took evening courses at Stoke School of Art, a government training school taken under the wing of the South Kensington Museum when it opened in 1857.† Probably through this connection, Lockwood then spent two years in London as an apprentice to J. Birnie Philip, a successful sculptor who worked, among other things, on the frieze on the podium of the Albert Memorial, and with Gilbert Scott on some of the modelling for Exeter College Chapel, Oxford. It is likely that from 1860 to 1864 Lockwood was working on the decorations of the new buildings at the South Kensington Museum, although the only clue is that today, in the museum's courtyard, the wall tablet showing the prime movers of the museum includes, very distinctly, a short, stocky, bearded figure that is completely unmistakable.[10]

Wherever he had been, by 1863 he was spending part of the year at the South Kensington Museum and part in Burslem (possibly supervising the terracotta decorations ordered by the museum). He

* Later his daughter was to write indignantly that he was born in 1838. The origin of this mistake was that Alice was three months older than her husband, and mortally embarrassed by the fact. She refused to give her date of birth ever after (even leaving instructions that it was not to go on her tombstone); her husband lied about his age to humour her, and general confusion was therefore created all round, much as Alice would have wished. There is no real doubt, however: the birth of John Kipling was registered in 1837 in the Pickering District registry of births.[8]

† The South Kensington Museum, set up with the profits of the Great Exhibition of 1851, changed its name to the Victoria & Albert only in 1899.

was a good companion, friendly, outgoing and yet calm. He never lacked for friends who described him fondly. He was 'a little man [he admitted to five foot three] with a big head, and with eyes for everything';[11] 'a rare, genial soul, with happy artistic instincts . . . and a generous, cynical sense of humour'.[12] He was

in every sense a choice spirit; gentle, kindly and of remarkably even temperament. His knowledge of art, his wide reading, his extensive travel, and an interest in every phase of the world's doings, made him a rare conversationalist, when inclined to talk, and an encyclopaedia of knowledge as extensive as it was accurate.[13]

It was rare for someone *not* to comment on his breadth of knowledge – later one of Fred's daughters nicknamed him 'Enquire within upon everything'[14] – but it was Edie who best understood the attraction he had for Alice: their temperaments contrasted and at the same time did not clash. Instead Alice's quickness found a response from the rarely excited but always comprehending Lockwood. Alice had a 'sprightly, if occasionally caustic, wit, which made her society always desirable, except, perhaps, to those who had cause to fear the lash of her epigrams'.[15] Lockwood could soothe her when she was overwrought, and match her when he chose. Her only comment: 'I ought to have met John earlier.'[16]

Once they had met, an understanding was quickly reached. The difference between Alice's previous engagements and this one was that she now had a partner who knew what he wanted, and was going to keep on until he got it.★ Within a month of their meeting he was visiting her at home in Wolverhampton. On one of his early visits, George was just beginning evening prayers. 'There was a man sent from God whose name was John,' he read as Lockwood appeared.[18] It was taken by Alice as an omen. The only problem

★ Despite the usual ups and downs of married life, he never wavered. Editha Plowden reported that in 1877, after more than twenty years of marriage, the morning after Alice left India on a trip to England Lockwood looked 'as though he had cried all night. His voice seemed to have fallen half a tone, and he spoke with a languor that made my heart ache. His office walls were lined with casts from the antique, and, looking at the Venus torso, he said listlessly: "I think I will take her home to live with me." '[17]

was that Lockwood was not earning enough to marry and, as with Burne-Jones in 1856, it was not clear when he would be.

In addition, things were no easier at home. First, while Louie was in London in the summer of 1863 she came down with smallpox. Fortunately it was a mild dose, and Aunt Pullein took over the nursing – a lucky thing, given that George in Wolverhampton not only was no better but was now much worse and it was impossible for Hannah to leave him. Alice came down to London to help with Louie, and at the end of three weeks her sister was well enough to travel. She and Alice then left for Ramsgate, where they stayed for more than a month, until Louie had gained a little strength. They then returned to Wolverhampton, where in the interim George, aged only fifty-eight, had finally had to acknowledge that he would never be able to work again. This meant another move, as a new minister would be needing their house. To lighten the load, for Hannah, was the thought that her itinerant life was finally over. She would need something to cheer her, because there was shortly bad news from the Burne-Joneses in London.

By the spring of 1864 Georgie was expecting her second child, and before the birth she, Ned and Phil went to have a short holiday in Littlehampton with Burne-Jones's father, the Morrises, Faulkner, and Faulkner's mother and two sisters. They had a splendid time – the practical jokes and games are a reminder of how young they were. One night they worked out an elaborate tease of Morris (who was the butt of most jokes). They stacked a deck of cards so that Morris appeared to have an unbeatable hand – but, no matter how wonderful it was, the others all had hands that were even better.

When they returned to London towards the end of October, Phil was unwell. By early November both he and Georgie had developed scarlet fever. At first things were not too bad; Burne-Jones kept the Macdonalds informed that things appeared to be under control. Then Georgie's baby arrived prematurely, brought on by the illness. Her condition worsened, and for eight days it appeared as if she might die; the baby, named Christopher, struggled on for three weeks before giving up and dying towards the end of the month. Hannah was torn between her invalid husband and her delirious daughter and dying grandson. She came for a few weeks, but had already returned to Wolverhampton by the time

Christopher died. (It may be because of this that there was no talk of burying him in the extra space in Carrie's grave – he was buried at Brompton Cemetery too, but separately.)

The Burne-Joneses' friends all offered support in their own ways. Edward Poynter, Frederick Burton (soon to become a colleague in the Old Society of Painters in Water-colour), and William de Morgan (a ceramicist) came to support Burne-Jones in his vigil; Ruskin ordered straw to be put down in the road outside to muffle the horses' hooves – an old custom that had almost died out, but was remembered kindly by Georgie. Rossetti, from Paris, sent his love via Swinburne, who was beside himself with anxiety – Georgie was his confidante, and he had an overwhelming fondness for small babies. He wrote pathetically to Burne-Jones, 'how very grateful I should be for any chance of being useful'.[19] As soon as she was able to travel, Burne-Jones took Georgie and Phil to Hastings to recover in the sea air (which, given that it was December, must have been overpoweringly bracing).

After Hastings, Georgie could not bear to go back to London: the room where she had been ill became an 'incarnate terror' for her, and it was decided that, rather than face it again, they would move. With their (as they had thought) increasing family, a new place to live had been in the air for some time. They had talked of building a wing on to the Red House and living next to the Morrises. Now illness and death had brought down that castle from the air. Burne-Jones had done no work for four months; doctors were expensive; there was no money to spend on building. What was more 'all the spirit seems gone . . . out of our country plans'.[20] He broke the news to the Morrises, and began house-hunting in London. Morris responded characteristically, apparently more concerned about the possible loss of his working partner than about the death of Burne-Jones's son, or his friend's consequent distress:

As to our palace of Art, I confess your letter was a blow to me at first, though hardly an unexpected one – in short I cried; but I have got over it now. As to our being a miserable lot, old chap, speaking for myself I don't know, I refuse to make myself really unhappy for anything short of the loss of friends one can't do without. Suppose in all these troubles you had given us the slip what the devil should I have done? I am sure I couldn't have had the heart to have gone on with the firm: all our jolly subjects would have gone to pot – it frightens me to think of, Ned . . . I need hardly tell you how I suffered for you in the worst of your troubles; on the Saturday I had begun a letter to you but it read so dismal (as indeed I felt little hope) that I burnt it.[21]

While her husband was searching, Georgie went to Wolver-hampton with Phil for Christmas. With the help of Crom Price, Burne-Jones's friend from Birmingham days, who was now back in England and a master at Haileybury, the public school near Hertford,* a house in Kensington Square was taken on a three-year lease and it was decorated and their goods were moved in before Georgie returned at the beginning of January 1865. Edward Poynter, who had earlier taken over their rooms in Russell Place, now took over the Great Russell Street rooms.

Kensington Square was a vast improvement. For the first time they had a house with a garden, even if this was tiny and mostly a place for the local cats to congregate – to Burne-Jones's fury. To compensate he had two good-sized rooms to himself as studios, and space for others to stay besides – there would be no more overnight guests sleeping in his painting room. Allingham visited early, as did Rossetti, for the first time in two years breaking his seclusion to visit them. Val Prinsep and Frederick Burton lived around the corner. The house was done up with pomegranate wallpapers and Sussex rush-bottom chairs from the Firm; Morris gave them a Persian 'prayer-carpet'.†

In addition, for the first time Georgie could begin to housekeep properly. No more makeshift dinners. Of course, this brought its own problems – including vermin. Housekeepers were given very elaborate instructions to stop insect infestations: they were to fill all

---

* Price had given up his earlier medical ambitions and instead had gone to work as a tutor to a family in Russia.

† The Firm was becoming well known to the discriminating: soon it would be recommended in guides for the newly married. Modern furniture, brides were informed, could be bought at Liberty, Maple's, the Junior Army & Navy or the Baker Street Bazaar, but it was the Firm that 'offer[s] special advantages to those who know the difference between artistic and non-artistic forms, and do not mind paying for what they admire'.[22]

holes with cement, then scrape out the old mortar between bricks and replace it with more cement. Then carbolic acid should be used in scrubbing water every day, and beetles would be entirely eradicated. Otherwise they 'will multiply till the kitchen floor at night palpitates with a living carpet, and in time the family cock- roach will make raids on the upper rooms, travelling along the line of hot-water pipes . . . the beetles would collect in corners of the kitchen ceiling, and hanging to one another by their claws, would form huge bunches or swarms like bees towards evening.' Rats and mice, on the other hand, 'are nice, pretty, clever little things, and not objectionable unless allowed to get ahead. They are our friends, acting as scavengers, and are to me in no wise repugnant . . .'[23]

While being able to do laundry at home does not sound exciting to a modern audience, in an age in which contagion was a chronic worry many people disliked sending laundry out, for fear of infec- tion and vermin being carried back in the 'clean' clothes. And, as Georgie now had a full-time servant (possibly two; it is not clear when the cook arrived), for the first time she could do the household laundry at home, in the way her mother had taught her. This was no light undertaking. All the water had to be boiled on the kitchen range, which generally meant that the range could be used for no other purposes – no hot water for the rest of the house that day; often no hot meals. An average household wash took four days to do, either once a week or once a fortnight: clothes and linen were 'firsted' or washed through once in boiling water, then 'seconded' in clean hot water with washing soda and soap. Then they were again boiled in the copper for a while, before being rinsed in water with the addition of blue-rinse, which counteracted the yellowish tinge produced by the soaps of the period. They were rinsed again to get rid of the blueing. After each of these stages every piece would have to be wrung out – back-breaking labour with the larger items, and involving boiling water. Only then could things be hung out to dry. With luck, this was all achieved on Monday. On Tuesday the clean items were folded, sprinkled with water, and made ready for man- gling and ironing. (Mangling was a preliminary process to get the bigger creases out before ironing.) Non-washable clothes, such as woollen and silk dresses, had to be taken to pieces, then stains were removed with spirits of turpentine. Most cleaning materials were home-made. A recommended method for cleaning silk was to rub the material with a sponge dipped in an equal quantity of honey and soft soap, mixed with spirits of wine. Starch was dissolved in hot water, and items were dipped in it before they were ironed. At least two irons were in use at once: one heating over the fire while the other pressed clothes as quickly as possible before it lost heat. Wednesday was reserved for any mending or other needlework which was necessary after the rigours of the laundry, and for fine finishing: for example goffering irons, which looked like modern hair-curling irons, were heated and used to press ribbons, lace and trim, especially on ladies' and children's clothes. On the last day everything was aired before open fires to remove any residual dampness.★

With their improved social position, this was the kind of household routine that Georgie was now presiding over. They were moving up in the world. Burne-Jones described it all to Ruskin:

as for Georgie she is growing rather grand in her chintz room. She wears a chintz dressing-gown and looks like a part of the furniture, and as if you could order any number of her in the Tottenham Court Road. Phil also has a nurse all to himself now whom he calls 'my cook' and altogether Spartan virtue is giving way to fashion . . . Saturday his mama extemporised an organ for him out of a small bonnet box – to her presently enters Phil with an infuriated countenance: 'Do you know you've given me such a thing as a step-mother would have gave me, something no bigger than a little fly upon the floor.'[24]

Phil was aware early on of the keen financial and social niceties that were to occupy him so much in later life. Hat-box organs may have been good enough to play with in Georgie's childhood, but by now good-quality toys were available inexpensively. Wooden animals, carts, rocking horses and train sets, plus games such as dominoes (which remained a favourite pastime of Burne-Jones to the end), Ludo, Happy Families and others, were all mass-produced, together with new, coloured children's books: Hans Christian

★ Early on, appliances were created to ease the burden. By the 1880s a 'Canadian prize washing machine' substituted rollers turned by a crank for the scrubbing board; a wringing machine with rubber rollers pressed out moisture; and various drying and airing machines were patented.

Andersen was a great favourite of the period; Edward Lear's nonsense poems were published in 1846, and from the 1850s a new
genre – adventure stories for boys – began to appear. 'Museums'
(keeping odd objects on a special shelf) and stamp-collecting were
middle-class pastimes that parents approved of – they kept the
children quiet and had the added benefit of being 'educational'.
Zoos and circuses fell into the same category: Wombwell's Circus,
the most famous of the period, advertised itself as 'the wandering
teachers of Natural History'; Sanger's Circus specialized in military
recreations, including, in the 1880s, the Relief of Khartoum and
the death of General Gordon.[25]

Alice came down from Wolverhampton soon after Georgie
returned, to see her into her new house. Also to see Lockwood,
who, it now appeared, might be closer to earning enough for them
to marry. Following the Great Exhibition of 1851, when Indian
artwork had been shown to great advantage, Henry Cole had
bought the East India Company's entire collection of Indian art for
the future South Kensington Museum. In 1859 Ruskin had lectured
there on Indian art. Eight years earlier he had admired Indian works
of art that were 'almost inimitable in their delicate application of
divided hue, and the fine arrangement of fantastic line'. Now he
was shocked by the deterioration he saw in imports. (He was
probably also embarrassed by their overt eroticism.) It was claimed
that, with India flooded with British goods, native craftsmanship
was dying. British-run schools training Indian craftsmen would not
only 'set the natives on a process of European improvement' but
would also 'improve the taste of the native public as regards beauty
of form and finish in the articles in daily use among them'.[26] Schools
had duly been set up in Madras, Bombay, Calcutta and Lahore, and
British artists and teachers were being recruited. John Lockwood
Kipling was a natural for a job – in February 1863 he had won joint
first prize in a competition for the ceramic decoration of the
Wedgwood Institute, a commission so prestigious that Gladstone
came to lay the foundation stone. His work at the South Kensington
Museum meant that he had plenty of access to the old East India
Company collection. By October 1864 he and Alice were talking
about India as a distinct possibility. In December a Bombay High

Court judge, who was in England for the purpose, wrote to the Chief Secretary of Bombay confirming that he had found the right man,[27] and in January 1865 Lockwood signed a three-year contract as an 'Architectural Sculptor' and Professor of Modelling at the Sir Jamsetjee Jejeebhoy School of Art and Industry in Bombay,* where he was to be one of three English tutors, with a monthly salary of 400 rupees, £36, which, while not lavish, was enough to support a wife and family.[28]

George's illness precluded the wedding being held at home – Hannah now referred to herself as a prisoner with a 'poor afflicted husband'. Georgie, only weeks in her new house, stepped into the breach. Fred travelled to London to give Alice away; Louie and Agnes came to stay beforehand. It could be the last time the five siblings were to be together for what might be years. Hannah baked a veal cake and sent it down, as her contribution to the festivities. Finally, on 18 March 1865, with only a few mishaps (Brown, known for muddling names, called John Kipling 'John Gilpin'; Lockwood on his way to the ceremony mislaid his key and left all his money behind; Alice, busy getting Louie and Agnes ready, found that the carriage was at the door before she remembered she herself wasn't dressed),[29] Alice was at last married.† Louie rather sniffily described Alice's wedding band as 'as thick as a coster-monger's',[30] but Alice was happy. The Kiplings made a quick dash to Wolverhampton to say goodbye, and three weeks after their wedding they were on board the SS *Ripon* bound for Egypt and, ultimately, Bombay.

'. . . daybreak, light and colour and golden and purple fruits . . . There were far-going Arab dhows on the pearly waters, and gaily

---

* It was also known as the Bombay School of Art. For convenience I shall refer to it this way throughout.

† It is stated in many biographies of Rudyard Kipling that it was in the marriage register that John Kipling became John Lockwood Kipling for the first time. However, some time in 1863 or 1864 he had made a jug for Fred on which he painted 'To FWM from JLK'. (It also included a poem in praise of beer: 'Twin child of Ceres, Bacchus's daughter,/Wine's emulous neighbour if by stale:/ Ennobling all the nymphs of water/and filling each man's heart with laughter – / O give me Ale!' It would appear that Fred was no more teetotal than his father.)

dressed Parsees wading out to worship the sunset.'[31] The memory is Rudyard Kipling's, and was recorded more than seventy years after his parents first stepped off the ship in Bombay in May 1865. But the startling colour and light, the dazzling new world spread out before them, were also their first impressions of this new continent. Lockwood later said that Bombay was 'a blazing beauty of a city . . . I never see it but to renew my conviction that it is the finest city in the world so far as beauty is concerned.'[32]

Lockwood immediately found a whole new world to explore and try to understand. Nothing was too small or too widespread to escape his attention. He could spend more than an hour watching two lizards play on the warm floor of a south-facing verandah, or he could describe, in a letter to Louie, how he 'stood in the thick of a dense native crowd watching the gas lighted the other night and grieved deeply that I could not understand the buzzing conversation round me'.[33] An old India hand they met soon after they arrived said that 'From the first [they] took a very intelligent interest in everything connected with the people and country, and even in their Bombay days [they] were better informed on all matters Indian – religions, customs and peculiarities – than many officials who had been long in the country.'[34]

In general Alice was less immediately concerned to explore her surroundings, and more worried about finding a home. In Lockwood's letter to Louie, her urgency is explained: Alice was pregnant, expecting their first child at the end of the year. They needed to move into a house, and Lockwood needed to settle in at the school, which was a 'school' only in so far as teaching went on there. There were no permanent buildings yet. Depending on whose information you believe, the Bombay School of Art was either in a tent or in a temporary building★ – the main buildings were not to be completed for another thirteen years. Their house was no more ready than the school, and for some time the Kiplings

★J. J. Rivett-Carnac, in *Many Memories*, goes for the tent; A. W. Baldwin in Gross, *The Age of Kipling*, is on the side of buildings. Rivett-Carnac does not strike me as hugely reliable – he is far too concerned to make sure that the reader knows how important he is. (The Kiplings were not much more impressed: Trix Fleming was later to rename him 'Trivet-Claptrap'.) On the other hand, he was there; A. W. Baldwin was not born for another half-century.

lived in one of a row of brightly coloured 'tents' (actually made of plaster) on the Esplanade.

There, on 31 December 1865, Joseph Rudyard Kipling was born – 'Rudyard', suggested by the romantic Louie, who had agreed to be godmother, to commemorate his parents' meeting; 'Joseph' to conform to the Kipling family tradition of naming alternate first sons 'Joseph' and 'John'. Alice had a difficult birth, and now a proper home was ever more imperative.

Alice set to work, organizing everyone – she had 'a fine gift for finding out what anyone could do and setting them to work'.[35] Lockwood had a good salary but not a lavish one, so it was essential to find local workers to produce furnishings and furniture, rather than shipping things (expensively) from 'home'. With Alice's managerial abilities and Lockwood's trained eye, they not only created an individual house, they also solved some of the problems that beset the English in India. For example, because of the climate, ceilings were high and windows were under the roof, usually covered with drapery or hangings. But Lockwood

devised an art print, at a price of only a few pence a yard . . . A dull red was the predominant colour and the general impression, and the print was divided into a series of horizontal strips above and rectangular patterns below. One of the horizontal stripes having a whitish ground was decorated with lines of marching men, elephants and horsemen, conventionalized into a restful pattern. In the rest free use was made of the geometrical and floral conventions. For a modest number of shillings you had a dado five feet high round the indecently bare flanks of your sitting room . . .

Here was the product of knowledge and ingenuity on several different planes: the work of a man who knew the purses and the tastes of a European, the conditions and capacities of the Indian craftsmen, and the adjustment which would yield the artistic result. If wit could have saved Indian art out of the deluge of combined economic and social change, Lockwood Kipling would have done it.[36]

These domestic refinements were produced in his not very copious spare time. He had a full-time job at the Bombay School of Art, and he had also to find extra pupils to supplement his basic pay, which covered only the necessities. To Alice's irritation, they did not automatically move in the 'best' circles – Lockwood at this point had not formally joined the Indian Civil Service and, even when he did, art teachers were not high on this conventional, hierarchical society's list of people to see and be seen with. So he accepted many other jobs that brought him into contact with those in government. He worked, together with his students, on architectural decorations for Crawfurd Market in Bombay (built between 1865 and 1871), designing and supervising the making of the reliefs on the building and the fountain. He visited Simla to organize a series of sketches that was wanted for a Department of Commerce report. He drew, at the government's request, pictures of craftsmen at work, for display in London. He travelled to the Central Provinces to make sculptural casts of the rock temples. He spent time in small villages in order to report on Indian handicrafts.

Lockwood, in fact, very quickly made a name for himself as a man who could make things happen. He also crusaded for the preservation of local styles and techniques against commercially weighted persuasion to switch to Western methods. When he arrived, Indian students were being taught European techniques by European teachers.[37] Three years later he acknowledged the damage that had been done to traditional crafts, and noted, 'As a rule, those of my students who have come to me . . . direct from native towns, without having received any instruction in the School of Art, are decidedly the best.' His ideas were radical for the time, but the results were appreciated early on. In 1873 Colonel H. St Clair Wilkins, aide-de-camp to the Queen and architect of the New Secretariat in Bombay, wrote to him:

I consider you were the pioneer of your art in this country; for, eight years ago, when I first met you, artistic sculpture of natural objects was unknown in India. In 1863 an architectural design of mine was said . . . to be out of the question owing to the introduction of foliated capitals and carving. In 1865 you had, I believe, performed that which in 1863 had been pronounced impossible.

★

These were modest gains compared to those of his artist brother-in-law back in London. In 1865 Burne-Jones had been made a member of the Old Society of Painters in Water-colour (the 'Old Water-colour Society' – more prestigious than it sounds). This gave him an annual exhibition showcase, and also some confirmation of his professional standing. Morris, Marshall, Faulkner & Co. had also been put on a slightly more professional footing. Charles Faulkner had decided to return to his Oxford mathematics fellowship, and the Firm's books were now taken over by Warington Taylor, who tried to stop Burne-Jones using the Firm as his personal bank. Burne-Jones had been in the habit of drawing cash against commissions. Taylor was ever-vigilant: 'What does that £60 owing by Burne-Jones mean? He never had £60 to pay anybody.'[38]★ In addition he prevailed upon Burne-Jones to hire a studio assistant – the first of many attempts to speed up a very slow worker. Charles Fairfax Murray – known as 'the boy' – arrived at a salary of 25s. per week, or £65 per annum, which is a vivid indication of how Burne-Jones's income had soared.

While all this had been going on on the work front, the home front had not been quiet either. Edward Poynter had been a friend, part of the large and lively group around the young Burne-Joneses, ever since they married. Now he began to draw closer. Agnes was growing more and more beautiful, with exquisitely delicate features, beautifully modelled; Lockwood had referred to her as 'tyrannously beautiful'. In the fashionable world, women had taken to wearing bright new colours only recently made achievable through the discovery of aniline dyes.† They also wore large crinolines, which grew in size as cheap sprung-steel hoops replaced the earlier, and heavier, whalebone versions, or the even earlier layers of petticoats. This created the large bell-shape that today says 'Victorian'. Georgie never wore anything of the kind. From the beginning of her marriage she had gone completely Pre-Raphaelite

★ Although Burne-Jones was beginning to earn good money, and certainly had more work than he could keep up with, his lack of financial sense meant that immediate cash was often a problem. By 1868 he owed the Firm over £120. This was only partly eased by a small legacy from an uncle.

† For example magenta and solferino (an acid green), named in honour of Napoleon III's victories over the Austrians.

– or, as it was becoming known, 'Aesthetic' – and her dresses were all uniformly unfashionable serge, neatly gathered at the waist, with perhaps some embroidery at the throat and wrists to lighten the flat, muted colours.* Agnes, however, embraced the new and desirable lures, despite the many difficulties caused by the excessive space the skirts took up – an overenthusiastic gesture could upset a small table or chair, and Agnes found that at the Red House her bedroom was too small for her to get her crinoline in. Edward Poynter had, despite his calling, never lost his desire for convention-ality, and Agnes, a beautiful young woman suitably dressed for society, looked just the wife for an ambitious man.

Poynter was ferociously ambitious. He had started on his life as a painter early, being in many ways born into it. His father was Ambrose Poynter, a successful architect; his great-grandfather was Thomas Banks, an eighteenth-century sculptor.† He had gone to study in Rome in 1853, where he began a friendship with Frederic Leighton that lasted their lifetimes, and he then went on to Paris to study under Charles Gleyre, a disciple of Ingres. (Monet studied with Gleyre at the same time. Sadly nothing rubbed off on Poynter's art, which always remained resolutely academic. It is very difficult to remember that, outside the insular British art world, Manet was exhibiting *Le Déjeuner sur l'herbe* and *Olympe* two years before Alice married.) During those Paris days of the 1850s Poynter had shared a studio with George du Maurier, Thomas Reynolds Lamont and Thomas Armstrong. Among their friends were James McNeill Whistler and a Greek named Alexander ('Alecco') Ionides, later to play a role in the life of Poynter's brother-in-law.

These friends were remembered and caricatured by du Maurier decades later when he wrote *Trilby*, his novel of bohemian Paris

---

* The current use of vegetable dyes for dress was oddly at variance with the practice of the earlier Pre-Raphaelites. They had been among the first painters to add the new synthetic pigments to their palettes.

† Banks, according to Nicholas Penny, then Keeper of Western Art at the Ashmolean Museum, 'had no interest in the ornamental, and little ability at running a studio, but was devoted to the elevated ideals promoted by academic theory'. Penny adds that, having 'obtained two major public commissions for St Paul's . . . and having devised beautiful reliefs for their pedestals [Banks then] created ludicrous figures on top from which no reputation could easily recover'.[39]

which gave the world Svengali. Whistler was so incensed with his portrait there that he threatened to sue; Armstrong joked that as he was the only one left out of the story he too was going to sue.* In some ways it was a shame that *Trilby* was not written until 1894: du Maurier's reading of Poynter's character was fairly close to home, and it might have given Agnes pause for thought. Poynter is Lorrimer, 'the industrious apprentice' who hoped to become 'the duly knighted or baroneted Lord Mayor of "all the plastic arts" (except one or two perhaps, here and there, that are not altogether without some importance)'. He was a 'painstaking young enthusiast, of precocious culture, who read improving books, and did not share the amusement of the quartier latin, but spent his evenings at home with Handel, Michael Angelo and Dante, on the respectable side of the river'. And this stiff, humourless, driven young man is more or less what landed up on the Macdonalds' doorstep.

Poynter's career had not taken off as swiftly as Burne-Jones's. Like him, he had had to find something to boost his income while he waited for patrons to clamour for his paintings. Burne-Jones had the Firm; Poynter the illustrated magazines and book work. By 1861 he was working for *Once a Week*, illustrating serials. In addition, he made engravings of old masters, which, before mass-market photography, people hung on their walls. In 1863 the Dalziel brothers, engravers, printers and publishers, engaged him to produce drawings for their big project, an illustrated Bible, which would keep him in some financial security while he worked on what he confidently expected to be his *magnum opus*. He had 'got in a toile ten feet by six feet for his Egyptian picture to which he intends to devote two years, never expecting to sell it'.[40] With this Egyptian picture he hoped to make his name.

While he was working on this, he continued to mix in London mainly with his Paris friends, even though he was always something of a detached onlooker at the revels – the 'chevalier de la triste

* For those who might like to read this charming period piece, the key is: 'The Laird' was Lamont; Joe Sibley, 'The Idle Apprentice', was Whistler; Little Billee was an idealized self-portrait of du Maurier; Taffy was Val Prinsep. Alecco Ionides was rechristened Poluphloisloiospaleapologos Petrilopetrolicoconose – this is not a book that is willing to miss a good 'comic foreigner' joke.

figure', du Maurier called him.[41] The Ionides family saw that he
was kept properly fed, having him and du Maurier to Sunday lunch
every fortnight or so. They also gave him tickets for concerts.
Music was the main way he socialized: he had people to his rooms
for dinner, and they sang after; or he and his friends visited his sister
and brother-in-law, and they played the piano and sang. It was
usually quite informal, du Maurier explained to his mother: 'Sometimes of an evening in Poynter's room or mine, where there are
pianos – and a dozen jolly fellows, *l'élite* . . . they will make me sing
for two hours at a stretch.'[42]

Agnes and Edward shared a love of music. Her piano playing
was more than just good, her voice was by amateur standards
spectacular – well above basic drawing-room level – and she took
both very seriously. For example, around the time of Alice's marriage she was working on a sonata by Hummel, Spohr's *Faust*
and Mozart's Jupiter Symphony (a piano transcription, perhaps).
Poynter's musical interests meshed with hers, and as early as 1862
his friends knew where his affections lay: 'Had a jolly Evening
at Burne-Jones's, who's got the jolliest wife and sisters-in-law
imaginable (Poynter head over years [*sic*]).'[43]

A month after Alice's wedding in March 1865, Poynter took the
plunge and wrote to George. By the middle of April Agnes and
Edward were formally engaged, and visits to the prospective
mothers-in-law on both sides took place. It was now just a matter
of waiting to see if Poynter's latest 'big' picture, selected for the
Royal Academy Summer Exhibition, was the kind of *succès d'estime*
that could set an artist up for life. And successful it was. *Faithful unto
Death* – a depiction of a soldier who, when Mount Vesuvius
erupted, remained at his post on duty at Pompeii because no
one had ordered him to stand down – became one of the most
famous images of Victorian art. It encapsulated the virtues the
Victorians admired – duty, obedience and fidelity – all in one
simple image.

Initially it looked as if the next wedding was to be Agnes's alone.
Louie had been working intensively on wood engraving, and
Morris was very impressed with what she had produced. She spent
some time at the Red House, talking to him about producing
engravings of Burne-Jones's illustrations for Morris's most recent

work, *Earthly Paradise*. Then, as always seemed to be the case, 'love and marriage claimed her instead'.[44] Alfred Baldwin, who had quietly been calling on Louie for at least three years, wrote to Hannah and asked permission to marry her daughter. They were engaged only six months after Agnes and Edward, in October 1865.

Alfred Baldwin was the first prospective husband for any of the girls who was even moderately prosperous. There was no waiting in order to secure an income. Alfred's grandfather had moved to Stourport in 1788 after the Staffordshire and Worcestershire Canal had brought it within reach of the Severn. His father carried on the family traditions and was an iron-founder. He died young, of scarlet fever, leaving a grown family by his first wife, and a second family of eight children, of whom Alfred was the youngest and born after his father's death. On his majority Alfred inherited, as all the Baldwin men did, a share of three overlapping businesses in the area, held between his uncles, brothers and cousins.[45] His main business was in three of the family firms. E. P. & W. Baldwin, which began as a side venture, was from 1854 based in Wilden, a few miles from Stourport, and made iron, tinplate and metal sheets for the Birmingham metal-finishing trades. Alfred was therefore clearly a 'catch' in the worldly sense, although religious scruples had to be overcome – was he *too* worldly? Hannah was unsure. She wrote to him, after he had formally asked for permission to marry Louie, 'My dear Mr. Alfred . . . few things could have surprised me more than the contents of your note. The state of solicitude and perplexity in which my mind has been must be an apology for not replying at an earlier period.'[46] Alfred pressed his suit, writing Louie long letters explaining his religious viewpoint, and she shortly succumbed.

It was decided that, given the Revd Macdonald's parlous state of health, Agnes's wedding, scheduled for 9 August 1866, would be a double one, and that Fred would come to Wolverhampton to give both girls away. In the event it was a rather subdued affair. George was too ill to attend; Fred was distracted and had to rush off, as he was himself getting married in Burslem the next day. Burne-Jones had written Louie a comic note:

I am unchangeable in my love for you, don't doubt it: nothing will ever divide us – not chance nor circumstance will bring that about – but a little gloomy sulkiness is excusable in me. I only had two wenches, and they are both gone, and I am very much past thirty and growing selfish as Georgie will tell you. Tell the other wench [Agnes] she's another's and doesn't care for me.[47]

At least, it was supposed to be comic.

Then Georgie and Burne-Jones decided that they couldn't manage to get up to Wolverhampton for the wedding, and instead went on holiday for three weeks to stay with William Allingham in Hampshire. The question of who was abandoning whom is worth asking. True, Georgie had given birth to a daughter, Margaret, only two months before the wedding,* but if she was well enough to go to Hampshire, why not Wolverhampton? Had there been some sort of family breach or quarrel? Had something happened in the eighteen months between Alice's wedding and Louie and Agnes's? Or at Alice's wedding itself? Otherwise why did Fred marry the day after his sisters, in Burslem? It is understandable that his fiancée, Mary Cork, wanted to be married from her home, rather than travelling to Wolverhampton, but why the day after Louie and Agnes? There was no obvious benefit to be gained from this, and an obvious loss – the lack of his family, and a lot of belting about the country for Fred. Edie was clearly not very interested in Fred's wife – in her memoirs she misspells her name the one time she mentions it. Alice in India showed little more excitement about the weddings. Nearly two months later she was sending messages to Agnes and Louie through friends, saying she was sorry not to have written to them congratulating them on their marriages, and that she would do so 'soon'. There is nothing in any surviving papers to indicate an estrangement. It may have been nothing more than that with increasing age and the growing demands of their own families the distance between the sisters was widening.

---

* Burne-Jones had noted, 'So Phil's conjecture that it would be either a boy or girl was not unfounded.'[48]

7. 'Love enough to last out a long life'
1866–1871

After Louie and Agnes came back from their honeymoons in September 1866 (Scotland and Devonshire, respectively), they moved into their new homes. Poynter had taken a house at 106 Gower Street, not far from his old rooms in Great Russell Street, and in the heart of artists' studio-land. Louisa moved to Bewdley, in Worcestershire, where Alfred had taken a 'very large' house, as her mother noted. After settling in, she travelled to Wolverhampton to visit George and Hannah and, of course, Edie.

Edie was now eighteen, unmarried and still living at home. Her position in the family was not initially very odd. She had been a bright, enquiring child – a characteristic family story had it that one day she rushed into the room where her sisters were talking, 'saying, with shining eyes, "What about what?"'[1] Nothing was taboo to her: after Louie said grace badly one day, Edie admonished her: 'Say it again, O irreverent doggie!'[2] She had her share of the family musical talent: some of the songs that she wrote were published, and won the approval of M. T. Marzials, who ran the music library at the British Museum.

With increasing age, however, things began to change. There was no obvious reason for her not marrying. Maybe it was that the wit which was sharp in all her sisters had a razor edge in her case. Alice's many entanglements had been a running joke to her: when someone enquired about a visit from which Alice had, unusually, returned un-engaged, Edie tartly replied that there had not been a cloud over it, 'no, not so big as a man's hand'.[3] It does not appear to be just that she was sharp-tongued, however. Somehow she was always just overlooked. Hannah tended to mention her children's birthdays in letters, but, whereas the others appear in the main body of the text, Edie's are often scribbled in at the top, as an afterthought. When Alice got engaged to Lockwood, Hannah talked about 'my two daughters at home', referring to Agnes and Louie. When Louie returned from honeymoon and came to visit,

Hannah told friends how grateful she was that 'we have one child' who was nearby. She had one child actually in her house, so what was happening?

In large Victorian families there was usually one child – often the youngest, almost always a daughter – who did not marry and stayed at home to look after her elderly parents. That this happened to Edie was therefore not abnormal; the fact that she was somehow invisible, of no account, is more peculiar. It was almost as if by being unmarried she had somehow failed, and was therefore to be tucked away at the back of the family's minds. Georgie, towards the end of her life, noted that 'it has been her lot to have no life of her own'.[4] Fred writes about his travels in his memoirs, and particularly mentions a trip to Paris after the Franco-Prussian War, but he doesn't say that Edie was with him; in fact he doesn't mention her at all. There are no descriptions of what she looked like; she and Alice were the only sisters who were not painted by Poynter. Alice, in India, is an understandable omission. But Edie was there when Louie was sitting. It wasn't that she was actively disliked by her siblings: on the contrary, they wrote of her (when they remembered) with great fondness. It was just that she was single and had no career or particular talents; she was therefore not a 'success' as they were.

They *were* successful, in their chosen careers as wives and mothers. Agnes and Louie had a son each within a month of each other, and within a year of their weddings. Stanley Baldwin was born six days before his parents' first wedding anniversary, on 3 August 1867;* Ambrose Poynter arrived on 26 September. Their husbands were matching this with worldly success. Poynter had further acclaim at the next Royal Academy summer show: his painting *Israel in Egypt*, a vast monster showing the Hebrews building the pyramids, was bought for an astonishing 850 guineas.

Israel in Egypt is worth pausing at, simply because most people today have never knowingly seen a work by Poynter. The focus is on the historicity of the view: the architecture is all rendered with minute fidelity, although it ranges in date over three thousand

---

* In a burst of family feeling, Louie made Harry one of his godfathers. Both sides seemed perfectly happy to forget the transaction ever after.

years. It includes, among other things, Philae in Upper Egypt, the obelisk at Heliopolis, the Great Pyramid of Giza, the mountains at Thebes, the Temple of Seti I at Gourna, and the gateways of the temple at Edfu – a melange that could not possibly have occurred anywhere except in a Victorian's fevered imagination. The picture was already old-fashioned when it was painted, belonging to the school of history painting becoming outmoded in the 1820s and 1830s. Ruskin approved of the 'noble conventionalism' of the lions, which seems to be damning with faint praise,[5] yet this was no check to Poynter's rise. Shortly afterwards he was invited to create the mosaics for the walls of the South Kensington Museum lecture theatre.

The Baldwins had made the older Macdonalds happy by suggesting that it was time they left Wolverhampton and moved permanently to Bewdley, where they could be near Louie. This they did, and found a pretty red-brick Georgian house on the High Street only a few doors away from their daughter, son-in-law and grandson. They were leading a comfortable life, Alfred going off to the works, Louie and Edie visiting each other daily. As the Baldwins had the space and time, their house became a meeting point for the sisters in England, who now began to visit regularly – at least twice a year, often more.

The Burne-Joneses' finances were also improving at such a rate that, for the first time, Burne-Jones opened a bank account.* They were on the move again. They had wanted to stay put in Kensington Square, but their lease was up and the house was getting a bit small after Margaret's appearance in June 1866. This time they wanted to stay in the same part of London: they were settled and happy, near friends – particularly George and Rosalind Howard, whom they had begun to grow close to in the previous year.

George Howard was the heir to the Earl of Carlisle and in line to inherit Castle Howard in Yorkshire; his wife was a blue-stocking from an aristocratic family. George Howard wanted to be an artist, rather than the politician or the landed proprietor his birth had arranged for him. They owned Naworth Castle in

* Although, before he did so, his patron Frederick Leyland had to show him how to write a cheque. After this another of his patrons, William Graham, took over managing Burne-Jones's accounts.

Self & Family *by Burne-Jones*

Cumberland, and were also planning a house to be built in Palace Green, an elegant new outcrop of Kensington. Georgie wrote to Rosalind, 'we are very anxious not to leave this neighbourhood . . . I am sure you will believe that one of our chief reasons for wishing to remain in this neighbourhood is that we may not lose sight of you . . .'[6]

Finally the Burne-Joneses settled on the Grange, in Fulham, an eighteenth-century house with three-quarters of an acre of ground, big enough for a small orchard. It had once belonged to Samuel Richardson,★ and, as it was too large, and too expensive, an arrangement was made that Wilfred Heeley, temporarily back from India,

★ It has since been pulled down. The only remnant left is a council block called 'Burne-Jones'.

William and Janey Morris *by Burne-Jones*

should take half of it. The size was a worry to Burne-Jones. He wrote to Howard:

It is too grand and large and splendid for us: we have no right to such a place . . . I am frightened. It reminds me a good deal of Castle Howard – I should say rather it had the scale of that mansion combined with the more sympathetic aspect of Naworth: it is called the Grange, not moated however . . . there is a madhouse next door which is convenient, for I hate distant removes.[7]

By March 1868 the house was done up in showpiece Morris, Marshall, Faulkner & Co. style. Soon a grand housewarming party was held, and Brown remembered:

the house, being newly decorated in the 'Firm' taste, looked charming, the women looked lovely and the singing was unrivalled, and we all luckily escaped with our lives, for soon after the guests were gone, the ceiling of the studio (about 700 lbs of plaster) came down just where the thickest of the gathering had been all night. Morris was to have slept on the sofa on which most of it fell, but, by good luck, he went home to sleep with Prinsep.[8]

There may have been practical reasons for Morris sleeping at Val Prinsep's. But it was in Morris that the first cracks in all their youthful idealism were beginning to show. He and Janey now had two daughters, and some time after the birth of May, their second, Janey had retired to her couch, a permanent semi-invalid (or a semi-permanent invalid, as suited the occasion best). The diagnosis was vague: 'spinal irritation' was suggested, but nothing that would today be understood as organic disease. What is retrospectively implicit in this retreat is that she was unhappy. By the late 1860s she had started an affair with Rossetti, which was to continue until at least 1875.* Morris may have known; he may have refused to know – it is impossible to be sure. He certainly knew that Janey shared no interests with him, and that he was now more or less alone.† He as much as admitted this to various friends; he wrote to Louie, 'I have been a happy man *with my friends*' (my italics).[11]

Despite the domesticity that Georgie enshrined in her memoirs and implicit in the view that he liked to project of himself – always at home, unable to manage without his children, never going out, and having no interests outside the Grange and his work – Burne-Jones had a night life. It was not a particularly disreputable one by today's standards, but it was one that was quite apart from his family circle. He continued to see Swinburne, whose drinking had now reached a stage where he was often, as Georgie delicately phrased it, 'not quite himself',[12] and Simeon Solomon, who was well on his way to total disintegration.‡ (Oddly, Solomon had also

* It was Rossetti who created, as well as preserved, our image of Janey as the archetypal Pre-Raphaelite beauty, as her face peers out of his innumerable paintings of her. Henry James described her at the time: 'Imagine a tall lean woman in a long dress of some dead purple stuff, guiltless of hoops (or anything else, I should say), with a mass of crisp black hair heaped into great wavy projections on each side of her temples, a thin pale face, a pair of strange, sad, deep, dark Swinburnian temples, with great thick black oblique brows, joined in the middle and tucking themselves away under her hair . . .'[9]
† In 1883 he wrote, 'I married in 1859 and have two daughters by that marriage very sympathetic with me as to my aims in life'[10] – which can be understood to mean that his wife was *not* sympathetic.
‡ In 1873 Solomon was arrested with another man in a public lavatory, and charged with gross indecency. Rossetti set the tone for all his friends' response when he wrote to Ford Madox Brown, 'I hope I shall never see him again.' Swinburne agreed that Solomon had 'made it impossible for anyone to keep up this acquaintance' and was 'now a thing unmentionable by men and women, as equally abhorrent to either'. For some years Solomon lived on handouts

been a friend of the strait-laced Poynter, and in 1865 a portfolio of his risqué drawings had been issued with a dedication to Poynter. As his behaviour became more erratic, and Poynter's more Establishment, the friendship withered.) Solomon and Burne-Jones scribbled lewd illustrations to Swinburne's more Sadean poetry, to themes, Burne-Jones wrote, 'that Tiberius would have given half his provinces for'[14] (although Burne-Jones was careful to destroy all these drawings and any letters to and from Swinburne he could get his hands on). Richard Burton, like Swinburne known for his interest in flagellation, was another bachelor friend, as was Luke Ionides, a patron of the Pre-Raphaelites. Together they visited pot-houses, music halls and theatres, including a trip to see Kate Vaughan perform her notorious skirt-dance at the Gaiety Theatre.

At home things were rather more settled. Georgie was ensconced in her new house. Alice, pregnant once more, was on her way back to England with two-year-old Ruddy to await the birth of her second child. In 1868 Poynter was elected an Associate of the Royal Academy, the first step on the road to full membership as a Royal Academician, or RA, de rigueur for the successful conventional career in art. But somehow, even with that, nothing seemed to go right. Louie, in Bewdley, was beginning a situation similar to Janey's. Hannah regularly reported Louie's various ailments – inflammations, irritation of the 'mucous membrane', 'neuralgia' in her arms and legs – and from January to March 1868 she spent most of her time in bed, rarely coming downstairs: the beginning of a lifelong trend. In July, Georgie wrote Rosalind Howard an apology for not answering a letter, 'but if you had known all my

from his relations, but gradually he became an alcoholic vagrant, ultimately selling shoelaces in the Mile End Road. The Burne-Joneses continued to support him, much to their friends' disgust. Rossetti reported in 1880 that 'Ned Jones looked in for a minute and a half the other day and told me that poor SS. wrote to him from an hospital. He did not answer, but wrote inquiries to his doctor and learned that S. had arrived at the hospital not only ragged but actually without shoes! I must say Ned's conduct as a correspondent is hardly consistent with the penultimate piece of news he gave me on the subject: viz: that he and his wife had judicially gone to view this Hebraic phenomenon at a friendly meeting! . . .' After Georgie's death, Phil found 'a doleful little bundle' of begging letters from Solomon. With a careful eye on posterity, he burned them.[13]

circumstances you would not wonder':[15] a precursor to a major crisis which would not come to a head for another year. Alice's baby had been born at the Grange on 11 June 1868 in an unexplained atmosphere of tension and worry. It was not an easy birth – Louie referred to it as a 'grimly' incident, and hoped that Alice would never have another child.

Ruddy had been left in Bewdley with his grandparents. It was not, to put it mildly, a successful visit. Countless biographers of Kipling have dissected his grandmother's diary entries about his stay – he was wilful, spoilt, rambunctious, they conclude. It is hard to feel anything but sympathy for him. He was two years old, in a strange country, in a strange house, with strange people he was supposed to love. His mother was away, and his ayah, who had constantly attended him in India, had vanished, and no one had replaced her. In addition, his grandfather was dying. It is difficult to imagine in what way he could possibly have behaved that would have won the approbation of his distracted grandmother, who was rarely cheerful at the best of times. By November, Alice, baby Alice* and Rudyard were on their way back to India. Six days after the boat sailed, Alfred and Louie were woken in the middle of the night – George Macdonald, after an interminable illness, had died.

Hannah now went into mourning, a formal ritual with clearly defined rules. It was not something new for her. Four of her eleven children had died, three of them in infancy – a higher percentage than average, which was at this time 5 infant deaths per 1,000 live births, or half of one per cent. But mourning for a child lasted only twelve months. For a husband it was more elaborate, with a dress code for the next two and a half years. For the first twelve months non-reflective black paramatta and crape were worn; then for nine months dull black silk trimmed with crape ribbons. For the following three months the crape could be removed, and for the final six months 'half-mourning' was required: greys, lavender, black or white only. In addition, apart from 'commemorative pieces', or diamonds or pearls set in black, no jewellery could be worn in the first year. After that, jet jewellery was allowable.[16] This

---

* Young Alice was never known by her Christian name. Shortly after her birth Lockwood noted that she was a very tricksy baby, and Trix she became ever after. She was not, despite many references to her thus, named Beatrice.

was the formal guidance, but in middle-class families women tended to make special mourning dresses only for 'best' wear. For everyday clothes they retrimmed old dresses, dyeing them black if necessary.

In addition, no invitations could be accepted for the first year, except from immediate family. Public gatherings were avoided. Mourning also had a community aspect.★ It was considered 'ill-bred' to wear bright colours if someone in the house was in mourning. (After a royal death Queen Victoria said, 'I think it quite wrong that the nursery are not in mourning, at any rate I should make them wear grey or white or drab and baby wear white and lilac, not colours. That I think shocking.')[17] So Edie, who officially came out of mourning for her father after twelve months, may well have worn black for longer, as an acknowledgement of Hannah's loss. Music was not be played in the house for the first three months, and for a while after that family members limited themselves to religious works.

George's death was only the beginning of a year of trouble. Louie miscarried early in 1869. She continued unwell, and Hannah began to tell friends that she had trouble with her spine – that worrying catch-all that had affected both George Macdonald and Janey. She may have had another miscarriage at the end of the year – it is clear that Hannah was worried once again, rather than continuing to be worried, but she is not specific, and it is hard to say precisely what happened. For the entire year Louie went back and forth to doctors, and in between suffered from a dizzying range of illnesses.

Alfred was not doing much better. He had been a stalwart of the local Liberal Party, canvassing door to door, taking part in the rough and tumble of a political scene that owed much to its Georgian ancestry: Victorian decorum was some years away, with the coming of the 1872 Secret Ballot Act. Until then, the war cry 'Vote Early and Vote Often' probably best described the mood of elections. The previous year Enoch Baldwin, Alfred's cousin, had

---

★ Mourning was generally observed for public figures. For royalty the populace wore, if not full mourning, at least black ribbons or black gloves and hatbands. When Prince Albert died in 1861, the shops were shut for a day, and street railings were painted black; for a lesser royal figure shops remained open, but sports and leisure activities were suspended briefly by the entire population.

been duffed up by the Tories during a political scuffle.* In January 1869, amid Tory objections to ballot scrutiny, Alfred was arraigned for bribery and intimidation, while the local MP was unseated for bribery and corruption. (This sounds today much worse than it was – the charges were political rather than criminal, and were considered almost a routine part of the struggle for power.) By August there was more trouble: *The Times* reported that Stanley, Alfred's brother, and the senior partner, had gone bankrupt, owing £20,000. The paper was forced to retract and print an apology within the week, but there was a small nugget of truth lodged inside the greater falsehood: business was not good. Stanley was not the head of company that could be wished for, and, as Alfred found his feet, a conflict between them grew nearer.

As a final touch, Harry suddenly showed up from New York. He arrived in the early spring, and appeared inclined to make a long stay of it. Hannah was delighted, Alfred rather less so. Harry's business abilities were, to say the least, meagre. After his initial work as a proofreader for the *New York Times*, he had found various jobs in stock brokerages. He never stayed with any one company for very long, and, although there is no indication that he was ever booted out, there is also no indication that anyone tried very hard to keep him. In addition, he had become a heavy drinker. During his stay in Bewdley he fell and cut himself badly, and no one doubted that he had been drunk at the time. Louie had that Macdonald disregard for smoothing over the rough places which contrasted so oddly with their dislike of talking about unpleasant facts. She bluntly advocated the removal of his liver under anaesthetic. And so – with a grieving and widowed mother-in-law, an invalid wife, a charge of bribery pending, a cadging brother-in-law, and general business worries – Bewdley cannot have been a cheerful place for the Baldwins. That may be why they were not of more help to Georgie. The crisis that had been looming for the Burne-Joneses since the previous summer was now out in the open, and apparently unstoppable.

What became known as the Mary Zambaco incident grew

* Enoch Baldwin, later to be Alfred's partner in Baldwin, Son & Co., was elected Liberal MP from 1880 to 1885 for the old parliamentary borough of Bewdley and Stourport.

slowly. The Burne-Joneses had become friendly with various members of the Greek community in London. Alecco Ionides, Edward Poynter's friend from Paris days, was descended from a clan of merchants and bankers who had moved to England years before. His father, Alexander, was the patriarch of a heavily inter-related group of families. Mary (or Maria) Zambaco was the daughter of 'Hadji' and Euphrosyne Cassavetti, and a first cousin to Alecco Ionides. She was a remarkably beautiful woman and, according to George du Maurier, a rich one. He had met her six years earlier, and described her and her behaviour to his mother:

Funny thing rather, there is a certain beautiful Greek girl of great talent and really wonderful beauty, with a small fortune of *her own* of 80,000£. She is supposed to be attached by mere obstinacy to a Greek of low birth in Paris and is of that rudeness and indifference that she will not even answer those who speak to her; and about 2 months ago when I met her for the first and only time, she and I had quite a talk to everybody's astonishment . . . Well, the other day as I was walking through Kensington Gardens I saw a group of ladies and little girls talking and in one glance recognised the beautiful Cazaretti [*sic*], but pretended not to know her through her thick veil and walked on. What does Cazaretti do but leave her friends and with a little girl for a chaperone just follow me about the Gardens, I apparently very innocent of it all, but dodging about everywhere, and she still following and passing me. The thing was evident, and from a girl of her position and peculiar indifference the performance was rather significative [*sic*].[18]

Clearly this was a woman who was rather more forward and open than was considered quite nice at the time. In 1863 she married the 'Greek of low birth' – in actuality simply a Greek doctor named Zambaco, who practised in Paris. By 1866 she had left him, with her three children, and was back in London. She was soon coming to sit regularly for Burne-Jones: she had wonderful red hair, and a skin so fair it was practically phosphorescent, said an infatuated cousin.* Burne-Jones was in retrospect clearly besotted, but at the

---

* This was Luke Ionides, who it has been suggested was a spurned lover of Mary's.

Maria Zambaco and Self *by Burne-Jones, c. 1870*

time nobody noticed anything. He once sent George Howard, who often came to paint with him at the Grange, a muddled note: 'the only two days at all engaged are Tuesdays and Saturdays when Mrs Zambaco comes. And there is no reason why you should not come then if you want except that the room would be so full and I can't work so easily with many by'[19] – in brief, you can come except you can't.

In between periods of euphoria, his spirits – never terribly stable – veered alarmingly. Howard, his closest friend of the period, was on the receiving end of dozens of notes along the lines of:

dear fellow, Webb tells me bad unfaithful things of you – that you asked strange questions about me – don't tell him I told you he told me – that you asked even if I cared as much for you – which was unfaithful of you – I have been ill all the year – really ill, ill in head and every way, and have been poor comfort to any friend – all have been merciful and remembered me at my best and forgiven me – I have tried everyone this

The Reverend George Browne Macdonald in early middle age;
Hannah Macdonald, his wife, *c.* 1865.

Four of their children: Harry in New York, *c.* 1860; Caroline shortly
before her death in 1854; Fred soon after his ordination, *c.* 1862; and
Edith in the late 1880s or 1890s, at Wilden House, home of the Baldwins,
where she lived after her mother's death.

The Macdonald sisters:
Alice in middle age (she disliked
being photographed, and rarely
was); Georgiana, on her engagement
to Edward Burne-Jones in 1856;
Agnes, shortly before her
engagement to Edward Poynter;
Louisa at the age of sixteen.

Burne-Jones in many of his
drawings used his fiancée's family as
models. *King's Daughters*, 1858, may
show all the sisters: it has been
suggested that (*from left*) Alice is the
woman with the buttons on her
dress; Edie the small child; Georgie
at centre; Agnes on the balcony at
left; and Louie at the extreme right,
carrying a rabbit.

(*Right*) Alice and Lockwood Kipling, *c.* 1864–5, shortly before their marriage. (*Below*) Rudyard, aged four or five, in Bombay. (*Far right*) A drawing of Georgie by Dante Gabriel Rossetti, made in 1860 to celebrate her marriage to Burne-Jones. (*Far right, below*) A woodcut by Georgie before she gave up to, as Ruskin put it, 'echo' her husband's art, which could be done 'without too much disturbance of feminine thought and nature'. (*Right, below*) Burne-Jones in the early days of his marriage.

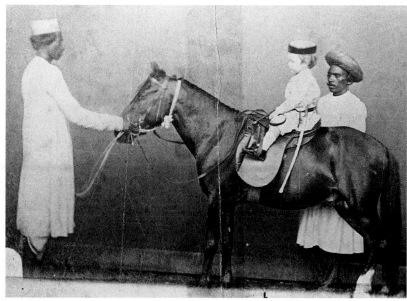

Georgie at the piano, drawn in the early 1860s by Burne-Jones. She was a talented musician, with a better than average voice. The piano was given to the Burne-Joneses as a wedding present, and decorated by Burne-Jones. It is now in the Victoria & Albert Museum.

In the garden at the Grange, *c.* 1874. (*From left to right:*) Richard Jones (Burne-Jones's father), Margaret, Edward, Philip and Georgie Burne-Jones, May, William, Janey and Jenny Morris. After scarlet fever and the death of her child in 1864, Georgie always looks prematurely aged. She is in fact a year younger than Janey Morris.

Agnes, in a painting by
her husband,
commissioned by Louie
shortly before the sisters'
double wedding. Edward
Poynter in 1883. He
enjoyed his eminence as
both director of the
National Gallery and
president of the Royal
Academy, and was the
first to hold this dual
role.

Louie, also painted by Poynter, in 1868, shortly after the birth of her son Stanley, seen here in 1876. Alfred Baldwin in later life.

year – if I could have pointed definitely to heart disease, or cancer, or consumption or something clear and obvious it would have been bearable to my friends, but I have had no such luck – only I have felt intensely melancholy and depressed – the result of a good couple of years pondering about something . . .[20]

A remarkable letter, but no alarm bells rang.

Finally, things were brought to a head by the oldest means in the book. When tidying Burne-Jones's clothes, Georgie found a letter from Mary in a pocket. It was clear from the letter that she and Ned were lovers, and had been for some time. This was when Alice had come to stay with Georgie to wait for Trix to be born. It is hardly surprising Georgie wrote to Rosalind Howard that she was sorry not to have written,

but if you had known all my circumstances you would not wonder. However, the worst is over now and I draw breath . . . [Ned] makes it a matter of difficulty even to go . . . to fetch Phil from Bewdley. The small man has been there for more than a month, and we want him back sadly, but he was obliged to go away whilst the house was so full.[21]

The line added at the end did not bode well: Ned 'has not been working at all hard'.

The situation was impossible: Burne-Jones was unable to leave his mistress even to fetch his small son home; he was doing no work; Alice and her newborn baby were *in situ*, observing, as Georgie and Ned desperately pretended that nothing was happening. By September 1868 Georgie had fled to Clevedon with the children, and stayed for over a month, valiantly lying: 'I was not well – but I was not ill either, but very tired with all I had gone through in the way of other people's babies &c.' And again, Ned 'has nothing to shew for this year scarcely'.[22]

Nothing was resolved. Burne-Jones did not want to stay with Georgie, but he did not want to leave her either. Then in January 1869 everything blew up. Rossetti, who was now, with Ford Madox Brown, somewhat estranged from Burne-Jones, wrote to Brown with a certain relish:

Private. Poor old Ned's affairs have come to a smash altogether, and he and Topsy, after the most dreadful to-do, started for Rome suddenly, leaving the Greek damsel beating up the quarters of all his friends for him and howling like Cassandra. Georgie has stayed behind. I hear today however that Top and Ned got no further than Dover, Ned being now so dreadfully ill that they will probably have to return to London. Of course the dodge will be not to let a single hint of their movements become known to anybody, or the Greek (whom I believe he is really bent on cutting) will catch him again. She provided herself with laudanum for two at least, and insisted on their winding up matters in Lord Holland's Lane. Ned didn't see it, when she tried to drown herself in the water in front of Browning's house &c. – bobbies collaring Ned who was rolling with her on the stones to prevent it, and God knows what else.[23]

Rosalind Howard was a little more coherent:

we hear that Mme Z. when Jones refused to fly with her produced a poison bottle and said she would drink it at once a struggle ensued – J. tried to take it from her – the police came up – at that same moment appeared Lucas Ionides – her former friend and he explained matters to the police and walked off with Mme Z. Jones walked away and then fainted – a regular drama – I suspect Ionides followed her to see what she was after and from anger and jealousy repeated the story.[24]

Burne-Jones had planned to run away from all the trouble he had created by fleeing to Italy, taking Morris with him to hold his hand. But, as on his honeymoon, he broke down, and had to return ignominiously from Dover.

As can be seen from Rossetti's letter, within days the story was all over town. Rosalind was the only one who did anything practical. She and her husband drove over to the Grange and left £50 for Georgie, 'thinking [she] might need it'.[25]★ Georgie was holding herself together with difficulty: 'Forgive my reserve the other day

---

★ Rosalind may have had a difficult manner – she described herself as 'brusque ... aggressive in my speech ... opinionated, fault-finding, pugnacious and techy'[26] – but she was the only one of Georgie's friends who did anything apart from gossiping.

when you came, but I am obliged to shew it in time of trouble or I should break down.'[27] By now Burne-Jones was back home, being nursed by his long-suffering wife. Finally she unburdened herself to Rosalind:

Georgy had a private talk with me – was very loving – seemed overdone and harassed in mind said she never could be unreserved because there were certain things in her married life she could not talk about because asking for sympathy would seem like taking part against her husband. I think she refers to his living apart which he does for her good so as to avoid many children; but it is a mistake.[28]

Georgie's friends were all anxious – Agnes and Louie sent worried letters to each other about her; Agnes came and kept her company; the novelist George Eliot, a new friend, sent tactful enquiries via Rosalind – but she was determined to keep her misery to herself. Burne-Jones was more forthcoming: he wrote to Howard that their discussions must remain 'a profound secret', spoiling the effect more than a little when, after four repetitions of how secret everything must remain, he added, 'I have written to the same effect to Morris, Webb, Rossetti, Howell.'[29] Finally Georgie could stand no more. She took the two children and moved into lodgings in Oxford. She told Burne-Jones that she had taken them for a month, and then would see how things stood.

Once there, she was able to take stock. If Burne-Jones was prepared to try again, so was she. In a letter to Rosalind her self-renunciation is painful to read.

No words can explain any difficult relation of any human beings to each other and none but God can sum up a case and see it clearly. I know that you are generous enough to take me on my own terms, and to forgive me where you think them mistaken – reserving your judgment as to my mistake – and I am very thankful to you for this because I love you, but I hope you will be able further to bear with me if I appear as tiresomely reserved as ever on some subjects. I have made up my mind to this, long ago, and mean to keep to it. At the same time, please never be afraid of saying anything to me . . . or anything you think might help me, directly, or indirectly, for I need help. Indeed, my dear, I am no heroine at all –

and I know when I come short almost as well as any one else does – I have simply acted all along from very simple little reasons, which God and my husband know better than anyone – I don't know what God thinks of them.

Dearest Rosalind, be hard on no one in this matter, and exalt no one – may we all come well through it at last. I know one thing, and that is that there is love enough between Edward and me to last out a long life if it is given us . . .[30]

Georgie returned to the Grange in March, and in July went to Naworth to stay with the Howards for a much-needed break.* Given the circumstances, it might have been expected that she would be sympathetic to Mill's *On the Subjection of Women*, which she read on its publication this year, but she found it 'too exaggerated on the unpopular side of the subject'.[32] 'I do wish I cared a little more about the female suffrage question – it seems such a piece of indifference to the troubles of my "sister-woman".'[33] Eventually things at home settled down, with Burne-Jones deciding to stay. However, there were intermittent eruptions for another four years at least, and Georgie never recovered the pleasure and equilibrium she had experienced earlier in her marriage. Tellingly, in 1869 Phil was given a toy printing press, and with it he printed a story which began, 'Once upon a time a little boy said to his mama, "Mama, why do you look unhappy?"'[34] In 1904, over thirty years after the event, Georgie could not bring herself to discuss any part of the year 1869 in her memoir. The chapter covering 1868– 71 is the only one in her otherwise year-by-year account to have

*Rosalind was a lifeline for Georgie, and Georgie gave Rosalind a warm friendship which she otherwise lacked. In 1868 Rosalind commissioned Poynter to paint Georgie for her, as he had painted his own wife, and Louie. Georgie wrote to Rosalind, 'I have stipulated that your little locket shall be distinctly visible in it and though no one will know what it means when we are dead and gone you and I shall while we live.' It was a little heart set with pearls, enclosing a lock of her hair that Rosalind had given her friend, and engraved 'Georgie Jones from RH'. In the early 1900s Georgie wrote to Rosalind, from whom by then she was distanced, asking if she could buy back the portrait, so that 'The three sisters in effigy would then remain together amongst their own people long after the originals have disappeared'. Rosalind refused, rather huffily, but after her death her daughters gave it to Georgie's daughter.[31]

any time unaccounted for, and its epigraph says everything: 'Heart, thou and I are here sad and alone.'[35]

Agnes and Louie, paired off in childhood, married at the same time, were now finding that their married lives were moving very much in tandem too. Agnes spent a great deal of time at Bewdley with Louie, going regularly for visits of up to four weeks, three or four times a year sometimes. Their children – Stan and Ambo, as they were always known in the family – were of an age, and their mothers had much in common: ill health, consumerism, and ambitious, successful husbands.

Louie, within striking distance of Birmingham, and Agnes, in London, were enjoying the advantage of the new 'stores' that were opening up to meet the demands of the newly prosperous. In 1841 Manchester had had one shop for every 146 people; by 1871 it was one for every 83.[36] Burberry's, Derry & Toms, Whiteley's, Marshall & Snelgrove, Barker's, Harrod's, John Lewis, Bentall's, Liberty, the Army & Navy all opened within twenty years of each other. Shops were now a place where finished goods were sold, rather than a place where craftsmen created individual pieces. There was no legislation to regulate their hours, and in the cities they often opened at 7.30, for people on their way to work, and did not close until the pubs and theatres closed, after ten at night. They were accessible to all – putting things 'on account' was the norm, and the more prosperous were billed only once a year (although the careful housewife paid in cash, for which she received a discount). Debenham & Freebody, which opened in the prosperous town of Cheltenham in 1870, offered five different services for its women customers: they could have their clothes made to measure, in the 'high-class dressmaking salon'; they could buy part-completed clothes, which were either taken to a dressmaker for finishing or completed at home; there were ready-to-wear dresses; there was a dressmaking service which supplied fabric and patterns for home sewing; and there was a mail-order facility for the whole country. Agnes and Louie participated keenly in the new shopping rituals. Louie went regularly to Birmingham, as well as to London more rarely, and they sent each other notes about 'a good French dress-maker' and suggesting places for materials and other items.

Such activity was becoming easier as they became more prosperous. In 1870 Alfred bought out his brothers George and Stanley and started, with enormous success, to drive the family business forward on his own. Stanley had not proved to be a good businessman, while Alfred was the exact opposite. Where the money came from to buy out his brothers (and, apparently, pay off the outstanding debts) is not clear, but Alfred had been appearing on the Birmingham Exchange for some years, and it is probable that one or two Midlands businessmen saw him as the powerhouse he soon became, and backed him.

As befitted his new status, Alfred was now ready to move his family into a larger house, and one that was more convenient for the works. For years he went every morning from Bewdley to Wilden, a matter of three miles, either in a local fly or on foot. Now he proposed to relocate entirely. Wilden House was across the road from the works, and was traditionally the home of the brother who ran the family firm. It was larger than the Bewdley house, and had a big garden that ran up to a coppice on a hill at the end. The less attractive side of the move was that they were now virtually living 'over the shop'. If the wind blew from the wrong direction, smoke from the works covered the house and its contents with black smuts. But, Alfred said, 'it was their bread and butter, and they accepted the dirt along with the fortune it carried'.[37] By November 1870 the move was completed and, although Hannah and Edie mourned the loss of their neighbours, the distance was small enough to make very little change in their visiting habits.

In 1871 Poynter was made Slade Professor of Fine Art at University College London. This was a new professorship, and when in March the appointing committee met they decided that few would qualify for the post, and the few who might had not applied. Poynter was approached, and, in typical Poynteresque fashion, by the time he was interviewed he had already drawn up a memo on how he would run the school. Weighing heavily in his favour was that he had taught at neither the Royal Academy nor the Government School of Design – both of which disliked the idea of the Slade, as diluting their control over how art and design should be promoted. Two years later he was also made principal of the National Art Training School at the South Kensington Museum, consolidating his grip as arts administrator *extraordinaire*, although he later admitted privately, 'I feel I have rather cheated Univ: College who hoped to rival South Kensington through me.'[38] However he didn't let this – or anything else – stop him.

Agnes was valiantly bobbing along in his wake, although Rosalind Howard had noted that she was only 'clever in a way'.[39] In 1870 a move had been called for. Gower Street might be all right for an up-and-coming artist, but now he had reached a certain eminence Poynter deemed a house in the newly developing suburbs more appropriate. As the recently enriched middle classes built themselves new houses to match their affluence, so they needed to decorate them, and art (and art advisers) were increasingly important further along the social scale. In turn, those artists and advisers rose. So Gower Street was left behind, and the decorously named Beaumont Lodge, in Shepherd's Bush, was taken. It was one of only a single line of new houses on one side of Wood Lane, all with large gardens backing on to meadows and orchards.* The Poynters were very much part of a mass expansion. The population of the suburbs grew by nearly 50 per cent in every decade between 1861 and 1891.[40] This was due partly to the overground railways (which most people took to, unlike Ruskin, who referred to travelling by train as 'screaming along at the tail of a big tea kettle'),[41] and partly to the new underground railways. The first line had opened in 1863, between Farringdon Street in the City and Paddington on what were then the western edges of town. On the first day it carried 30,000 people. By the 1860s the underground was extended further west from Paddington to Shepherd's Bush, and both Shepherd's Bush and Kensington, which had once been rural, were now conveniently connected to the West End.

Beaumont Lodge had much more space than Gower Street, and when the Baldwins visited London they could now be accommodated here as easily as at the Grange. Louie and Agnes continued to visit back and forth, drawn even closer by their increasing ill health. They went together to the seaside on short trips with their children, always looking for that elusive cure. This was the age in

---

* Nothing remains of these houses now – they were built over at the beginning of the twentieth century by the Central London Railway.

which the seaside town came into its own (Brighton pier was erected in 1866), and for the first time hotels began to cater there for the middle classes. Louie and Agnes followed the older style of taking an apartment for themselves and their children. They would buy their own food, which the landlady and her servants would cook for them. As they became better off, a house was rented, and Alfred and Edward would join the women and children for a short break and for weekends. The sea air never did much good, and the sisters continued to exchange letters suggesting remedies for their ailments. Louie once wrote to Agnes that to stave off collapse she had had a whole bottle of champagne that day, and the following day she would follow a regime that included eggs beaten in wine. She also drank stout, for the iron. Agnes reported that Stan was so used to seeing his mother in bed that, aged three, he brought her cushions for her back and, imitating her, sat in a chair with another cushion and announced, 'Stanley poorly back.' Meanwhile the same phrases occur again and again in their letters, and in others' comments on them: Louie is a 'great invalid but wonderfully cheerful considering that character'; she is in 'continued collapse' and 'of course' too ill to go out. She has varyingly tic, neuralgia, a bad back. Agnes needs a month at the sea to 'build her up'; she is recommended blisters for 'counter-irritation to the spine'; she is 'crushed by the sudden pain'.

One diversion in all this woe was that in the spring of 1871 the Kiplings were back in England. Alice had had a third pregnancy in India the year before, which had ended in a stillbirth. A respite from the hot weather was needed, and, now that Lockwood was writing regularly for an Anglo-Indian paper,★ money was not stretched quite so tight. It was time, according to the prevailing wisdom, that the children were taken back to England to start their schooling. The plan was for Alice and Lockwood to take them 'home' and settle them in, after which Alice could recuperate a bit.

Alice and Lockwood had seen a newspaper advertisement placed by a couple in Southsea named Holloway, who boarded the children of expatriates. They decided that Southsea would be the best

---

★ 'Anglo-Indian' today means part-English, part-Indian. I use the phrase as it was used in the nineteenth century – 'of or about the English community in India'.

place for Rudyard and Trix to spend their primary-school years. No one has ever come up with a reason for sending the children there rather than to their many relatives. Hannah offered to take them, but, perhaps remembering their previous visit, this was rejected. Louie, Agnes and Georgie all had households with children of roughly the same ages. Besides Alice's family, Lockwood's mother in Yorkshire lived quietly with two of her daughters, whom afterwards Trix remembered with affection, but staying there also seems not to have been an option. The only surviving comment on why none of these relatives was regarded as suitable was that, said Alice, staying with them led to 'complications'.[42]

Quite what these complications might have been may be imagined. Louie and Agnes were semi-invalids. The last time Alice had visited the Grange, Ned and Georgie had been in the middle of the Mary Zambaco crisis. And, it must be considered, Alfred, Poynter and Burne-Jones were all much more successful than Lockwood: Alfred ran a prosperous business; Burne-Jones was fast becoming one of the leading painters of the day; Poynter was a university professor. Lockwood, although busy and well liked, was only an art teacher in a vocational training school. Was there a sense that, if their children grew up in these houses, they would start to make unfavourable comparisons? That they would have expectations that could not be met at home? It is possible. In the event, we simply do not know why Alice and Lockwood chose to send their children to stay with strangers; but they did.

Years later Rudyard wrote a short story about his time in Southsea. 'Baa Baa, Black Sheep' is a horrifying account of the systematic abuse, both physical and mental, of a child sent from India to an English seaside town. The raw pain, the trauma unburied, is terrifyingly portrayed. The question of what was real and what was emotional truth, as well as those details imaginatively recreated for the purposes of the story, needs to be explored. The facts are these. In May 1871 the Kiplings arrived in England. The spring and summer were spent between Worcestershire and London, with Lockwood visiting his family in Yorkshire for a short time. In October their parents took Rudyard and Trix to Littlehampton. They stayed two weeks, then, without warning, Alice and Lockwood took the children down the coast to Southsea and left them with the Holloways – for the day, Rudyard and Trix thought. However, Alice and Lockwood returned to London, and within a month they were on their way back to India. The children were to remain with the Holloways for the next five and a half years.

Lockwood and Alice had decided not to tell them that they were to stay in Southsea when their parents returned to India. The first Rudyard and Trix knew of it was when, at the end of their first day there, their mother failed to return to collect them. Alice may have not known how to tell them; she may have been too upset; she may even have thought it would be easier for the children (Rudyard was nearly six, Trix was three) not to have this incomprehensible event hanging over them. But, as Trix noted later,

Looking back I think the real tragedy of our childhood days . . . sprang from our inability to understand why our parents had deserted us. We had no preparation or explanation; it was like a double death . . . every-thing had gone at once . . . They doubtless wanted to save us, and themselves, suffering by not telling us beforehand that we were going to be left behind, but by so doing they left us, as it were, in the dark with nothing to look forward to . . . We felt we had been deserted 'almost as much as on a doorstep' and what was the reason? . . . they had gone back to their lovely home, and had not taken us with them.[43]

The standard account of this period says that Mrs Holloway terrorized Rudyard; her son viciously persecuted him; they made his home life unbearable, and his school life too. He was beaten, isolated, made to appear in school wearing a placard marked 'Liar'. Trix was petted but, young and powerless, was unable to help her brother. Some of this was undoubtedly the case, but just how brutal the Holloway regime was is difficult to assess. Rudyard neither forgot nor forgave; he took his wife to see the house fifty years later, and 'talk[ed] of it all with horror'.[44] There is no question that the children were desperately unhappy. But two things need to be set against this. One is a comment of Trix's to her cousin Stan, nearly seventy-five years after the event. Stan was preparing Kipling's entry for the *Dictionary of National Biography* (which in the end he did not write), and Trix warned him not to attach too much importance to Rudyard's version of events:

if you remember Loughton [where the children were taken after they left Southsea in 1877] you will agree with me that he was no drooping lily then, but distinctly a soaring boy – special with devilry. Very much between ourselves, dear Coz, I think that in some ways 'Auntie' [Mrs Holloway] saved his soul alive. He was about as spoilt as he could be when he came home in 1871. Six and a half years old [sic] and he had never been taught to read! I don't know what the parents were thinking of . . . Mother had a very strong will – but there were curious streaks of sand in her marble – I still suffer from some of her foolishly fond concessions granted in 1878![45]

She also noted elsewhere that in 'Baa Baa, Black Sheep' 'Dramatic licence added some extra tones of black to intensify our grey days.'[46] This is likely, but it must be noted that Trix also left an undated typescript which was less convinced of the redemptive nature of their time in Southsea. Particularly worrying, in light of her later life, was the comment 'anything that hurt or frightened [me] could not be forgotten . . . pain or terror, especially terror, seemed to dig a groove into [my] brain'.[47] It seems that, after all, terror was a part of her life as a child.

The second point is that child-rearing is one of those areas that has changed so radically in the last hundred years that it is almost impossible to look back, with our values now, without feeling that much of what happened then verged on the criminal. A few examples of Victorian childhoods, all from stable and loving homes: Lady Frederick Cavendish had a governess who was 'over-severe and apt to whip me for obstinacy when I was only dense . . . At Brighton I used to be taken out walking on the parade with my hands tied behind me, terrified out of my wits by Miss Nicholson's declaring it was ten to one we should meet a policeman.' Lord Curzon wrote that his governess

practised on us every kind of petty persecution, wounded our pride by dressing us . . . in red shining calico petticoats (I was obliged to make my own) with an immense conical cap on our heads around which, as well as on our breasts and backs, were sewn strips of paper bearing in enormous characters, written by ourselves, the words Liar, Sneak, Coward, Lubber and the like . . . She forced us to confess to lies which we had never told, to sins which we had never committed, and then punished us savagely, as being self-condemned. For weeks we were not allowed to speak to each other or to a human soul.

Queen Victoria's daughter Vicky was punished for lying 'by being imprisoned with tied hands'.[48]

If these appear to be the privileges of the upper classes, Dickens describes a very similar situation in *Little Dorrit*. Mrs Clennam, from a lower-middle-class background very like that of Mrs Holloway, says:

You do not know what it is . . . to be brought up strictly, and straitly. I was so brought up. Mine was no light youth of sinful gaiety and pleasure. Mine were days of wholesome repression, punishment and fear. The corruption of our hearts, the evil of our ways, the curse that is upon us, the terrors that surround us – these were the themes of my child-hood. They formed my character, and filled me with an abhorrence of evil-doers . . . My father impressed upon me that his bringing-up had been, like mine, one of severe restraint. He told me that besides the discipline his spirit had undergone, he had lived in a starved house, where rioting and gaiety were unknown, and where every day was a day of toil and trial like the last . . .[49]

This is not to say that Rudyard created the story out of thin air; nor that therefore the Kipling children's childhood was happy; just that it was not unusual. Which may, at least, be a partial answer to the question always asked in Kipling biographies: Why did Alice's family notice nothing, do nothing?

Alice, in India, was pining for her children, but conventional wisdom said that it was better for them in England, and she felt that Lockwood needed her with him. She left a poignant verse reminder of this dilemma. (The fact that it barely scans in places somehow makes it more, rather than less, moving: Alice was perfectly capable of writing competent verse at other times.)

To the Children at Home

Once there was a little Boy,
(Mother's darling treasure,)
Always laughing, full of joy,
Everybody's pleasure –
He would shout, and about
All the house, run gaily:
In and out, such a rout
Little Boy made daily.

Once there was a little Girl,
(Mother's bonny baby.)
Pretty darling, pink and pearl,
Sweet as a child may be!
She was fair and her hair
Framed her face completely,
And her eyes, like the skies,
Bright and blue shone sweetly.

Little Boy and Girl are gone,
Leaving Mother lonely:
What they shout and run about
Now remembered – only –
He and she, o'er the sea,
Finding other pleasures,
Scarcely miss, Mother's kiss
Rich in childish treasures.[50]

8. Spartan Mothers
1872–1877

It must not be thought that Alice's family ignored the two small children in Southsea for the next five years. Far from it – which is what makes the whole episode so much more puzzling. In September 1872 Hannah, Louie and Georgie, with Margaret in tow, went to Southsea for a week, to see how their niece and nephew had settled in. They noticed nothing worthy of comment. In addition, Rudyard came to the Grange for several weeks every Christmas. (Not Trix. There appears to have been no thought of her going, and no one wondered at this. When Rudyard came back from the Grange he would reduce her to tears by calling her 'Margot'.) Once he went to Wilden for a month. This was not repeated, although there was no suggestion that it was not a successful trip. Agnes never had either of the children to stay: her husband and child took all her energies, and nothing much was penetrating from the outside.

While the Kipling children were not neglected, they were not coddled either. They had nothing like the comfortable, happy home lives their cousins took for granted: trips to *Bluebeard* at Covent Garden, to see Hermann the Conjuror, to Hampton Court, to Kensington Palace to see the Thanksgiving Procession set out for St Paul's★ (Burne-Jones was by now a friend of Princess Louise, Queen Victoria's artist daughter). There was even a trip to Paris with his father for Phil. If Alice and Lockwood had decided to send their children to strangers to avoid setting up a situation where their circumstances could be compared, they had unintentionally created a scenario where nothing else was possible.

Georgie was finding relief after the Mary Zambaco scare in turning to her children and other interests. She taught Phil at home in his early days. Although she had been taught in this way herself,

★ This was to mark the Prince of Wales's recovery from typhoid in February 1872.

it was unusual in families at their new level in society. She enjoyed it, and Phil was thrilled. He was a small, nervous child and had great difficulty mixing with other children. Everything worried and frightened him. When he was ill, Georgie reported, she 'had to keep to his room and assure him constantly'.[1] Georgie also decided to return to her studies herself. She studied Latin and French with a French émigré named Andrieu; she began to learn to play the organ, practising on the Howards' instrument at Palace Green; she joined a choir. She was soon to add Italian to her list.

All this was played out against a background of establishing a new relationship with Burne-Jones. Things could never be as they were before, and both parties knew it. The repercussions were widespread. Burne-Jones's Aunt Catherwood had died, leaving them £3,000, but Burne-Jones had done very little work over the previous year, and money was still tight. In addition, his painting *Phyllis and Demophoön* caused a scandal when it was exhibited in 1870. The story it depicts is that of Phyllis, Princess of Thrace, who falls in love with Demophoön. He promises to come back for her, after returning home to settle his affairs, but when he fails to do so she commits suicide and is turned into an almond tree. Demophoön returns and, after showing suitable remorse, is embraced by the tree/Phyllis in token of forgiveness. The face of Phyllis is unmistakably that of Mary Zambaco, and the Latin inscription on the reverse of the picture in Burne-Jones's handwriting no doubt also relates to her – 'Tell me what I have done, except to love unwisely?' It is doubtful that the news of his affair had reached far enough to be the reason why the Old Water-colour Society asked him to alter the picture. The problem was that Demophoön's genitals are not covered. That, and the subject – 'the idea of a love-chase, with a woman follower, is not pleasant'[2] – created enough of a stir that Burne-Jones felt he had no option but to remove the painting, and himself from the membership of the society. Thus he lost his one public exhibition arena.

He needed his friends to gather round and offer support, but here was another problem. William Morris, Burne-Jones's oldest and greatest friend, had suffered silently in his own unhappy marriage for a number of years. Now he had found an emotional outlet – Georgie. It is almost impossible not to read much of his writing of the time as unspoken conversation with his best friend's wife. In 1869, right in the middle of the chaos at the Grange, Morris began a novel, which his first biographer (and Georgie and Ned's future son-in-law) claimed was strongly autobiographical. It was about two brothers who both fell in love with a Methodist minister's daughter with grey eyes:

Amidst apparent coldness they would be tender, O how tender with love, amid apparent patience they would burn with passion, amid apparent cheerfulness they would be dull and glassy with anguish. No lie or pretence could ever come near them, they were the index of a love and greatness of heart that wielded the strong will in her and that serious brow which gave her the air of one who never made a mistake, an [*sic*] look which without the sanctification of the eyes might perhaps have given an expression of sourness and narrowness to her face.[3]

He sent a fragment 'to Georgie to see if she could give me any hope: she gave me none, and I have never looked at it since'.[4]* His dismissal of his marriage can be read into *News from Nowhere*, when the hero, William (born in Walthamstow, as Morris himself was), notes that he had suffered from 'calf-love, mistaken for a heroism that shall be life-long, yet early waning into disappointment'.[6] Others saw it too. Charles Eliot Norton, a friend of the Burne-Joneses from Cambridge, Massachusetts, wrote in his diary:

Went with Burne-Jones to Oxford. Much interesting talk with him on the way, of himself, of Rossetti, of Ruskin, of Morris. I asked him if Morris had ever suffered deeply. 'Oh yes, he has had to bear a long, monotonous, bitter grief. But he took it as part of the great order of things, felt as if it brought him more into the currents of life, bore it as if it were the pain of one in the thick and heat of the hard day's fight, quite uncomplaining and steadily.' The sorrow, I fear, goes on.[7]

---

* It is not clear whether she condemned it because it was too obviously a picture of her relationship with Morris, or because she thought it no good. Morris himself came to the latter view, describing it to Louie as 'a specimen of how not to do it . . .'tis nothing but landscape and sentiment: which thing won't do'.[5]

Georgie, in return, described Morris as 'altogether the most remarkable man I ever saw'. With her meticulous gradations of human behaviour, she added, 'I don't say [he is] the greatest, though I think him great, but certainly [he is] the most remarkable.'[8] Contrary to everyone else, who thought him unattractive (Prinsep wrote that he was 'a truly grotesque figure' with a head that was too big for his body),[9] Georgie thought him 'very handsome'.[10] There is no indication that there was anything other than an extremely close friendship between them. Morris may have suggested something more and been rebuffed, or he may have been content to have a friend with whom he could share his thoughts.

In late 1872 the Morrises moved to Turnham Green, within walking distance of the Grange. Morris began to go over every Sunday for breakfast with Georgie and Ned, and then a morning's work with Ned in his studio (a custom they were to keep up without pause until Morris's death nearly twenty-five years later). This solved Morris's problem that, with Burne-Jones still in a spin over Mary Zambaco, he was seeing less of Georgie – 'not from any coldness of hers', he hastened to add.[11]

In 1871 Morris had gone on a trip to Iceland, and on his return he presented Georgie with the fair copy of the journal he had kept while he was there. To Georgie, and not to Janey, nor to Burne-Jones, his 'best' friend. This is perhaps understandable. Morris had taken up illuminated manuscripts before his trip, and had made two copies of the *Rubáiyát of Omar Khayyám*, a work of totemic significance to the Pre-Raphaelites. He presented one to Georgie, one to Ned. Georgie's was with her belongings when she died; Ned immediately passed his on to Frances Graham.

Frances was the daughter of one of Burne-Jones's most enthusiastic patrons, William Graham.★ She was about eighteen or nineteen, and Burne-Jones was heading for forty. While he had put the emotional intensity of Mary Zambaco behind him, he could not resist young, pretty girls who looked up to him. Georgie noted drily that 'Two things had tremendous power over him – beauty and misfortune.'[13] He had succumbed to both with Mary. From

★ Graham was enthusiastic, but Mrs Graham was less so – she was devout, and didn't like nudes. Once, when Graham bought a female nude, his daughters referred to it as John the Baptist, and she never knew any differently.[12]

now on he settled for beauty, allied with money and an upper-class background. He began an intense friendship with Frances as she grew up, dining at her parents' house in Grosvenor Place two or three times a week, having her sit for him regularly, taking her to picture galleries and theatres. He established with her a relationship amorous in writing, passive in action – a safer proceeding than his previous way, and one he was to keep up (though with different women) always.

Like the Burne-Joneses, the Baldwins too were discovering divergent interests. Superficially, Louie's constant illnesses made her ever more dependent on Alfred; he was happy to fulfil the role of strong protector. However, he now began to return to political life, which he had more or less abandoned after his run-in with the electoral officials in 1869, serving on various local committees, becoming passionately involved once more. For the first time Alfred began to travel without his wife. After 1870, when George and Stanley Baldwin had withdrawn from the works, Alfred's share had grown substantially, as had the business itself. With politics, it became the driving passion of his life. Despite her illnesses, and her claim to have no occupation, Louie filled her days now that her husband had found so many outside interests. She started German lessons, and music lessons.

In addition, she was beginning to write. She and Alfred had always been great readers, ranging widely from the history of the early Christian Church, through Jane Austen, Charles Dickens and George Eliot's novels in parts, as they came out, to Charles Darwin's 'new book' (*The Descent of Man* was published in 1871). Louie in addition read Scott, Carlyle, Ruskin and, of course, Morris. She was inspired to try to do some writing of her own, and Morris encouraged her in her aims:

Please send the M.S.S. and take my thanks for your putting it in my power to be of any use to you . . . I know you are clever and thoughtful, and are not likely to be wrong about it: forgive this piece of personality and be sure that I shall be really pleased to have the M.S.S. Withal Georgie told me you were writing a story, and praised it to me: and I think she is a better critic than I am – don't tell her I said so though.

As to publishers; I can show the work to Ellis (mine) and if it is not in his way to publish it, no doubt he can set the thing on foot for you: I should think however he would publish it, on some terms or another, though it is like enough you may have to risk the expences [*sic*].[14]

Before any of these talents could be put to use, however, everything was suddenly placed on hold. Hannah, who had been failing for some time, became dangerously ill. She had settled very comfortably into her life in Bewdley. She had become devoted to her garden; enjoyed her grandchildren on their visits; had grown deeply attached to her son-in-law Alfred (and he to her – he sent her a birthday note: 'The quiet happiness so often felt in the eve of a well-spent life, and for years to come, may it be yours').[15] But long years were not to be hers. Aged sixty-five, she was told by her doctor that there was nothing more to be done. Louie, bedridden again, was carried in to say her farewells; Agnes and Georgie arrived three days before her death on 2 March 1875. With Edie, they made five wreaths, one for each of them and one for the absent Alice. (At least Alice was remembered – it took another sixteen days for one of them to write to Harry to tell him his mother was dead.) A stained-glass window was designed by Burne-Jones and paid for by Alfred, to be erected at the local church in her memory. There are few written records of their mother's death, and none that discuss their feelings. Some documents may have been destroyed, but in general the Macdonalds did not discuss their emotions, and Hannah's death did not change that.

No longer were Alice, Georgie, Agnes and Louie daughters: now they were wives and mothers only. Edie was neither a wife nor a mother, only an 'accidental person', as Morris called Janey's unmarried sister.[16] Hannah had left everything to Edie, but as this amounted to less than £450 it was neither possible nor considered desirable that she should set up on her own.* The options were to

---

* Hannah's will actually left everything to Edie on condition she remained unmarried. As there was no further clause saying who should inherit if Edie were to marry, it is probable that this was simply so that any fortune-hunter (for £450!) who came along could not get his hands on her money. The Married Women's Property Act of 1870 would, as it happened, have protected Edie from this fate, but, although Hannah died after it was passed, the will had been written two years before and not revised.

become a governess or to go and live with one of her siblings. Louie and Alfred made the decision easy by offering to take her as soon as Hannah died. With Louie ill, Edie immediately became the surrogate housekeeper and companion and even mother, looking after Stan, making sure that he did his lessons (he had a tutor, with whom he studied the normal boyish subjects – French, Latin, etc. – and also music and drawing). She also sat and sewed or read to Louie, keeping her company in the house and going on outings with the family that were too much for her sister. She took Stan skating on the Stour when it froze.

Despite servants, housekeeping had become only marginally easier than when Hannah had had to struggle with her young family. Hygiene had improved: the arrival of geysers in the 1860s pushed plumbing in more prosperous homes out of the kitchen and up to the bathrooms. The invention of the S-bend made it possible to have sanitary drainage indoors without risking an overpowering stench through the house. But prosperity brought its own dirt. A large house could use up to a ton of coal a month, in as many as fourteen fireplaces. Oil lamps were most commonly used, and the lamps needed 'winding up' and trimming at least twice in an evening, depending on draughts. The globes that surrounded them had to be washed with monotonous regularity, as the oil gave off a sooty black vapour that gradually covered the glass. It was estimated that the fires and lights could keep a single servant occupied full-time. The amount of coal dust and dirt from the lights meant that spring cleaning was a necessity after a long, dark winter. Mrs Beeton noted that spring cleaning did not just mean an extra-good clean. It included 'turning out all the nooks and corners of drawers, cupboards, lumber-rooms, lofts, &c. . . . sweeping of chimneys, taking up carpets, painting and whitewashing the kitchen and offices, papering rooms, when needed . . .'[17]

In addition, it was generally accepted that servants had to be supervised constantly and closely. 'Good housekeeping' produced not just a comfortable house, but a frugal one. The kitchen was the place where the woman of the house particularly needed to be ever vigilant. Leftover food should be practically non-existent: fish heads and bones, vegetable leaves, plate-scrapings and wine left in glasses were all to be used to make soup; broken or dry bread was used for bread puddings for the nursery or for breadcrumbs; tea leaves were used for sweeping or to clean glass; cold tea made good eye lotion; potato parings went to feed the chickens; eggshells were used as compost in the garden; dripping was sold to fried-fish shops; other grease was boiled down for soap. Anything left over was put into a bucket and the 'wash' man came to collect it, to be sold to pig farmers – hence 'hog-wash'. Here the housekeeping guides are very firm. If the improvident housekeeper is not careful, the cook will say that she has to pay to have the wash taken away, while actually selling it, thus receiving money from both the homeowner and the wash man.

Controlling all this would have been Edie's responsibility, not to mention disposing of the rest of the household waste. (Wastepaper was sold by the hundredweight: ledgers and account books (without covers) 7s.; covers of ditto, 1s.; old letters, envelopes, invoices, circulars, old music, etc., 4s.; old printed books, old magazines and old newspapers, 3s. Empty biscuit tins went for 3d. each, empty wine bottles and jam jars 6d. the dozen; champagne bottles with the labels were worth more than without – even champagne corks were worth something.)[18] Above all, her overriding role was to be useful and cheerful. She clearly filled it well. Georgie reported to Rosalind Howard that Edie had been to stay with her, 'and I am sorry to lose her, for she was pleasant in the house and so easily amused and pleased as to be quite touching'.[19]

It was good for Georgie to have company, as towards the end of 1874 both Phil and Margaret began school. Burne-Jones's financial position had strengthened in the previous year, although the precipitating factors were distressing. Morris had decided that the Firm had grown unwieldy, and in order to bring it more firmly under control he proposed to dissolve Morris, Marshall, Faulkner & Co. and start again as Morris & Co. The artists broke into two groups: Burne-Jones on Morris's side, Brown acrimoniously siding against them, together with Rossetti, who was now Brown's daughter Lucy's brother-in-law (she had married Gabriel's brother, William Michael Rossetti, the previous year).* Brown told anyone who

* An indication of the trouble to come can be seen in Morris's letter to Louie a few days before the wedding: 'Sad grumbling – but do you know I have got to go to a wedding next Tuesday: to wit Lucy Brown & William Rossetti, & it enrages me to think that I lack courage to say, "I don't care for either of you &

would listen that the artists had carried the Firm when it was not profitable; now it was beginning to make money, Morris wanted it all. There was probably some truth in this, as there was in Morris's view. Burne-Jones, to his regret, got caught in the middle, trying to make Rossetti and, through Rossetti, Brown see reason. His letters to Rossetti to try to sort things out became increasingly plaintive:

I know Brown has fantastic ideas of the money value of the firm and he may be justified in that idea as I in my equally decided one that it never can pay much – but which of us is nearest the mark could soon be proved by the books of the firm – in short it is only this that is wanted that he should meet us – if we could have a meeting in which *you* and all the members were present I believe we could avoid an evil result yet.

Meantime the state of things is intolerable – Brown tells you and who knows whom else besides that at a meeting a few of us voted a big sum of money to Webb for nothing at all – when it is in the minutes of the firm that he himself proposed and Marshall seconded that very vote.

Although one can understand Burne-Jones's increasing irritation, he perhaps was not particularly diplomatic in expressing it:

Will not Brown meet us or at least meet Morris? That does not seem such an unreasonable thing to ask – for heaven knows what reason he has been very unfriendly to me for a long time – I hear through third and fourth people from time to time of his wrongs at my hands – as I hear them they are all fabulous and untrue he has never once had the – regard for old friendship to state them to me and give me the opportunity of denying or explaining anything that hurt him – now he is treating Morris in the same way; refusing to see him face to face, picking up any odds and ends of reports, stating his unjust suspicions to mutual friends as facts

you neither of you care for me, & I wont [*sic*] waste a day out of my precious life in grinning a company grin at you two old boobies" (for they *are* old Louie, I mean for that sort of folly) . . .'[20] They were certainly older than the average newly-weds at the time – Rossetti was born in 1829, Lucy in 1843 – but their age was clearly only an excuse for Morris's grumbling.

– in short behaving to my mind not only in a very unjust but a very unmanly way . . .

I do want to get out of the firm for the reasons I have said – I want it more than ever now.[21]★

Burne-Jones felt he had outgrown the work he was doing for the Firm, and wanted to leave. (He wrote to his friend Mary Gladstone Drew, daughter of the future Prime Minister, about a stained-glass window he was designing: '[It's a] poor little art that pleased people when they were all babies.')[24] In the end he and Morris were the re-formed company's two main designers, with consequently a greater share of profits coming to Burne-Jones than before. This meant that, among other things, Phil could be sent to public school.

This was an abrupt break for him. As the eldest of the group of children, and one of the few boys, he had been used to being the leader. (The records of the secret society he and Margaret formed with the two Morris girls meticulously noted, 'May Morris was created Honorary Secretary, Jane Alice Morris, Captain . . . Margaret Burne-Jones Standard bearer; Philip Burne-Jones being the Leader . . .')[25] Now this shy child was to be inserted into a large rough and tumble group of boys. His parents had chosen to send

★ The 'fabulous and untrue' stories that Brown was telling about Burne-Jones consisted in part of Brown's fixed contention that, when his son Nolly died, Burne-Jones had been uncaring and insufficiently sympathetic. This may or may not have been the case – it is certain that sometimes Georgie's extreme reserve and sense of privacy could appear as indifference: she wrote to Mrs Armstrong on the death of her child, 'I never *dared* to enquire from you about the illness of your precious child – The very idea of his danger seemed too sad for any but an intimate friend to put into words.'[22] She had known the Armstrongs for forty years.

Several years after the breach with Brown, Rossetti summed up for Janey his ideas as to its cause: 'The grievance I believe is not at all a bitter Greek matter which wd. now be ridiculous, but partly on account of the privation of income which B[rown] suffered from loss of custom work, partly on account of the ridicule with which Burne-Jones had for years – not in the least maliciously but very pertinaciously and very thoughtlessly pursued Brown – and partly on account of the very marked indifference which poor Nolly's undervalued genius met with from the same quarter. I must say I cannot think the feeling quite causeless on Brown's part.'[23]

him to Marlborough, without seemingly giving any thought to how the son of an artist would fare in a caste-ridden group of children from landed families. Swinburne was acute when he reflected that Phil was now at a school where the headmaster was 'a cur who writes against Me',[26] one of Burne-Jones's oldest friends: artists were still dangerous radicals who could corrupt. Burne-Jones was mainly concerned that Phil meet the right kind of people, and prepare for his future career at Oxford. It was the old story: the son was to have the advantages that had not been available to the father – whether he wanted them or not.

Phil did not flourish. He and his parents suffered acute separation anxiety, which was never to improve, and was to blight both Phil's and his sister's lives later on. Burne-Jones wrote to Louie:

Don't send little Stan to school, Louie, it's much worse than you would think, and I don't feel sure at all of the compensating good. It is really a constant blank and source of small heartache losing one's little companion. Two months are gone and I am much less like an antique Roman than at first. Did Georgie tell you, but of course she did, how, like a Spartan mother, she inspired him to fight, and got him a big black eye for her pains? But the black eyes wouldn't matter – the loss of daily sight and hearing seem to me things never to be paid for.[27]

The black eye probably mattered rather more to Phil. Burne-Jones wrote attempts at encouraging letters:

I know you will get happy soon: after all dear it is the world in little, for when you are a man it will be just the same – only backs of hair brushes are not used, but things more tormenting – you have not more discomfort at school than I in the world, or feel its nastiness, meanness and unkindness more or its little tyrannies and wanton mischievousness – grown-ups are like it really . . . cannot bear kindly for a few years ways different from theirs, or understand that any can have different desires or hopes or pleasures or thoughts even – no nor bear them to wear different hats or colour shirts . . . the world means it dear – and your being at Marlborough means that you may learn it – and if you learn how to bear it and ever understand it, it will be more worth learning than much Caesar and much

Ovid . . . the world of men is just the same if afterwards when your nature is matured you get any great enthusiasm in it, people will only mock, if you drop it to please them, they will still mock, if you were to die for it they would have no other way of expressing themselves – and still don't mean any evil but are only thoughtless and pitiable – I was also very miserable at school and still more at college, and every way I had that was not quite like the ways of men about me was only derision to them . . . I know if you take all this well and bravely, reflecting upon what it means, resolving never to do the like to others nor to bear malice for what is done to you (for it is only stupidity and no more) it will be what school means – and what life means – it will make you stronger than ever kindness would – I want you to know the world – and to know more evil as time goes on than you can guess, that nothing afterwards may take you by surprise or make you falter in your steadfastness . . .[28]

Not, perhaps, the most reassuring letter a twelve-year-old ever received: don't worry if you find the boys stupid, brutish and unkind – the adult world will be even worse. Poor Phil! Things never got much better for him. Three years later Georgie noted with happiness, 'It is worth anything for Phil to make the acquisition of two such nice boys . . . for he does not seem to find any to care for out of his 500 and odd fellow scholars.'[29]

Margaret did better. She was sent to a day school more in keeping with her family background: the children of merchants and professional people predominated, together with the daughters of clergymen.* This was the Notting Hill High School Limited (where, said Burne-Jones snidely, she received 'a limited education').[30] It probably was fairly limited. According to one Victorian, the average girl of the period spent 640 hours studying arithmetic, and 5,520 studying music.[31] Georgie hoped that Margaret would go on to one of the new women's colleges (perhaps Newnham College, Cambridge, where Helen Gladstone, sister to their great friend Mary Gladstone Drew, was vice-principal), but she failed to do anything to encourage it – Georgie thought women's education began in the home, studying alone as she did. Competing for scholastic certificates was an indication that the

* Walter Sickert's daughter was a pupil too, at roughly the same time as Margaret.

future held governessing or schoolteaching; there was a lot to lose socially by achieving distinction at school.

Academic distinction was for boys, and the Kiplings were beginning to think about where Rudyard should go once his primary-school days were behind him. As the poor relations, they could not think of Marlborough – or Harrow, which the Baldwins were planning for Stan in a few years' time. Instead, Alice wrote to their old friend of Birmingham days:

> My dear Crom
> If your old friends no longer call you by that familiar name pardon my using it, and take as an apology the assurances that the friends of twenty years ago are still remembered by me as I used to know them . . . I saw in yesterday's *Pioneer* an advertisement of the 'US Proprietary College' and was delighted to see your name as Head Master.[32]★

The United Services College, known colloquially after the village it was located in, was a small school recently established in the failed seaside resort of Westward Ho!, Devon.† Created as a feeder school for Sandhurst and Woolwich, it was for the Army-bound sons of those who could not afford the grander public schools. (Haileybury, where Crom had previously been a housemaster, charged approximately £80–£100 a year. Crammers in London could cost as much as £300.)[33] Rudyard could not think of the Army – poor eyesight, as well as his temperament, precluded that – but a combination of their old Birmingham friend and low tuition fees made Westward Ho! an obvious choice.

For, in India, money was still a problem, even though Lockwood was finally moving upward in that world. In 1875 he was made a

---

★ It is interesting to note how isolated from the Burne-Joneses and home Alice was. The Burne-Joneses had never lost touch with Crom, and had Alice heard from them more often it is unlikely she would have had to ask if he still had his nickname, or learn from a newspaper of his new appointment.

† The resort was named after Charles Kingsley's hugely successful novel of 1855, concerning a Devonshire seaman fighting the Spanish Armada. The novel is notable today mainly for its viciously anti-Catholic tone, and its appalling comic-opera violence.

fellow of the University of Bombay, in recognition of his contribution to the artistic life of the city. In addition he had now left
schoolteaching behind. In April of that year he was appointed
principal of the Mayo School of Art in Lahore, and curator of the
Lahore museum. This was a big step up socially. Lahore had only
seventy English families, plus various military men posted there,*
and the serried ranks of hierarchy that had frustrated Alice in
Bombay were less rigid here. But first the move from Bombay to
Lahore had to be made.

Alice sounded a great deal like her mother after the move. She
wrote to her great friend Editha Plowden, seventeen days after
her arrival at Lahore, complaining that the new house was ugly,
inconvenient, badly decorated, and in a bad 'situation'. 'I declare I
can hardly bear to recount the doings of the station so dreary and
monotonous do I find them . . . take the women all round they
have not brains enough to make such a cutlet as I ate at breakfast
this morning! And how I am going to exist here God knows – I
can't imagine . . .'[34] The house in Lahore was actually a pleasant
one, opposite a semi-abandoned house owned by the Nawab of
Mundot, and looked out at a pretty eighteenth-century mosque.
For some reason the road was said to be haunted – when forced to
use it late at night, the coolies sang to scare away the 'bhuts'. The
house itself was a square white bungalow, with four big centre
rooms, and smaller rooms at the corners. It was surrounded by wide
verandahs, which looked out over grounds that had had all their
vegetation removed: Lockwood was convinced it bred disease.
Because of the resulting scorched-earth appearance, local comics
nicknamed it Bikaner Lodge, after the Bikaner Desert in central
India. Even after everything was redone to her satisfaction, and at
her wittiest, Alice never forgot this beginning. A visitor looking
around commented, 'I say, Mrs Kipling, your house is simply A.1.'
'Ah,' replied Alice, 'you should have seen it B.4.'[35]

At least when Hannah moved house she was in her own country,
surrounded by her family. Alice admitted, 'I am homesick worse
than I ever was in my life. I *cannot* care for this country – or even

---

* In 1875 the census listed 128,491 people living in Lahore and its suburbs; of
these, 1,723 were English.

seem to do so . . .' Nothing was right for her there. A caller was worthy of note only for his (unattractive) appearance: 'My dear he has grown quite fat – a double chin – and – if you will excuse my mentioning it – a double stomach.'[36]*

Lockwood, as usual, fitted in immediately. He had a big job ahead of him, and one that he was passionate about. The Mayo consisted of a few pupils in a small house; by the time of his retirement eighteen years later it was in a new building (designed by Lockwood) with a flourishing tradition of applied arts and design.† He had gone to Lahore ahead of Alice to start work while she closed up their house in Bombay, and stayed in the Punjab Club. Nearly fifty years later he was remembered by the man who had stayed in the next room as 'one of the sweetest characters I have ever known . . . When I think of the lines: "His little, nameless, unremembered acts of kindness and of love", I think of wise and gentle John Lockwood Kipling.'[38]

Six months after Alice arrived in April 1875, Lockwood came down with typhoid. They were newcomers; they knew few people in the community (and it would take strangers some time to find their way past Alice's astringencies); they had no women servants (why is not clear). Alice was on her own. It was a harrowing time, and one she would always remember. It was four months before Lockwood pulled through and was out of danger, the only vestiges of his illness then being that afterwards he was 'grey and bald and prematurely old looking'.[39]

Lockwood recovered and soon returned to work, but Louie's illnesses in England were a much more time-consuming operation. By now she had been intermittently bedridden for five or six years. Alfred's business was in good shape. Now that Hannah was no

---

* One is irresistibly reminded of a comment of Edie's as a child. When told by her father that the stomach was an organ, she said, 'O Papa, then yours must be a barrel organ!'

† His work there was not forgotten. In 1906 Lockwood wrote to Editha, '[I] hear from Lahore that the Sch: of Art is booming along at a great rate. More numbers, more money . . . and all my pet schemes being carried out. They want my portrait to hang up as their Venerable Founder – they don't use those words – sacred to that strong old John Wesley, but similar like.'[37]

longer nearby and needing care, that splendid Victorian standby, travel in search of health, was on the cards. Sea air, mountain air, sunshine – all were regarded as sure ways to cure various ailments. Different places cured different illnesses: 'In parts of Italy, the principal effect of the atmosphere was sedative; in areas of the Franco-Italian Riviera, it was mildly tonic; elsewhere still, it was extremely exciting.'[40] Spas in particular were recommended, being 'designed to ease the mind while regulating the functions of the body'.[41] Water was the focus: ritually swallowed, or in baths taken 'medicinally'.

Such a regime was what Alfred and Louie decided on. They left Stan with the Poynters and in July 1875 headed off to a Prussian spa town. They did the same the following summer, after yet another specialist had confirmed 'irritation of the nerves of the spine'. The year after that Madeira was the chosen destination for six weeks. (This time Stan came too, as did Edie and the Poynters.) Then the next four years were France and Germany again, always in the name of a cure. It is easy to sound cynical about these trips. Whether mentally or physically Louie was suffering. But when a partial itinerary includes a trip down the Rhine, then Mainz, Nuremberg, Regensburg, Passau, Linz, Vienna, Budapest, Vienna again, Munich and Frankfurt, even before they started the trek home, the idea begins to form that Louie could find the strength to do what she wanted to do when she wanted to do it. This is not to say she was not ill. It is just to query the origin of the illness.

Louie had had one, possibly two, miscarriages after the birth of Stan. She came from a family of eleven children. When she had been growing up and forming her ideas of what constituted a family, anything less than seven children was small; 30 per cent of all households contained over half the population.[42] This was changing, but for professional people three children were the norm. A woman's primary job was to be a child-bearer, then a help-meet to her husband. Louie and Agnes had produced only one child apiece. Their husbands showed no sign of needing either their moral support or their economic support in the way that their mother's had been needed – making clothes, educating a family, stretching an already overstretched income – or in the way that Georgie looked after the accounts both for her household and for Burne-Jones's work. What then was left?

Delicacy, fragility, passivity – these were the stereotypical attributes of the Victorian woman. Illness is the epitome of the first two of these: an invalid is doubly delicate, entirely fragile. But passive? As illness represented the middle- and upper-class image of Victorian femininity, it is possible that women actually dominated their households through the sickroom. This different way of representing themselves helped them to create a persona that gave them the control they otherwise lacked. It was easy for Victorian women to be ill. Illness was their natural state: medical conditions requiring special care included puberty, menstruation, pregnancy, childbirth, breastfeeding and menopause. Lack of pregnancy (through either infertility or celibacy) was also an illness. There was not much time left in which a woman could be regarded as healthy.*

Men had historically been able to suffer from nervous illnesses without it being a cause for shame. Burne-Jones suffered badly from recurring depression. Just before Phil went to Marlborough, Burne-Jones had been invited to Naworth to stay with the Howards. As usual, Georgie was there to fight his battles for him:

he is extremely unwell. Please, dear Rosalind, treat him as you would a man recovering from a serious illness – don't make any plans or excursions for him, but let him wander about and breathe in fresh strength if the sweet air will give it him. I feel a ceaseless anxiety about him until he shews more decided improvement, so forgive me for sending you this hint as to his state – he needs rest (if he can take it) and quiet at any price – two things impossible for him in this house, poor boy. He still has very bad nights, with bogie dreams and no doubt more painful thoughts in the waking times from them – you'll put him in a room not too far from fellow creatures, won't you? I fear this seems half impertinence to you who will I know be as kind to him as you were to me when I was there with you – but I shall have many sad anxious thoughts about him and wanted to say this to you.

---

* In many women, treatment for these ills probably caused physical illness where mental illness (or unhappiness) had previously been the underlying complaint. Quinine, arsenic and strychnine, given up to three times a day, were tonics for those needing 'strengthening'. Then there was the standard bleeding, purging and blistering. Not many systems could stand up to these remedies.

Four days later she fired off another note:

I have not at all exaggerated the need for rest and care with regard to
Ned. Dr. Radcliffe is graver about him than he has been for many years
past . . . If it isn't fidgeting you (which I know it isn't) may he have his
usual glass of warm milk with a tablespoonfull of rum in it before rising
in the morning?[43]

Georgie's attitude was becoming old-fashioned, however. As
initiative and drive became the prevalent cult, and muscular Christianity called for self-control in all things, depression started to
appear selfish and a result of lack of will power. Rosalind was
very much of this viewpoint, disapproving of 'mollycoddling' the
delicate. She thought that it was good for nervous people to have
their sensibilities 'blunted'.

While Burne-Jones had no trouble talking about his depressions
– 'about every fifth day I fall into despair as usual';[44] 'I sorely want
a companion to say to me ten times a day, "never mind", "stick to
it", "don't give in", "peg away", "it's worth the while" . . .'[45] –
Poynter, who suffered from the same problem, felt unable to talk
about it at all. Agnes said that he 'sinks utterly both morally &
physically, which is impossible for people of other natures to
understand . . . He groans & travails over his work & does nothing
easily. He says there is nothing the matter.'[46]

Even the son of Alice and Lockwood – neither of whom showed
signs of depression themselves – did not escape the family taint. By
December 1876, when ten-year-old Rudyard arrived for his annual
trip to the Grange, it was clear that something was wrong. In 'Baa
Baa, Black Sheep' a friend of the family simply discovers on a visit
to Southsea that 'the little chap's nearly blind!'[47] There is (a bit)
more to the story in Rudyard's autobiography: 'Some sort of
nervous breakdown followed, for I imagined I saw shadows and
things that were not there, and they worried me more than the
Woman [Mrs Holloway]. The beloved Aunt [Georgie] must have
heard of it, and a man came down to see me as to my eyes and
reported that I was half-blind.'[48] This is a nice piece of concealed
revelation, moving seamlessly from 'some sort of nervous breakdown' and apparent hallucinations to mere myopia. Although

Kipling did have terrible eyesight, and wore very thick glasses from this time onwards, something more had happened. Georgie remembered later that she began to worry about what she called 'optical illusions': 'He would suddenly run across the room and touch the walls, and when I asked him why he did this, said "to see if they were there!"'[49] This is rather more than myopia.

Georgie wrote at once to Alice, saying that Rudyard had suffered 'a sort of breakdown', and by March 1877 Alice was back home. She collected the children from Southsea, and took them (with Stan for part of the time – there was scarlet fever at Wilden) for nearly eight months' break to a farm in Epping Forest. Rudyard was under strict instructions not to read, not to think, simply to play and be a child for a while.

Alice was probably glad of the break too. On New Year's Day 1877 Queen Victoria had been proclaimed Empress of India, and the Delhi Durbar set out to commemorate the event in suitable fashion. Val Prinsep had been sent out from London to produce an official painting of the assemblage. Despite his closeness to Georgie and Ned, there is no indication that he visited the Kiplings, or that there was any communication at all, even though Lockwood, the man who got things done, was in the thick of things. At the last minute Lord Lytton, the Viceroy, had had the bright idea of giving each of the seventy native princes in attendance a banner of his own. Lockwood was to design them, and Alice showed the local tailors what he wanted, sewing the more difficult bits herself. They were finished in time, although it was a very close-run thing.

When Alice arrived in London, she found the same sort of frantic preparation going on at the Grange. Since his resignation from the Old Water-colour Society seven years before, Burne-Jones had had no regular exhibition space, relying instead on his faithful group of patrons to buy his pictures as he finished them. Up to a point this worked, but he was pleased to be invited to exhibit in a new gallery that was about to open.

The Grosvenor Gallery in Bond Street became one of the most famous exhibition spaces of the day, mostly because it was perceived to be a leader in the new 'Aesthetic' movement that was emerging. Sir Coutts Lindsay, the owner, had been an army officer before deciding to become a painter. Although he had some success at the

Royal Academy summer shows, he wanted to create a gallery where the Royal Academy's notorious selection and hanging rituals could be obviated. He planned an annual exhibition, with daily visitors and season-ticket holders, just like the Academy. He added to this an elitism that manifested itself in the creation of a space that looked like the homes of those who bought the pictures that were hanging, in 'Sunday afternoons' where Lady Lindsay played hostess to 'notable people in Literature and Art', and in intimate suppers for artists and patrons together. (All this was helped along by the fact that Lady Lindsay had been born into the Rothschild family.)

The first show, in May 1877, included Burne-Jones, Poynter, Watts, Millais, Whistler, Albert Moore, Alma-Tadema, Holman Hunt and W. B. Richmond. The gallery was run by Joseph Carr, an art critic, and C. E. Hallé, the son of the Sir Charles Hallé who had founded the Manchester – now Hallé – Orchestra. Although as a public forum to show his works the Grosvenor Gallery was to suit Burne-Jones for many years, the first exhibition caused him nothing but trouble. It was about the Whistlers on display★ that Ruskin launched his now famous attack: 'I have seen, and heard, much of Cockney impudence before now; but never expected to hear a coxcomb ask two hundred guineas for flinging a pot of paint in the public's face.' Whistler immediately sued for libel, and Ruskin called on Burne-Jones to be one of his expert witnesses.

This was not something Burne-Jones could easily refuse. For many years their relationship had been strained. When Burne-Jones had been the postulant and Ruskin the master, things had gone well; as Burne-Jones found his feet, he was not always in agreement with his old mentor, and this was not something Ruskin found easy to accept.† There had been a serious breach over Burne-Jones's

★ The pictures were *Nocturne in Black and Gold: The Falling Rocket* (this was the prime offender), *Harmony in Amber and Black*, *Arrangement in Brown*, *Arrangement in Black No. 3*, *Nocturne in Blue and Silver*, *Old Battersea Bridge*, *Nocturne in Blue and Gold* and *Portrait of Carlyle*.

† Their dissimilarity of character didn't help, either. One day, when visiting Ruskin at his parents', Burne-Jones began – in desperation one imagines – to read them the story of the barber from *The Arabian Nights* to amuse them. Amusement had never been high on the Ruskin family's list of desiderata, as Burne-Jones reported: 'His mother . . . said she was always interested in the Egyptians because of their connection with God's chosen people. I thought that

infatuation with Mary Zambaco, when Burne-Jones had interpreted Ruskin's attack at the time on Michelangelo's 'dark carnality'
which 'substitutes the flesh of man for the spirit' as an attack on his
own life and work.[51] Despite his dislike of controversy, it was
impossible now to refuse Ruskin's request. He joined the witness
list, together with William Powell Frith (painter of *Derby Day*, the
sensation of the 1858 Royal Academy exhibition) and Tom Taylor,
a journalist.

In retrospect, Burne-Jones did not cover himself with glory. He
told Ruskin's lawyers that 'scarcely any body regards Whistler as a
serious person', that Whistler's art was founded on 'the art of
brag', and that Whistler rarely 'committed himself to the peril of
completing anything'.[52] Not only is this not attractive, from our
perspective it is almost wilfully blind to the way in which art was
developing. (It is notable that Frith, Ruskin's other 'expert' painter,
was by the time of the trial completely out of fashion.) This is not
just hindsight; even his contemporaries noticed it. Walter Crane,
once Burne-Jones's assistant and by the time of the trial a well-
regarded children's illustrator, commented, 'I was rather surprised
to find, however, that Burne-Jones could not, or would not, see
[Whistler's] merits as an artist, or recognise the difference of his
aims. He seemed to think there was only *one* right way of painting.'[53]

---

funnier even than the story of the barber. It was a difficult evening and I wished
I hadn't begun . . .'[50]

9. Faith and Works
1877–1882

In 1877 Alfred Baldwin took the plunge and formally moved over to the Conservatives.[1] He had never been a particular supporter of Gladstone, rather a slightly Whiggish Palmerstonian. Over the next decade he moved effortlessly into the heart of the landed families who ran the Conservative Party, becoming a Justice of the Peace in 1879, and an active and valued member of the Worcestershire Conservative executive and other regional and national associations. He was instrumental in renewing the party's local organization after the many electoral reforms of the period. Two major events had precipitated his break with the political party his family had supported so steadily. The political motive was what became known as the Eastern Question. The moral impetus was the radical pressure for Church disestablishment.

The Eastern Question began to preoccupy the minds of Britons in the summer of 1874. A Russo-Turkish treaty permitted Russia (Britain's traditional enemy) to approach the Sublime Porte, or Ottoman government, on behalf of Russian Orthodox Christians living under Ottoman jurisdiction. The British, always on the alert for signs of expansionism, saw this as one more attempt to spread Russia's power and influence. Then several waves of Balkan uprisings, which led either to severe repression or to appalling atrocities by the Turks (depending on your political viewpoint), brought the question to ignition point. The Treaty of San Stefano, signed at the end of the ensuing Russo-Turkish war (1877–8), was thought by many to be inadequate to protect British interests in the region. Gladstone felt that the solution lay not in supporting Russia or Turkey, but in promoting autonomous rule to the people of the Balkans. Many in Britain, including Alfred, felt that, by not supporting Turkey, Gladstone was by default supporting Russia.*

* In January 1879 Lockwood created an illustrated menu card for a 'Conservative dinner party' at Wilden. It shows Gladstone on a camel, following a signpost 'To Russia', suggesting where his natural allies were. (Dinner consisted of: Mock

Burne-Jones, on the other hand, was passionately with Gladstone over his stand on the Eastern Question. It was the first (and last) time he was to become personally involved in political agitation. While it lasted he was totally committed. Gladstone gathered most of his support from the intelligentsia and the Nonconformists, seeing the matter as a moral rather than a political one. In 1876 the Eastern Question Association had been formed to ensure the dissemination of information for the cause. Morris became treasurer of the association, and Howard and Burne-Jones joined in, together with more political types – Carlyle and the MP John Bright among them. That year Burne-Jones helped convene a conference at St James's Hall, where Gladstone spoke; in 1878 he continued his involvement, organizing with Morris and Crom Price a Workmen's Neutrality Demonstration at Exeter Hall to discuss the same question. In 1882 he was instrumental in getting the government to take action on reports of systematic persecution of the Jews that were starting to come in from Eastern Europe. But by this time Burne-Jones was becoming disillusioned – the amount of time and energy it took to create the smallest change in public perception, much less in government policy, was overwhelming. He took this personally, and could not accept the equanimity with which the government could oversee what he understood as injustice and cruelty. Morris relished his first immersion into politics and began to become seriously involved with the socialist movement. At this Burne-Jones drew back – by 1890 he was so detached that he was fined for refusing to do jury service. He said, 'I have no politics, and no party, and no particular hope: only this is true, that beauty

---

Turtle Soup, Turbot with Lobster Sauce, Oyster Patés, Stewed Kidneys, Boiled Turkey Tongue with Oyster Sauce, Roast Haunch of Mutton, Pheasants à la Gitana, Roast Hare, Plum Pudding, Mince Pies, Jellies &c., Cheesecakes &c. This was fairly typical dinner-party fare. Puzzlingly, etiquette books of the day suggest 'the best of dinners should not be prolonged beyond an hour and a quarter'. How this amount of food was eaten in that space of time perhaps explains the prevalence of spas and other places to cure digestive problems, as well as purgatives such as Frompton's Bill of Health, which promised 'long time efficiency for correcting all disorders of the Stomach and Bowels, the common symptoms of which are costiveness, Flatulency, Spasms, loss of appetite, sick headache, Giddiness, Sense of Fullness after meals . . .' A 'sense of fullness after meals' as a worrying symptom is particularly charming.)[2]

is very beautiful, and softens, and comforts, and inspires, and rouses, and lifts up, and never fails.'[3]

Georgie was with him in his earlier political forays, getting passionately involved herself. Over time, however, their attitudes revealed their essential differences in character. Burne-Jones became progressively disenchanted with the political world: Georgie was a sticker, and remained faithful to her initial enthusiasm always. In addition, Burne-Jones was to move steadily rightward, while Georgie remained a proud socialist to the end of her days. Louie, on the other hand, showed no interest in politics at the beginning, and it would appear that Alfred's initial withdrawal from politics had much to do with his marriage in its early days. After he returned to the fray, Louie retired to bed; it was only after her son was grown that she recovered enough to take an interest, as the wife of a Conservative stalwart.

Alfred saw Gladstone and the Liberal Party's policy on the Balkans as a betrayal. When some Liberals also began to work towards separating the Church of England from the governance of the state, it was one step too far. Alfred could not contemplate this, and could stay with the Liberals no longer, distrusting their 'infidelity' as well as their 'socialism'. His break with the Liberals over Church reform is important in understanding his character. Louie and Alfred were the two members of the family who continued to be regular communicants, for whom religion was at the core of their beings. Lockwood, on his branch of the family's church-going, simply said, 'None of us, by the way, ever go.'[4] Later, in an attempt at fiction, he elaborated:

I have knelt with my brow pressed against the back of a rush-bottomed chair in ritualistic Churches in England. I have bowed my head in baize-lined pews of Dissent; I have knelt at the amateur prayer-meetings of those evangelical ladies and gentlemen who proposed to 'unite in prayer' as godless people propose 'to have a little music' or a hand at whist . . . I have marvelled at the ravings of methodist ranters round weeping and snuffling victims at the 'penitent bench'.[5]

Georgie was crisper: 'Going to church seems to me so poor a substitute for religion.'[6] This was shorthand. Art had been her religion from adolescence, while she maintained a strong core of orthodox belief. She wrote a condolence letter to a friend who had lost his sister:

I cannot write or feel sadly about her death any more than I could about her life, for the one is part of the other to me and I am sure was not different so far as you could see . . . year by year I feel more certainty of life beyond.[7]

Burne-Jones felt the same way, although he expressed it differently:

There was a Samoan chief once whom a missionary was bullying. Said the missionary: 'But have you, my dear sir, no conception of a deity?' Said the Samoan chief: 'We know that at night-time someone goes by amongst the trees, but we never speak of it.' They dined on the missionary that same day, but he tasted so nasty that they gave up eating people ever after, so he did some good after all . . .

When Burne-Jones was asked about his beliefs, he just repeated the words of the Samoan: 'We know that at night-time someone goes by amongst the trees, but we never speak about it.'[8]

Alfred and Louie, on the other hand, not only spoke about their beliefs, they acted on them. In 1878 Alfred set up a local Sunday school. In 1879 he laid the foundation stone for a new church at Wilden, to be called All Saints. He financed it in the main, and was its first churchwarden.★ He tithed his income to the church, and gave substantially to charity. Alfred had left the Nonconformism of his family in his early twenties, and by the time he married he described himself as 'high church'. It was not that he was extreme, just that he had come a long way from the low, almost

---

★ The Baldwins long maintained their connection with All Saints. They were the lay patrons of the church, with the right to nominate the vicar; in 1895 Louie gave a jewelled communion plate; in 1910 the Memorial Clock was formally started by Stan's son Oliver; in 1921 the war memorial was unveiled by Stan, and in 1930 he attended a service to mark the church's fiftieth Jubilee year; in 1940, for its sixtieth year, he gave the address. The vicar in 1940 was the man Alfred had appointed curate in 1896.[9]

Dissenting, Church of his childhood. Rather than being attached to the high Anglicanism of the Oxford movement, he was convinced that the traditions of the Church of England, its position as the 'national' Church in the unity of the nation, were what was important.

In addition, faith as part of daily routine sustained Alfred. Until his death he professed himself a disciple of Charles Kingsley, who believed that religion and secular pursuits were not separate, and that both together made up a full Christian life.[10] It is in this world, not the next, that the Christian man engages and struggles with God's purposes. Alfred was a wholehearted admirer of these ideas, 'exalt[ing] practice over theory', 'in the world ... [but not] of the world'. Duty was the important point. A man had to work because it was his duty to do so, serving God and his fellow men by performing his job to the best of his ability. It was a religious and ethical, as well as social, necessity. Success was given to man by God, and it was man's moral obligation to serve God well by using his wealth and position for the greater good of his fellows.

This makes Alfred seem to some modern eyes to be rather a dreary character, although contemporary accounts show that he was clearly much loved, as well as greatly respected. He drove his family firm forward without the ruthlessness of the great capitalists. He knew all his workers personally. He was patriarchal, but in the sense that his workers were an extended family, 'that the connection between master and servant should be something beyond one of mere cash and that a master's interest did not cease when he had paid his workers on Saturday night'. He was the first Midlands ironmaster to allow his workers eight-hour shifts, instead of the standard twelve-hour day. Safety, hygiene, housing, medical care, guaranteed employment – all were part of the duties Alfred saw as his.

Louie was the wife of the owner, and as such, when her health allowed it, carried out her role: exemplar to the women of the community. As well as a church and a Sunday school, Alfred built a school for the children of his employees; Louie and Edie (and later Stan) lectured and taught at the Sunday school and at the various groups and societies set up for worker improvement –

works bodies and also a 'friendly society', which organized, on a voluntary basis, mutual insurance for the workers.* Family events were events for the whole workforce – when Stan turned five, a tea was given for over 200 women and children from the village and the works.† Wreaths and banners were put up, a band played, and Stan received presents ranging from some fruit or a cake to toys and books.

Georgie found herself in sympathy with Alfred. Although her religious beliefs were less overt, her ideas of practical Christianity coloured much of her life. Unlike Burne-Jones, she had remained on close terms with Ruskin. In 1874 Rose La Touche, Ruskin's former pupil, with whom he had been in love, had died after several years of nervous breakdowns and suffering most probably from anorexia nervosa. For the following two years Ruskin was in an increasingly odd state of mind, which Whistler's libel suit only exacerbated. When Ruskin returned from Italy in late 1877, it was clear he was heading for a major collapse. Georgie went to Brantwood, in the Lake District, to be with him in January 1878, taking Margaret with her. By February he was violent and completely divorced from reality: his diary shows his thoughts whirling around evil, Rose and sex. Georgie remained one of the faithful, only commenting years later, 'Now and then his brain gave way under the strain of thoughts and feelings that were beyond his power to express – I wonder more people don't go distraught when they realize how much of life is a hand to hand fight.'[13] Nearly forty years after she had first met Mary Zambaco she saw life as travail. Then she had asked a friend to 'Help me to rail at Fate a little, and then to bear it'.[14] Now life was a fight to the death.

---

* Alfred was later president of the Wilden Works Mutual Improvement Society (1902–3), and Stan vice-president. Among the talks they gave, Stan spoke on 'England 100 Years Ago' and 'The Fiscal Question', the Revd Theodore Baldwin on 'The Age of Chivalry'; and even Edie lectured, on 'Venice – Illustrated', though she had been there no more than her audience had.[11]

† The population of Wilden at the time was about 500 to 600 people, although with the agricultural depression of 1879 it began to shrink. In 1886 an informal census of Wilden shows the Baldwins living with four servants – the only people in the village with any servants at all.[12]

Things were, on the contrary, becoming easier for the Kiplings. Alice had stayed in England since she had removed Rudyard from Southsea, while Trix had been returned, happily, to Mrs Holloway for another year (another indication of how carefully Rudyard's version of events must be treated) before being brought to London to attend Notting Hill High School. Rudyard was sent to Westward Ho! at the beginning of 1878. He had difficulty settling in at first. Although, unlike Phil at Marlborough, his background was not different from that of the other boys,[*] he missed the love and friendship he had become used to in the nine months since Alice had returned. Trix later remembered, 'for the first month or so he wrote to us, twice or thrice daily (and my mother cried bitterly over the letters) that he could neither eat nor sleep . . . I remember my mother going in tears to my aunt, Lady Burne-Jones, who told her that her son had written exactly the same sort of letters but was now very happy.'[16]

Not precisely happy. By September 1878 Phil had more or less given up on school, and Georgie was looking for a tutor for him in the time before he could go up to Oxford. He was painting a bit, and to encourage him he was given the little studio over the dining room, which Burne-Jones had outgrown. He remained a worry to his parents. Withdrawn as a child, unhappy at school, as he progressed to maturity he came to be no more comfortable in his skin. By January 1879 he was in a state, and Burne-Jones was speaking 'in a rather wild way', saying 'that [Phil] has given up all thought of Art'.[17] By July Georgie was in despair. She spoke unguardedly of her lack of confidence in Phil's abilities to Rosalind Howard, and then had to write asking her

to keep to yourself what I said to you about Phil on Saturday morning, for I feel as if I had been unjust to the boy to say as much as I did, and certainly that there is no need for me to feel while he is 17 as much disappointment as I might if he were 21. He is a dear and good son to us,

[*] The *United Services Chronicle* for Westward Ho! in 1881, the year before Rudyard left, lists 189 boys in the school, of whom 72 were born in England, 8 in Scotland, 11 in Ireland, 4 in Wales, 76 in India, 2 in Jamaica, 2 at the Cape, 4 in New Zealand, 2 at Aden, 1 in Ceylon, 1 at Gibraltar, 1 in St Helena, 1 in Egypt, 2 in Italy, 1 in Switzerland, 1 off China.[15]

and I cannot bear the idea of labelling him with a fault. He has buckled
to work with his tutor with a good grace and neither hope nor patience
are exhausted in my heart.[18]

A shockingly harsh indictment of a child – and Phil was little more
– implying a considerable burden of expectation. By twenty-one,
clearly, it was expected that Phil would have found his way in life;
if not, he would remain a 'disappointment'. Margaret was judged
by equally exacting standards; nor were her shortcomings kept in
the family. When her daughter was eleven Georgie wrote to Charles
Eliot Norton, their friend from Boston, that she had received a pair
of shoes his daughter Sally had embroidered for her: 'long would it
be before Margaret could equal their art'. Sally also plays the violin,
while 'Margaret learns only that maid of all work the piano'. A
letter from Margaret is forwarded to Sally 'with all its probable
imperfections of spelling, about which the address forbids me to
affect no anxiety.'[19]* Any one of these comments would mean
nothing, but the ceaseless barrage is daunting.

In the summer of 1878, before Phil left Oxford, Georgie had
taken her second trip abroad, going with Margaret to France, where
they met Ned and Phil, who had been spending some time in Paris
and Normandy. For the first time the Kiplings were able to give
their children similar treats. Lockwood had arrived in England in
March. As well as having some well-earned leave, he was charged
with responsibility for the Fine Arts of India Pavilion at the Exposition Universelle of 1878.† Lockwood and Rudyard spent five
weeks together in Paris: a chance for Lockwood to acquaint himself
with his son, just as Alice had done the previous summer. Lockwood's French had always been good – Trix remembered him
reading aloud from books in French, translating as he went, with
never a pause to think, or grope for words[22] – and now he could

* Oddly, Georgie's formidable personality, which allowed her to deviate not an inch
from what she saw as the 'right' way through life, allowed her at the same time to be
vastly more forgiving than many of her friends. In 1872 she braved the 'Insane Ward'
of the Marylebone Workhouse Infirmary to visit a friend who had ended there.[20]
† The fair was extremely popular with the British in particular. Thomas Cook
& Son took 75,000 customers over to Paris during its run, as well as selling
400,000 tickets for the fair: a third of all admissions.[21]

show Rudyard around and then give him his first taste of freedom, allowing him to roam at will. After the Exposition, Lockwood returned to England, where he stayed until October 1879, before returning to Lahore via Venice – where he may have gone with the Poynters, who were certainly there that month.

This was a much-needed break for Agnes and Edward. In 1876 Poynter had decided that his responsibilities in central London – at University College, and at the South Kensington Museum – made the journey from Shepherd's Bush every day too difficult. In addition, the job at South Kensington gave him a studio, and so a large house was no longer as necessary as it had been. As he had inherited his first rooms from Burne-Jones, so now he passed the lease of his house on to Walter Crane, who would benefit from the studio he had built in his garden. Crane had lived round the corner from them, and was close to Poynter, often coming to paint in the Beaumont Lodge studio when his own proved too small for the commissions he had on hand.* He now took it over permanently, and the Poynters moved briefly to a house in a small turning off Knightsbridge, Albert Terrace. By 1878 they had moved again, just down the road, to 28 Albert Gate. This had a much smaller garden than Beaumont Lodge, but it opened out at the back on to Hyde Park.

The size of the house had become less important, as had the garden, as in the autumn of 1878 Ambo went off to prep school. He and Stan were sent together. Agnes had spent so much time with Louie at Wilden that their sons were the closest of all the cousins. It was decided not to separate them, and to send them to a prep school in Slough – Hawtrey's, which was a feeder school for Eton. Stan took the separation from his parents calmly. His father wrote, 'You were a very good, brave boy this afternoon, and I was very pleased with your manly way. If you will be as good in your work as you are brave in your play while you are at school, you will indeed do well.'[23]

One of the great advantages of Hawtrey's was that the boys were

---

* Poynter helped Crane with more than his house: in 1879 he made him an examiner at the South Kensington School of Art, a useful source of regular income; and in 1888 Crane was elected to the Old Water-colour Society through Poynter's patronage.

not far from London. Now that they had relocated to the centre of town, the Poynters could share in the family pastimes more easily, and Stan could join them. The Poynters' drawing room was just the size for theatricals, and in January 1879 the large group of children – Burne-Joneses, Poynters, Morrises and various cousins and others – colonized Albert Gate. In their 'in-house' magazine, the *Scribbler*, they reported in their Drama section: 'On the evening of the 17th instant a large and fashionable audience assembled at 28, Albert Gate, to witness a performance . . . we allude to the performance of Bluebeard, in twelve tableaux designed by and produced under the personal superintendence of, Messrs. E. J. Poynter and C. E. Hallé.' Bluebeard was played by Ambo 'in blue garment of eastern design – the turban absolutely gleaming with turquoise jewellery'. Miss M. Bell (Poynter's niece) was Sister Anne, and Margaret was Fatima. There was a Stop Press: 'We are sorry to hear that the performance of "Cymbeline" which was contemplated at the Grange Theatre, Fulham, has been abandoned; we trust only temporarily.'[24]

The mixture of popular and classic is revealing. The Poynters, the Baldwins and Georgie had a taste for opera and concerts – Edward and Agnes had a regular box at the opera and, in a long-standing arrangement, Georgie went with them. She also went to regular Monday concerts, taking Rosalind Howard's tickets whenever she was out of London. The Poynters and Georgie went to Shakespeare as much as possible – taking the children to 'suitable' plays, with the Baldwins eager to join them whenever they were in town. Burne-Jones, on the other hand, found opera as dull as he had when he had first gone to Italy with Ruskin, and he was not much more interested in Shakespeare. He went instead with his bachelor friends to Gilbert and Sullivan, and sent George Howard an enthusiastic report: 'I screamed and Armstrong screamed and Sanderson . . . I shall take Morris and Georgie there but I shan't enjoy that – for they won't laugh at all I know – indeed they say they won't.'[25] And indeed they didn't. Morris reported glumly that he 'thought [it] dreary stuff enough in spite of Burne-Jones'.[26] It gradually became accepted that it was better to keep their outings separate than suffer each other's tastes.

★

In 1880 Alice prepared to return to Lahore. Trix was brought back from Southsea to attend her new London school, and lodged with some 'ladies' nearby – there were apparently still too many 'complications' to ask Georgie to look after her, even though Trix and Margaret were to be together at school. This may have been because the Grange was in a state of upheaval – a semi-permanent situation. The architect W. A. S. Benson was building a new studio across the end of the garden, and hot-pipes were being laid, although only to heat the studio.* Nor was Rudyard to stay at the Grange with his 'beloved Aunt' when he was not at Westward Ho! Early in his schooldays he spent part of his holidays with Fred's family. This was clearly enjoyed by Rudyard as well as by the Macdonalds. One gets a glimpse of the devilry that Mrs Holloway had been at such oppressive pains to eliminate. His cousin remembered when, after being scolded for his grubby appearance, 'my mother gave him sixpence to go to the hairdressers . . . When he came back his head was shaved and my mother said to him, "Ruddy, what *have* you done?" "I am sick of all the fuss about a parting . . . Now there isn't going to be one." '[27]

The Burne-Joneses were fully occupied, and they didn't seem to have room for a nephew and niece. Georgie, said Ned half admiringly, half despairingly, 'is tremendous and stirs up the house into a froth every morning',[28] so that it smelt of 'Soap and washing so that I dread going into my studio for fear Rachel [the housemaid] should have washed my pictures'.[29] Although Burne-Jones claimed never to go anywhere, and never to see anyone ('it is very dull'),[30] a list of Sunday callers taken at random from one of his letters shows Morris arriving for breakfast as usual, followed by Walter Crane and the Slade Professor at Cambridge, Sidney Colvin, in the morning; four guests for lunch; then 'callers', unnamed, in the afternoon.[31] In addition, in 1879 Burne-Jones was invited to Hawarden, Gladstone's house in Flintshire. He claimed not to have wanted to go; and to have hated it while he was there

---

* This new studio was to replace the studio indoors that Phil was using. It was also much larger. Until now Burne-Jones had been sharing Watts's studio in his house in Melbury Road, Kensington, when he worked on his largest canvases – not very convenient.

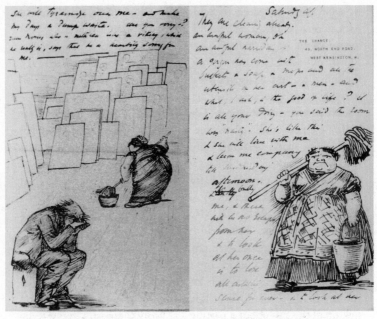

*A letter from Burne-Jones with caricatures of himself in his studio
with the cleaning lady*

('from the dawn when a bore of a man comes and empties my
pockets and laughs at my underclothing and carries them away
from me, and brings me unnecessary tea, right on till heavy
midnight . . .').[32] But he went, and he made sure everybody knew
where he'd been.

The Grange was not Georgie's only concern. The Burne-Joneses
had become accustomed to going down to the south coast
whenever they felt they needed a break, or a change. In 1880
Georgie found a cottage in Rottingdean, then a tiny village outside Brighton, which they quickly bought. It was small, without
being either the 'mean cheap contemptible' house Burne-Jones
described to his friends or the 'mansion' Rossetti snidely referred
to.[33] Prospect House (later to be renamed North End House, in
honour of the Grange, on North End Road) was pleasantly situated,
away from the day trippers who besieged Brighton, while it was
near enough Brighton station to make running down for a weekend

feasible.★ There was a cottage next door that could be rented when the Baldwins came to visit, which they began to do fairly regularly. Money was now plentiful for the Baldwins, and they were spending several months a year in London at a small hotel. Alfred was beginning to have commercial reasons to be there, and Louie was, as always, in search of health. Doctors were to be found in London; invigorating sea air in Rottingdean.

Georgie was probably pleased to have Louie nearby more often. For the last decade she had had one great woman-friend in George Eliot. They had first met soon after the Burne-Joneses had moved into the Grange, and during the Mary Zambaco crisis Georgie had become closer to both George Eliot and G. H. Lewes, spending time with them at Whitby in the summers. Georgie was 'Mignon' and 'dear little Epigram' to Eliot's 'Lady Theory' and Lewes's 'the good Knight Sir Practice'. By the late 1870s Georgie was going to Eliot every Friday, when no other visitors were expected, and Lewes was suggesting sharing the Christmas holidays. When Eliot and Lewes went to Wiltshire on holiday, they called in as a matter of course at Marlborough to see Phil; Georgie and Eliot shared similar tastes in books and music, and for more than a decade had gone to concerts and lectures together. When Lewes died in 1878, Georgie, defying the convention that women did not go to the burial of even their closest family, had attended his funeral. Then, suddenly, in 1880, she received a note from Eliot telling her she had eloped with 'Johnny' Cross, twenty years her junior. Eliot knew what a shock it would be, and wrote:

If it alters your conception of me so thoroughly that you must henceforth regard me as a new person, a stranger to you, I shall not take it hardly, for I myself a little while ago should have said this thing could not be . . . I can only ask you and your husband to imagine and interpret according to your deep experience and loving kindness.[35]

★ The 'day-tripper' side of Brighton can be seen even in the sheet music of the time: a 'tender narrative' song has a picture on the front cover of people fighting to get into a train marked 'Brighton'.[34]

Georgie's response initially seems as spontaneously open as Eliot could have hoped for:

I have been away with the exception of one clear day . . . when I returned and found your letter . . . and I cannot sleep till it is answered. Dear friend, I love you – let that be all – I love you, and you are *you* to me 'in all changes' – from the first hour I knew you until now you have never turned but one face upon me, and I do not expect to lose you now. I am the old, loving Georgie.

It becomes clear, however, from her next letter to Eliot, six weeks later, that she had not sent this letter – nor any other:

Dear Friend
You will see by the enclosed [the letter cited above] that I answered your letter at once and that I was grateful for it – but when my answer was written I put it aside, hoping to find more and brighter words to send. Forgive it if they have not come yet, and let me send those first ones . . .
    Give me time – this was the one 'change' I was unprepared for – but that is my own fault – I have no right to impute to my friends what they do not claim. Forgive what would be an unforgivable liberty of speech if you had not said anything on the subject to me or if you had not also looked closely into my life.[36]

As Georgie drily noted to Rosalind Howard, 'Mrs. Lewes's marriage has been a great shock to me – but I am obliged to fall back on the undoubted fact that she had a perfect right to do what she thinks fit in the matter.'[37] Georgie never had a chance to resolve this sense of betrayal: by December Eliot was dead, and Georgie's final comment on her great friend was a sad little 'I loved her vy much – more than I loved her work – and I miss her out of the world sadly.'[38] She should have remembered Eliot's response when she had talked of her reticence: 'Ah! Say I love you to those you love. The eternal silence is long enough to be silent in.'[39]

Added to this loss was an increasing worry about Louie. Certainly she had been unwell for most of the last dozen years – often in a bath chair, unable to get downstairs for breakfast for years at a time. Yet within these very confined parameters she had managed to lead a relatively normal life. (When one of Alfred's brothers died in 1881, at the young age of fifty-five, leaving behind several children, Alfred and Louie took in the dead brother's son, Harold, who was almost the same age as Stan.) In October 1881 Louie's illnesses worsened. Stan had left the month before to start his first term at Harrow. Almost immediately afterwards he promptly came down with scarlet fever, and was forced to remain at school because his mother was lying flat in a darkened room, being fed by a tube. Agnes spent over two months at Wilden, looking after her sister with Edie and sending bulletins back to London. Louie had been living 'at too high pressure', she had 'exhausted' her brain. Georgie reported 'no distinct disease, but prostration so agonising that for a day or two they almost despaired of reviving her'.[40]★ By December things were getting worse – Louie now needed a trained nurse (or Alfred, Edie and Agnes did); Georgie was summoned; Stan returned from school. There was little change, and gradually they disbanded. In January, Louie, with the nurse, followed her sisters to London, where she stayed, neither better nor worse, for another three months.

Agnes's presence for so long in Wilden was a kindness. In addition to getting Ambo ready for Eton, where he went in September, she was, much to her (and everyone else's) embarrassment, pregnant again. In January 1882, nearly fifteen years after the birth of Ambo, she had another son, Hugh. To add to the general air of farce, she went into labour at a dinner party, and had to be carried home. Alice, in India, took the whole thing personally. She wrote to Editha Plowden:

You will be amused to hear that up to this time your letter is the only one that has brought one tiding of my sister Agnes. But for your little PS I should even yet know nothing but what I have seen in the papers and from a para. in the *World* . . . I won't pretend that I am not very much amazed by having had no letter from any one of my sisters. They treat

---

★ Many years later Georgie described Louie's 'path through life [as] that of a Fly on a window-pane – six steps forward and five back . . .'[41]

me in this way and are yet surprised when I say that out here I feel cut off from them all! I shall not mention the matter in any home letter until I hear from some one . . .[42]

It is not clear if Alice had not heard about the birth in what she considered good time, or if she had not been aware that Agnes was pregnant. The latter seems incredible, but it may be possible. Before she had had time to post the letter, however, she had heard from both Rudyard and Georgie:

Last night brought a letter from Mrs Burne-Jones from which I am glad to learn that badly as poor Aggie managed her affairs they might have been worse and that she was going on all right. Ruddy writes very *funny* about it. He says he saw the news in the *World* and adds 'Est-ce que mes tantes sont donc folles? . . . At first I had a confused idea that I was an uncle or a grand-papa, but on mature reflection I find that I am only another cousin . . . Can you imagine Uncle Edward's face?' All this shows a very just appreciation of the situation.

If she knew of the pregnancy and had simply not had news of the birth of Hugh, then the postal system would have been the main cause. The mails to India left England every Friday; letters then took eighteen days to reach Bombay, and at least a week after that to reach Lahore (it took a person three or four days by train). From the fact that two letters arrived while this one was being written, Georgie had written to let Alice know within a fortnight of the birth. Alice's letter may be general grumbling, or it may have a more specific cause. Alice was worried about Trix. Rudyard, said his mother, reported that

a sensitive plant is pachydermatous by comparison to her. She seems to have got – who knows how or where – some morbid religious notions and is tormenting herself with the fear that we shall be disappointed in her in some way . . . If you would see her sometimes and try to cheer her . . . My sisters seem too much occupied to take much notice of her – she had not up to last mail seen Mrs. Poynter's baby – and I know she is feeling lonely in a crowd.[43]

In addition, she and Lockwood were now concerned about Rudyard's future. He was approaching sixteen, and had no ideas for a career. Although he 'fairly pelt[ed]' her with poems and letters, 'I always open his letters with a feeling of trepidation, though I don't know why.'[44] One reason may have been guilt. Stan was at Harrow, and was planning for Cambridge; Phil had been at Oxford (although he had lasted only a year and, like his Uncle Harry, had gone down without a degree, to his parents' distress); Ambo was planning to follow his grandfather's path and become an architect; Georgie was even talking about university for Margaret. It must have been hard that Alice and Lockwood, like their parents before them, knew that economics meant they could not hope to send their children to university. But they couldn't – despite the fact that Alice had started writing 'Simla gossip letters' for the *Bombay Gazette* and the *Civil and Military Gazette* around this time. These would only help pay for their time in the hills to avoid the hot weather – there wasn't nearly enough for anything else.

Alice and Lockwood took their anxieties once more to Crom Price. Rudyard had an 'easy-going general interest . . . in all things', and 'journalism seems to be specially invented for such desultory souls'.[45] The idea, once planted, grew steadily. Not only had Alice and Lockwood an 'in' with various papers in India, a job there would also enable them to have Rudyard living with them again. They even began to contemplate Trix's return:

We should be together as a *family square* for a few years at any rate . . . John would grow younger with his son and daughter by him – a process he sorely needs for he is getting so dreadfully absorbed in things that he is rarely now the conversational companion he used. For me the companionship of these bright young creatures would be new life – I have never been cheerful except by excited spurts since I came out last and I often wonder if this dull depressed woman can be the same she was in England . . . if there were no other reasons for it there's the pecuniary one – that is strong enough. Our income which would be a good one if we were all here under one roof – does not bear division and sub-division . . . we are really feeling a pinch at present.[46]

Lockwood had been working flat out preparing for the Punjab Exhibition, designed to display to the rest of India the arts of the north. Alice, as always, worked closely with him – she had charge of the textile section – and they were both exhausted.

It was hard for them to hear news from home: Poynter, from his position at the South Kensington Museum, was offering Queen Victoria advice on portraitists; Burne-Jones had received an honorary degree at Oxford, which put Lockwood's University of Bombay fellowship in the shade. Even acknowledging this, it is clear that Alice's sharpness was now turning into outright harshness. She made no allowances for anyone. One did not have to offend her directly to be on the receiving end of her strictures:

Mrs. Molloy (née Miss Townsend) was down . . . looking as she always did, like a good little housemaid. Our new young ladies are rather a failure. Mrs. Black's daughter is a dumpy girl – who I believe speaks some when spoken to and we thought her rather plain till Mrs. Parry Lambert's daughter came, and by her transcending ugliness made Miss Black seem almost beautiful. You remember Major Lambert who is no beauty? She is like him – but much plainer. Her eyes are slits and her mouth a gash, the upper lip doesn't cover the teeth. The nose turns up and the cheeks are large and shapeless – she is short, dumpy and has large hands – altogether she might be an Irish maid of all work in a lodging house . . .[47]

Despite this, Lockwood retained touching faith in his wife's social skills. When Editha was in trouble he 'hope[d] you told Mrs. Kipling something of your affairs. Besides sympathy, you would get the brightest sense put in the most convenient form for reference.'[48]

Two years before, in 1880, Fred had gone to the General Conference of Methodist Episcopalian Churches in America. There he had visited Harry and his wife, and to his regret discovered that as 'we had seen nothing of one another during a long period in which each of us had changed and developed . . . All the memories we had in common were those belonging to our earliest days.'[49] That is, they had nothing in common, and not much interest in catching up. None of the Kiplings would be returning to England – 'home' – for many years, but perhaps the same situation was what Alice feared for her children – and herself.

III

Empty Nests

10. The Families Square
1882–1884

Alice could be consoled by the fact that the decision about Rudyard's future had been made, and he was to come back to India to go to work as a journalist on the *Civil and Military Gazette*. In 1882 he left Westward Ho! and, not quite seventeen, set off for the country of his birth, which he had last seen aged five. On landing at the dock at Bombay in October he found himself in a dream, 'moving among sights and smells that made me deliver in the vernacular sentences whose meaning I knew not'.[1] The Bombay mail took him to Lahore, where his 'mother, always quicker than anyone else in both sight and speech, cried "Look, look, there's Ruddy . . ." '[2] He arrived the proud owner of a small moustache, which Alice, apparently by will power alone, had him remove almost before he was through the door. (It soon reappeared, and is indissolubly part of our mental image of Kipling.)

As Rudyard began his adult life, his cousin Stan, although just two years younger, was in only his second year at Harrow. Although Stan and Ambo's prep school was intended to prepare boys for Eton, in the end Alfred and Louie had chosen Harrow, perhaps because H. M. Butler, its headmaster, was a follower of Charles Kingsley, as Alfred had been for so long. Unlike Rudyard, with his bad eyes, Stan was athletic, which made it easier to find his feet in this new place. He had loved cricket from early days, and now took to football as well.* Long after, he remembered wistfully, 'I never felt a tithe of the pleasure or excitement when I was offered [an award in public life] as that I felt when I got my first colours [at

---

* When he had stayed with Rudyard and Trix in Epping Forest after they left Southsea, he had brought his cricket bat and tried to teach the Kipling children the basics; but they weren't interested – too many rules, they declared.[3]

football] at the age of about fifteen.'[4]* Stan was comfortable in an atmosphere of striving to create in daily life the epitome of Christian virtues. It was very similar to the atmosphere in his own home, and initially he flourished: he regularly won prizes, and was often first in his form. Ambo, in contrast, despite having spent his prep-school years being guided towards Eton, at a school where Eton games, Eton slang and the Eton ethos were fostered, made little mark once he actually got there – he was in none of the house teams, and no prizes are listed against his name.

After Stan was first settled at Harrow, Louie had remained in London for three months over the winter of 1881–2, and then decided that a trip to France would do her good. Alfred had commuted from Wilden to London during the winter and now found time to go with her to France for a month from early August 1882. The year before they had also been to France for a month, and had travelled about a good deal – to Paris, Bordeaux, Bayonne, Saint-Jean-de-Luz, Saint-Sébastien, Biarritz, Angoulême, Poitiers, Tours and Paris again. This time it was decided that just two places might be better suited to the invalid, and so Dieppe and Amiens were chosen. By October Louie was back in bed, and by December she was in a nursing home. Again, no medical details that survive in her sisters' correspondence match anything we might now recognize as an organic disease, and the one treatment mentioned – a skimmed-milk diet – gives few clues. Boredom or unhappiness strike us today as obvious culprits. In twelve months, Louie was away from Wilden for as many as six – travelling, in the nursing home, staying in London for months at a time.

Alfred did his best to be with her, even when his multiplying interests made that difficult. His wide range of posts – wide both in function and in geographical range – shows how far afield his interests had spread. He was elected to the new county and parish councils that were being created in the 1880s; in 1879 he had been made a Justice of the Peace in Worcestershire, and, unusually, in

---

* This may have simply been part of the Victorian fashion for looking at one's childhood as a time of unrecapturable joy. Burne-Jones had written similarly: for Queen Victoria's coronation, when he was four, he had been 'allowed to wave a banner in the air in front of the house, and that gave me more happiness, I think, than anything that has ever happened to me since'.[5]

1883 he was made a JP in Staffordshire as well. In 1884 he was to be offered candidatures for a seat in Parliament in four different districts (all of which he refused). He also served as a member of the local school board and the local hospital board; he was shortly to become a director of the Great Western Railway and the Metropolitan Bank; he joined the London Chamber of Commerce. All this in addition to being the senior partner (what today would be the managing director) of Baldwin, Son & Co.[6]

Then came an incident at Harrow that brought disgrace on the whole family, although it is rather clouded and uncertain in outline. Early in 1883 Stan, to general consternation, was discovered in possession of what was referred to as 'juvenile pornography'.[*] It is unclear what it was – a salacious story? dirty postcards? – or how it had been obtained. Did the boys buy it? Write it themselves? Did Stan write it? Whatever it was, he had sent it to Ambo, and it had been intercepted somewhere along the way. The headmaster immediately telegraphed for Alfred, who arrived the next day. Stan was punished, not expelled, so it is possible that the very act of hushing the matter up has made it appear worse than it was: afterwards Alfred always said that the whole thing was 'much exaggerated'. The one long-lasting effect it had was that Stan was never comfortable at Harrow afterwards. He stopped winning the prizes that had been his so effortlessly before; his ranking slipped down the form.

There was at this time a great change happening to Louie, and this too may have added to Stan's air of uncertainty, which became observable now. It may have been owing to Alfred's increasing preoccupation, or the increased amount of time he and Louie were spending apart. It may have been the realization that Stan was not going to come home again – he was heading towards adulthood, with Cambridge and 'real' life beckoning. Whatever the cause, in the spring of 1883 Louie suddenly found herself cured. She had not done anything differently, not been anywhere. The medical prognosis remained unchanged. Then one morning she just woke up restored to health. And that was that. She returned to Wilden

[*] Stan's son, in his biography of his father, loyally says that this had been supplied by 'a friend', but isn't that what any child would say about his father? Indeed, isn't it what any child would himself say when caught in this type of misdemeanour?

full-time, started teaching in the Infant School, took in hand the local Girls' Friendly Society branch, and generally became the active wife of a prosperous and increasingly powerful businessman once again. Stan's response was not the expected one. His son records that when Louie returned from her last 'cure' and ran up the stairs to the front door where Stan was waiting for her, instead of being carried up as she had been for so many years, onlookers thought he was going to faint. From this period onwards he began to manifest the same nervousness that Alfred had been at pains to suppress in himself for so long. Now any sudden noise, anyone calling out unexpectedly – anything unexpected at all, it seems – had the power to disturb Stan disproportionately.

It is not possible at this distance and with the available material to work out what happened to Louie. It is worth considering that, just as her first bout of long-term illness began when Alfred renewed his interest in politics, her return to health occurred towards the end of Stan's time at school. When he went to Cambridge in 1885, Louisa's acute ill health finally receded completely. Did she fade as she felt herself superfluous to her husband's life and as she saw her child set out on his own path? Did she recover when she began to find time for writing, which was more interesting than being ill? No one at the time made any connections, and it may very well be that there is none to be made.

Alice arrived in England in July 1883, in time to witness this transformation. She had come to collect Trix, who was now fifteen. It was unusual for girls to go (or return) to India until they were 'out' in society and ready for the marriage market. But Alice and Lockwood found that having Rudyard home again was so pleasant that they decided they could not do without Trix any longer. They agreed that it would be all right for her to return if she did not come out for another two years. In the meantime, if the others were invited out in the evening, at least one of them would stay in with Trix – though for years she 'merely thought how nice it was that Ruddy was always disengaged when both parents dined out'.[7] Before they sailed to Bombay Alice spent some time with her sisters – made easier because the Baldwins had taken the next-door cottage in Rottingdean while Alice and Trix stayed with the Burne-Joneses.

Burne-Jones was going through one of his periodic crises. Frances Graham, with whom he had had a close emotional friendship for years, had married a man named John Horner. Despite the fact that Burne-Jones was himself married, and had no intention of changing that status; despite the fact that at her age, and in her social circle, nothing else was to be expected, Burne-Jones was devastated. She had modelled frequently for him;★ they had for years exchanged letters daily, and Burne-Jones had written of running away and living 'dishonoured in lodgings'.[8] He knew his distress at the event was comic, but still he could not help himself. He broke off all communication with her, and did not speak to her for two years.

This was the second blow in two years. In the summer of 1882 old Mr Jones (Burne-Jones's father) had, at the age of eighty, suddenly upped and married his much younger servant. This was at least partly his son and daughter-in-law's responsibility. They had decided that he was too old to be left alone in Birmingham and had moved him to lodgings in Ealing. With no friends nearby, no one to talk to all day, it should not have been a great surprise that something like this happened, but it was. Edie wrote later that the family always had a 'tacit understanding never to discuss the points on which we entirely differed',[9] and Georgie followed this principle now. Burne-Jones did what he usually did at any sign of trouble: he ran away – or, as Georgie put it more diplomatically, 'Edward came quickly away.'[10] Mr Jones, with wife/servant, was bundled back to Birmingham, to live out his days with only the minimum of communication from his child.

Burne-Jones had an air about him which led people to assume the best. A contemporary of Phil's described him thus:

He might have been a priest newly stepped down from the altar, the thunder of great litanies still in his ears . . . but as one gazed in reverence

★ As well as painting a portrait of her, Burne-Jones used her as a model in *The Golden Stair* (she is holding a pair of cymbals, near the bottom of the picture), as the bride in *The King's Wedding*, as a nymph in *Perseus and the Sea Nymphs* and as Eurydice in a cycle of drawings on the story of Orpheus and Eurydice that he did as a preliminary study for the decoration of a grand piano for William Graham.

the hieratic calm of the face would be broken by a smile so mischievous, so quaintly malign, as to unfrock the priest at once and transform the image into the conjuror at a children's party.[11]

This is what people saw at first. His humour, drollery and puckish charm led them to overlook the steel in him. He was a man who had as many enemies as friends – or, if not enemies, certainly people who did not like him and were not terribly concerned if things did not go his way. He was kind and coaxing when it suited him – he gave money to beggars freely (when Comyns Carr of the Grosvenor Gallery reproached him for his largesse, saying, 'Can't you see that it's only acting?', Burne-Jones's response was 'Well, my dear, I've paid ten-and-six to see worse'),[12] and wrote endearingly child-like letters to get what he wanted. When it was his turn to play host at the regular dinners he and his artist friends had in Soho, he wrote:

Oh, dear Carr, save my honour. I know no more what dinner to order than the cat on the hearth – less, for she would promptly order mice. Oh, Carr, order a nice dinner so that I may not be quoted as a warning of meanness . . . yet not ostentatious and presuming such as would foolishly compete with the banquets of the affluent. O, Carr, come to the rescue![13]

He used the same tone to Val Prinsep:

Who the ****** shall I get for the Artists Benev: this year? What the ****** shall I do? Nobody wants to, nobody likes it – everybody hates it nobody answers my letters – everybody says they are out when I call. I am turning all my friends into foes. Oh Val, you would be so nice as a steward – so handsome, so imposing but Phil says you won't – what had I better do.[14]

Usually someone was there to tell him what to do, how to order his supper, to sort him out generally, so that he had to take on no responsibility at all. His friends acknowledged, even celebrated, his childish side. (For his fifty-first birthday, Crom took him to a toyshop and bought him a fur parrot.)

But when it suited he could be ruthless. He wrote, 'I cut old friends when they fit no more. I can't wear the clothes I had when I was a child.'[15] Charles Eliot Norton, the Burne-Joneses' Boston Brahmin friend, enquired about a man who was claiming acquaintanceship with Burne-Jones. The man would have done better without, as Burne-Jones left no room for misinterpretation:

I know that Beak – a sort of poor relation of mine – do you know I think you would be disappointed in him, but I would gladly bring him to you if I did not fear nausea setting in presently – these funny fellows are hardly company after a little time . . . and they are better chained up than let loose – but as I said he is a relation and perhaps I am not quite fair.[16]

Georgie believed in the same kind of plain-speaking:

O, let me not forget, a nephew of Edward Poynter's, one E. Hamilton Bell, is in America, playing in a poor play called 'Vice Versa'* . . . We did not like to send him to you with a formal note of introduction, because we believe that though there is no harm in the young man there is little to supply the place of it . . . I hope he won't trouble you . . .[17]

Their standards were not easy to live up to, and it is not entirely surprising that many of Burne-Jones's friends became his ex-friends – Ruskin, Rossetti, Ford Madox Brown, even Janey Morris. As he entered his fifties his friendship with Morris was faltering too – the friendship which had been at the centre of his life since Oxford. As early as 1855, Crom Price had noted that 'Ted [*sic*] . . . and Morris diverge more and more in views though not in friendship.' Georgie, when she quoted this in her biography, added firmly, 'but divergence of aim never'.[18] This was wishful thinking. It was precisely their divergence of aims that was now driving them apart. Burne-Jones had joined the upper middle classes, and he enjoyed this new way of life enormously. Morris, haunted by the need to 'do good' that had been with him since he had planned to enter on the

---

* It would be interesting to know whether Burne-Jones too thought this play 'poor'. Written by F. Anstey, a *Punch* contributor, it was a farce in which a father and son reverse roles. When Burne-Jones was still young himself, Georgie's sisters had noted the way his father called him 'old man' while Burne-Jones had children's names for his father.

religious life at Oxford, was drawn to the socialist movement and gradually gave it more and more of his time. Burne-Jones not only couldn't join him; he did not even want to try. He was happy with his place in the world, and content with a world that gave him such a place. He confided to Mary Gladstone Drew:

for my own sake I wish [Morris] could be out of it all and busy only for the things he used to be busy about. – I shall never again make myself such unhappy [*sic*] at passing events – it could be easy to break oneself to bits with [illegible] troubles. I shall try never again to leave the world I can control to my heart's desire – the little world that has the walls of my workroom for its furthest horizon – and I want Morris back to it, and want him to write divine books and leave the rest.[19]

Socialism was the superficial reason for their estrangement – 'I think better and better of him and less and less of his judgement about everything as time goes on,' said an exasperated Burne-Jones.[20] They could no longer even work harmoniously together:

I can't finish this letter my dear because your friend Mr. Morris is marching up and marching down and interrupting me at every turn and laying traps for me to say what quarter the wind is in so that he may say it just isn't – and wanting to quarrel about the necessity of rain, and wanting to talk about carpets (and I want ever as long as I live I won't do anything about carpets but walk on them) – so now – he has just asked what I am frowning at, and I shan't tell him – but if I am frowning it is at the word carpet.[21]

Nothing about Morris was right for Burne-Jones now. He got worked up about things Burne-Jones could not care about. In 1881 a fundamentalist in Egypt declared himself the Mahdi ('one who is guided by the Lord'), and agitated against Western influences. By 1884 he had most of the Sudan in his control, and it was decided to send General Gordon to help rescue what was left of the city and garrison of Khartoum. The whole thing was a farce, albeit a grim one, from start to finish: at Charing Cross at the beginning of the expedition Gordon discovered he had left his money and his watch at home. General Sir Garnet Wolseley gave him his own watch, and another member of the government had to be prevailed upon to buy the train tickets. Things never improved. Gordon became besieged; the Cabinet in England spent so much time debating what to do that by the time forces arrived to relieve the reliever he had been dead two days.[22] Morris was disgusted at the interference in the lives of other peoples; Burne-Jones could only grumble that Morris was wasting his time and talents.

To Burne-Jones, even Morris's size was alarming. Morris had always tended to put on weight, and in their early days this had simply been one more joke. Once, when Burne-Jones, Morris and Faulkner went boating on the Thames, when Morris was asleep Burne-Jones borrowed a needle and thread from the landlady and took in Morris's waistcoat, so he would think he had got hugely fatter overnight. In his account books with the Firm, Burne-Jones drew himself as a long, sad figure, and Morris as a fat, exuberant one. Now his horror of fat (and by extension, one feels, of Morris) became obsessional. According to his biographer, Rubens nauseated him; dreams of fat women tormented him; even the roast on Sunday, with its 'lappets of fat', made him ill.[23]

How much this had to do with the diverging aims of the two men is not clear. It is certain that Georgie and Morris's continued closeness exacerbated Burne-Jones's estrangement, even if it was not the reason for it. As well as his socialist activities, Morris's home life was equally troubling for his friend. Janey, probably initially egged on by Rossetti, disliked Burne-Jones.★ And much worse was the fate of Jenny, Morris's elder daughter. She had been a bright, vivacious girl. Then in 1876 a series of small accidents were finally diagnosed as due to epilepsy. This was not far from a death sentence, or at least a living death. There was no way of controlling the seizures, and if frequent and severe they produced progressive brain damage. Burne-Jones sympathized, while freely admitting that he really liked only beautiful women (intelligent, too, although that was of secondary importance). Jenny was bloated from the drugs

---

★ Rossetti, after years of self-imposed isolation and chloral addiction, had finally died in 1882, a ghost of what he had been. His affair with Janey was long over by his death, and she acknowledged that his opinions had not been reliable for some time: 'That Gabriel *was* mad was but too true, no one knows that better than myself.'[24] But she didn't like Burne-Jones any more for it.

she was given, and her once vibrant personality was shuttered. Burne-Jones could not help his friend.

Morris shouldered this as one more burden. There was to be no golden future for his much-loved child. Georgie, loyal and steadfast as ever, was there to offer what help and support she could. Morris's letters show that he talked to her of Jenny (which he couldn't to Janey, who could not come to terms with the illness) and of socialism (which Burne-Jones refused to hear about and Janey disliked). Georgie followed where she could, inviting the American socialist poet Emma Lazarus★ to the Grange, where she introduced her to Morris, and keeping up with the socialist press – although there was a slight domestic ruckus when the socialist magazines started to arrive. 'Please address Commonweal to Mrs. Burne-Jones, not to Mr.,' she begged.[25] She sympathized with his aims and his troubled home life, and kept her own counsel, although she admitted to Charles Eliot Norton that her sympathy for Morris's politics had limits: 'it grieves me not to go with such a friend, but I can't'.[26] She managed to maintain a meeting of minds, which was more than Burne-Jones and Morris could:

Morris comes regularly to breakfast on Sunday still unless he has to be away lecturing on Socialism – and is always our dear Morris, but alas some topics are all but tabooed between him and Ned . . . To me he talks more about his work, and is ever good and patient with me in my dis-agreements, and if we are walking side by side it is in a kind of labyrinth, with a high wall between us. This often makes me unhappy. I take in his Paper, because I want to see what he is doing, saying publicly.[27]

A situation where the wife and the best friend run off together is not that unusual. One where the status quo is superficially maintained because of the strength of the wife and (with regard to other women) the weakness of the husband is less so. It may be that Burne-Jones both recognized this and illustrated it when he began *King Cophetua and the Beggar Maid* at the height of his estrangement

★ It was Lazarus (1849–87) who wrote the verses that appear on the base of the Statue of Liberty: 'Give me your tired, your poor,/Your huddled masses yearning to breathe free,/The wretched refuse of your teeming shore./Send these, the homeless, tempest-tossed to me:/I lift my lamp beside the golden door!'

from Morris. Georgie was the model for the beggar maid, who sits, aloof and cold, scorning the wealth that surrounds her. The picture can easily be read as one of a marriage where the man has failed to live up to the austere morality set by the woman.*

Alice and Lockwood, on the other hand, now they had their children back, were happier than they had been in years. While Alice had been away, fetching Trix, Lockwood had spent most of his time working on the Jeypore Exhibition, another son-of-Great-Exhibition, this one to be held in Calcutta. Not quite enough of his time, Rudyard mock-complained. He fretted that living with his father alone was very troublesome: 'the pater is cutting me out of the hearts of all my old flames . . . that's the worst of a family I find'.[29] But he enjoyed their bachelor life: 'It's a collarless, cuffless, bootless paradise of tobacco, unpunctuality, and sloth. We both enjoy it and roam about the house like bears in just any garment that comes handiest.'[30] When Trix and Alice returned, the family was together for the first time in thirteen years, and they joyously settled down to learning about each other. The house was crowded: for so long it had held only Alice and Lockwood. Now there were Rudyard and Trix, and also Lockwood's pet ravens, Jack and Jill, and squirrels that Trix later remembered as sitting

on my book, or pull[ing] out little tufts of hair for nest lining. It was at Ruddy's suggestion that I hung up a tangle of woollen threads stolen from my mother's workbag. They understood and appreciated our good intentions at once, and selected the most suitable colours for camouflage. In a day or two only bright blue, red and purple threads were left.[31]

There were also Trix's Persian cat and her terrier puppy, and Buz, Rudyard's bull-terrier, 'all head and paws and grin'.[32] ('They all hate one another,' Rudyard noted laconically.)[33] Given that Alice didn't really like household pets (the last ones she had lived with

---

* David Cecil, in his monograph, has also drawn attention to the very Burne-Jonesian fact that, despite painting a beggar maid, the artist has represented her among worldly riches: poverty-stricken without stooping to the ugliness of poverty.[28] My feeling is strong that it is the rejection of the riches that is the subtext of the picture.

were the guinea pigs Louie and Agnes kept in the dark little yard
in Beaumont Street in 1859, twenty-five years earlier), it is clear
that happiness was allowing her to make great concessions. As
Rudyard noted, 'We are all spoiling the maiden* sadly – but she
won't spoil easily and brightens up the domestic shanty like a
"Swan's incandescent".'[34]

Rudyard was happily finding his feet after the horrors of Southsea
and the rigours of school regimentation. He settled quickly into a
routine at the paper and enjoyed the responsibility, later writing of
this time with great fondness, for example in 'The Man Who
Would be King'.

He soon found that the 'hot weather' made things rather less
enjoyable. Alice and Lockwood had only recently managed to
avoid it by going to the hills – for their first decade in India this
had been financially out of reach. Alice and Trix went to Dalhousie
first, and Lockwood and Rudyard – 'the men' – stayed on to work
through until their leave was due. In June 1884 Rudyard reported
that 'the iron of my giglamps [spectacles] has burnt a blue horse-shoe
over the bridge [of my nose]'.[35] By July the symptoms were no
longer just physical:

I assure you Auntie, that for one weary week my fear in the daytime was
that I was going to die, and at night my only fear was that I might live to
the morning. I wasn't seedy but I was washed out and boiled down to
the lowest safe working point, had lost my sense of taste, my temper and
all desire to keep alive for a moment longer than was necessary. The Pater
had gone to Dalhousie for a week and as soon as I was alone in the big
dark house my eyes began their old tricks again, and I was so utterly
unstrung . . . that they bothered me a good deal. I could only avoid the
shadows by working every minute that I could see.[36]

Worrying, in this family where seeing things was not unusual. From
their table-turning days in Birmingham, an interest in spiritualism
had been sustained among some of them. Alice described herself as
having psychic gifts. In Simla, where séances and other aspects of

---

* A reference to Trix. 'The maiden' sounds hideously affected to modern ears,
but was not a Kipling coinage – it was a common expression of the time, as were
'the mother' and 'the pater'.

the paranormal were popular pastimes of hill-station life ('we give ourselves up to prying into the future by cards', noted Rudyard),[37] she went to a séance held by a medium, although she claimed that the medium was a fraud. This may or may not have been the psychic who told Rudyard that he would shortly come into money. He replied, 'I ain't superstitious and least of all after dinner.'[38] His scepticism didn't dampen his mother's enthusiasm. She claimed to be the seventh daughter and therefore to have psychic powers.[*] She and Trix had what they called 'a poltergeist experience' once at lunchtime, although no details survive. Lockwood hated the whole subject and wrote optimistically in one of his articles in the *Pioneer*, 'To say this deliberate revival of the insanity of the dark ages is mischievous is perfectly true; but happily it also has a grotesque and comic side. A few more occult phenomenon and a few more lectures on them, will most probably bury the Theosophical Society to the tune of the inextinguishable laughter of the country.' Poor man. He was to learn the hard way far too soon.

Apart from this, life was good. Lockwood was getting more prestigious work than he had ever had before. In 1883 the Duke of Connaught, Queen Victoria's third son, arrived in India to command the Meerut Division of the Indian Army, and in December Lockwood was presented to him at the opening of the Jeypore Exhibition. The Duke did not fit the stereotype of the Englishman abroad, who had no interest in indigenous culture. In 1884 he and his wife came to visit the Mayo School of Art, and, with Lockwood's advice, the Duchess began to collect brassware. Discussions began for the creation of an 'Indian' billiard room at Bagshot Park in Surrey, their English home.[40] Ultimately, after a lot of heavy hinting, the Indian princes offered to have the decoration done as a wedding present. Lockwood was the obvious person to design the room. He had done a ballroom for the Lieutenant-Governor of the Punjab, 'charmingly decorated and painted in eastern Moorish

---

[*] Edie, who *was* the seventh daughter (although not of a seventh daughter, which is necessary), made no such claims. Nevertheless they were made for her afterwards: it has been suggested that she had the gift '(or ought I to call it the affliction?) of feeling so vividly what was in the minds of others that she suffered with their suffering ... approaching to a second sight of the contents of other hearts'.[39]

A wood-carver, John Lockwood Kipling, Simla, 1870

style'.[41] He now produced for the Duke and Duchess an eighteenth-century Punjab-style room with 241 carved wooden panels, plus a carved ceiling, window and door frames, mouldings, fireplace furniture, billiard-cue racks and all the other paraphernalia of a gent's room. In addition, the smoking room next door, an ante-room and the passage also got the Indian treatment. Everything was produced under Lockwood's supervision in the Mayo School of Art workshops during the next four years, ready to be assembled in Surrey on the Duke's return to England in 1890.

The glory of this royal connection meant that more and more was possible for Lockwood. He began to design a new building for the Central Museum at Lahore (it was finished in 1890). He became one of the moving spirits behind the *Journal of Indian Art and Industry*, founded to promote the arts of India both at home and in Europe. He may even have edited it for a while – it is not quite clear; his contributions cannot be doubted, and he was certainly the editor of the first, prototype, issue. He was chosen to be one of a six-man committee designated to establish a Punjab Public Library at Lahore. He collaborated on a book called *Lahore as it is and was*.★ Yet again, there was an exhibition to prepare – this time the Indian and Colonial Exhibition. Lockwood was in charge of the Punjabi section, which was to be set in a traditional carved courtyard, for the display of regional products.

Finally, to Alice's delight, the Kipling family achieved the higher slopes of Indian society. In 1884 a new Viceroy, Lord Dufferin, was appointed and set out to centre his government more closely on Simla than had previously been the case. After Lockwood's encounter with the royal family in the shape of the Connaughts, Lord Dufferin too consulted him on Indian art; he decided at the same time that Alice was charming company – 'Dullness and Mrs Kipling cannot exist in the same room,' he announced, and Alice made sure it was remembered.[42] At the same time, the Kiplings found themselves with more ready cash now the family was in one place again and Rudyard was Simla correspondent for the season for the *Civil and Military Gazette*, which paid him to visit the hills. In addition Trix was seventeen and, as a fully fledged member of adult society, no longer had to languish in a secondary hill station like Dalhousie (or 'Dullhouses', as she had quickly named it).

Trixie had grown tall for a Macdonald, and was described as 'a statuesque beauty'. 'Statuesque' is often code for 'not especially attractive', but this doesn't appear to be true of her from her photographs. It may instead refer to her shyness, which inhibited her in public and made her look withdrawn and haughty. Her facial configuration added to this: her father described her as having a family 'build of brow – helmet-lidded eyes and a vast space between lid and eyebrow, of itself a pathetic and wistful conformation'.[43] She was also well read, which she didn't trouble to hide, and this too might have hindered her social success; she was known as 'Nothing-if-not-critical'. Despite Lockwood telling Margaret Burne-Jones that, since Trix had returned to India, 'I find myself much more popular with subalterns than I used to be',[44] it is much more likely that he was more honest when he wrote to Editha Plowden, who knew the territory. He fretted that at a recent

★ This is not held in the British Library nor in any other copyright deposit library. The only reference to it is in *Notes and Queries*, 24 October 1942.

ball, given by Lady Dufferin, Trix had had only five partners, mostly older men; men her own age remained indifferent to her charms.

Later Trix made many claims for herself and her family in their India years, on which she could be regarded as the authority – the sole survivor of those who were there. It is well to be wary of what she said, as there is a definite sound of axes being ground in the background.* First she was very careful to make sure that everyone knew of her suitor (note the singular). She trotted him out at the drop of a hat, and by her very insistence made her claim about him appear weaker. According to Trix, Lord Clandeboye, Lord Dufferin's son, fell in love with her and proposed. She refused him, even though the match would generally have been considered an extraordinarily good one for her (and an extraordinarily bad one for Clandeboye). 'Lord D. loved me for my good sense, Lady D. never forgave me . . . Of course a penniless daughter-in-law was the last thing she wished for . . . but – if her "splendid Arch" was not good enough for me – she gave me up.'[45] She reminded Stan of the (non-)engagement when years later he wrote asking for information about Kipling in India for the *Dictionary of National Biography*: 'I assure you that it is entirely your poor cousin's own fault that she was not left that dreary thing a widowed courtesy countess after Ladysmith [where Clandeboye was killed in 1899 during the Boer War].'[46] The story then continues that Lady Dufferin suggested to Alice that Trix be sent to another hill station. Alice responded frostily that if anyone left it should be Clandeboye – and, to Simla's amazement and amusement, leave he did.

It is likely that Clandeboye did pay Trix some attention. She was very pretty; his father admired and enjoyed the company of her parents; his sister took drawing lessons from Lockwood – why shouldn't he be attracted to her? It may even be the case that his parents worried about a possible entanglement. But Trix's continued reiteration of how 'I drew the line against marrying' an Irishman makes one wonder.[47] She also repeated again and again that she and Rudyard had written the poem 'My Rival'

---

* None of these claims was made while her brother was alive: one assumes partly as a concession to his ferocious protection of his own privacy, and partly because he was someone who could – and would – contradict her.

together, and that it had nothing to do with her and Alice.[48] 'My Rival' is the lament of a young girl who is ignored while her older rival is admired:

> . . . I wish *I* had her constant cheek:
>> I wish that I could sing
> All sorts of funny little songs,
>> Not quite the proper thing.
> I'm very *gauche* and very shy,
>> Her jokes aren't in my line;
> And, worst of all, I'm seventeen
>> While She is forty-nine.[49]

It must be faced, however, that Alice was in social demand, Trix was a wallflower. Alice was witty, Trix was shy. Finally, Alice *was* forty-nine and Trix *was* seventeen when the poem was written.

Trix's concern with the status of her family, and the respect that was due them, was acute. She wrote to the librarian of the Kipling Society, 'I grow so tired of the falsehood that he [Kipling] was a scrubby little maggot from Grub St. – eating his way into the nut of "Indian Society". I wish our visitors' book in Lahore was still extant – it would show the sort of company his parents kept.'[50] The giveaway comes when she comments crossly to Stan that Lord Dufferin had put the Kiplings on the Government House free list, 'which meant invitations to *all* the balls and dances – and At Homes – and many dinners'.[51] Lord Dufferin was appointed Viceroy in 1884, which gave Alice and Lockwood nearly twenty years of *not* being invited automatically to those so-desired balls and dances and at-homes.

Their time on the outside had marked Trix and Rudyard as surely as it had done Lockwood and Alice. When they began to write together, they produced a collection of verse parodies of the society around them which slid off their pens with extraordinary ease. Parody assumes recognition of discrete groups, and it also assumes that the parodist is not part of those groups. *Echoes* was very definitely outsiders' work; it was not a comfortably secure civil servant who wrote in 'A Vision of India':

Mother India, wan and thin
   Here is forage come your way,
Take the young Civilian in,
   Stay him swiftly as you may.

Smite him with the deadly breath
   From thy crowded cities sped;
Still the heart that beats beneath
   The girl's picture o'er his bed.

Brains that thought and lips that kissed,
   Mouldering under alien clay.
Stir a stagnant Civil List,
   Help us on our upward way . . .

The seemingly idyllic was not always so. Rudyard wrote to Edie that

In these days [in Simla] have I returned to my Nursery and Trixie is with me, so that for one blessed month I am become a child again . . . Yesterday Trix dragged me out to the rubicon, a mountain stream cutting across a two foot road over huge boulders of granite and down into the valley below three thousand feet. There we danced on stepping stones; picked flowers and sailed boats of bark down the current, finally the game grew so fascinating that my only match box was converted into a boat which gave us amusement and excitement for ten [illegible] minutes before it dropped out of sight . . . we went home singing at the top of our voices, for the pleasure of hearing how far the sound carried. Fancy a place where you can sing and play at swimming boats in your oldest garments, no man making you afraid![52]

Poor Ruddy, to have been so afraid, and of so little. Is this fear the source of his parodies? The stories Rudyard was beginning to write, often about Simla society, took a very dim view of the machinations of men and women. Despite this, when *Echoes* was published in 1884 it was a great success, with Simla taking it to its collective bosom, gleefully identifying various local characters. This was followed by the entire Kipling family setting to to produce a supplement to the Christmas edition of the *Civil and Military Gazette*, to be called *Quartette*.★ (They particularly enjoyed it when a sonnet of Alice's entitled 'Parted' came back from the printer renamed 'Putrid'.)[54] From his Westward Ho! days, Rudyard had been used to sending stories to Jenny Morris, who was the editor of the *Scribbler*, the occasional magazine put out by the Morris, Poynter and Burne-Jones children over a period of nearly four years.† Collaboration was natural to him. According to Trix, Lockwood wrote the verse epigraph of Rudyard's 'On Greenhow Hill' (very suitably: it was a Yorkshire story, and owed almost its entirety to Lockwood's memories of his childhood). She also said that Alice wrote one of her son's most famous lines: 'Oh, East is East, and West is West, and never the twain shall meet.'[55] This seems completely implausible, Trix aggrandizing their part in her more famous brother's life. Then one reads the following passage (set in England a few years later) in Rudyard's autobiography:

I had been at work on the rough of a set of verses called later 'The English Flag' and had boggled at a line which had to be a key-line but persisted in going 'soft'. As was the custom between us, I asked into the air: 'What am I trying to get *at*?' Instantly the Mother, with her quick flutter of the hands: 'You're *trying* to say: "What do they know of England who only England know?"'[56]

It is clear that Trix was simply reporting what she saw.

★ Should anyone want to look up the issue, the unsigned articles can be allocated as follows: Alice wrote 'An Anglo-Indian Episode', 'Two Sonnets', 'Rivals', 'Parted'; Lockwood wrote 'Mirror of Two Worlds', 'My Christmas at Ajaibhaun Exhibition', 'Mofussil Jurisdiction'; Trix wrote 'The Haunted Cabin', and Rudyard did everything else.[53]

† There are many charming features about the magazine, including a response to a letter complaining of the high price of the *Scribbler*: 'The editor begs to offer an explanation. In the first place, the *Scribbler* is printed by a newly patented process, which is sure to act in the long run, though at present it is rather tedious and expensive, and involves a large staff of printers and mechanics, who, being new to the work, are somewhat puzzled and muddle-headed, and likely to sour the Editor's life . . .' The copies of the *Scribbler* in the British Library are part of the May Morris bequest (Add MS 45,337). They are all handwritten except for those issues which included stories by Kipling, where typewritten copies replace them because the originals were later sold by May to collectors of Kiplingiana.

Rudyard's views on women – overly sophisticated and curiously innocent all at the same time – came in for a certain amount of family criticism. He was not yet twenty, but living as an adult among adults. The confusion is hardly surprising, and Alice in particular made sure that he didn't go beyond certain limits acceptable to the society they lived in. Trix said that she and her mother would 'drop severely on things his women said . . . "No Ruddy, no! Not that." "But it's true." "Never mind, there are lots of things that are true that we never mention." '[57] Alice also acted as his mother, as well as his literary companion. A couple of years later he wrote to a friend in Allahabad, Edmonia Hill:

You ask what did Mrs. Kipling say to it – the Sermon. She didn't say much but she wrote a good deal. Here's an extract from her letter. 'It's clever and subtle and all that and *I* see the morality in it but, O my boy, how do *you* know it? Don't tell me about "guessing in the dark". It's an insult to your old Mother's intelligence.'[58]

To the outside world Alice defended him stoutly. When a Simla matron said to Alice, 'What a lot you must have taught your son about women,' she flashed back, 'On the contrary, what a lot my son has taught me.'[59]

As part of his liking for the collaborative process, for being in a family after so long alone, Rudyard took criticism well, from abroad as well as home. But it had to be from the family – comments from outsiders were definitely not welcomed. Kay Robinson, the incoming editor of the *Civil and Military Gazette*, noted that 'It was inevitable that such a family should, amid such surroundings, become a select Mutual Admiration Society with a forcing-house atmosphere of warm domestic approval.'[60]* Within the family, (almost) anything was permissible. Trix said

he used to read – or rather 'spout' – his verses to Mother and me while they were very much in the making. Sometimes indeed we found it a little hard to follow when 2 or 3 lines were eked out by 'Tum-tum-tee-tum' . . .

---

* Not too dissimilar an atmosphere to the one Fred Macdonald recalled of his own childhood.

I remember my mother saying once – 'Yes, Ruddy – that is a fine brick – well turned and baked – but I haven't taken in the whole plan of the house for it – yet.' And he would accuse us of 'losing our faculty'.[61]

From England Margaret wrote to him with her opinions, and he thanked her meekly. Or sometimes not so meekly:

Your epistles show me that you have a style about seven and a half times better and more powerful than mine . . . But . . . I have never seen Miss Margaret Burne Jones in print anywhere and consequently when she tells me calmly that she has been doctoring my prose I cock my editorial nose and cry: . . . Who the this and that is this Miss Margaret Burne Jones who takes a pen in her hand and ploughs over the work of a journalist of three years' standing?[62]

In exchange he encouraged her to write herself:

As the wop★ truthfully observes writing letters is one thing and writing books another . . . I give you three years – thirty-six calendar months – wherein to turn out something and a half year over. If at the end of that time you have *not* turned out any thing I shall go to Trix and say, 'Hi! you know that Wop of Europe don't you?' And Trix'll say 'Yes, Cousin o' sorts I write to . . .' And I shall answer: – 'Exactly. Don't you write to her never a line no more. We've disinherited her and cast her off for a Blazing Fraud' . . . And Trix will again make answer: – 'Thou fool. She has been married for the last year or maybe two and she has passed beyond your knowledge and comprehension and understanding . . .' And I shall lift up my voice and wail and wonder secretly whether the Wop *has* fulfilled her destiny and whether my Sister's words be true . . .[63]

★ A childhood nickname: Margaret was the Wop of Europe, Rudyard the Wop of Asia.

11. Leaving Home
1884–1888

What Margaret's destiny was, and how she was to fulfil it, was an open question. In 1884, aged nearly eighteen, she had left school, and had also finished with the part-time governess Georgie had arranged for her. Georgie's earlier ambition of university for her daughter as well as her son had disappeared – there is no mention of it once Margaret approached university age. Was she not clever enough, or simply not interested? Or was it that, Phil not having managed to stick it out, Margaret's attendance would have shown up her brother's lack of staying power?

Instead she began the daily life of a young lady of the upper middle class, which was by now the group the Burne-Joneses lived among. But, while they were in it, they were not of it. Though Burne-Jones may have dined with Princess Louise, or an MP like William Graham, he was aware, and his daughter was aware, that he and his family were invited because of his abilities. They did not feel that it was where they naturally belonged.

One way that their 'not belonging' manifested itself was in the clothes Georgie wore. She stuck to her simple Pre-Raphaelite ways all her life, although by now Burne-Jones would have welcomed her dressing more to suit her new station. She refused to bow to the convention of tight lacing, and to other uncomfortable fashions. Unlike Margaret. Clothes were an essential factor in divining status. In the 1870s the 'Princess line' came in – dresses fitted tightly from shoulder to hip, with narrow skirts. Beautiful, but walking was difficult. Wearing this style was an indication of how little one did. By the 1880s the tailor-made suit (jacket and skirt worn with a blouse) also made its appearance. This was more practical, and allowed women to do things that the Princess line had made impossible – getting on an omnibus, for example. Even so, such suits still were constricting, and only for the leisured. Collars were stiff, waists were laced tight, long skirts limited movement.

Nevertheless, suits were an improvement. The fashionable

clothes Margaret so admired had been burdensome in a very real sense: the *Lancet* campaigned against the heaviness of women's clothes, saying that many women who complained of tiredness during exercise were not fragile flowers, needing cosseting, but simply suffering the 'natural exhaustion from carrying a burden few strong men would care to bear'.[1] By 1881 the Rational Dress Society was campaigning to reduce women's underwear to a maximum of seven pounds.[2]

Women suffered, and so did children. In winter the typical middle-class girl wore a vest, a woollen binder,* drawers, a bodice, a flannel petticoat, a cotton petticoat and a flannel dress. In summer the outfit was the same, except that cotton was substituted for flannel. To break the rules was to court derision – the kind of muted, softly coloured 'Aesthetic' dresses that Georgie favoured were mocked in Gilbert and Sullivan's *Patience* as being, in the famous phrase, 'greenery-yallery, Grosvenor Gallery'. Mrs Beeton had firm strictures on the new aniline dyes: 'To Brunettes, or those ladies having dark complexions, silks of a grave hue are adapted. For Blondes, or those having fair complexions, lighter colours are preferable . . . The colours which go best together are green with violet; gold-colour with dark crimson or lilac; pale blue with scarlet; pink with black or white; and gray with scarlet or pink.'[3]

The importance of conformity to a woman of Margaret's background can be seen from the diary of Jeanette Marshall, a distant acquaintance.† She reported on an at-home at the Browns, 'The flood of "artistics" in everything hideous in the way of costumes was appalling'; at Lucy Rossetti's everyone was 'most singularly attired, the ladies sad & the gentlemen mad-looking'; the wife of an unnamed painter was 'as usual in mouse-colour and very sloppy'; Phil's friend Graham Robertson was 'frightful & all but imbecile';

* A binder – worn by children – was a cross between a corset (though less rigid) and a liberty bodice.
† Jeanette Marshall was the daughter of John Marshall, William Rossetti's doctor, who taught anatomy at the Schools of Art and Design at South Kensington (where he pioneered mixed classes of men and women). He was also doctor to the Alma-Tademas, the Holman Hunts and many in the Greek community. So Jeanette had a good vantage point. She wrote what the world thought when she noted, 'I like to see these queer folk now and then.'[4]

Holman Hunt's second wife 'looked a regular Judy'. Janey and May Morris – the epitome of Aesthetic chic – are described variously as 'witchlike' and 'horrid frights'. At a dance,

Mrs Morris and her 2nd daughter May were there, and the former looked very well, I thought, though very sloppy, in a cream crepe, sparingly trimmed with old gold satin, & made high to the throat. Her hair was fuzzy, and she had a white Indian shawl over her shoulders. When her face is quiet, it is fine & fascinating, but when she speaks she is spoilt. The daughter, in a brown-red bedgown with no tucker, was a guy everyone voted. She is excessively ugly.[5]

In addition to the Burne-Joneses' sense of being only marginally accepted, the ideal of the 'perfect wife' – which Georgie had grown up aspiring to, and which Agnes and Louie had abdicated from, where the woman was an active participant in the man's life, playing a vital role in the economic and social support of the family – was now obsolete. This was replaced by the idea of the 'perfect lady'. A perfect lady did very little apart from dressing herself, visiting her friends, and playing a bit of light music every now and again. She had no functions or responsibilities – a housekeeper ran the house, a nurse looked after the children, her husband's business was conducted entirely away from home – and therefore no real reason for doing, or not doing, anything much. Such purposelessness exacerbated Margaret's already extreme lack of self-confidence: 'I try to help [my mother] in a little way, but there does not seem to be much good in me.'[6]

Margaret had grown up to be a beautiful young woman – 'unfairly pretty'* was how one of Phil's friends described her.[7] She was, like her mother, tiny in stature – not reaching five foot – with a kind of miniature perfection that drew many admirers, although, oddly enough, like Trix she fascinated older men in particular. Ruskin – Phil's godfather, and a well-known little-girl-lover – had written Margaret letters that her own daughter later burned, describing them simply as 'the kind of letter that Mr. Ruskin ought not to have written'.[8] Burne-Jones's friend W. B. Richmond, only

---

* Rather as Agnes had been 'tyrannously beautiful' to an earlier generation.

two years younger than Georgie, was another admirer. He painted her three times before she was twenty-two and, despite Margaret's being a close friend of his daughter, cried when she told him she was engaged.

Even more than Trix, Margaret was overwhelmingly shy, self-contained to the point of invisibility – one of her friends later said that if she had to tell you what she'd eaten for dinner she nearly died of shame. Therefore when the Nortons arrived from Boston and invited Margaret to accompany them and their two daughters on their travels in England, Georgie was delighted for her to have the company. Burne-Jones, however, went through agonies at the thought of separation, as he had when Phil had left for school. He suffered from the absence of his children to an extent that verged on the pathological. When Margaret had planned to go to Scotland with Phil earlier in the year he worked himself into such a state that he decided she would not come back alive, and so he had her sit for her portrait before she went. The extent to which she was protected is apparent from something Georgie wrote to Charles Eliot Norton before the trip, regarding her expenses: 'As you love us you will tell us the charges you are at for Margaret's journeying and hotels, and so we shall not burden the child with a purse.'[9] (She was *eighteen*.)

On her return at the end of June 1884, Georgie felt initially that Margaret had 'gained in life by her time with you – her glance is freer and brighter, and she has less restraint of manners'.[10] But by the end of the month her 'old trouble' had returned, which needed 'strict care'. There is no indication of what this trouble might have been – Margaret did not suffer from any particular long-term ailments. The only recurring refrain was her severe introversion and lack of companionship. When Charles Eliot Norton's daughter Lily came to England the following year and stayed at the Grange, Georgie was 'thankful for the pleasure of her society to our rather lonely daughter'. It may even have been this visit that drew her out: 'Something lately seems as if it had been what the Methodists called "blessed to" Margaret, she is so much more expansive than she was a year ago.'[11] Margaret may have opened up a little, but Burne-Jones's fears remained, and, although frequently invited to stay with the Nortons in Boston, her parents refused on her behalf:

'The gift of imagining which is so great in Edward has a dismal side to it, making him imagine all evils in absence, and he has died a hundred deaths already by its means.'[12]

By the spring of 1885 Phil had moved his studio down the road and was officially independent: he 'has a studio of his own now, and a pompous cough to match',[13] Margaret noted shrewdly. Although he continued to live at the Grange, this marks a point at which all the sisters began to take a back seat. It was not that they suddenly thought, 'Our children are grown, our lives are over', but they began the imperceptible move into the background, understanding that the new generation would replace them, as they had replaced their own parents.

Phil exhibited his first picture in the following year, at the Grosvenor Gallery. It was a literary subject, taken from Henry James's 'Madonna of the Future'. It was well received, although Phil would probably have been more encouraged if another gallery had shown interest – one that didn't make a very nice income from his father's work. His attachment to painting was rather half-hearted. What he was really good at was comic drawing (as was his father). But, while Burne-Jones adored jokes in private life, he felt that humour had no place in art, that

wit is the opposite pole to poetry – not fun, but wit – I'll go to the stake on that. It keeps people from being pedants or bores, I think, and there lies its chief use. But some of the greatest beings ever born had none – nor humour either, and I often reflect that the books I most worship are as devoid of it as the paintings I worship. None in Homer, none in Aeschylus or Dante, none in the Morte d'Arthur. It isn't necessary – and though it betters a second-rate creature very much, and makes a first-rate one better company for the passing hour, it affects great work, I think, very little indeed.[14]

He asked Phil solemnly to swear never to use his comic abilities commercially – which is a pity: instead of another third-rate artist, the world might have gained a first-rate caricaturist. Phil was a good and dutiful son, and he promised. His chosen career being forbidden, he didn't give the one imposed on him the whole-hearted attention it needed – as Crom Price later noted when he reported to Rudyard that Phil 'would be greater if he were stuck on a desert island for a while with nothing but paints and canvass [*sic*] and no Society'.[15]

Georgie was frighteningly detached in her assessment of her child:

[Margaret] has inherited the love of books, but Phil is curiously without it: if he can learn a thing in *any* other way he always will. He certainly goes about keenly alive to outward things . . . It is a serious difference though, between people, that of not receiving impressions in the same way, and I have to tell myself that probably *he feels as great a want in me as I do in him*. We bridge over the distance with the plank of love as well as we can – and I remember that without it all the books in the world would not unite us.[16] [My italics]

Even when his first picture was well received, it was 'Poor Phil, I am so glad for him.' She added, 'now I hope he has found what will be an absorbing work for life'.[17]

This was important, because once again the family's finances were not as secure as they should have been, considering the prices Burne-Jones was getting for his pictures. William Graham had died in 1885. For many years he had overseen the business side of Burne-Jones's work. 'Before his death he went over our affairs as if we had been his own children, and left a plan of work in writing, which, if Edward's health lets him carry it out will produce . . . great relief of mind to himself.'[18] The key words are 'as if we had been . . . children', which Graham clearly thought the Burne-Joneses were in terms of managing their finances. Burne-Jones was a slow worker, and it took many years of intermittent work to finish each painting to his satisfaction. So the hope that Phil would have some sort of career must have been a small comfort.

Burne-Jones had always worked hard – even compulsively – and he painted every possible hour, but this was becoming more and more difficult. Between 1811 and 1820 the average number of days in the year affected by 'ordinary' fog was 18.7; between 1881 and 1890, with increasing urbanization and industrialization, it was a staggering 54.8 days a year – nearly two months out of twelve completely dark. An RA (and friend of Poynter), Luke Fildes, wrote to his brother-in-law in Venice in 1880:

We have endured and still endure the most awfully dark and hopeless winter that has ever been known in London, consequently the civilised globe. We had uninterrupted heavy fog for 5 consecutive days last week . . . it is too dark for painting and so dense that we have had to burn gas to get our meals by . . . Nobody is doing any work except a few at Hampstead.

And again, later that same year, 'All through the next 4 months I doubt if there will be 15 hours a week of light fit to paint by.'[19]

As early as 1878 the first electric lights had been installed, on Victoria Embankment, from Westminster to Blackfriars, but by 1884 the company that had installed them had gone bankrupt, and the Embankment was turned over to gas lighting again. Gas in itself was problematic indoors. Most books on domestic economy agreed that it was 'unwholesome', and it certainly burned with a yellow and smoky flame: 'The products of its combustion tarnish gilding, spoil the bindings of books, prevent plants from flowering . . . and soon make the atmosphere nauseous.'[20] Paraffin and oil were both cheaper and more pleasant. In the 1890s one gas burner cost 25s. a year to use, while oil cost only 13s. or 14s. (Electric light at home, by contrast, would have cost over £50.)[21] Because of this, gas was often not laid on in sitting rooms and bedrooms. The Grange was never particularly modern, and Burne-Jones continued to paint by candlelight long after gas was the norm in most houses.*

Like Phil, Ambo, who had left Eton at Christmas 1885, had no interest in going to university. Unlike Phil, however, he had a profession mapped out. He wanted to become an architect and, as had Morris before him, he saw that the best way to do that was to apprentice himself to a practising firm. After studying at both the South Kensington Museum and the Royal Academy Schools, he articled himself to the architect George Aitchison. As usual, there is no record of his parents' views, although as Poynter was very proud of his own father, a respected architect, the decision was probably welcomed, if not more. Ambo may have been pushed in

*During the First World War, Georgie commented enviously on her grand-daughter Angela's house, 'It is warmed and Lighted by Gas and Electricity, which means the saving of one servant . . .'[22]

this direction: Aitchison was a great friend of Leighton, as was Poynter.

Stan, by contrast, was still a student, just beginning on his Cambridge life. He had gone up to Trinity College that same year, where his cousin Harold joined him.★ Unfortunately, in the following year so did H. M. Butler, his quondam headmaster at Harrow, who became Master of Trinity. After the pornography incident, Stan had been uncomfortable at Harrow, so it cannot have pleased him much to see that that part of his life was going to follow him. He had chosen to read history, although early in his first term, coming under the influence of William Cunningham, the college chaplain, he announced that he wished to take holy orders. Alfred probably admired the sentiment, even if he did not want his only child to enter the Church. It was a relief when Stan decided to confine his religious impulses to extra-curricular activities. Cunningham was also a historian, and the author of *The Growth of English Industry and Commerce*. He was a strong influence on Baldwin into the 1920s.[23]

Studying history in the late nineteenth century was, much as it is today, intended to create a well-rounded person who might go on to do almost anything; creating historians was not its main function. University was not a breeding ground for academics: it was a place to meet the right sort of people (with whom one had probably gone to school anyway), to participate for the first time in some form of public life – university clubs, debating societies and so on being precursors of the clubs and societies of adulthood – and in general to prepare to take one's place as a leader of men. Stan did modestly well, achieving a third, which was then standard for someone whose future did not include the sitting of civil-service exams or hoping for a fellowship in order to remain in academia. He later said that Alfred had commented that he hoped he would not be third class in life, too. Whether this was meant for encouragement, or a spur, or a sharp comment, cannot now be determined. Alfred's faith in his son seemed unshaken. In 1888 he and Louie took Stan to France for four weeks, as a graduation present, to

★ Shortly after, Harold fell out of a window. Epilepsy was diagnosed, and, as with Jenny Morris, his life was afterwards severely curtailed.

introduce him to the world of art. They made a tour of Amiens, Rouen, Caen, Bayeux, Avranches, Mont Saint-Michel, Nantes and Paris – a museum, church and cathedral tour. In 1886, while Stan had been at Cambridge, Alfred had added to his various business interests and set up a new company, Alfred Baldwin & Co. Ltd. With this he built a new works in Monmouthshire; two years later he bought another steel-mill nearby and was expanding at a great rate.

Louie had also broken out of the home circle. For years she had written stories, which she had passed on to Alfred and to Georgie to read, but she had not done anything more with them. In 1886 she published her first novel, *A Martyr to Mammon*. It was traditional in form, a three-decker tale of love and romance, set against a business background. In it a young architect falls in love with a shipping heiress. Her guardian has other ideas for her, but, after many trials and tribulations (including that standby, a forced marriage to a rich old man), true love wins through. Many of Louie's concerns are developed in this first effort: the business scene is drawn rather hazily, but the 'mistaken' values of a world where money is worshipped are carefully set out. Many received opinions are mocked: 'in society, it was most prejudicial to a young lady's interests to acquire the reputation of differing in any respect from other young ladies of her own age and position'.[24] However, the mockery remains within safe bounds – no one could be disturbed by Louie's distrust of filthy lucre, or young ladies' education. She was against women becoming involved in politics; she was against the working class moving out of their station; farmers have 'a rustic inability to take in ... many ideas at once'.[25] The book was dedicated 'To A.B., who never failed me when we passed through deep waters', and it was modestly successful.

Louie was not the only one winning public recognition. In June 1886 Burne-Jones was elected an Associate of the Royal Academy, the first step to full membership as a Royal Academician. Most artists in Britain at the time thought membership of the Royal Academy the ultimate accolade, and connived and schemed to achieve it. It meant automatic acceptance of one's work to the summer show, which by the 1880s was drawing 355,000 visitors on average. Burne-Jones was unusual in being completely indifferent, and the thing had been pushed through by Leighton, as president of the Academy, without his knowledge or consent. His lack of interest was not taken kindly by others. Luke Fildes wrote to his brother-in-law:

I have no doubt it was a surprise to you . . . you will see by the voting there was a dead set for him. I have not the slightest objection to him being in the Royal Academy. I only feel there has been an indecent haste in rushing him in and a very slavish bowing down to him as soon as he graciously consented to allow himself to be elected. My idea about B. Jones is that he is not quite good enough to make such a remarkable demonstration about and it will only make all the Grosvenorites more offensive than before.[26]

Burne-Jones's own concern was that he should not be thought to be deserting his friends at the first sign of significant acceptance by the Establishment. He asked F. G. Stephens, the editor of the *Athenaeum*, whether a note in the journal would be helpful:

I do hope my election at the Academy will have no injurious influence on the Grosvenor Gallery – I feel so strongly that my first duty is there. They have been so courteous to me from the first and it is there that those who like my work have learned to like it that I feel bound to them in gratitude . . . Therefore if you have at any time any opportunity of saying that my election was unsought for by me and was a spontaneous act of the Academy it might put an end to any idea that I had abandoned old friends.[27]

Finally he decided it was 'a question of a kindness and sign of fellowship offered by a body of artists which it would be impossible to refuse without giving a rebuff – and so he said "thank you for the unlooked for honour you have done me, and I take it as a friendly act, and you will remember I have other engagements already" '.[28]

This was particularly emphasized as Burne-Jones was actually becoming increasingly unhappy with the Grosvenor Gallery, but he did not want people to think that he was leaving because of official recognition. In fact for the previous three years things had

not been going well there. Sir Coutts Lindsay, now separated from
his wife, had financial troubles, and for some reason he felt that the
answer to these was to bring in a new manager, Joseph Pyke, who
had previously been a jeweller. In 1887 Burne-Jones wrote to
ask Sir Coutts about the constant 'feasts, parties, advertisements,
placards and refreshments' that were now a permanent part of the
gallery's programme.[29] Walter Crane, the illustrator, noted that
'One heard that the frequent suppers and other entertainments'
were 'distasteful' to Burne-Jones, 'and it was even whispered that
labels announcing "soups" and "ices" were hung in front of some
of his pictures.'[30] Finally the normally reticent Burne-Jones cracked.
He wrote to George Howard:

Carr and Hallé have been on the point of resigning for a year and a half
past – my own feeling is that if they leave, all guarantee is over that the
place will be worth exhibiting in – a hundred changes are happening –
the dominant spirit of the place is one Pike [*sic*] – I don't know him –
and a lesser spirit before him but very potent is Wade, and our hierarchy
stands thus

Pike
Wade
Sir Coutts Lindsay
Hallé

Carr

and then the poor painters – and I don't like it – and Sir Coutts won't
change it – and Carr and Hallé won't stand it and Tadema definitely
won't stand any more . . . the Gallery is Sir Coutts's own to do what he
likes with it and I am my own to do what I like with me . . . We are
going to begin a new gallery if we can and want your help if you think it
right after having heard all the tale – but I don't want to influence you
. . . it seems to me I am always resigning something or other, although I
should have said I was a peaceable fellow enough.[31]

By May 1888, there had been a mass exodus from the Grosvenor
Gallery, as the artists followed Carr and Hallé to their newly created
gallery, the New Gallery.

★

Lockwood was more in harmony with officialdom at the moment. In the 1887 New Year's Honours list he was made a CIE – a Companion of the Most Eminent Order of the Indian Empire. Professional recognition was pouring in too, and in the same month he was asked to design the Memorial Hospital in Gwalior.* His little family, however, was beginning to break up. Rudyard was offered a bigger job on the *Civil and Military Gazette*'s much larger sister paper, the *Pioneer*, in Allahabad, and in November that year he moved there to take it. Trix had just become engaged. This all sounds very Happy Families, but in reality things were beginning to unravel.

Rudyard had been looking out for Trix, acting as a big brother should, ever since her return to India. In 1885 he had written to Margaret:

You being a mere woman can't understand my intense anxiety about the Maiden and my jealous care lest she should show signs of being 'touched in the heart' . . . Of course we can't hope to stave off the inevitable but I promise that unless he is a most superior man, I'll make it desperately uncomfortable for the coming man – *when* he comes . . .[33]

A year later he was no more resigned to Trix finding a suitor:

a brother journalist from the Northwest wrote to me some weeks ago telling me all about his 'feelings' in regard to Trixie and goodness knows what else and asking me if I thought the case hopeless. The audacity of some men beats me. He had only seen Tr. for four days and had certainly not impressed her in the least. Personally I liked the man . . . but that didn't prevent me from sitting down and sending him a brief and courteous epistle of an exceedingly unpleasant nature. Unofficially of course I was sorry for him because I knew how he'd feel but, officially and as a Brother, I was at some pains to thoroughly sit upon and end him. You

* A newspaper report was 'happy to find that Sir Lepel Griffin is in accord with us about the professional merits of Mr. J. Lockwood Kipling, who he has determined to entrust with the designing of the Memorial Hospital about to be erected at Gwalior . . . The cost of the work will certainly amount to several lakhs [hundreds of thousands] of rupees and will afford to Lahore School of Art . . . an opportunity of showing what they can do in applying Eastern architectural resources to Western requirements.'[32]

can't realize how savage one feels at a thing of this kind – an attempt to smash the Family Square and the child barely eighteen too![34]

By 1888, however, Trix had fixed her heart on Jack Fleming, an officer in the Survey Department who was ten years her senior. He came from an Anglo-Indian family – indeed, his mother's entire family excepting her had been murdered in the Indian Mutiny the year before his birth – and he had spent all his adult life in India. An engagement to Fleming meant that Trix's future would be entirely Indian – no returning 'home' until retirement. That would have been fine if everyone had been pleased about the match; but only Alice was. The engagement was broken off almost before it was made, then it was on again. Rudyard wrote of it pessimistically:

A queer walk . . . In the end the Maiden told me her little store of confidences. That objectionable cuss with whom she had broken, had another last-despairing interview with her yesterday morn, and very naturally with his appeals and protestations had shaken the poor darling grievously though she persists and persisted in her original intent. She talked to me and told me as much about it as a woman would ever tell a man and at last the blessed tears came to her relief and she cried all among the pine-needles while I lacked words that could give her any comfort . . . so we agreed that never since the world began was there any sorrow like to her sorrow and hunted for raspberries till the tears were dried and our fingers blue-red, and we began to steal from each other's vines and throw pine-cones at each other's heads as it was in the very early days. But somehow the fooling was not amusing and when Trix collapsed on a rock and said: – 'Oh how miserable I am!' I felt that we could not play at being babies any more. Wherefore we came home solemnly to tea and announced that we had had a riotously jovial afternoon.[35]

It was very different from the time they had sailed their boats and Rudyard delighted in no longer being afraid. And things did not get better. A week later Alice was ill in bed,* and

* 'The Doctor had said that it was *tonsillitis* . . . [but] our fear was the worser disease [diphtheria, a killer]. Where the Mother is concerned we are very easily upset . . .'[36]

just as the Mother was down with high fever who should turn up except the maiden's rejected lover – off his head completely. 'Could she give him a quarter of an hour? Only a quarter of an hour?' 'If the Mother's going to be real bad' said the maiden 'I'll get rid of this man between a poultice and a poultice.' So she dealt with him for the space of fifteen minutes and then he left and she was on the verge of tears but she had said very bitter things, and felt more at ease . . . 'It's *not* nice' said the maiden tearfully 'to have to make poultices with one hand and stave off an importunate lover with the other. Now if I could clap the poultice on his mouth' . . . Then we laughed and thought of fresh torments . . .[37]

Fleming was persistent, and a fortnight later Trix 'was making pathetic little attempts to be cheerful and moping because she wouldn't see him'. Most of the cause of the breach appears to have been Lockwood's and Rudyard's adamant opposition.

Under these circumstances I shook her gently but firmly, and demanded explanations. When I got 'em my heart smote me for it seemed that I was keeping two loving souls apart and who was I to do that? 'Only let him see me' said the Maiden 'and try not to hate him so and then – if there is another quarrel it will be all over – indeed it will.' The Mother said: – 'Let them see each other and get to understand each other and perhaps they won't care so much.' . . . Maybe under other circumstances I should have been more hard-hearted and backed up my father.[38]

This went on for another month, until in August Lockwood reported to Editha Plowden that

Trixie has renewed her engagement to Jack Fleming and I don't like it . . . Came the young man, eager for an answer, with their (Alice and Trixie's) sanction. What could I say or do? . . . He is . . . a model young man; Scotch and possessing all the virtues, but to me somewhat austere; not caring for books nor for many things for which our Trix cares intensely . . .[39]

Rudyard, over 600 miles away in Allahabad, received word from Alice that the date was now set for the following summer:

'Didn't you know?' writes the mother as though I had received a printed notification with every issue of the *Pi[oneer]* for the last month. No madam, I did *not* know and I ain't one little bit pleased, but console myself with Mrs. Kipling's practical philosophy. Here it is. 'The older I get the less inclined am I to bother about the future until it becomes the present. The future generally arranges itself.'[40]

So here was Trix, engaged to someone she was not sure she wanted to be engaged to, with her father and brother fiercely against it, while her mother was just as fiercely for it. Why did she go through with it? First, because being married was what she was trained for. Second, because despite the loud protestations about the loving 'Family Square' that they all wrote of, despite Trix saying that those years in India were 'the happiest time in both [her and Rudyard's] lives',[41] the truth of her feelings for her family may have been rather different, as a contemporary document suggests.

In 1891, under the not-very-pseudonymous pseudonym of Beatrice Grange, Trix was to publish a novel, *The Heart of a Maid*, which tells the story of May Trent, a young girl who marries Anstruther, whom she does not love. It is facile to suggest that May Trent is a portrait of Trix – even an indifferent artist has imaginative powers. There are, however, little details which make one feel that certain parts of the story reveal rather more than Trix would have wanted. The narrator comments that

Between May and her mother there was very little sympathy, a result probably of their never having lived together until the girl was eighteen. When mother and daughter – comparative strangers, having scarcely met since the latter's early childhood – are put to the test of living together, without the links of custom to bind them, disagreement, even constant quarrelling, is too often the result.

(It is worth noting that in neither this novel nor Trix's next does the heroine have a happy childhood or a sympathetic mother figure.) The narrator goes on, 'half the hasty, ill assorted marriages that take place have for a cause the fact that the girl was not happy at home'. And then, 'Two years . . . with Mrs. Trent would have been enough to convince a not very strong-minded girl that marriage was the only career to look forward to.'

Did Alice alone in the family want Trix to marry Fleming because she thought they were suited to one another? Or had she succumbed to the Simla disease of believing one's daughter was a failure if she was not married within a specified number of seasons? Had Trix learned to believe the same thing? Or was she just anxious to escape? The two men of the family thought Fleming completely unsuitable* – but Rudyard had a way out if he was not happy at home. He was a man, and he had a job.

Was Rudyard, too, unhappy at home? Kipling's feelings about his home life, like everyone's, were mixed. He was, to his own way of thinking, happy to be with his parents, and he was a loving son to them. He protested it often enough, and it is likely that he believed it. He told Margaret, only partly as a joke, that

The mother's care and . . . attentions have completely demoralized me and . . . I have decided that when I marry it must be a lady well versed in domestic knowledge, not less than twelve years my senior, and by preference, some other man's wife. Thus only can I hope to pass gracefully from the comforts of the foursquare hearth to the comforts of my own.[42]

In turn his parents wanted to make up for the childhood that he and they had missed: two years after Rudyard had first begun working, his father called his salary 'that boy's pocket money'.[43]

In 1884, when Rudyard had first been offered a promotion to working for the *Pioneer* in Allahabad, his primary concern had been how to manage on his own, without his family square. He had never lived alone, never looked after himself. There were of course many men in India who 'shifted for themselves', in the phrase of the time, but they were more to be pitied than imitated. His chaste passion for Mrs Edmonia ('Ted') Hill, seven years older than he and the wife of meteorologist Professor Alexander Hill, and his lack of interest in any more suitable women, meant that marriage, the

---

* And they proved in the long run to be right.

obvious solution to his housekeeping dilemma, was not immediately a possibility. The next possibility was to look for one of those
'superfluous' women to take care of him. Aunt Edie was the family
member who fitted that description, and now that Louie was so
much better, and with Stan at university, she could probably be
spared. Rudyard wrote to her:

best of Aunts, what would you say if I were to ask you at some future
time to come out and keep house for me through a season at Allahabad?
When the evil day of my transfer comes as come it must if I go on happily,
some one will have to look after me. I'm helpless as a babe by myself; and
I have fended off the prospects with the direst threats of instant matrimony
whenever it has been discussed. I think we might manage a six months
together fairly successfully . . .[44]

How Edie reacted to the idea of changing her life and travelling to
India, and all for six months (clearly a trial period, with the possibility of being returned as unsatisfactory at the end), is unknown. The
Hills offered Rudyard a room in their house and, given his feelings
for Mrs Hill, it was snatched at — although Alice as usual put the
sharpest spin on it, as Rudyard reported: ' "Well," said the mother
judicially . . . "it would be good for you because you'll have to be
moderately genial and interested in things. I don't know what the
Hills are like but I don't think they'll tolerate your moods and
blue-devils and falling into clouds. Yes, you'll have to be civil." '[45]★

   The reintegration into a family had been no simpler for Rudyard
than it had been for Trix. Alice's tongue was not curbed just because
she had her children home. In the hot weather, Rudyard was
reunited in Simla with the small dog who had gone to the hills with
the women seven months before:

None of us thought that she would remember and I own that I had quite
forgotten; but she belied us all — dear little beast. In a moment of
expansiveness I said egotistically: — 'I shall think better of myself hence-

★ Mrs Hill commented, 'The mother's estimate of the boy was so true — he was
impossible at times — but we knew him quite well before he came, and so could
make allowances.'[46]

forward.' 'Hear him!' said the Mother. 'Anyone but a man would have said that he would think better of the dog.'[47]

Before that, her acid comments on what, to a young man, immature and uncertain with women, are the most difficult aspects of life may have made the move to Allahabad appear attractive. Rudyard told Mrs Hill, 'I am going up to Simla *foi de gentilhomme* to make love to Mrs Edge!!!! Hereon my mother with brutal frankness: – "*I* shan't hinder you but she's a yellowish green just at present and like a daguerreotype only shows in certain lights. It doesn't say much for your taste." '[48] That sort of thing is fine if you don't care deeply about the woman – which in this case Rudyard didn't. But if you are uncertain about yourself, which Rudyard was, it can be excruciating.* Lockwood was less tart about another girl Rudyard had conceived a passion for from afar, although only after he realized that his son was not truly affected. Rudyard ruefully reflected on it later:

She has the face of an angel, the voice of a dove and the step of the fawn. I worshipped her blindly till I found she was the Cantonment Chaplain's daughter. My love was proof against this also and I said; – 'I will go and listen to her Papa on Sundays.' I went once . . . He preached. I went a second time for I saw that she was lovely and I hoped peradventure that her Papa might have been drunk. But he preached a second time and I drove home . . . and laid the mangled heads of Her Papa's sermon before my Papa. And he said: – 'My Son – there must be hereditary insanity in that family. Avoid it.' And I avode for I was of the same opinion as my Papa.[50]

On the whole he appeared content. There are, however, three events that contradict his later descriptions of his supremely happy relationship with his parents. The first is a small one. In 1885, three years after his return to India, while he was living in Lahore, he wrote to Margaret, 'I have written to you more freely, my sister, than I have *ever spoken* to any one I know.'[51] Those are his own

---

* Emotionally, Rudyard was uncertain; in terms of his work and his social status he was extremely confident (it seems wrong to say 'overly confident' only because of his great talent). Mrs Hill described him as 'dash[ing] about Allahabad with his protruding cleft chin out-thrust, as though it were leading him'.[49]

emphases. The claim might, of course, be hyperbole, a moment of warmth. But, when set beside a comment he made to Professor and Mrs Hill three years later, the words take on added significance: 'You shouldn't have taken me in, dear people, and showed me what a happy home life is like. It makes one exacting.'[52] This is harder to overlook. It is an extraordinary form of words to choose; he is saying, Without you I would not have known how to be happy in a family, for I had not learned this at home.

The final clue to Rudyard's inner unhappiness is overwhelming. In 1886 Rudyard had been saying to Kay Robinson, editor of the *Civil and Military Gazette*, that

I look forward to nothing but an Indian journalist's career . . . My home's out here; my people are out here; all the friends etc. I know are out here and all the interests I have are out here. Why should I go home . . . I shall have to go through a rough time of it if I prefer a life that I don't know to the broad margins, uncut edges and pleasant type of my daily existence in this land.[53]

Maybe in the next few years he did go through a 'rough time of it'; maybe the Family Square had become overpowering; maybe it was just the natural consequence of growing up. Whatever the reason, by 1888 Rudyard was planning to leave India. He did not just go. He also made certain that he could not come back, by detonating some carefully placed bombshells on his departure. He wrote a poem, 'A Job Lot', about the Commander-in-Chief, Lord Roberts, which suggested that the most desirable jobs were being handed out to Roberts's own friends; he wrote a nasty squib against Lord Dufferin, and another on the rarefied privileges of Simla as compared to the Indian peasants' lives. The final explosion was 'Baa Baa, Black Sheep', which, bizarrely, he published as a Christmas story. Looking back at his young adulthood from old age, Rudyard wrote that, until their deaths, it had been his parents who 'made for me the only public for whom then I had any regard whatever'.[54] If they were his most discerning public, this barely disguised story of Trix and Rudyard in Southsea – abused, neglected, unloved – must have been shattering to them. Not only were Alice and Lockwood forced to contemplate how damaged their child was – he ends the story, 'when young lips have drunk deep of the bitter waters of Hate, Suspicion, and Despair, all the Love in the world will not wholly take away that knowledge'[55] – they were also forced to recognize that, such was Rudyard's success in Anglo-Indian society, all their friends would know it too. There was no turning back now – Rudyard could not live any longer in India.

His leaving was planned as a round-the-world trip which, after a jaunt to America, would end in England, where he would try his luck as a writer. Emotions now came to the surface, on both sides. Alice was devastated to be parted once more from her son, and she wrote to Georgie, 'There was so much to do and with maternal egotism I fancied no one could do things as well as I. Indeed, it was good to be busy, for when the heart is full and the hands are empty it is hard to get through the last days of anything.'[56] Rudyard sounded as if he might be regretting his demolition job when he wrote to Margaret:

She, the Mother, is very anxious to see me again and I confess that I should like to feel her arms round me once more before I go. I can get as much praise as I want in these parts but love is a scarce commodity and I hold the best is a mother's. Thank your God Madge that you have never had to live alone without help or sympathy except what comes by letter. If I live I see a long stretch of solitary years before me . . . At present the prospect rather wearies me. I've been there before, y'know, and know what it means.

His emotional, and consequently physical, state, which brought on this allusion to childhood trauma, was fragile. He also used it to justify his leaving:

The last month has been to me one long stretch of 'fever an' ague' coupled with violent sickness and mental depression, yea even to the verge of hanging myself. It was never bad enough to spoil my work or at least to stop it but it put me 'down in a gulf of dark despair' . . . The doctors say that unless I wish to leave my bones in the country . . . I had better quit.[57]

He left in March 1889, despite the fact that it was only three months before Trix was due to marry Jack Fleming. It may have been real anxiety about his health; it may also have been his clearest comment on the marriage.

While Alice and Rudyard were saying their farewells in Lahore, Alice reminded him of her brother Harry in New York, whom she wanted him to visit.* When Rudyard, working his way across America from west to east, finally arrived in New York in September 1889, he reported, 'after searchings manifold [I] captured my long lost uncle in a building in Wall Street. It was a queer meeting for we had to talk family affairs for an hour with the ticker reeling off the prices of stock in our ear . . .'[59] Rudyard was uncomfortable and Harry was querulous: 'My uncle reminds me pathetically from time to time that I am the only one of his blood-kin who has come to him for thirty years.'[60]† It was not a relationship that Rudyard was anxious to develop. He was finding various members of his extended family embarrassing to the bluff-young-reporter-about-town image he was now cultivating. For example Margaret, only a few years earlier the cousin to whom he told his innermost secrets, had now become 'a maiden . . . who lived in an entirely different life from mine – all among the aesthetic fold and the writer-men of Oscar Wilde's epicene stamp'.[61]‡ It is most likely that the precipitating factor in this volte-face was not only Rudyard's new life, but also that in the previous week he had heard of Margaret's engagement, 'to a portentous prig'.[62]

---

* In the odd words of Charles Carrington, Kipling's authorized biographer, Alice '*recalled* that she had an elder brother in New York'[58] (my italics). This may be simply the form of words he decided to use, but Carrington was chosen by Elsie Bambridge, Rudyard's daughter, and he saw papers that she later destroyed. In considering Alice's relationship to her siblings, the distance implied in the word 'recalled' is worth bearing in mine.

† Not true, of course. Fred had visited him ten years before.

‡ This is nearly a decade before the notorious trial, when Wilde's name became unutterable. It is a comment on the Aesthetic movement, not on homosexuality.

12. The Cousinhood
1888–1892

In 1881, when Burne-Jones had been awarded an honorary doctor-ate in Civil Law at Oxford, the twenty-two-year-old winner of the Newdigate Prize that year had recited his winning poem at the ceremony. This was Rudyard's 'portentous prig', J. W. (or Jack) Mackail. Mackail had been born on Arran in 1859; his father had been chaplain to the Black Watch in Malta, then to the Free Church in Calcutta before returning to become a minister in Ayr; his mother had died when he was four. Jack was a phenomenon, arriving at the University of Edinburgh at the age of fifteen. He then went on to Balliol and looked set for academic glory. Instead he moved to London and joined the civil service: he worked in the Department of Education, and for a time was private secretary to an MP.★

Georgie was thrilled when he and Margaret became engaged in February 1888. She had loved looking after him when he came to visit, and she mothered him, making much of the fact that his parents were both dead and his sister married, 'so he came to us a homeless man', she wrote to Charles Eliot Norton when giving him the news. 'I feel as if what I have to tell you must have shone through the envelope before you could open it . . . our dear Margaret is going to marry the one man in the world Ed: and I would have chosen for her if we might . . . we are on our knees for thankfulness.'[1]

She had initially written 'the one man in the world I would have chosen for her if I might'. The 'I's had been crossed out and 'Ed: and I' and 'we' substituted. Was this simply because Georgie wanted

---

★ This was Lyon Playfair, one of those extraordinary Victorian whirlwinds of energy. A chemist by training, and the discoverer of nitro-prussides, a new class of salts derived from prussic acid, he was subsequently a prime mover in the organizing of the Great Exhibition, then Postmaster-General, then Deputy Speaker of the House of Commons, while an MP first for the universities of Edinburgh and St Andrews, afterwards for South Leeds.

her friend to see her marriage as completely united? Or is it reading too much into this small change to see Burne-Jones's feelings about the match showing through? By July, Georgie noted, he had made himself ill at the thought of 'losing' his daughter. This is all of a piece with his liking for young girls, his fear of growing old – the ultimate indication of age, after all, is when one's children marry. Georgie saw it somewhat differently. He was suffering a 'fit of good hearty green-eyed jealousy' which 'blinded him for a time'.[2]

It is interesting that Georgie, who accepted her increasing age, did not see her story as played out, whereas Burne-Jones, that Peter Pan, saw that the focus was now on his children's lives, not on his generation any more. This first engagement for any of the Macdonald sisters' children marks an important transition point, as had the sons' beginning to leave home. Women were never, of course, in the forefront of society, but after they had fulfilled their 'biological destiny', in both bearing and rearing children, they were expected to retreat even further. And this is what the sisters did. They were a long way from death; indeed, by today's standards they were no age at all, ranging from Alice at fifty-one to Louie at a mere forty-three. Nonetheless, they now began a sort of mental disappearing act, even if in a more corporeal sense they continued to live active, busy lives. It is hard to convey this duality but it is abundantly obvious that from now on, with only two-thirds of their lives over, the women themselves, as well as society as a whole, thought their function was fulfilled.

Although Burne-Jones admired and also came to love his son-in-law very much, there was between them a certain wary distance he never bridged. He called him Jack with some difficulty; in private he wrote it 'Djaq'. If he had done so only once or twice, this distancing mechanism could be passed off as a (not particularly successful) joke; but Burne-Jones kept it up until he died. Rudyard, as has been noted, thought Jack self-satisfied (although quite what his opinion was based on, from his distant vantage point in India, it is impossible to say). There were other dissenting opinions on the man as well. A Glasgow newspaper referred to him as 'the greatest classical scholar to hail from the Isle of Bute',[3] which shows an unexpected level of mockery. Cynthia Asquith called him 'the most complete walking encyclopaedia I've ever met'.[4] He was staid and sure of himself, very much part of the Establishment.

Whatever the general opinion, the immediate family was delighted with the match. Phil, after a time to readjust, was pleased (he had been in Oxford pursuing his desultory university career when Jack was winning plaudits there). As usual, Georgie left him severely alone emotionally; she did not try to help him come to terms with the idea that his sister was moving out of his orbit, although she clearly recognized that he was having trouble with this: '[I] left him quite to himself . . . and himself is triumphing.'[5] As the wedding drew nearer Burne-Jones continued to fret about 'losing' his daughter, although less so as it appeared that Jack was happy at the Department of Education, and that they had found a house in Kensington, within walking distance of the Grange.* A story that has been reprinted several times is that the idea of procreation so distressed Burne-Jones (perhaps especially in relation to his daughter) that it was quietly removed from the marriage service to avoid upsetting him. This may be true, although no source is ever attributed to it.[6] It is easy to see how the legend grew up – Burne-Jones was not happy about his daughter leaving home, however good a gloss he put on it: he and his children were abnormally close. This is not to say that there was any suggestion of what would today be considered abuse, but the emotional closeness does appear pathological; even Georgie commented on the 'exceptionally strong attachment',[7] and, unlike when Phil went to school or Margaret visited Scotland, this separation was not going to end. After the ceremony on 4 September 1888, at the appropriately named St Margaret's in Rottingdean, Burne-Jones freely told everyone that he was 'pretty doleful'.[8]

Rottingdean was a happy place for the ceremony. Ned and Georgie had settled down very comfortably in the little village. In 1889 they decided to buy the cottage next door to Prospect House,

---

* The address was 27 Young Street, which ran (and still runs) off Kensington Square, only yards from the house where Margaret was born. Many of the landmarks the Mackails' daughter Angela Thirkell noted in *Three Houses*, her memoir of her childhood, are still present: Thackeray's house across the road, the pub next door, Mrs Patrick Campbell's house round the corner in Kensington Square.

knock through, and make one larger house. Margaret was pregnant with her first child,★ and if they could gain some more space the cottage could continue as a family holiday house, with all of them under one roof. There was also a slightly less attractive reason put forward by Georgie: 'We should not have done this however for anything short of compulsion, we are so fond of our tiny home here – but there was a likelihood of very tiresome neighbours taking it and that would have spoilt our comfort as we are so very close to each other, and we were obliged to do it.'[10]

They arranged for W. A. S. Benson, who had designed Burne-Jones's garden studio, to merge the houses, making a new entrance and creating a studio upstairs for Burne-Jones – until then he had not had anywhere to work if the light was bad.† Rottingdean was still a rural idyll. There was no gas laid on in the village at all until the late 1880s, and the high street was not surfaced until the turn of the century. North End House, as the enlarged Prospect Cottage was now renamed, was situated facing a little village green, where there was a carp pond, and two large houses, the Dene (owned by the Ridsdales, a prominent Liberal family) and the Elms (which at this stage still had a cowshed against its north wall. Here 'Trunky' Thomas, who in summer had charge of the bathing machines, which were drawn in and out of the water by horse, to enable the ladies to bathe in decent privacy, kept his cows in the winter).[12] Although only a few miles from Brighton, the village could not have been more different from that popular seaside resort, and the Burne-Joneses felt both the difference and its superiority. The main route to Brighton, even into the 1890s, was by omnibus:

★ Although she may not have known it yet. Twenty years before, the generally accepted signs of confirmation of pregnancy were given as: (1) 'ceasing to be unwell' (that is, ceasing to menstruate); (2) morning sickness; (3) shooting pains and enlargement of the breasts; (4) 'quickening' of the foetus in the womb (in the seventeenth to nineteenth weeks); and (5) increased size. A woman was often five months pregnant before she could be certain. In the absence of more advanced diagnostic tests, a wait-and-see approach was the only available method.[9]

† It remained an artist's house for a long time. After Georgie's death the house was sold to Sir William Nicholson, the painter (and father of Ben), and then later to Sir Roderick and Lady Jones. Lady Jones published under the name of Enid Bagnold, and it was here that she wrote *National Velvet*.[11]

A two-horse 'bus, driven by Walter Holden, popularly known as 'Scribbets', made the journey twice a day to Brighton, and its departure from the old White Horse Inn . . . was heralded by the village boys . . . Later a four-horse 'bus with George Thomas handling the ribbons and Charlie Tuppen, in pink coat and grey topper, tootling the horn, did the journey in great style four times a day, starting from the Royal Oak.[13]

When the Burne-Joneses first arrived Scribbets was a child, but the bus was the first sign of a growing encroachment upon their retreat.

Georgie particularly loved the house: her garden was 'a haven of sweetness with sweetbriar and wallflower, and quite blue with irises, bluebells, borage, periwinkle, and thousands of forget-me-nots'.[14] Burne-Jones was less enamoured: he was neither particularly interested in nor moved by nature in the raw, unmediated by art, unless it related to something he was painting, or to the work of an artist he admired. One writer on Burne-Jones has suggested that 'the sight of visible beauty distracted his mind from the contemplation of imaginary beauty'.[15] Whether or not that is the case, he used North End House more rarely than Georgie, restricting his visits to recuperative ones – after a busy period of work, or when he was on the mend from one of his many ailments – or to the times when Margaret and Jack were there.

They had set up home in Kensington very happily, and the Burne-Joneses visited them every day. Jack, at the Department of Education, had ample time for scholarly work – civil servants worked from ten to four or from eleven to five, and they were one of the privileged elite who received paid holidays every year. Margaret was much taken up with setting up her home 'properly' – everything had to be in accord with upper-middle-class mores, and be just right. She had had a surprisingly short engagement for a girl of her background. A year was more usual, to allow for the purchase of a complete trousseau. A sample list for a girl on a 'moderate' income:

only 3 nightdresses, silk, cotton, or woollen, as desired; 4 to 6 shifts, or combinations if of longcloth, 3 if woollen; 8 pairs of worsted stockings, 3 woollen, 3 black silk, or Lisle thread, and for evening wear, a couple of pairs of white silk or lace; 2 corsets, 2 summer vests (low); 4 winter, 2 high and 2 low; 3 white petticoats, 2 good and 1 handsome (other petticoats according to habit); 2 evening bodices or slips (camisoles are best, drawing up), and 2 coloured woollen or linen bodices (high) or both; 6 pairs of boots and shoes will be wanted, all told, for bad weather and bright day wear and evening and fireside slippers; 1 dressing-gown; 1 toilet jacket of flannel; 12 collars, or a few yards of frilling; 12 towels; at least 2 dozen pocket handkerchiefs – 12 for common use, say 12 finer, and a few lace ones besides are as well . . . cuffs and gloves as required; last, not least, nice handsome travelling-trunks and well-fitted dressing-bag . . . the foregoing list represents the minimum.[16]

It may be that, with Margaret so occupied, Georgie had more time alone; another reason she may have been glad to have a bolt hole in the country is that there is a possibility that Burne-Jones was again involved with Mary Zambaco. There is only one reference to this extant: the diary of Jeanette Marshall. The drawback to relying on this is that Marshall was spiteful and enjoyed unpleasant gossip, which means she may have exaggerated rumours for the pleasure of it. Nevertheless, this particular diary entry looks as if it is based on fact. In November 1888 she wrote:

We are all rather exercised about Mme Zambaco. When M[ama] and I went to her studio in Campden Hill Road the other afternoon, & found it all shut up, a man offered to ring the bell for us, and while waiting, he volunteered some information. There are only 2 studios side by side, and one is Mme 'Zambago's' (like lumbago!) & the next Mr. Burne Jones', 'Royal artist' added our informant with a flourish. Now knowing that B.J. has a large studio at the Grange, & that Mme Z. did not know *we* knew of her studio there, (wh. P[apa] found out by many enquiries at her former rooms,) & remembering the set out there was between them before, it looks *very* odd! I feel quite disgusted to think that she is going on agn. in the same old style. It is a shame! If I were Mrs. B.J., I wd. soon have her wig off!! P[apa] actually mentioned the man's remark when he and M[ama] called at Shepherd's Bush to Mme Z., who looked uncomfortable, wh. I don't wonder at. How very inopportune! – I don't like the look of it at all.[17]

There is nothing further, but it may be an additional explanation for the expansion of North End House, and the increasing amount of time Georgie spent there while Burne-Jones was in London.

Although Margaret had now left home, briefly Georgie had had another family member to look after. Rudyard had arrived in England in October 1889, and for a few weeks, until he found his feet, he stayed at the Grange with the 'beloved Aunt' and Ned, whose knowledge of art he looked up to only slightly less than Lockwood's. ('[He is] a mine of wisdom on letters and Art. He is one of the best talkers I know when he cares.')[18] Although not widely known in England, Rudyard had arrived with a respectable body of published work behind him: *Departmental Ditties* and the collection of stories *Plain Tales from the Hills*,★ which had been reviewed in England in several important journals. His small Indian collections† were now pulled together into two larger ones, *Soldiers Three* and *Wee Willie Winkie and Other Child Stories*, which drew approving notice. Rudyard also established a good relationship with *Macmillan's Magazine* and started writing for the *St James's Gazette*. It was not long before he woke to find himself famous, and all before he turned twenty-five.

Rudyard had arrived in England an engaged man. While he was in the States, staying at the home of Edmonia Hill's father, in Pennsylvania, he had somehow become engaged to her sister, Caroline Taylor. 'Somehow' is the correct word. There are no surviving letters to show any great feeling (or really any feeling at all), and the whole thing appears to have been a bit half-hearted. It is likely that, given Rudyard's unspoken yet unmistakable passion for Mrs Hill, the engagement to her sister, just as he was physically

★ The dedication to this book is of endless fascination to biographers. It reads, 'To the wittiest woman in India, I dedicate this book.' Trix claimed that this was Alice, and it is true that in her copy Rudyard had written, 'The Most Excellent Lady of the Dedication/From/her unworthy son'. He had also written before publication to the original of Mrs Hauksbee, Isabella Burton, 'If I put on the title page, *sans* initials or anything, just this much, "To the wittiest woman in India I dedicate this book" will you, as they say in the offices, "initial and pass as correct"?'[19] It would appear that Rudyard had carefully chosen a most elastic form of words.

† For which Lockwood had probably designed the covers. They are credited to 'The Mayo School of Art, Lahore'.

moving out of Mrs Hill's ambit, was an attempt to stay attached to her. Caroline came to London at the end of the year, and the engagement survived only until the following summer. In the meantime, Rudyard was setting himself up on his own for the first time in his life.

After a few weeks at the Grange he found two small rooms in Embankment Chambers, Villiers Street, behind Charing Cross station. The rent was £55 per annum, and Burne-Jones agreed to be the reference for the lease. In 1890 Rudyard signed on with an agent, A. P. Watt. Watt was not absolutely the first literary agent, but he was the first truly effective one. He had previously been a publisher, and had seen the increasing need for a go-between for the benefit of both writers and publishers. Authorship was becoming professionalized, just as painting had been twenty years before. Rudyard got the full benefit, as between January and March that year, with the help of Watt, his earnings doubled.

Rudyard had never looked after himself before – in India his manservant had even shaved him before he woke up – and he found it a 'sore trial'. His need for company, for friendship, ensured that he rediscovered his English family after seven years away. His letters to Mrs Hill are full of lines like

[I] ran into Aunt Aggie's house at Knightsbridge where I had tea and played railway tricks with the small boy Hugh – a late arrived cousin whom I persist in regarding in the light of a nephew. Passed on by special invite to meet my unmarried Aunt Edith Macdonald, Jack Mackail and Margaret at Aunt Georgie's where there was a family gathering.[20]

Phil, his elder by four years, was now to Rudyard's mind in need of care. Rudyard had succeeded in this new and alien world; Phil, for all his cigar-smoking, society ways, lived at home and painted indifferent pictures that no one showed much sign of wanting. His judgement was not all it should have been, either. After less than two months in London, Rudyard was already rescuing Phil from what he had decided was a gutter-press journal:

[It was] a mean little rag which professed to publish the lives of 'Eminent Workers'. With the eternal vanity of the artist Pip had allowed himself to be roped into the show – had forwarded an autobiography and had sat for a likeness!! . . . One glance at the first number of the horrible journal was enough for me . . . and I schemed to pull that phool Phil out of the disgraceful horde. Ran back to his studio in Kensington High Street, told him he was an ass, and that he had better give me a power of attorney to interview the unprincipled editor and get Phil's M.S. of his own life back again, since he was in more than shady company and his foes would scoff. Pip promised . . .[21]

Phil was apparently given no choice, and the relationship was set at this level.

Rudyard also took to Ambo. Ambo was only eighteen months his junior, but to hear Rudyard it was eighteen years:

young Poynter my cousin aetat 22 came with me to my rooms and he spoke till one in the morning, never so he says having had a soul to talk to before. The trouble is an old one. Young man in his father's house, just growing up and inheriting his father's nervous temperament, unhappy, lonely, doesn't quite know what he wants . . . felt sorry for him.

Then, some days later,

Young Poynter who insists on regarding me as his father confessor thrust into my hand on leaving his M.S. volume of poems and A FIVE ACT TRAGEDY IN BLANK VERSE! . . . Such a queer pathetic written letter accompanied the thing . . .
  . . . the poor boy had evidently been struggling with religious difficulties thro' it all – complicated with budding flirtations which, most naturally, plunged him further into the maze of doubt and uncertainty . . . Very naturally he estimates all his poems *not* by the thing actually put down in black and white but by all the glorious inchoate fancies that flashed through his brain when his pen was in his hand. He wants my verdict not so much on his poems as his psychological condition. If I put it down in writing I shall offend him. I will e'en ask him to dinner – or a pipe – and talk things over – verily the soul of a young man is awful cur'ous.[22]

Although the tone Rudyard used in these letters to Mrs Hill was worldly-wise and elderly beyond even an elderly man's years, Ambo obviously did look up to him. Rudyard was as good as his word. He took Ambo out to dinner and a music hall, and listened and said little while Ambo unburdened himself until two in the morning. He relished being part of a group of closely knit relatives, and enjoyed himself even if the meetings did not go entirely as planned.

Dined at the Burne-Jones's to meet my Uncle Fred Macdonald the Methodist preacher and his Nephew George* a weedy sucking solicitor . . . Aunt Georgie had stuck the pallid boy George with his back to the fire. He was much too polite to ask for a screen so he was! Then he drank two glasses of clinging clammy Saumur. (I love my Aunt Georgie but I don't drink her wines.) Then when the ladies . . . had retreated, George wrapped himself round one of Burne Jones's best Havanas! (I love my Uncle Ned and I *do* smoke his cigars when I can get 'em.) That didn't agree with George. He was – not to put too fine a point on it AWFUL SICK! . . . Phil ran for the slop bowl and I ran for the hall. Fred evidently was used to the hair-trigger stomach of his offspring for he left Phil to doctor the poor boy . . . Now the shame of the performance is this. Ten or eleven years ago when I had last seen George a rickety scrofulous child he was being sick up and down his father's stairs. Today, nothing in the wide world will convince me that he hasn't been continually sick ever since. And yet he must have had some lucid intervals or he would not have passed his examinations . . .[23] †

His Aunt Agnes, as the mother of a small child and also chronically ill, was less available than Georgie, although Rudyard visited her at home, where he enjoyed playing with the baby. He also spent time with Poynter, interested in the background to art. He reported going to see Poynter's new picture, *The Queen of Sheba's Visit to King Solomon*, just before Christmas 1889 – although he perhaps didn't take it as seriously as Poynter took things. He described it to Mrs Hill:

It's Old Brer Solomon coming down the steps of his throne to welcome Sis Sheby as she comes along with apes and peacocks and all that truck. I

* A slip. George was Fred's son, and Alice and Georgie's nephew.
† Rudyard recovered from this reintroduction, and George acted as his solicitor for many years.

never saw such a blaze of colour or jumble of notions in my life. Sol is in stamped blue and red Peshawurlac cloth. Sheba in Delhi . . . 'I thought it was oriental' says Poynter 'and no one knows any better here.'[24]

Rudyard was shortly to begin work on a novel, *The Light That Failed*, and he used many of Poynter's reminiscences of his time in Paris at Gleyre's atelier in the 1850s.

Agnes's one contribution to settling Rudyard in was to try to find 'nice' girls for him (another sign of quite how wishy-washy his engagement to Caroline Taylor was). One evening he went

with Aunt Aggie . . . over to a dance at 27 Rutland Gate . . . A tiny drawing room was cleared out . . . A crowded room cannoneered impartially all round. Then even as I looked the whole thing wearied. Arrived at No. 2 danced one waltz with Aunt Aggie who dances lightsomely, saw three girls to whom she purposed introducing me; saw a glimpse of Phil Burne-Jones who showed me another girl. I am I hope strong but their eyes scared me . . . and so quit while No. 4 waltz was beginning and walked home in the night. But Phil found time to tell me one tale which was worth many dances. There was a man last season who, smitten of Heaven for his sins, was suddenly at a crowded dance violently sick over his partner!! He did not commit suicide – not he. He lives but he has no given name. Everyone calls him 'The man who was sick'.[25]

It was more than just the dances that were beginning to pall. The publishing world was showering Rudyard with attentions, but after less than six months at 'home' Rudyard was refusing such eminences as Edmund Gosse, saying feebly that he had got his diary 'into such a beastly tangle' that all he wanted to do was bolt.[26] The reason was less the quantity (or quality) of engagements, and more the fact that Rudyard was descending once more into depression. The Poynters rallied round and took him to stay in Rottingdean in February 1890, but by June, when Trix arrived in her newly married state, she found her brother very low. His engagement to Caroline Taylor had ended (given its lack of importance to both sides, this was probably as a result of the depression, rather than the precipitating factor). Being at Rottingdean at this time probably made the breaking-off appear worse than otherwise it would have. Margaret

Mackail had just given birth to her first child, Angela, in January
1890, and, as Lockwood had noted, Rudyard was 'crazy' about
babies. He was also ill – he wrote in an undated letter to an
unknown recipient, 'Just at present am engaged in spitting blood.
It's sensational but it comes out in serial numbers too often for
me.'[27] Finally, during the summer, he sent a telegram – desperate,
panicky, while disguising it as a joke – to Alice and Lockwood. It
read, 'Genesis 45:9.'[28] As any child of a Methodist minister would
have known, Genesis 45:9 reads, 'Haste ye, and go up to my father,
and say unto him, Thus saith thy son Joseph, God hath made me
lord of all Egypt: come down unto me, tarry not.' (It makes more
sense when it is remembered that Rudyard's first name was Joseph.)

Alice and Lockwood did not tarry. Now that work was coming
in in great quantities for Lockwood, Rudyard was earning an
extremely nice living, and Trix was the financial responsibility of
her husband, they could take some of the leave owing to them
and head home. They recognized the anxieties behind Rudyard's
playful stratagem: even before they had received the telegram,
Lockwood had written to him:

I won't pretend, dear boy, that we have not felt very anxious about you
. . . Let me beg of you, dearest Rud – not to worry yourself about our
lodgings before we come . . . though I understand and can sympathize
with your loving wish to have a place ready for us – it distresses me to
think of your being bothered about all that when you are not well.[29]

For the first time, the Kiplings could afford to rent a house, in
the Earl's Court Road, and not be dependent on the more successful
members of the family. In addition, they arrived in the autumn of
1890 trailing the glory of a royal commission: the billiard room at
Bagshot was successful – so much so that

I was sent for the other day to Buckingham Palace to see the Duke and
Duchess of Connaught and it was arranged that I should go to Osborne
to see the Princess Louise who, being artistic, is keen on having a room
of the new wing now building there done in the Indian manner . . . I
went to Osborne . . . and had long discourses with the Duke and Duchess
of Connaught, the Princesses Louise and Beatrice and the Queen and the

net result is that one of our Lahore men is to come over for modelling and general get up of a *plastered* room, and after another is to come for colouring. I want to take a back seat and show that young Indians trained to study Indian work can design it.[30]

Ultimately Lockwood supervised the design of what he called 'a sort of Hinduized version of the work of the Akbar period'.[31]

Before Lockwood could settle down to work on the project, his brother-in-law Fred received a letter from Harry in New York. At the age of only fifty-five, Harry was desperately ill. 'My first thought', he wrote,

was that I would at once wind up my affairs here and come with my wife to England that I might see you all once more, die among my own people, and be laid by father and mother. But my doctors tell me that I should not survive the voyage, but be buried in the Atlantic. So, if it is at all possible, come at once, my dear brother, and see me for the last time.[32]

Alice and Lockwood decided that the sea voyage would be good for Rudyard in his present state of health, and so he and Fred set off at once for New York. Harry died on 11 June 1891, two days before they landed, and achieved none of his last wishes – he died among people not his own, was buried beside none of his family, and did not even manage to see his brother one last time. It is a summary of his sad, short life – so little desired, even less achieved.

Lockwood was achieving rather more, and was at the peak of his creative life at only two years younger than Harry. In the spring of 1891 one of his men came out from India to supervise the job at Osborne. A sixty-foot-long room, of teak, heavily ornamented in both woodwork and plaster, had been planned and agreed.[33] Lockwood noted in a new 'diary' (which he managed to keep for just two weeks) that 'Ram Singh arrives at Victoria from Lahore by the train at 7.10 and to-morrow I suppose I take him on to Osborne . . .'* He then moved on to rather more exciting news:

* Queen Victoria, always taking a particular interest in her Indian subjects, had earlier instructed Lockwood to arrange for Ram Singh to postpone his trip until the summer, as she feared the cold for him. (In true imperial fashion, she queried when he could come 'home' – meaning England – even though he neither was

Yesterday Watt [Rudyard's agent] met me at E[mbankment] Chambers
and took away with him type-written examples of the Beast book and
sketches; writing in the evening that he had shewn it to Macmillans who
seemed impressed . . . Must confess to feeling anxious and a little excited.
Probably the reason why I did not sleep last night but read Solomon and
Job instead.[35]

The 'Beast book' was a manuscript Lockwood had been working
on for some time, to be called *Beast and Man in India*, a lively
collection of legends, folk tales, superstitions, retellings of Indian
myths, all graced with his own animated sketches. The nervous and
excited author was accepted by Macmillan.* It is pleasing to know
that Lockwood's final, sad little entry in this mini-diary was this
time fulfilled. He wrote, 'Could wish for more of the things I ask
for.'

Beast and Man was published towards the end of the year, dedicated to 'The other three'. Sadly for Lockwood, the main review
it received in England was written by Sir George Birdwood, a civil
servant and self-proclaimed 'India expert'. Even when he had
written the handbook for the Indian section at the Exposition
Universelle in Paris that Lockwood had organized over a decade
before, the two men had not seen eye to eye. Birdwood had
pronounced that 'it is not for Europeans to establish schools of art
in a country, the productions of whose remote districts are a school
of art in themselves, far more capable of teaching than being
taught'.[37] He attributed good Indian design to the traditional structure of the guild and, despite this being precisely the model that

English nor had ever been in England before.) He was ultimately at Osborne for
over two years, working on the room. The Queen had a cottage on the estate
allocated to him, where he could do his own cooking – she was aware of the
difficulties that might arise if he had to eat food prepared by others. At Christmas
1891 he was invited to Osborne for five days, and given a gold pencil-case by
the Queen-Empress herself.[34]

* Macmillan were his son's publishers, but they chose this manuscript on its merits
too – it did well for them, and was reprinted. Rudyard later advised his father on
it, and Lockwood meekly bowed to his superior judgement: 'When my son was
here in the winter he spoke of the paragraphs being, in many cases, too long and
wanting separation where there is a change of subject. It is true I think, but I am
not sufficiently expert in correction to indicate how it should be done . . .'[36]

Lockwood had used in the building-up of the Mayo School of Art, continued to carp from the sidelines. Lockwood appeared detached about the review of his book – 'It will be hard to make a reply – full of unpleasant facts . . . The writer cuts his own throat so effectively in two or three cases that a reply is unnecessary – Also it is hard to deal with the writer's ecstatic irrelevancies without an appearance of frigidity and banality.'[38] He also tried mockery to deflect the criticism: 'Sir George Birdwood said the other day that he would be delighted if an earthquake would swallow up all the High Schools and all the schools of art in the country. But in spite of this most reasonable utterance Indian education is bound to go on . . .' However, the fact that he wrote Maurice Macmillan, his editor, three letters in three months (or rather there are three letters that survive in Macmillan's files – Lockwood may have written even more often) goes some way to indicating his distress.

He clearly was very distressed. Lockwood was informed, intelligent and extremely competent, but he was not particularly confident. He described himself as a 'jibber' – 'not altogether incapable of going when once set in motion, but apt at unexpected times and places to refuse to start'.[39] And it was not as if Birdwood was going to go away. Lockwood was putting together one more exhibition – this time for Chicago – and, after the 'toil', 'all the credit we shall have will be to be told by Birdwood that we are ruining everything'.[40] He tried to keep this melancholy side of his nature hidden, but Rudyard, as a fellow sufferer, recognized it easily – 'The Pater . . . is *not* a sanguine soul'[41] – and Lockwood himself occasionally let it peep through: on his way to England the previous year a man had jumped overboard. 'Leaning over a ship's side most people have felt how easy it would be on a little provocation to have done with things – I, for one, have occasionally found it better to walk away and – change the subject.'[42]

Then anxiety set in in earnest. In October 1892 Lockwood was diagnosed with an 'ailment of the Aortic valvular arrangement of the heart, and I am ordered to drop all work that involves worry, fatigue, and anxiety and to go to sea at once, and am gazetted for six months' special leave'. He therefore planned to miss the opening of another Punjab Exhibition – not that one exhibition out of so many he had organized could bother him, but he had also set up a

conference on Indian art, and he did regret the loss of that. Now
he was to 'coast . . . from Kurrachu [*sic*] to Calcutta, Burma and up
the coast of Mandaly'.[43] The typhoid he had suffered in 1875
had permanently weakened him, and this new illness brought the
beginning of the end of Lockwood's Indian career. It also marks a
change in the relationship between Lockwood and Alice. The
children had gone to Southsea partly because Alice had felt that she
needed to be by Lockwood's side, to help him advance. Now as
he moved towards retirement, with further ambition halted, he
began for the first time to travel alone. It may be that, like Georgie,
Alice recognized a new phase in her life, and was not resistant.

But first, with Alice and Lockwood in London, the immediate
priority was to get Rudyard well again. He and Lockwood planned
a short trip to Devon to visit Crom, almost as soon as the Kiplings
landed. They also went to Rottingdean, where they could visit
Georgie, and Agnes too, for the Poynters had taken a house nearby,
as Agnes was

by no means so well as those who love her would like. The influence –
which so far as I can make out, seems to be a high polite name for bad
malarious fever – has left her with a deplorable tendency to rheumatism
of a painful sort, and generally worn and weak, which is sad to see in one
so bright.

They were happy to spend time with the family: 'Hugh is a dear,
nice boy. He has conceived a strong friendship for Rud, who is
crazy about children . . . Ambo is turning out a notably fine young
fellow of a fine mental quality and good of his hands and at
his work. Also, he has first-rate common sense, and very good
manners.'[44]

The Poynters and the Baldwins had been particularly close ever
since Agnes and Louie had spent so much time together when their
children were small. In 1888 Stan had left Cambridge; he and Ambo
renewed their friendship, with Ambo spending weeks at a time
with Stan in Wilden. Stan, like his cousin Rudyard, had passed
from school to adulthood with none of the troubled times that
Ambo was undergoing. On returning to Worcestershire he
immediately assumed the role waiting for him: heir apparent. He

formed an artillery battery under the aegis of the Volunteer Force, joined friendly-society lodges and courts, and co-founded for the Conservatives the local habitation of the Primrose League (Louie ran the 'Dames'' Kidderminster habitation). His twenty-first birth-day was celebrated by the entire village, although the festivities had had to be postponed because he was in camp with his artillery battery on the actual day. There was a dinner for forty-five people, and also banners, races, a banquet, and an illuminated address for Alfred and Louisa, as the proud parents. It was a works event through and through, for Stan had already joined Alfred at Baldwin's.

Initially, according to his cousin Harold, Stan hated the idea of going into business. Two months after he began, Stan was 'evidently awfully depressed by this damnably dull business life, and he hates it as cordially as I do; poor old chap, it is terrible for him, and as one looks forward the view is gloomier still'. Three years later Harold noted, 'The way in which he has settled down to business amazes me; he's almost as keen on it as his Father, and at the same time from the bottom of his heart detests it; he's wonderfully quick and grasps a situation in no time.'[45] Perhaps the situation Stan had grasped most clearly was that he was his father's son, and that his duty was to his parents, and therefore to their business. This was what his upbringing, and his religion, had taught him, and Stan was not one to shirk. He later noted that he and Rudyard had 'common puritan blood in us and [Rudyard] said a thing I have so often acted upon: "When you have two courses open to you and you thoroughly dislike one of them, *that* is the one you must choose, for it is sure to be the right one." '[46]

One bonus of Stan's work was that, for the first time, he began to travel. He had previously gone with his parents on some of Louie's trips for her health, but mostly he had stayed at home, or with the Poynters. When he was eighteen, Lockwood and Rudyard had tried to persuade Louie and Alfred to let Stan spend some time with them in India, but Rudyard drily noted that he did not 'for an instant suppose that Aunt Louie would let that paragon with a horror of fast girls go away for a year'.[47] Nor did she. But in 1889, after he had been at Baldwin's for a year, Edward Poynter offered to take him with him on a trip to Switzerland and Italy. Stan was close to his uncle as well as to Ambo, and was grateful for this introduction to cultural life. The following year he went to Canada and the United States for Baldwin's, with introductions to the Burne-Joneses' friends the Nortons in Boston, and to friends of the Kiplings, Lockwood and Meta de Forest, in New York. Georgie, as usual, was blunt:

He was a plain, pink, thin boy when you saw him with his parents that day at Rottingdean years ago, and is now a plain young man, but a good one, and the hearts' delight of his parents . . . [he] had to take his place in his father's business (he is an ironmaster) because there is no other son to do it. I bet it was a hard thing for him at first, for he likes books, but he saw the justice of it, and applied himself to office work with all his might, and is already so helpful to his father that he will soon be admitted into full partnership.[48]

Louie was still going strong with her own interests. In 1891 her second book was published, again a three-volume novel designed for the circulating libraries. *Where Town and Country Meet* is set in 'Sturminster', an amalgam of Stourport and Kidderminster. It concerns a farmer, jilted by his fiancée, who finds happiness with Ruth, a girl from the local manufacturing town who takes in sewing to support herself and (in a touch we recognize as standard Victoriana today) her small blind sister. Before the farmer declares himself, Ruth is tested by being given too much money in her pay, to see if she is honest enough to return it. Perhaps as a link with this stalwart woman, the book is dedicated to Georgie, 'my friend and sister'.

Louie now spent even more time in London than she had previously. Alfred's ever-increasing business interests made this a necessity, and they had taken a house in Albemarle Street, ending their years of staying in hotels. Stan too travelled up frequently, and he and Rudyard began to get to know each other, really for the first time. Rudyard felt he had a lot to prove: unlike Stan, who was entirely comfortable as his father's son. When Rudyard made his first £1,000 (a vast sum), what he most wanted, he remembered half a century later, was that 'my people should come over and see what had overtaken their son'.[49] He was nervy and depressed, even after *Life's Handicap* was published in 1891 to tumultuous acclaim. His parents' arrival the previous autumn had not helped as he had thought it would, and as late as July 1891 he was still 'recuperating' in the country, all work of any kind forbidden.

In *Life's Handicap* Rudyard had written that the tales had come from all over, and that 'a few, but these are the very best, my father gave me'. However, he recognized that his father had to return to India, and that his own future was in England. He found a new collaborator: Wolcott Balestier. Wolcott had been born in Rochester, New York, the grandson of an immigrant from Martinique on his father's side. His maternal grandfather was equally well travelled: Erasmus Peshine Smith had spent several years in Japan as the Emperor's adviser on international law. Wolcott first worked for the Rochester *Post Express*, before having some stories published. Recognizing that writing was not his forte,★ in 1889 he became the London representative of an American publishing house, bringing with him his sister Caroline (Carrie) to housekeep for him. His charm was clearly considerable, for he arrived without fanfare and within six months had most of literary London pressing invitations upon him. Carrie wrote triumphantly to her mother, 'We have discovered to our satisfaction that we can get Henry James when we really want him and so we are going to indulge him and let him stay away except when he is really needed to impress.'[50]

Wolcott was (one assumes) less obvious: he later claimed that when the new sensation Rudyard Kipling was recommended to him he asked who – or possibly what – that was. Soon this 'carefully dressed young-old man, or elderly youth'[51] and Rudyard were such close friends that they decided to write a novel together, echoing Rudyard's collaboration with the Family Square. This was to be *The Naulahka*, a 'tale of East and West' – Rudyard to supply the

★ His novel *A Victorious Defeat*, among many other flaws, shows the same snobbery that was later to afflict his sister so ferociously. Set in a late-eighteenth-century Moravian community in New England, it deals with the second son of a baronet, who 'had done an undeniably peculiar thing' in marrying an American. Her 'high breeding' is 'easily accounted for' by the fact that her English father was 'of an irreproachable family'. The book is pretty unreadable, filled with sentences like 'The sun is not a perfectly amiable body with us, but it has its humane impulses.'

East, Wolcott the West. Before it could be finished, Wolcott went
to Dresden for his firm, arriving in the middle of a cholera epidemic.
By 6 December 1891 he was dead, just a week before his thirtieth
birthday. Rudyard was devastated. Wolcott may very well have
been his first close friend, outside schoolmates. Over two years later
a friend noted that 'Wolcott's name could not be mentioned to
him, and his photograph was never in evidence'.[52]★

   Henry James went to Dresden for the funeral, both for his friend
and to support Carrie. Carrie talked to him at some length, and he
wrote afterwards to Edmund Gosse, 'One thing, I believe the poor
girl will *not* meet – but God grant (and the complexity of "genius"
grant), that she may not have to meet it – as there is reason to
suppose that she will. What this tribulation is – or would be, rather,
I can indicate better when I see you.'[53] This is obscure, even for
James. Leon Edel, his biographer, believes that James foresaw what
was to happen next, and dreaded it. Carrie sent a telegram to
Rudyard, who had just arrived back in India to visit his parents.
He immediately turned round and returned to England. Only
weeks after his arrival, he and Carrie were married at All Souls
Church, Marylebone, on 18 January 1892, just five weeks after
Wolcott's death.

   The wedding was a grim affair. Carrie's letters notifying her
friends of the event went out on black-bordered mourning paper.
Mrs Balestier and Carrie's sister Josephine were too ill with flu to
attend the ceremony, as was Phil. The witnesses – and sole guests –
were Gosse, Henry James, Ambo, and the publisher (and Wolcott's
great friend) William Heinemann. Alice and Lockwood were in
India, but there is no indication of why neither the Burne-Joneses
nor the Poynters were there. Gosse called the small wedding procession a 'cortège'; James described the wedding party as a 'scanty
group . . . as huddled and shivering in the big bleak church as a lost
sheep on a moor'. He added, 'They strike me as a little couple in
some ways intensely matched and I hope they won't do each other

★ Martin Seymour-Smith, one of Kipling's biographers, has suggested that Rudyard's extraordinary attachment to Wolcott betokened a homosexual relationship
(overt or latent). It is worth noting that when Rudyard heard of Robert Louis
Stevenson's death he took to his bed and could not write for three weeks. As he
had never met Stevenson, it is unlikely he was having a relationship with him.

any harm.'[54] Hardly more enthusiastic was Lockwood. He thought Carrie was 'a good man spoiled', and added gloomily, 'if I had been in [Rudyard's] place I think I should have preferred the younger and prettier sister'.[55]

13. Settling Down
1892–1894

Carrie and Rudyard left on honeymoon, planning an around-the-world trip after first taking a look at Vermont, Carrie's home state. This meant that they would miss Stan's wedding.

Stan had been spending more and more of his free time in Rottingdean. The attraction was no longer his Aunt Georgie, rather it was her friends across the way. Mr Ridsdale was an assay master at the Mint and Mrs Ridsdale was a force in village life, 'sailing down the village street, commanding of figure, a large silver-topped leather bag always hanging at her side, a word for everyone, an eye to everyone's business'. They were the terror of the neighbourhood, their 'alarming frankness of speech' reducing outsiders to jelly. 'In any other family the torrent of criticism and plain speaking which burst out would have meant a violent family row. But with the Ridsdales it was merely a family conversation.'[1]*

Into this atmosphere came Stan. Stan had always been shy, diffident. Like his father, he suffered from a facial twitch, and in addition he had a nervous habit of snapping his fingers: not precisely the kind of personality that would be thought suited to the Ridsdale rough and tumble. It was Stan's love of sport that had brought him into contact with Lucy Ridsdale, known as Cissie, two years his junior and a stalwart of the Rottingdean ladies' cricket club. Village cricket was taken extremely seriously by the whole family: Cissie and her brother Arthur wrote a description of it which nicely captures the flavour – a combination of wildness, great seriousness and charming eccentricity:

John Sladescane, 'Civil John' as he was called, landlord of the Plough Inn

*One of those who must have produced many of these family 'conversations' was Cissie's brother, Sir Edward Aurelian Ridsdale GBE, later to become Liberal MP for Brighton from 1906 to 1910. He was, unlike the rest of the family, a freethinker, and the author of *Cosmic Evolution*.

. . . supplied the cricket luncheons on Beacon Hill, or 'Bacon Hill' as the villagers called it, to home and visiting teams at 2/6 a head, with a barrel of beer on tap all day.

The luncheon table, forms, mugs, barrels, etc., were all carted up to the top of the hill via the windmill and a booth erected. There was a long table and cloth, with forms but no chairs except for the scorer.

This booth was covered with canvas with a place at the side where you bought glasses of beer on tap from a barrel, ginger beer, shandy-gaff, etc. The booth was always counted as a boundary, which the villagers called 'a boother'.★ Dandy Hyde, one of the old characters, often tipsy, was an enthusiast and always attended matches: he some-times stood umpire and his attire for those occasions was a grey square bowler hat, frock coat and light trousers. He was not employed for serious cricket, for when appealed to 'How's that?' he never said 'Out' or 'Not Out', but would turn to the batsman and say, 'If 'ee do it again, I shall give 'er out!' Old Trunky Thomas, the bathing man, was another of our 'umpires'.[2]

Because of the slope, Beacon Hill was not ideal for cricket, particularly in those pre-boundary days. Its topography lent itself to one of the many shaggy-dog stories that vie to describe the most runs ever scored off one ball. The ball was hit down the hill. When it was finally retrieved, it was thrown hard at the stumps, missed them, and rolled all the way down the opposite slope, to allow a staggering sixty-seven runs for the batter.

All this was irresistible to Stan. His emotions were bounded by home, Church and cricket – and here was Cissie, a member of a large, loving family, with a religious cast of mind, and a demon fast bowler to boot: not a combination to be found just anywhere. He was besotted, and allowed his affection to pull him out of some of his shyness: on his way home from one visit he sent Cissie a telegram from every station between Brighton and Worcester. He kept his feelings to himself, as was his habit, and told his parents only in April 1892, when he had already proposed and been accepted. Even when he was planning to make the break from his family home, he

★ This term was actually in common usage in this period, when boundaries were only beginning to appear. There were no boundaries at Lord's until 1866, and they didn't appear in the revised edition of the Laws of Cricket until 1884.

remained the dutiful son. He told Alfred and Louie that he hoped
he and Cissie would 'live to be half as good to everybody & as
much of a blessing to the community as you'.[3]

Louie arrived at the Norfolk Hotel, Brighton, in August, nearly
a month ahead of the wedding, in preparation. Agnes came down
too, and Georgie was of course at North End House. This was a
sisterly reunion, something that was getting rarer all the time as
they grew older and their family demands remained while their
energies decreased. On 12 September 1892 Stan and Cissie were
married from Cissie's home in Rottingdean. The honeymoon was
of a seriousness appropriate to such a serious man – a tour of the
cathedral cities of the West Country. They then moved into a
house that Stan had rented not far from his parents, Dunley Hall,
where they were to spend the next ten years. They settled down
to the life of a prosperous businessman and his wife, and Cissie
learned to modify her behaviour to suit Stan's temperament. If she
called out suddenly, if she coughed too long, if they had to drive
in foggy weather, he became worried and afraid. She stopped
appearing in amateur dramatics, because he found it too distressing.
Anything could become an ordeal – a speech, reading the lesson in
church, going to the dentist, even speaking to his workers. His son
claimed that any of these horrors could make him turn white, sweat
profusely, feel nauseous. An orderly, quiet life was what he needed,
and what Cissie gave him.

The Rudyard Kiplings were not the only ones to miss Stan's
wedding – Lockwood and Alice had returned to Lahore towards
the end of 1891. With them went Edie, invited to spend a few
months in the Kiplings' now childless home. Lockwood worried
that 'Alice of that ilk would be considerable lonely now her Trix
is gone, and she will be glad of a companion in the long days when
one is at work.'[4] It did not work as well as they had hoped. Edie
herself said on her return to Wilden that she had found the climate
'not kind'; Lockwood was more forthcoming. He clearly felt for
Edie, even as he realized how funny she was:

In this little shanty we have been a good deal drawn towards gruesome
thoughts because of poor Edie Macdonald who has been very near death
during the past week and at the moment is only better in that the fever

has left her – pretty much as the surf leaves a swimmer after a battle for life, high and dry on the beach, but exhausted. She had remittent fever (which really had no intervals) for fifteen days . . . she has been conscious all the time – perhaps better for her, but very serious for her nurses (Alice and Trix [who had come home to help her mother], with a professional lady). Because in the clearest way and with perfect self-possession she has, as Trix says – 'bossed her illness herself, ridden on the whirlwind and directed the storm', giving instructions at most frequent intervals and constantly announcing her most immediate dissolution. The Bishop . . . has been most kind. He gave her the Holy Communion during one of these convictions of death and was much struck by the terse, calm . . . way in which she spoke of herself in extremity and just about to go . . . Alice and Trix are a good deal worn . . . by the incessant watching and nursing, for not half an hour passes but she asks for something. Both doctor and nurse say they had never seen a case like it, for fever so bad and so long continued generally leaves the patient with very little will . . . But with Edith, her constant cry is – 'Now give me something, I am sinking', – and she has been able to take nourishment and stimulant enough for a man at work . . .[5]*

Far from India, its fevers and family, Rudyard and Carrie now decided that, rather than return to England, they would make their future in America, and they bought a parcel of land in Brattleboro, Vermont, on which they planned to build a house. In the meantime they settled next door, into the aptly named Bliss Cottage, lent to them by Carrie's brother Beatty Balestier, and awaited their first child. There had been some talk about going to India – on a trip or for longer is not clear – but this was aborted, ostensibly for financial reasons. It may partly have had to do with the fact that Carrie was pregnant; it may equally have had to do with another fact, which was that Carrie and her mother-in-law were, to say the least, not soulmates but rather two strong women fighting for control of one man, who only wanted a woman to look after him.†

---

*Rudyard was even more unkind. He thought at the time that Edie 'rather cultivated her maladies', and in later years remembered that she had received the last sacraments as 'one of her diversions'.[6]

† It is indicative of this that in his autobiography Rudyard calls the chapter that deals with his time in England before his marriage 'The Interregnum'.

(Carrie, throughout her married life, adopted Rudyard's name for Lockwood – the Pater – while she resolutely called Alice 'Mrs Kipling' until the day she died.) She and Alice were alike in dominating their menfolk, but Carrie's slow, rather prosaic mind was never a match for Alice's barbs, which clearly stung. She took her revenge in disparaging Alice to anyone who would listen. Soon after her marriage she wrote to her mother, 'Mr. Kipling said last night, "Cant [sic] we make the mother [that is, Mrs Balestier] come". But he cant make his mother either . . . but it is quite for a different reason for she is selfish about it.'[7] Carrie was never one to worry about beams while discussing other people's motes.

There was enough to keep her occupied. She and Rudyard had an architect draw up plans for their house, which measured ninety by twenty-six feet and had eleven rooms. Rumours of its lavishness and cost were to reach ludicrous proportions. Beatty later claimed that it cost $50,000.* Rudyard was rather more realistic. He wrote to the editor of the *Ladies' Home Journal*, 'When are you going to bring out a set of articles "Housekeeping in all Countries" – with weekly bills appended. You owe the innocent public some amends for luring them to financial destruction with $1000 and $1500 houses. I know these cheap houses. They end by costing from $5600 to $11,374. I built one.'[8] Even this was an enormous sum, and it is an indication of how well Rudyard's writings were doing. In addition, a more permanent occupation came their way. Josephine Kipling was born a few days after Rudyard's twenty-seventh birthday. One source (admittedly prejudiced) claimed that the father was disappointed the baby was not a boy;† if this had been the case, within days he was infatuated. Mary Cabot, their friend and neighbour in Vermont, went so far as to say that

---

* By the time he gave this figure to the *Chicago Record*, Beatty had no interest in doing justice to Rudyard and Carrie.

† The only mention of this 'fact' comes from a strange little book called *Rudyard Kipling's Vermont Feud* by Frederic van de Water (New York: Haskell House Publishers, 1974), p. 25. The book's main aim is to show that, in the later notorious battle with his brother-in-law, Rudyard had behaved badly in all ways. More of this later.

Josephine 'was Mr. Kipling's idol'.[9]★ He had always been fond of children; four years later he commented to a friend in England whose wife had just given birth, '*Now* you are a complete man.'[10]

As their children moved into their adult lives – settling down with wives, husbands, children, houses – the earlier generation accepted the shift in focus, but did not necessarily feel their own lives were over. Before the 1892 general election, yet again the local Conservatives offered Alfred a parliamentary candidature in the division of his choosing. Unlike 1884, when he had refused, this time he accepted, choosing West Worcestershire, the safest seat. He was returned with a plentiful majority.† Alfred saw parliamentary office not as a route to advancement, but rather as an obligation – a duty conferred upon him as part of his role as leader in the community. One of his fellow magistrates, who had served with him for many years, understood this well: 'He was a man that one rarely met with in this world . . . His great idea and one that he fully carried out was to do his duty to God, his King and his country, and therefore to humanity.'[11] Alfred rarely spoke in the House, but was a busy and useful committee member, in particular in dealing with special interest groups that he knew intimately through his business life. He was no longer simply an ironmaster, even a prosperous one: in London he was now a director of the Metropolitan Bank. He also became a director of the Great Western Railway, based at Paddington.[12]

Louie, in the midst of all this business activity, continued on the path she had set for herself, publishing her third book, *Richard Dare*, in 1894. By now the pattern of Louie's novels must have been obvious, maybe even to her. As usual, in *Richard Dare* there is one man who is caught between two women. This time he is a doctor. In her next novel, *The Story of a Marriage*, published the following year, it is a young upper-class man interested in 'social

★ An ominous note was struck in this same memoir. Mary Cabot reported that, after the death of one of the Cabot children, Rudyard said 'that if it were Josephine, he would never be able to think or speak of her again'.
† In fact the seat was so safe that from 1892 until Stan finally relinquished it four decades later the other parties often did not bother to field a candidate.

questions' who must decide between two women. Again, as in the template set in her first book, all the men choose wrongly at first, only to be redeemed by the love of the good woman in the final chapters.

It may have been her inability to break out of this rut that led to Louie finding an 'adviser'. She began to send material to her nephew Rudyard for his comments. Over the years he patiently, endlessly, went over her work, pointing out her strengths and weaknesses. Dozens of letters from him survive, all along the lines of 'It's good work well conceived but, as usual, the descriptive part is much weaker than the dialogue. When your characters get to talking they live and move all right but you must look out for new adjectives and new cadences and new methods of approaching common objects in your descriptions.'[13] He gave her advice about how to publish short stories; he asked publishers of his acquaintance to read her manuscripts. If nowhere else, his fondness for her shows through in these letters – never impatient, always treating her as his equal in the writing game. It was more than ordinary kindness, particularly as Alfred felt, now that his wife was a published author, he could not discuss her work with her. In token of thanks, Louie dedicated her collection of ghost stories, published in 1895, 'To My Friend and Kinsman, Rudyard Kipling'.

The letters to Rudyard found him wherever he settled. He and Carrie had nearly finished their house in Vermont, which was to be named Naulakha, after the novel Wolcott and Rudyard had begun together, and presumably in Wolcott's memory. In March 1893, although they had not yet moved into the new house, Lockwood was for the first time able to travel to America to see them. He had been unwell for almost a year, and was now anxious to retire. Alice too was keen to leave India – despite nearly thirty years there, she had grown no fonder of the place than she had been when she first arrived. The only catch, as usual, was money. Officially, Lockwood had not worked for the civil service for his first three years in India and he worried that he would have to work an additional three years in order to collect his pension. Five months before he had written to Rudyard that he would leave the next day if it were not for that, 'but I have a morbid horror of going abegging',[14] and he would not pull strings. This may have been an oblique way of asking Rudyard for help. If it was, it worked. Rudyard spoke to some people who spoke to the Viceroy; Lockwood's long service and distinguished career were taken into account, and by the early spring of 1893 Lockwood and Alice were preparing to return home for good.

On her visits to England, Alice had become particularly friendly with the Burne-Joneses' friends the Wyndhams. They had been building a house outside Tisbury, in Wiltshire, for several years, and Alice decided that this would be the perfect place for herself and Lockwood to end their days – near their friends, and in a less expensive area than they would find around London. It is notable that Alice did not consider either Rottingdean or Worcestershire. As with her children's education, perhaps she thought being near her family would still cause 'complications'. From Liverpool, where she landed, Alice travelled to the Grange and stayed with Georgie and Ned until she had found a house; Lockwood went straight on to New York to spend six months with Rudyard, Carrie and Josephine.

Lockwood, as usual, made himself agreeable, and was immediately at home. Carrie reported to her new friend Meta, the wife of Lockwood's old friend from India and near-namesake Lockwood de Forest:

The father is vastly pleased with everything he sees and his sober judgement of me and things is delightful. He has the keenest eye for all the differences in ways and means and immensely admires our handy ways . . . He . . . is at present most occupied painting pictures of all the animals on cotton cloth which I cut out and button hole onto a large square of cloth which is to be used for little Jay as a rug when she sits on the floor. He is so patient with all our inconveniences and little difficulties of living that I am much less unhappy than I could have hoped to be over his being in these small quarters . . .[15]

Finally, however, Carrie decided that the men were more trouble around the house than they were worth. When the time came to move from Bliss Cottage to Naulakha, she sent them to Quebec. Lockwood was a bit shamefaced about it to de Forest:

To the outer world I suppose that the spectacle of Father and Son mooning round appears decent enough, – but I'm not sure that the severe moralist might not find serious fault with the conduct of two fairly able-bodied men who have both deserted their wives and a severe domestic crisis. Rud: is sent away because he would be very much in Carrie's way now that like General Wolfe storming the heights of Abram [*sic*], she is attacking and driving out the French (carpenters and painters) from the new house, and I am keeping away from England to give Mrs. Kipling a free elbow in getting in to the little shanty she has taken near Salisbury.

It is sad from the moralists' point of view, I fear, – but amusing from mine.[16]

Ten days later, when the de Forests received a letter from Rudyard solemnly telling them that 'when the workmen take to drinking malt extract out of the refrigerator besides stealing the lard to grease their saws with, it seems to me that a man *must* stay by his wife',[17] they probably knew whom to believe.

It was not only with his family that he was agreeable – Lockwood made friends everywhere, by the age-old formula of being interested in whatever he saw and heard. On a train

I noticed a gold mohur hanging on a man's watch chain in the 'smoker'. So I beguiled him to talk and he told me he was in Calcutta for some years, – the last representative of the Tudor Ice Company that used to import . . . ice, Kerosene, apples and lumber &c, and he further declared himself a sworn admirer of the works of one Rudyard Kipling. I found it very amusing to listen to this, but at last I told him I knew that author.[18]

Then the gadding about ended and in October Lockwood returned to England, where Alice had found a house for them, although it would be some time before they could move in. Still, it had 'hot and cold water and bathroom and many more conveniences than one is apt to find', and all for £33 a year – a very reasonable price.[19] In the interim she had not made Lockwood's easy conquests, for she never had his ability to fit in wherever she found herself. At the end of her three months with Georgie and Ned, Ned wrote of his relief that the visit was over, although 'it rather

Alice in India. Lockwood and
Rudyard in 1883, the year after
Rudyard returned to India. Bikaner
Lodge, their house in Lahore.

Simla at play: Alice (*extreme right*) taking part in amateur theatricals; Trix with her *sais*.

Lost children: Elsie, John and Josephine Kipling, 1898.
Josephine died of pneumonia, aged six, a year after this
picture was taken. Rudyard with his son, John, in 1909, a
mere six years before John's death at the Battle of Loos.

The garden of the Grange, Georgie's home from 1867 to the turn of the century.

Philip Burne-Jones,
c. 1900, looking every bit
the man about town he
aspired to be.

Margaret Burne-Jones in 1886, aged twenty. Angela Mackail, her daughter, with Burne-Jones, c. 1892.

Poynter 'at home' in his studio at Albert Gate, *c.* 1884. As is clear from his surroundings, this was not his working studio – he had space at the National Art Training School, South Kensington Museum, where he was principal. (*Below left*) Ambrose Poynter during the First World War. (*Below right*) His brother, Hugh, *c.* 1885, younger by fifteen years.

Alfred Baldwin in 1897, as MP for West Worcestershire. He held the seat from 1892 to his death in 1908, when Stanley was nominated to the vacancy. Stanley Baldwin, c. 1909. Both photographs are by Sir J. Benjamin Stone, taken outside the Speaker's Gate at the House of Commons.

The Macdonald sisters: (*above left*) Alice aged fifty-three, in 1890; (*above right*) Georgiana at sixty, in 1900; (*left*) Agnes in the 1890s, in her fifties; and (*below*) Louisa, some years before her death at the age of seventy-nine, in 1925.

touched me that she did not see I was not in harmony with her – yes, I'm glad it's over'.[20]

He was writing to Mrs Helen Mary Gaskell, known as May, the final woman he was to romanticize. As with Mary Zambaco and Frances Horner before her, she was younger than he – this time twenty-five years younger (he was her father's age, and his second grandchild, Denis Mackail, had just been born). She was married to a captain in the 9th Lancers, and had children nearing adulthood herself. As now suited Ned, she moved easily in the moneyed world where he had grown so comfortable. The Gaskells had three homes – near Marble Arch in London, in Lancashire, and in Oxfordshire – and they travelled between them. With May away so much, he wrote to her every day – and often half a dozen times a day.[21]

He set out to be amusing. He sent her cuttings from newspapers ('At Westminster Police-court, John Thurston, a boy of twelve, residing with his parents at Lower Sloane Street, was summoned under the Police Act, at the instance of Inspector Noviss, for discharging a missile, to wit, by spitting from Chelsea Bridge at a passing steamboat on the 7th inst. – The defendant pleaded guilty.')[22] He regained some of his youthful interests: 'The lady whose shoulders are tattooed with the Last Supper is in town – is at the Aquarium – and I am going with [Luke Fildes] to see her. On Saturday he [Luke] saw her – the tattooings are still perfect – only she is somewhat fatter, and all the faces of the Apostles are a little wider, and have a tendency to smile.'[23] ★ He also turned some of what he considered to be the travails of life at the Grange into amusements for his upper-class friend, who, he seemed to feel, would not have to undergo such indignities herself. A new char came to work at the Grange: 'Mrs. Wilkinson and I have had a very interesting conversation, and I see we shall get on well together for life. She said "Good morning sir" and I said "Good morning" and I think this has cleared the air.'[25]

Despite this new love, Burne-Jones had been depressed for months, and he had begun 1893 no more happily. In February he

★ The tattooed lady was Emma Frank. She had, as well as the Last Supper, a necklace tattooed around her neck, a crucifixion scene, a Union Jack and a Stars and Stripes (she was an American), an open page of the Bible, and a pair of eyes on her thigh.[24]

had decided he could no longer remain a member of the Royal Academy. He confided to May, 'It is an honour to be associated with about 6 of them – and nothing at all to be associated with about a dozen more of them, and positive disgrace to be allied with the rest.' Despite his assurance here, he had recently been going through one of his periodic crises of faith regarding his work:

I have worked so badly this morning that I even took the model into my confidence, and said I wished I had never been born – indeed what a solution of trouble that idea suggests – and who would have been the worse off? Georgie? Well, it would have been much better for her – she could have married a good clergyman – Phil and Margaret? Well, I don't know what they would have been, it is outside practical politics, even practical metaphysics . . . My friends? They would have been in the same case as Phil and Margaret. They would never have known their inestimable loss – and be none the wiser, nor foolisher. My purchasers? Oh, they could have saved their money – The art of the country? There is no art of the country – I have only bewildered it. The public – OH D—N THE PUBLIC and the public be d—d. A few art critics, god help them poor creatures, would have earned a few less pennies-a-line. I really think they are the only ones to whom the least difference can have happened – and it would be morbid to lament their case.

    . . . I must have cost such a lot in food, too . . .[26]

He may have been reduced to the depths by the sight of Ford Madox Brown. Brown was fading fast – he would be dead by October – and he had never received the recognition Burne-Jones felt he was due. A couple of years before, Burne-Jones had had to encourage his friends to club together to buy a painting, anonymously, to ensure that Brown had some money to live on. 'It is sad', he wrote to Val Prinsep, 'to think of the dear old fellow at the end of life, alone and unlucky.'[27]

    That was one form of patronage – the kind one hoped never to need oneself. The other sort, putting a word in with influential friends, was different, and Burne-Jones had no problems with that. In October 1893 he wrote to the only person he knew with Oxbridge contacts, his friend Mary Gladstone Drew. Mary's sister Helen was still at Cambridge, and might be expected to know what was happening in Oxford as well. He asked 'if the Greek Professorship at Oxford is a settled thing already – more likely it is – and if you said "Yes, it is all arranged" then it would save Angela's papa from much labour in his already over-taxed days – but if it isn't he would try I think.'[28] Little did he know his daughter. Mackail was anxious to return to academia, but, whenever it was mooted in the coming years, Margaret – normally the softest, quietest of women – showed that she was her parents' child. She combined her mother's determination with her father's nervousness, and tears, hysteria, long periods locked in her room were guaranteed until the danger was past. When Mackail gave up the idea of leaving London, she would emerge, smiling, and return to her place as the shy wife of a rising civil servant. Even the Mastership of Balliol was refused so that Margaret could stay near her father, where he could drop by regularly, listen to her practise her music, play with her babies, stroll in the neighbourhood with her. They were no less attached than they had been before his marriage – Burne-Jones described to May a typical day in which he had gone to visit Margaret in the afternoon, 'then I came home to dine. We grew restless and went back to look at Margaret for another hour and so back to bed.'

If it did not work for Mackail, Burne-Jones was always willing to lend his influence to other family members. In 1892 the question of who was to replace Sir Francis Burton as director of the National Gallery when he retired in 1894 came up for consideration. George Howard, now Earl of Carlisle and a trustee of the gallery, wrote to Gladstone to say that he felt strongly that the new director should be a painter, not an administrator. Poynter, via his brother-in-law, made it known that he would be interested. Burne-Jones wrote Mary Gladstone Drew a preliminary note:

I wonder if very soon would not be the time to present the substance of that letter about the Directorship of the National Gallery – I heard your father had given over this matter to Sir William Harcourt – but that might be rumour – if so it would be useless for me to plead I suppose, for I do not know him and my partisanship might be injurious – I wonder if you know or could discover – the new appointment will be made, I am told, at Christmas . . .[29]

He must have been given some encouragement, for in August the following year he wrote to her again, in a letter clearly intended to be passed on to her father:

[This] is a sort of business letter – pray thee observe that it is dated – it was no trifle to find the date, for to ten days or so I never know how any month goes on. – It is a subject I do want you if you can, to mention to your father – and it is to save him if it were but one letter that I ask you to be my mouthpiece and to bring the matter before him at a fitting moment – It regards the appointment of a new Director of the National Gallery – which I learn from Sir Henry Layard⋆ may probably take place before long. Burton having done his work finely and being full of years and deserving of rest – I want to say, if it is any use my doing so, that I believe Edward Poynter, whose name has from time to time come up in connection with the idea of a successor to Burton, is so admirably fitted and equipped for the post that I should like your father to be aware of the fact.

I need not say this opinion is as it were a public one – based upon private knowledge of his qualities and capacities – the fact of his being a connection of mine does not count in it – this I may say to you for you would believe me – and indeed is it human to call a brother-in-law a relation at all? That wouldn't influence me one way or other you will believe, I know. But he would do splendidly for the post – he is a good man of business, has a great knowledge of ancient art, indeed I think he has no superior in that science – and of modern too – with a very wide sympathy for good work at all times and schools – moreover he is a most conscientious fellow – and laborious and painstaking beyond word in all that he does.

I know Layard, who is Senior Trustee and Lord Carlisle have a very high opinion of his fitness knowing both the place and the man, and as I have lately learned that he himself would be willing to accept the position if it were offered him, I determined to say what I could on his behalf before any names are mentioned – for honestly I don't know that a better man could be found.

He does not know that I am writing this, nor would he ever push himself forward in this or any other matter that affected his own interest – so his friends must do for him what he would never stir a step to do for himself – for he is a most proper gentleman.

⋆ Sir Austen Henry Layard was both a politician and the excavator of Nineveh; he was also a trustee of the gallery.

It is a most serious matter to creatures like me, of whom there are probably too many, who shall be the next chooser of treasures – but I do hope I am not asking you to do anything you will really dislike . . . Layard told me that he himself had no idea that Poynter would take the place if it were offered – and that unless he would come forward in the matter it might be assumed he was indifferent to it – it wouldn't [*sic*] be like him. I have never seen anyone who would do so well there – and on the strength of Layard's hint, I wrote and definitely asked him if he would accept supposing it were offered to him – and he said yes but in a voice so low that it might have been an offer of marriage, and there I must leave it in your judicious hands.[30]

With this letter, Burne-Jones shows himself to have been a shrewd judge of character. A civil servant or a businessman might have wanted to get his protégé the job out of self-interest; an artist, he is saying, is surely above that, and he proves he is an artist at the very start: his mind is on higher things – only those whose minds run on the mundane know such tedious things as the date. In addition, he emphasizes what he knows will be considered Poynter's strengths for the job: he has two strings to his bow – both working artist and, as Slade Professor and director of the Art Department at South Kensington, a known administrator. (He does not, it is clear, think that it is worth spending much time discussing Poynter's ability as an artist, but the two together are useful.) And then the final consideration: Poynter is 'a proper gentleman' – who could hope for more?

As an artist, Poynter had been made prominent by controversy. He was still producing his sub-Alma-Tadema-ish pictures of the domestic lives of ancient Greeks and Romans – Caesar and Calpurnia at home, that sort of thing. Historical painting was, despite the rise of the Aesthetic movement nearly a quarter of a century before, continuing to be publicly well received. The *Art Journal* in 1896 wrote that people in historical pictures 'are beautiful types of humanity . . . undisturbed by any sordid emotions. Their lovers' quarrels and reconciliations, their partings and welcomes, and all the other small events of their placid lives, are presented with a gentle suggestion of properly ordered passion which recognizes the importance of obeying the laws of self-repression laid down by good society.'[31] In addition, it was clear that a lot of work – both scholarly research and actual painting – had gone into each canvas, and the influence of Ruskin held: the amount of work involved in any picture in part determined its artistic value. By this measure Poynter's work was meritorious, and it may have been in reference to this that Burne-Jones described him as 'laborious and painstaking beyond word'. In general, his pictures were received without great enthusiasm. The technique and the research that went into them were praised, but no one ever went into raptures over his canvases.

In 1885 there had been as usual a large number of 'antique' pictures on display at the Royal Academy Summer Exhibition, including Poynter's *Diadumenè*, a painting of a young girl binding up her hair before stepping into her bath. It was based on a pose inspired by a sculpture by Polyclitus, discovered in the 1870s, showing a male athlete binding up his hair before entering a competition. Poynter's reworking of the subject should therefore have been sanctified by its connection to the antique, but 'A British Matron' wrote to *The Times* following the opening of the exhibition, saying that the 'indecent pictures that disgrace our exhibitions' were 'an insult to that modesty which we should desire to foster in both sexes'.[32] Others sprang to the artist's defence – 'An English Girl', 'Common Sense' and 'A British Parent' all wrote to support Poynter the following day, and John Brett, a landscape painter, suggested that 'the lady calmly assumes that purity and drapery are inseparable . . . that decency and indecency are dependent on a textile fabric'.[33] After another two days of battles in the letters column, even Jerome K. Jerome weighed in:

Sir – I quite agree with your correspondent, 'A British Matron', that the human form is a disgrace to decency, and that it ought never to be seen in its natural state. But 'A British Matron' does not go far enough in my humble judgment. She censures the painters, who merely copy Nature. It is God Almighty who is to blame in this matter for having created such an indelicate object.[34]

But Poynter did not want a public dispute. He certainly didn't want one that looked as if it might turn into a joke. He had, as always, the courage of others' convictions and added clothes to the offending figure, despite writing to *The Times* himself to claim that the purpose of the picture had been to show what a Greek or Roman bathroom might have been like – art as social history, which would 'lift my figure out of the category of baigneuses of the French Salon'.[35] He was not in the market to offend anybody.

In his theories on art he was grandiloquent, if unhelpfully vague. A modern critic has commented intelligently on his lectures:

Since Greek painting has perished entirely and is known only through a very few Roman imitations of doubtful accuracy, it might seem difficult to create a genuinely Hellenic style of pictorial art. The Victorians were not so easily deterred . . . Poynter was able [in his *Lectures on Art*] by some mysterious insight to draw detailed comparisons between the developments of the Greek and Italian schools: Polygnotus was the Orcagna of Greek art, producing works 'in a severe style, without perspective . . . possibly of one colour', while Zeuxis probably combined 'the pictorial and monumental character in about the same degree as the exquisite little picture of the Graces by Raphael . . . or, may we venture to bring in for comparison, at least as regards simplicity of arrangement and perfection of composition, the *Creation of Adam* and the *Creation of Eve* in the Sistine Chapel?' These speculations combine apparent exactitude with an enormous vagueness: if one can compare an artist equally well with the heroic grandeur of Michelangelo and with Raphael at his most miniature and precise, one might as well admit to ignorance.[36]

At the time, however, Poynter's theories went down remarkably well,* and he had his supporters for the National Gallery job. The Earl of Carlisle said that his training in France would be useful. France remained the mecca of serious art, and Poynter's background would enable him to value what came out of that unwholesome place better than one who knew it less well. Some people in England were demanding that, of all ridiculous things, Impressionist paintings should be bought for the nation, and Carlisle noted that this 'discloses a real danger, and one which can be best guarded

---

* Even Kipling thought that this sort of thing made his uncle a scholar. When Poynter pronounced on a picture, Kipling said, 'The verdict from a man of his knowledge we may take as conclusive.'[37]

against by the director possessing, from his own training and study, a criterion which will enable him to resist the demands of temporary crazes and modern fashions'.[38]★ But there were others equally prominent who did not support him – Morris put forward his friend (and Burne-Jones's old studio assistant) Charles Fairfax Murray; Carlisle himself wavered in the two years before the appointment was made and in the end supported another candidate. When Poynter's appointment was announced, in April 1894, Sir Frederic Leighton, president of the Royal Academy, wrote to Lord Rosebery that 'on public considerations . . . I deplore the appointment more than you can possibly imagine'.[39] This is interesting, as Poynter and Leighton had been friends since they were students in Italy together in the 1850s, and Poynter was wont to boast that he was the only man Leighton allowed in his studio when working.

Whatever the hesitations, the appointment was made, and as far as Burne-Jones was concerned

the Nat. Gall is safe for a time – and the newspapers routed, and the wire-pullers dismayed † – good news for me and I am heartily glad. Lord! What a peril it has been, and who really cared? All those treasures – irreplaceable – the pick of centuries – who minded whether they were imperilled or not . . . at any rate Poynter will buy beautiful ancient art . . . and he's a fine fellow to consent to put by part of his own work for the public good – public good – no d—n the public – private good – the good of the half dozen who really care.[40] ‡

★ Burne-Jones's views on the Impressionists had been made clear during the Whistler trial. Phil's were – and remained – no more advanced. As late as 1905 he was writing articles in which he condemned the 'experiment' of Impressionism as though it were still in progress – a full year after Picasso's blue period was complete and he had already moved on to work towards *Les Demoiselles d'Avignon*.

† Himself not included, we must assume.

‡ This form of elitism wasn't particularly unusual: the National Gallery was often avoided by the middle classes as its lack of admission charges meant that the working classes might be present in the building. The gallery's restorer reported that a sort of grease was commonly found on the surface of National Gallery pictures. 'That deposit seems to proceed very much from the class of persons who visit the National Gallery . . . More copious emanations and exhalations would arise from their clothing than from that of other persons who went decently dressed, and for the real purpose of seeing the pictures.'[41] One would

Agnes's views on the scandal of *Diadumenè* are as unknown as those on her husband's advancement – there is, as usual, no mention of her in any of his correspondence, and her own has vanished. There are very few direct instances where Agnes's thoughts are available. Her voice, rather depressed, rather depressing, can perhaps be heard in one of the few scraps to survive. She wrote to a friend who had asked her to pass on information about an entertainment she was getting up at home:

I will certainly do what I can . . . but I am very much afraid it is *too* far away to be of much use to people in from town. I am quite sure that many people don't know where Powerscourt Park is and in any case it takes half an hour to get there. However I daresay you have thought about all this as well as I and I hope it will be a success.[42]

Reading someone's life from their art is a very dubious business, and it should be allowed only to influence, rather than initiate conclusions. It is, however, striking that much of Poynter's art depicts women who lure men to their deaths. He painted sirens (in the late nineteenth century commonly used to mean prostitutes), Medea (who murdered her children for love of a man), Orpheus (who was destroyed by his love for Eurydice). Nothing definite can be made of this. But, given the paucity of material reflecting Agnes's own thoughts, and noting that contemporaries found Poynter a chilling personality, it may be useful to bear in mind the women he chose to represent. It can be noted more specifically that Agnes did not stay in London long enough to watch him become settled in his new job. By July 1894 she and Hugh had gone to Tisbury, to stay with Rudyard and Carrie, who had come over with Josephine and taken a house near Alice and Lockwood for three months in the summer.

News about Burne-Jones was rather more discussed by the families. In November 1893 Mary Gladstone Drew had written to see if he would accept a baronetcy if it were offered by her father. He replied that he and Georgie had consulted briefly, and then

---

like to think that this was the only time the class of the viewer was considered to have an effect on the pictures themselves, but it probably is not.

Georgie . . . said she wanted to be no hindrance to anything Phil would prize. So I am writing to say yes to the Question – it is a brief time, of necessity, in which it could affect me, a long time please God in which Phil would be affected by it, and if to maintain an honour that has been done to me would be a fine incentive to him, as it will be, it would prove a great future. So it will be yes, and I would sooner receive honour from your father than from any living man.[43]

Not an enthusiastic acceptance, but an acceptance nonetheless.

In February 1894, just before formal notification of the honour, Burne-Jones finally changed his name officially, from Jones to Burne-Jones. Nine years before he had still been explaining away the usage: 'I have just stuck in at the point the name "Burne" having long ago, in the natural yearning of mortal man not to be lost in the millions of Joneses put another family name before it – not from pride . . . but solely from dread of annihilation.'[44] Now he had a baronetcy to explain away too. Phil was his explanation, and probably was most of the reason. From his twenties, Phil had gone 'out a great deal in the highest of the high world and move[d] in circles one can scarcely mention without a gasp'.[45] He mixed with the Prince of Wales's set, visited at country houses, dressed the part, and 'dandled', in the phrase of the time, after married women. A baronetcy would make all the difference to the smart set's view of him, it appeared, and he certainly enjoyed it to the full. Over fifty years later his niece remembered that he had always 'insisted on all the right forms' for a baronet.[46]

One very interesting reflection on Phil's self-image, compared to that of an older generation who had had to make their own way in the world, is the responses he and Lockwood gave at different times regarding permission to use their work. Macmillan got in touch with Lockwood in 1895 to say that a firm wanted to use his illustrations from *Beast and Man in India* to decorate luggage labels: would he agree? He replied:

it is a pity to put illustrations to their uses: – but, as they might have used the illustrations for their tickets without asking leave, with scarcely any chance of detection – (for it is only the Manchester warehouse people and the Indian piece-goods dealers who ever use these blazing labels,) and, as, after they had re-drawn and coloured them it would be almost impossible to recognize them, – I thought it would be an encouragement of virtue rare in Manchester to allow them to pay for such use as they can make of the sketches.[47]

By contrast, Phil wrote in a rage about Longman, the publisher, who had asked to reproduce something of his, 'that it is quite impossible. Did he seriously expect that he would get permission to reproduce this design as an illustration to an unknown "author's" work for a guinea!'[48] It may be the inverted commas around 'author's' that give most offence. But Phil's opinion of himself was always higher than others'.

Burne-Jones had known that for a long time. He had told May Gaskell, before accepting the baronetcy,

I do love Phil – I ought to please him – I am responsible for his life – and it is the first time I have been called upon to do a thing I dislike for his sake.

I do dislike it and shall for a long time, and it might happen you know . . . Dear fil [*sic*] – when I told him I had made up my mind to say yes – he was quiet a good time and then came behind me where I was writing to you and sd. 'I know you have done this for my sake.' I said O no fil, not at all – and he gave me a cuddle round the neck and cried a bit – so I wasn't sorry . . . I'll give Ralph [Mrs Gaskell's butler] £5 a year always to announce me as Mr. –

Oh! I shall hate it if it ever comes to pass –

And when it did come to pass he replied to people who congratulated him, 'don't mistake – it's Phil who's the baronet – I am but Phil's papa'.[49]

This was the way the baronetcy was explained to Morris too. Morris was Burne-Jones's greatest worry over this change. He had now left all his socialist work behind and was deeply involved in his latest enthusiasm, the publishing house the Kelmscott Press, but his views were the same as they had always been. Burne-Jones was too afraid to tell him of the honour, and left him to hear about it on his own. Janey commented:

The baronetcy is considered a joke by most people, we had not heard of it before seeing the announcement in the papers – my husband refused to believe it at first, but afterwards when the plain fact was known, he said, 'Well, a man can be an ass for the sake of his children' – it seems that Phil was the chief culprit – I did hear that Sir George Lewis started the idea – in case his daughter wanted to marry Phil, so that he might be their *equal in rank*. It is all too funny, and makes one roar with laughing – I have got over the sadness of it now – it seemed to me such an insult to offer the same to a man of genius and a successful publican, and then for him to accept.[50]

This was probably partly true – it seems likely from what we know of him that Morris had initially refused to believe that Burne-Jones would have accepted a baronetcy. The notion of Sir George Lewis starting the idea is probably partly spite, but it is most likely that Morris's views were neatly captured at the end. Georgie, whose political ideas were far more radical than her husband's, merely noted in her memoir, 'The honour was accepted.'[51] The terseness says it all.

14. Separations
1895–1898

Rudyard and Carrie were now well set on their careers of becoming difficult people. So many stories fly around, about Carrie's snobbery and need for control in every situation, and about Rudyard's almost paranoid anxieties about invasion of privacy, combined with a strong sense of his own worth and importance, that one would like to be able to disprove them. Many were related by people with whom the Kiplings fell out, and must be handled cautiously; however there are also an almost equal number which were related by their friends, or told unthinkingly by themselves, and it is harder to discount these. They cover almost every aspect of the couple's lives, from their earliest days in Vermont.

Mary Cabot remembered how, after Josephine's birth, when the Bishop arrived for his annual visit they asked him to baptize the baby. '[The Bishop] commented with disapproval on the presumption that it took a Bishop to christen the child of a Kipling, and he refused.'[1] Even more grandiosely, Kipling asked President Roosevelt if a private post office could be set up for him near Naulakha. The amount of mail was the overt reason; unstated were Kipling's dislike of mixing with the locals and his desire to keep his business away from what he saw as ever present prying eyes. Roosevelt gave his permission, and Rudyard sent out letters pointing out the new address with some pride. But it was difficult to maintain a good level of service for only one customer, no matter how much mail the customer received, and the facility was shortly discontinued.

Carrie made heavy weather of housekeeping, as she herself acknowledged to Meta de Forest: her visit to the de Forests in New York had made a 'change from the little cares which grow heavy when one is tired. I mean now to make them take their right place ... The ease with which your house seems to be run with all your other demands is a lesson to me and I shall start over tomorrow.'[2] She never did. Everything had an equal weight of importance, big questions and small: at one point she admitted she wanted to add to their letterhead, 'Visitors kindly mention number and size of trunks.'[3] She designed Naulakha so that her desk was outside her husband's study; no one could approach Rudyard except through her. She insisted that they dress for dinner in a country where no one did – in order that her British servants would not think less of them. ('I wish I needn't,' Kipling said under his breath, but only under his breath.)[4] She expected small services to be done by her friends as a matter of course: Meta de Forest arranged her servants from New York; Lockwood de Forest was asked to get silver-plated a brass tray for a tea table, which Trix had sent as a wedding present. ('I shall feel most swagger with a silver tray'[5] – Trix had evidently not known that brass was infra dig.)

Even when they were trying to be kind, the oddness of their situation, and the oddness of their mindset, breaks through. They were no longer connected to the lives that everybody else led. The Kiplings' stable boy was working his way through the University of Vermont. At one point he approached Rudyard for help. 'He heard me through. Then he said, "I'll have to ask my wife." He came back, beaming, and told me: "It's all right. I can take ten thousand dollars." '[6] It was clearly so kindly meant, but ten thousand dollars? That was ten years' salary for a doctor. What *was* he thinking? On the other side, the fear of being taken advantage of, of someone pulling a fast one on them, was always present. Meta had yet again arranged for an agency to send Carrie a servant. The agency sent the bill on to the Kiplings, and Rudyard wrote to ask Meta if she had already paid it, adding, 'Of course there was no reason why you should but perhaps the office has been trying to get paid at both ends.'[7] The offensiveness of the idea, and of asking, did not strike him.

In Tisbury, where they rented a house for the summer of 1894, things were no easier. Rudyard and Carrie were rather taken aback by the English summer – they had forgotten how much it rains – and then there was the friction between Carrie and Alice, which was only ever muted; it never disappeared. It is unclear whether there was any specific reason for it, or whether it was just that, as this was the first time they had lived within calling distance, it now became clear how much they disliked one another. Alice did not comment – or her comments have not survived – so only Carrie's views remain. She wrote to Meta that she was

very low in my mind as well as my body . . . Mrs. Kipling has been away for three weeks recently and then I was away a week so until today we have not met for five weeks and I think she has been thinking matters over a bit for she was more human and nurse tells me she came twice to see baby while we were away and she is dressing a doll for baby I hear also. So after all the coming may have been of use. One hopes so. It has taken it out of me in a most dreadful fashion so I feel it must count somewhere.[8]

By the end of the three months it may have been with mutual relief that Rudyard and Carrie set off for America while the elder Kiplings prepared to leave their rented house. The latter had decided the previous year that if possible they would look for some sun, and, as their new house was not ready, in November they left for Florence, where they stayed until the following June. This meant that, when Trix headed for England in the spring, they could arrange to meet her at Marseille and travel back to England with her, when they could finally move into the Gables.

On their return they found that Georgie had been elected a parish councillor in Rottingdean, taking a part in public life for the first time. Over eighteen months before, she had given notice of this change in a letter to Rosalind Howard: 'We do live in wonderful times. The changes I have seen! My faith increases yearly in the progress of the world, and in the idea that all things and all people help toward it . . . I am quite out of the political world . . . but am intensely interested in the struggle going on in it now, which is a type of bigger thing.'[9] Morris, of course, was strongly behind her. He asked her for copies of her election pamphlet, 'which is as good as the subject admits of, and for the first time makes me know something about the parish councils'.[10] Oddly, given his views on the merits of decorative over practical or intelligent women, Burne-Jones was equally enthusiastic. He wrote to his friends:

I want you to read Georgie's letter to the parish council electors of R'dean – I think it is so well done – so luminously put and so simple –

all the crabbed legal hideousness got out of it and put into easy words of one syllable for simple people – so I send it by the same post as this . . . Georgie's love – she is so busy – she is rousing the village – she is marching about – she is going like a flame through the village.[11]

She was, of course, doing nothing of the kind. She was however taking the first opportunity to represent the village she now regarded as home. The Local Government Act of 1894 had created elective parish councils, and also enfranchised married women to vote and to stand for election. Morris was encouraging: 'Well now, I hope you will come in at the head of the poll; and I hope we shall beat our Bumbles . . .'[12]

Their relationship was as it had been for years, a close, rewarding friendship. His home life continued unhappy – as well as Jenny's illness, Janey had now begun an affair with Wilfrid Scawen Blunt, a minor poet, independently wealthy and a hanger-on of the literary great. He had married Byron's granddaughter, and from his diaries[*] it is clear that Janey's main attraction for him was that she had been Rossetti's muse. In addition, the Kelmscott Press meant that Morris now needed Burne-Jones again, as illustrator-in-chief for his new baby. (Burne-Jones also relied on the Kelmscott Press: Morris agreed to publish Jack Mackail's *Biblia Innocentium: Being the Story of God's Chosen People before the Coming of Our Lord Jesus Christ upon Earth, Written Anew for Children* – not Kelmscott's usual run of things at all.)

Burne-Jones observed his wife and his best friend together fondly. It was as if they were the long-married couple and he their oldest friend: 'when he calls Georgie "old chap" she likes it very much and accepts it as a high compliment'.[13] Now that Burne-Jones could write about him to May, and Morris had stopped worrying him about socialism, Morris's general ebullience, and his size, had stopped revolting Burne-Jones and had become charming to him once more:

Georgie who is not very well to-day and has taken some chill was nursing one of those horrible grey indiarubber water bottles – the sight of which

---

[*] He published an expurgated version in his lifetime. The full, unexpurgated, diaries can be consulted at the Fitzwilliam Museum.

so disgusted him that he cried out upon her 'What the devil is that for Georgie?' – and on her explaining he added 'Oh – I remember one time when I was staying in a country house for my sins when I plunged my feet down in the bed on to something soft and warm, and thought Good God have I had a baby?' and he looked so fat and funny as he said it . . . that I had hysterics.[14]

At the same time, Burne-Jones was curiously blind to Georgie and Morris's deep-rooted love of each other. It was *he*, after all, who was Morris's great friend, and if it was clear to him that they no longer had a communion of souls, that was not because it had passed to Georgie but because Morris communed with no one:

I suppose he minds [in the sense of 'cares'] for me more than for anyone, yet the day I go he will lose nothing, only he will have to think to himself instead of thinking aloud – no more than that. Yet side by side at Oxford it looked as if we had just the same thoughts about all things.[15]

The sisters' families were moving apart as well. Stan was now settled in married life. After an earlier miscarriage, Cissie gave birth to their first child, Diana, in 1895. (She was to have five more children over the next dozen years: Leonora in 1896, Margot in 1897, Oliver, their first son, in 1899, Betty in 1902, and Arthur Windham in 1907.) In 1898 Baldwin's moved from being a private partnership to incorporation as a company. Alfred was chairman, and Stan the 'governing director'. He was very much part of the business community, becoming a leader of a trade association, as well as taking on further political affiliations – he was by now the Worcestershire divisional secretary of the Primrose League, and soon to become a member of the executive committee of the West Worcestershire Conservative Association. These two parts of his life he saw as one. With politics, as with business, he was a pragmatist. His concern was to keep the business of business, and the business of politics, running smoothly and efficiently. He was less interested in theory, or in ideology.

Alfred had always merged these two sides of his own life, and now he headed a Conservative consortium to buy Berrow's Worcester

Journal, a company that owned most of Worcestershire's news-papers. This was purely a political decision: it ensured that the papers would be active on behalf of Conservative interests in the area. In the greater business world, Alfred was reaching ever greater heights. In 1901 he was made chairman of the board of the Metro-politan Bank of England and Wales, which brought with it a seat on the Committee of London Clearing Banks. It had been a local Birmingham bank, and one that was failing badly. Alfred turned it around and made it a powerful voice in the financial community within a few years of his appointment.

He was not greatly changed by these forays into the world of high finance. His religion – increasingly important to him as time went on – kept him grounded. He continued to tithe his income to the church (as did Stan), and from 1892 he became the lay representative for the Worcester diocese to the Canterbury Convo-cation, a position he held for more than fifteen years. To his way of thinking, this was simply another form of service, as were his political appointments. As a new MP in that same year he took on various other positions – chairman of the Midland Union of Conservative Associations, High Sheriff of Worcestershire – and in 1898 he would also become Deputy Lieutenant of the county. Louie and Cissie both worked for women's branches of various Conservative groups – charitable activity that extended the work they did for the church and Sunday school, as well as the local infirmary. Burne-Jones referred to them as 'the most solid characters in Worcestershire',[16] and there is no reason to read any mockery or condescension into his description.

Louie was not well again, and in 1896 Alfred interrupted his new duties to take her abroad once more to search for the elusive cure. This was the first time that they had needed to do so for several years. In 1890 Agnes and Louie had jointly decided that European travel would improve their health, and Alfred had taken the two of them – Poynter being too busy, or too indifferent, to go too – to Germany via Brussels. They had spent some time at a German spa, then travelled to Frankfurt, to Heidelberg, through the Black Forest to Freiburg, to Strasburg, and back to Brussels. It is likely that the trip six years later was similar, although this time Agnes was not with them.

Instead it was Poynter who began to travel. In October 1895 he went to Milan and Paris on purchasing trips for the National Gallery. It was business, and so perhaps not surprising that Agnes did not accompany him, although at one point he did take Hugh with him: family jaunts were clearly not out of the question. As it was, Poynter now went regularly to examine pictures that might come up for sale, or to attend sales in order to fill out the collection. He was in his element, laying down the law, separating the sheep from the goats – he was one of those people who *knew*, while everyone else just held opinions: 'You may be sure if I want it it is a good picture,' he announced grandly to the Earl of Carlisle, a trustee of the gallery.[17] One Goya he had gone to Spain to look at was 'about as good as a weak Gainsborough'; another was 'not as good as a good Ibbetson'. In fact, said Poynter, dismissing the painter from further consideration, Goya was 'coarse and vulgar to a degree'.[18] This certitude was not something that had suddenly come upon him with rank. When he was only in his thirties he could be found informing Sir Henry Layard of some pictures for sale. The Italian ones, he urged, should be saved for the nation, but there were also 'some Bouchers and Greuzes wh. will probably fetch very high prices . . . [and] might very well go to improve the taste of the Americans, and be no loss to anyone here'.[19]

His certitude was clearly admired by his contemporaries. In 1896 Frederic Leighton died,* and the race was on for his successor as president of the Royal Academy. Poynter, now head of the National Gallery, no longer had to have his friends put him forward: he was automatically considered one of the front runners. In the end it came down to Poynter and Briton Riviere, an Academician who specialized in animal pictures (especially lions). Poynter won, and in November was elected 'to the honourable position of head of the Royal Academy',[20] as he so orotundly put it. He decided, much to everyone's surprise, that being president of the RA did not necessitate his leaving the National Gallery, and so now he had much of the London art world under his control – the National Gallery, the Royal Academy and, soon, the Tate.

---

* He was created Lord Leighton the day before he died – the first artist to be so honoured.

The Royal Academy position was very much to his taste. For years Poynter had wined and dined those he thought useful to him – or, as he would have seen it, to art in Britain. (Rudyard was more brutal: 'He is ex-officio member of about every uninteresting society in England and spends his evening eating with bores.')[21] His Eating for England policy had helped him to the pinnacle: he received a knighthood to go with his new position, and he was now at the summit of art administration in the country. The Royal Academy also had a prominent social role. When Sir Joshua Reynolds had founded the RA, he had organized an annual dinner with invitations sent to those 'high in rank or official situation, to those distinguished for superior talent, and to patrons of high art'. Poynter continued this tradition, expanding the guest list to also include 'Cabinet Ministers, the great officers of the State and of the Royal household, the heads of the Church, the Army, Navy, Law, and Civic authority'.[22] It is notable that artists were becoming an even smaller minority of those invited.

As well as purchasing art of previous centuries for the National Gallery, he now had responsibility for acquiring contemporary works for the Royal Academy via the Chantrey Bequest. This was a fund set up in 1876 to purchase art by artists living in Britain, although this rapidly came to mean art by Britons living and working in Britain at the time of painting. (In 1904 Poynter noted that one of Holman Hunt's pictures was 'not all painted in England [and so] it is clearly ineligible'.)[23] The distribution and spending of this money caused controversy from the beginning. The funds were administered by the Academy, and essentially the Academy bought nothing but Academicians' pictures, at extraordinary prices. Less than a decade after he took over, 105 of the 110 paintings that had been purchased by the bequest – for the staggering sum of £60,000 – had been painted by Academicians.[24]

Now this jobs-for-the-boys ethos was to be spread further. The saga of the creation of the Tate went back to before Poynter's directorship of the National Gallery. In 1889, Sir Henry Tate, of Tate & Lyle sugar fame, offered to give to the nation (that is, the National Gallery) his collection of contemporary British art. The nation, as always, was ungracious in the extreme – the gallery turned it down for lack of space. The Earl of Carlisle and others thought that extra galleries could be added at the South Kensington Museum, although the government refused to give any money to create the space. In 1890 Tate offered to give the money as well – some £80,000 towards building costs, in addition to the collection, valued at £75,000. The newspapers were as charming as the art Establishment and the government:

Tate's sugar is getting a better advertisement now than ever any soap secured, and the proprietor must chuckle at the success of his boom. But the public should discriminate between sugar and art. Because a gentleman has purveyed 'crystal loaf' with success for many years it does not follow that he knows anything about pictures. Yet we are asked to accept some sixty canvases from Mr. Tate, build for them a palatial gallery, and presumably reward the generous donor with a peerage . . . And now the sixty pictures go begging, and can find no roof to hide their shame under. For which the art world offers many and fervent thanks, for indeed the pictures are sad examples of the worst style . . .[25]*

Finally it was agreed that the old prison on Millbank could be converted into a gallery, and the money and the collection were graciously accepted. Poynter, in his dual role, was to be in charge of the new space as well: the Royal Academy, through the Chantrey Bequest, was to control the financing of new purchases; the National Gallery was to donate works from its collection. Poynter and his colleagues finally decided that the work of British artists born after 1790 would go to the Tate. This would enable the National Gallery to keep all its Turners and Constables – a major sticking point. It was not only Poynter who felt that the Tate was a dumping ground for the second rate. Alfred de Rothschild, one

---

* The quality of Tate's pictures is still open to question. Certainly his tastes were what today we would see as old-fashioned, and heavily influenced by the Royal Academy exhibitions of the day. The bulk of the collection was made up of landscapes, animal studies and genre pictures with titles like *A Foregone Conclusion* and *Faults on Both Sides*. But the pictures were admired as examples of their kind. Luke Fildes's picture *The Doctor* was considered a masterpiece when it was first shown, and through much of the remainder of the century. Even now, of Tate's initial donation, Millais's *Ophelia* and J. W. Waterhouse's *Lady of Shallot* are two of the gallery's images most loved by the public.

of the National Gallery's six trustees, 'objected *in toto* to the English pictures going to *enrich Mr. Tate's* Gallery, but afterwards qualified it by saying that if there were any pictures that were not worth keeping here that we wished to get rid of there was no objection to sending them down to the Embankment'.[26] When the Burne-Jones Memorial Fund presented the nation with *King Cophetua and the Beggar Maid* in 1900, it specifically noted that it wished the picture to be hung at the National Gallery for six months.[27]

Unlike his uncle's, Phil decided that his career was not getting on as it should. He knew that his social life was taking up far too much of his time and energies, and decided to go to Brussels for a while, as Rudyard wrote – astonished – to Charles Eliot Norton, '*in earnest* to study from the life'. Rudyard added, 'I can't fit Phil and Brussels together somehow. Has there any news come to your folk *why* he has done this'?[28] There is no answer surviving, but one possibility was Phil's lack of success with women. In his late twenties and early thirties, Georgie wondered 'what daughter of Heth Phil will present to us'. Now he was heading towards forty, and 'He does not seem ever to think of marrying.'[29] There are odd references scattered in his parents' letters – Frances Horner is unkind to him, or 'he is making up his sorrowful mind for flight' (from what?). Burne-Jones wrote to May Gaskell, 'How good of you to write to Phil, in his loneliness – oh dear, this hardish time will be the best thing in the whole world for him . . .' The veiled allusions suggest various entanglements, even while he is always reported to be alone – 'not that I think he will ever marry now – he seems to dread it so'.[30] Margaret and Jack Mackail had had a third child, Clare, in 1896, but Phil never even reached the 'possible' stage with anyone.

That same year Rudyard and Carrie had also had another baby, Elsie, but otherwise things were not going smoothly for them. The relationship between Carrie and her brother, Beatty, was deteriorating fast. Carrie was a control freak, wanting – needing – everything to be just so. She was formal, distant, aloof. Beatty was a drinker, a convivial, muddling type, liked by everyone, but not up to much. He was also careless with money – his own and others'. Despite having been paid by the Kiplings for the work he had done on Naulakha, he was permanently broke, and in March

1896 a petition of bankruptcy was filed against him. The banks were moving in, and at their suggestion Rudyard found a Dun and Bradstreet reporter, George Calvin Carter, to look at Beatty's situation. Carter said:

I had never seen anything like the financial situation in which he was floundering. His statements were wild, far from the truth and his values based on what he imagined he could sell the items for . . . He did not know how much he owed and he did not care . . . I rounded up all of Beatty's liabilities including some he had forgotten about and reported to Kip that his brother-in-law was hopelessly insolvent but did not know it, and that in business matters, because he was a dreamer . . . he would end up in bankruptcy. I told Kip that in my judgement he was stuck for every note he had endorsed.

As for Beatty . . . I found him increasingly loud and noisy, explosive, sarcastic, bombastic and brutal. In spite of Caroline's apologies for him and her attempts to bring him to his senses, I predicted he would grow worse rather than better.[31]

More important than his finances was that several times, in Carter's hearing, Beatty threatened to kill his brother-in-law. Rudyard wrote of violence on the North-West Frontier, but he knew nothing of it in actuality. He believed Beatty, and when Beatty cornered and threatened him on a lonely road he had him charged with 'assault with indecent and opprobrious names and epithets and threatening to kill'. Rudyard could only lose, even if he won. Journalists began to circle, scenting a good story. The rich man oppressing his poor brother-in-law was never likely to go down well, and when Beatty, in a stroke of public-relations genius, refused to pay a bond, and said he would rather go to jail, Rudyard saw what was ahead. As usual, he had worried himself into a state approaching breakdown. Finally, in June, he and Lockwood de Forest fled to the Gaspé Peninsula in Quebec to do some fishing. Carrie hoped he would there 'gain . . . some of the nerve and strength which was frittered away in so unworthy a cause'.[32]

He didn't, and in August the Kiplings packed up for England. Ostensibly it was for a change of air, a change of scenery; in reality it was headlong flight. They left all their possessions behind, planning to rent a house in England on a temporary basis, but they never came back to Naulakha, where they had hoped to raise a family and grow old. By September 1896 they were installed in a house near Torquay, chosen by Carrie and located, one assumes, to be out of visiting distance of Alice. Torquay was a strange place to settle on – Rudyard loved the sea, but there was nothing and nobody familiar there. Rottingdean, also near the sea, had Rudyard's much-loved aunt and uncle, and was far enough away from Tisbury to be safe for Carrie. Carrie was perhaps more like Alice than she would have cared to think: Alice had possibly chosen to live in Tisbury for the same reasons.

One thing that may have ruled out Rottingdean was that the Burne-Joneses, in London, were completely taken up by the sad decline of William Morris. A month after the Kiplings moved to Torquay, Burne-Jones was writing to Mary Gladstone Drew, 'My dear friend, I should have written . . . but I am in such distress of mind that all business is very difficult for me – I am afraid my dear Morris is drawing near to an end – I cannot leave him or go away at all . . . I dare not go away.'[33]

In 1891 Jenny had had a serious attack of brain fever. Morris had always been close to his desperately afflicted daughter, and after she recovered he himself became ill: 'the shock of Jenny's illness was too much for him . . . he is much better, but not nearly recovered . . . I fear it will be a long time before he is anything like his former self.'[34] He never did become his former self. 'I cannot say that I think I am better since I saw you a week ago', he wrote to Georgie in April 1896, 'but I hope I am no worse.'[35] In June 1896 he was taken down to Folkestone for sea air. It did not answer, and in July he was sent off on a cruise, which produced no better results.

Janey and Georgie had never had any particular fondness for one another – their husbands were close, Georgie and Morris were close, but Janey's friendships with Rossetti and Blunt, and with others such as Ford Madox Brown, who disliked Burne-Jones, kept them apart. They grew no more affectionate now. Janey wrote to Blunt, 'Georgy Burne-Jones has passed the last four days with us – she proposed having a nurse, which gave great offence – she considered that his food was not always as carefully selected as it ought to be, which is true enough, but no nurse could force him to eat what he refuses to look at.'[36] It does not sound as if Georgie had been particularly tactful. Had her anxiety for the man who had loved her so faithfully for so long made her even more direct than usual? Or had Janey been wounded as she watched the husband she had betrayed for the last twenty-five years find comfort in the nearness of his dearest friend? In September, a month before his death, his final letter to Georgie arrived. It read in its entirety, 'Come soon. I want a sight of your dear face.'[37] Morris was valiant to the end. His last letter was to Jenny and ended with a heart-rending postscript: 'I believe I am somewhat better.'[38]

He was not. On 3 October 1896 he died. Burne-Jones cried and told Georgie, 'I am quite alone now. Quite, quite',[39] which, hurtful to one's wife at any time, was a body blow right after her own loss of her friend. (This may partly be the reason for her sharp comment in a letter to Charles Eliot Norton the following year: '[Morris's] death has left Edward a very lonely man in his work.'[40] Only in his work, not in his life? Or was the loss of a friend, rather than a colleague, hers alone?) Georgie had never attended church services on a regular basis since leaving her father's house, but her belief in God, and in the afterlife, was strong. When Charles Eliot Norton's sister had died, she had told him:

I have given over wondering at any death or seeking to explain it to myself but year by year feel more certainty of life beyond it. I think about it very often, for myself as well as for others, and cannot feel a dread of it . . . How often I have recalled what you once said about the value of the love of those our own age – soon after your chief loss ★ – it is worse to lose it than anything – but we must follow out the story.[41]

Georgie had 'hopes that go beyond [death]',[42] but death was ever present with her. She confessed to Rosalind Howard, nearly thirty years after the event, that 'I had a little shadowy babe before I knew you, that stayed with us three weeks, though I was too ill to know anything clearly about it – but as every year comes round I keep its birthday and death day and a shadowy son of seven and twenty

★ Norton's wife had died five years before.

sometimes exists a moment for me.'[43] In this Georgie was old-fashioned. Earlier in the century families wrote memorials, a sort of detailed diary of days spent at the deathbed, describing the religious resignation which the dying showed, and also recording their physical deterioration. These memorials were kept and treasured, to be reread for spiritual comfort in later years. Georgie's remembrance of her dead baby is much more like Hannah's ceremonial noting of her daughter's death than the behaviour of a contemporary. The Earl of Carlisle, just before his own death, remarked that 'no one ought to be called on to see a man die'.[44]

Burne-Jones, in keeping with his times, wrote to Carlisle quite sparely:

Morris died this morning. Since Tuesday a change came and we all saw that the end was near, it came today and yesterday I saw him for the last time. I don't think there was much pain ever – but the weakness was pitiful and for the last day or two I do not think he knew us. A loving band of friends nursed him and sat up with him at night always.

Georgie was more expansive, in the old way:

I write for Janey, to tell you of the death of our dear Morris. It was 20 minutes past 11 this morning, in the most blessed peace and quiet. There was a relapse, with fresh haemorrhage on Tuesday last – he was put into his bed, and there was no rallying power. But he will never die, and we who are still here will talk of him and keep his memory green as long as there is one of us to do it.[45]

Her feeling was that this was the way to handle death; talking about death and the dead kept them alive. She wrote to May Morris, who had not been at the deathbed, 'Darling May, I am coming to you on Monday – with a heart full of love, and I shall be able to talk to you about your dear father's most painless leaving of this life where he has worked so gloriously. Let us all give thanks for him.'[46] After his funeral, she said, 'now we turn from his grave and find him still living'.[47] To ensure this continued, his friends and Janey planned for a biography celebrating his life and work to be begun right away.

Less than a year after Morris's death, Jack Mackail had been chosen as biographer. Now fissures that Morris's personality had kept in check began to open. Janey refused to allow the Icelandic journals that Morris had kept and given to Georgie (not, of course, to his wife) to be included, or printed separately. 'Affairs here have been discouraging,'[48] Georgie confided to Sydney Cockerell (who during Morris's lifetime had been the Kelmscott Press's secretary; since then he had become the executor of Morris's estate, and secretary to Janey's lover, Wilfrid Scawen Blunt).* Janey kicked up again when it became clear that Mackail was going to note in passing in the biography that she had been born into the working class. She even objected to the inclusion of a picture of the house from which she married, as being too much of a giveaway of her earlier social status. In general, Morris's death released her. She told Blunt three days after Morris's death that she had never loved her husband. Blunt was also unsparing of Morris's reputation. He wrote in his diary:

He was not selfish in the sense of seeking his own advantage or pleasure or comfort but he was too absorbed in his own thoughts to be either affectionate or actively kind. I suppose he had affection for Burne-Jones, they saw each other constantly and spent their Sunday mornings always together and I have seen him tender to his daughter Jenny and nice with her and with his wife but I doubt if he thought of them much when he did not see them and his life was not arranged in reference to them . . .

Phil with whom I had also a private talk gave me curiously enough, the exact same impression of Morris as that which I wrote in this diary yesterday, his impersonality, his lack of personal affection for anyone except perhaps for his, Phil's, father. 'As for myself,' he said, 'he took no interest in me at all. Not long ago I tried to cheer him by talking of this, that and the other, the theatres and amusements and at the end of half an hour, he said bluntly, "there is not a single thing in all you have been telling me which interests me in the smallest degree, I wish there were not such things as amusements".' Phil is humble about himself and very careful and good about his father. His father dropped his

* In 1908 he was made director of the Fitzwilliam Museum.

napkin at luncheon and Phil at once jumped up and picked it up for
him.[49]

Phil was humble and good when comparing himself to his father,
and to his father's great friend, but it is hardly surprising that a man
on his deathbed should baulk at having to listen to gossip about
people he had cared nothing for even when he had been in full
health.

Phil was beginning to be someone everyone was a little
contemptuous of. Rudyard wrote him off as 'fat and forty' (he
was thirty-five – four years older than Rudyard). He painted a
few society portraits, but, despite his time working in Brussels,
was going round in circles. He knew it himself. As he once
wrote to Henry James, having found him out when he called,
'Well, I deserved no better luck, but I've been so accustomed
all my life to getting more than my deserts, that I feel it just the
same.'[50]

The Ruddies, as Georgie called them, had now given up Torquay
as too wet and dismal, and in May 1897 had been invited to stay at
North End House while Carrie awaited the birth of their third
child. They accepted with pleasure, although that did not stop
Carrie complaining that 'the house is beyond words inconvenient
there is no bathroom, the nurseries are on the 3rd floor the kitchen
a cellar really in the basement'.[51]* Josephine was sent with her
governess to Alice and Lockwood for the duration. Aged four, she
was the centre of Rudyard's existence. His letters are full of her
sayings and doings, and she does appear to have been delightful. The
governess was an innovation, he reported: 'We've got a governess to
look after Josephine, only Josephine doesn't exactly see it that way.
She prefers looking after the governess, and that bewilders the
governess.'[53] She had recently paid her first visit to friends, and
'came back inarticulate with delight – a small flushed woman
of the world'.[54] It was therefore judged that she would enjoy

---

* Carrie's odd, breathless style and lack of punctuation are reproduced exactly.
She wrote to a friend at one point that 'I wouldn't marry a literary man for the
world. They are always doing too much and one can only give them help by
being hopelessly dull, so they may rest their minds in the security of our stupidity.'
Carrie was not stupid, although she was not remotely literary.[52]

her visit to her grandparents while her parents waited for the new baby.

Rudyard was superficially deprecatory when the new baby, John, arrived in August 1897.* He wrote to Jack Mackail: 'Tell [Denis] John snorts. This will fix John in his mind and indeed John does precious little else. He has ferocious eyebrows and doesn't say grace before meals . . . John is no fairy-floweret either, but rather in the nature of a reddish pig.'[55] Delighted as he was to have a son, he was enchanted with his girls. He wrote to Alfred that 'after all it takes a lot to beat a daughter. I saw the meeting between your two grandbabies and our Elsie – all three in p'rams. They hauled alongside like Roman galleys . . . and solemnly and systematically began to try to pull each other overboard.'[56]

Georgie may have been glad of the distraction at home. Her husband, desolate at the loss of Morris, was – as always – writing half a dozen times a day to another woman. Her son had no career, no desire other than to shine in society, no motivation: 'His very love and reverence for his father', she noted, 'has in a way crippled him.'[57] Her daughter was wrapped up in her own husband and her babies. Her eldest grandchild, spoilt silly by Burne-Jones,† was turning into what at the time would have been called a proper little madam. (Aged seven, Angela looked at a family portrait and commented, 'Why do I look so defiant? & Clare so hopeless? & Den like a cowering stag? We all look like something except Ba [Mackail]. He's not there.'[58] It is not surprising that her Baldwin and Kipling cousins nicknamed her A.K.B. – Angela Knows Best.)

One response was for Georgie to occupy herself more fully outside her home than she ever had before. She claimed constantly that she rarely went out – 'it is entirely out of my way', and 'the habit is formed of not going about much'[59] – and Burne-Jones emphasized her 'little store of strength', which 'she spends . . . in five minutes'. It may have been the case that she was frail. What is

---

*Rudyard and Carrie followed the Kipling family tradition of alternating the names John and Joseph down the generations. John Lockwood Kipling had named his son Joseph Rudyard.

†Burne-Jones and Gladstone used to compete to see who indulged their grandchildren more. Burne-Jones won hands down when he said he took Angela her breakfast in bed.

much more likely is that she was venturing out of the house on projects of her own for the first time, and he didn't like it: 'Nor will she be advised or coerced – boundless liberty is her motto and badge.'[60] As well as the local council in Rottingdean, she joined the council of management of the South London Fine Art Gallery, a community project being set up in Camberwell.

This – one of the first local community projects – had started life in a small shop; then, as artists were induced to lend pictures, it gained its own premises. Gradually a council was formed, consisting of Leighton (in the few months until his death), Watts and his wife, Sir James Linton, Sir Wyke Bayliss, president of the Royal Society of British Artists, Walter Crane, president of the Arts and Crafts Exhibition Society, and the Burne-Joneses. Despite Leighton heading the committee, it all became a little too radical for Burne-Jones, and he was not interested in public works anyway. Crane had been a stalwart of Morris's socialist days, and under the influence of Georgie and Crane the gallery added a library for the local community. Eventually the building included the Arts and Crafts School of Camberwell, and the plan was to re-form it and hand it over to the local council. Crane and Georgie begged and borrowed pictures from artists and patrons, and persuaded Poynter (both Georgie's brother-in-law and Crane's friend and mentor) to reopen it in its new municipal reincarnation.

All this was a distraction from home, where Burne-Jones was writing to May Gaskell, 'Ah me, I do hate marriage and I think it a wicked mechanical device of lawyers for the sake of property and such beastliness.'[61] He acknowledged, at least implicitly, that he had not treated Georgie well – 'I have been a bad man and sorry for it, but not sorry enough to try to be a good one.'[62] He was not even sorry enough to treat Georgie kindly in his letters to May. Instead they are a litany of complaint. After a visit to the Grange, he wrote:

Were you in time for your music? The crimes of this house are multiplying – a nasty room to take you into – a watch that doesn't watch but cheats and makes you late – a drawing room that makes you say 'O for God's sake take me out of this, the upstairs room is better.' I'm very sorry. But I never thought it was good enough for you.

Georgie's faults were legion. She didn't dress properly – 'she gets horrid hats and bonnets – Baptist bonnets she gets – midland counties Nonconformist hats and bonnets and frocks she always gets'. When other people made unpleasing comments, it was somehow her fault:

Yesterday [Angela] tucked me up warmly and fondly on the sofa, and when she had finished she crept up to my ear and whispered 'You won't let any of the others – no other little girl – wrap you up, will you?' . . . Where can she get that turn of jealousy from? It must come from Mackail's family – or perhaps Georgie's – I have little sympathy with it.

And, most unkindly, even in his dreams somehow Georgie failed to live up to his needs: 'I seldom dream of anyone I love – have never yet dreamed of Margaret – sometimes of Georgie who is always unkind in dreams.'[63]★

We have no idea how May responded to these letters – after the Mary Zambaco crisis was precipitated by Georgie finding a letter in his pocket, Burne-Jones had learned to be careful. He told May that he only ever had her last two letters, which he kept until another one came; then he destroyed the first: 'it always hurts but is best'.[64] Georgie, for her part, had stopped caring. After May visited one day when she was out, and Burne-Jones gave her a shawl of Georgie's, he simply reported that she thought the gesture 'nice'. Which may or may not have been the case. Ten years before she had written to Charles Eliot Norton that in Burne-Jones 'There is somewhere, deep within, a spirit of eternal youth, which, having never been clothed upon with mortal body, cannot grow old. This me, which grows old, goes to look at it sometimes – unlocks the garden, unseals the fountain, and then, having seen that the spirit is still there, closes both again, and goes on its way.'[65] One reading of this is that Burne-Jones was eternally young; another that he was

---

★ It may not have been to May only that Burne-Jones confided this sort of thing. Frances Horner's niece by marriage told me that she had been told by her husband that Georgie Burne-Jones was a terrible liar. There is simply no evidence of this anywhere – every single source testifies to Georgie's almost painful veracity. Given that Frances Horner's main connection to the family was Burne-Jones himself, this piece of information could have come from only one place.

permanently adolescent, always longing for what he could not have, while she had moved on, and away from him.

His letters to May were now full of little jokes and stories that seem aimed at underscoring this latter impression:

I heard yesterday of a widower ... on the day of the funeral of the departed he was proceeding to enter one of the coaches when the undertaker rushed to intercept him, observing that it was customary in such a case for the widower to ride with his mother-in-law. 'Indeed,' said the functionary, 'it is *de rigueur*. It would be much commented on if you were not so accompanied.' 'Then all I can say is,' said the bereaved one, 'my day is spoilt.'[66]

It is only a funny story, but when added to other remarks he made to Georgie – he asked her if she thought marriage was a lottery, and when she said yes, said, 'Then as lotteries are illegal, don't you think it ought to be suppressed by law?'[67] – and to his studio assistant, Thomas Rooke, it indicates a very decided viewpoint. He told Rooke that 'A painter ought not to be married'; that 'There will have to be a separation of things that a man does because of a woman from other faults he may have'; and that 'Women ought to be locked up. In some place where we could have access to them but they couldn't get out from.'[68]

Perhaps Burne-Jones's thoughts on his life were best summed up in a sort of coded letter to May:

I am so tired suddenly of all the past years – of the long years between twenty years ago and two years ago – tired of them as if they had worn me out – which is silly, for they are past – but I don't want to think of one hour of them – nor of one hour of the seven years before that – I have but my work to show for those years – of life I had none – nor any happy hour to remember and think upon. – but there were eleven years that were bonny years and of those I love to think – years of the beginning of art in me and Gabriel every day, and Ruskin in his splendid days and Morris every day and Swinburne every day, and a thousand visions in me always, more real than the outer world – and eleven years is a great number of years to have been happy in.[69]

The code is simple, although it was not one that May could have been expected to understand: 'two years ago' was when Burne-Jones had met May; 'twenty years ago' and 'the seven before that' take him back to 1868, when he first broke with Mary Zambaco, after which he had had not one 'happy hour to remember'. The eleven 'bonny' years were from the time he and Morris came to London to the end of his relationship with Mary Zambaco.

Perhaps his most cutting comment on the state of his marriage in 1896 was to Georgie's friend Sally Norton:

We have had a poor time this year – Georgie has borne her fate, how 'nobly' you can guess – I bore mine very badly – I was so sorry for Ned – he lay on a sofa for nearly two months – doing nothing but being sorry for Ned – a poor occupation. As for competing with Georgie it can't be done.[70]

After his death, Georgie, in her very quiet way, was even more damning. She wrote to Val Prinsep, 'It *was* a good time for about three years, '56–'59, wasn't it?'[71]

IV

Old Age and Death

15. 'A pack of troubles'
1898–1906

Burne-Jones had a wife everyone admired, although he was unhappy. By contrast Rudyard had a wife few liked, while he relished his married state. After Rudyard and Carrie's son was born at North End House, where they had been so happy, they decided that the Elms, across the road, at three guineas a week, should be their permanent home. Rudyard wrote to a friend:

I believe it is good for all but a few men who are bachelors by instinct to be married after a decent and discreet age and in our business more than in any other who gets himself a good wife gets a good thing ... If marriage makes your life to you one half as good and wholesome as it has made mine to me, you'll be blessed.[1]

Mary Cabot had already noted in Vermont how much of his daily life Rudyard placed in Carrie's management; he told her, 'I am no more than a cork on the water, when Carrie is with me.'[2]

He may have bobbed along in her wake, but Carrie felt the weight of managing things. Rudyard's mood had not picked up after the Vermont breakdown, and it was suggested that a winter in England was not going to do him much good. They decided to go to South Africa for four months, taking Lockwood with them, and Carrie told Meta de Forest, '[Rudyard] won't go without me and I can't leave the children – so we all go and what an undertaking it is ... It must be done and so I am doing it.'[3] This is a summary of the marriage: he couldn't manage without her; she could manage, but not manage to enjoy managing. It is true that they didn't exactly travel light – 'two wheels, some baby carriages, and about half a ship load of baggage'[4] – on the other hand, Carrie didn't exactly do it single-handedly: they took with them a nursemaid, a governess and Carrie's maid.

Before they set off they spent Christmas 1897 at the Elms. Lockwood and Alice came from Tisbury, and brought Trix and

Jack Fleming with them. The Flemings had arrived back in England for a long home leave a few weeks before. They had a family reunion to celebrate, and also Trix's second novel, *A Pinchbeck Goddess*, had just been published, this time under her own name (with a bit of reflected glory from Rudyard's: 'by Mrs J. M. Fleming (Alice M. Kipling)' coyly declared the title page, and the book was dedicated 'To my Brother Rudyard').

The story was similar to that of *The Heart of a Maid*: an unhappy young girl, who is brought up this time by an unkind and repressive aunt, eventually meets and falls in love with an artist. There is a parallel story of a couple in an unhappy marriage, and it is tempting to read into this a commentary on Trix's own state. The husband feels it 'his duty to discipline' his wife, and 'She was growing accustomed to her image as he showed it to her in the distorting mirror of his mind.' He bullies and punishes her, often refusing to speak to her for days. Many years later, Trix's great-nephew Colin MacInnes* felt that the couple were very probably a portrait of his great-aunt and -uncle. According to MacInnes, by the time he knew them Trix had the upper hand. Jack Fleming

was that much mocked, admirable personage, the English – or Scottish – military gentleman: kind, good, honest, unimaginative and timid. And how aunt Trix teased him, cruelly almost, like a cat with sharpened fangs! Always arriving late for meals (which exasperated him), her breast clattering with necklaces, her fingers glittering with rings, she talked, and talked, and darted witty shafts, and chattered on and on until he cried out in despair, like an Old Testament prophet in the depths of torment, 'Oh, woman! Woman!' Whereupon she wore a sweet smile and raised her brows.[5]

This was, of course, nearly half a century later; it is revealing, nonetheless.

Perhaps as a result of being together in Rottingdean, Phil and Rudyard started to get on better once more. Rudyard had been inclined to dismiss him – that phool Phil – but now he agreed to a

* MacInnes, Angela's son by her first marriage, became a cult novelist of the new black youth culture of London in the 1950s. His best-known books are *City of Spades*, *Absolute Beginners* and *Mr Love and Justice*.

collaboration. For a while Phil had been a follower of Mrs Patrick Campbell, and for a while she had responded to his overtures. Then he was suddenly dropped, without ever knowing why (according to his account). He planned a vampire picture which some saw as a 'spiritual' portrait of Mrs Campbell, revenge for her treatment of him. It is probable that Rudyard was not aware of the subtext when in 1897 he agreed to write verses to go with it.★ After all, Phil's pictures were shown in all the right places – his portrait of his father was about to be sent to the Royal Academy. ('I hear from my uncle (Poynter, the President) that they have given it a very good place,' Phil importantly told Norton.)[6] When Phil not only asked him to sign 250 prints, but also to write a formal guarantee that he would not sign any more, thus increasing the value of the limited edition, Rudyard began to get a little tetchy. The picture was a scandal for a while, although it did nothing for Phil's career – a year later he wrote, 'The Show has *not* been a success . . . It was just a chance – it *might* have "caught on".'[7] *The Vampire* didn't sell either – three years later, in New York, Phil was still trying to find a customer for it.

Rottingdean quietened down after Christmas. The Ruddies went to South Africa with Lockwood; Alice returned to Tisbury; the Baldwin cousins left the Ridsdales and went back to Worcestershire. Even Georgie, tired out by the long winter, in January went on one of her rare trips abroad. The year before, when she had failed to persuade Burne-Jones to leave his work (and May), she and Cockerell had gone on a cathedral tour to Abbeville, Amiens and Beauvais. This year Burne-Jones again insisted on staying at home, so Phil took Georgie to Bordighera, on the Italian Riviera, where Janey Morris and the Howards used to winter. George Macdonald, Fred's son, was there, and Georgie spent five months in the sun: the most time she had spent apart from Burne-Jones in their entire marriage.

She returned in the summer of 1898, and divided her time

★ The verses have long survived the nine days' wonder of the picture. The poem is called 'The Vampire', and it begins, 'A Fool there was and he made his prayer/ (Even as you and I!)/To a rag and a bone and a hank of hair/(We called her the woman who did not care)/But the fool he called her his lady fair –/(Even as you and I!)'

between Rottingdean and the Grange as she had before. Burne-
Jones was working feverishly on a big canvas, and it was only with
great difficulty that he could be persuaded to spend some time in
Rottingdean, resting – his health was once more giving cause for
concern. In London on 16 June 1898 the Burne-Joneses' friend and
the Kiplings' Tisbury neighbour, Percy Wyndham, called, and
spent the afternoon with Burne-Jones, who was in high spirits,
playing 'Bear' on the carpet with the children. That night he awoke
in pain. He called for Georgie, who went to him, and 'before
doctor or child could come he had answered the call and was gone'.
'O, what a kindness to let him die alone in my arms.'[8]

Georgie accepted his death with the same 'air of determined
resignation' as she had accepted Morris's two years before: 'We
must pay for the wine we have drunk,' was all she said.[9] Burne-
Jones's body was cremated – a new practice, and one usually
requested only by atheists. Cremation had not been permitted in
England until 1884, and it was performed now at Burne-Jones's
own desire. He and Georgie had different views from the general
on the subject: Georgie later referred to cremation as being 'purified
by fire'.[10] Phil brought the ashes down to Rottingdean, and the
family began to gather. The Mackails, Rudyard and Carrie were
already there. Alfred, Louie and Stan went to the Ridsdales; Lockwood, Poynter, Agnes and Ambo, Fred and two of his sons came
down on the day of the funeral. Neither Alice nor Edie travelled
to Rottingdean; instead Edie went to Tisbury, where they spent
the day together.

The ashes were taken to the church the night before; Phil,
Mackail, the Burne-Joneses' friend Harry Taylor, Stan and Alfred
took it in turns to keep watch through the night. In Stan's watch,
between two and four a.m., so Rudyard told Norton, Georgie and
Margaret came in, 'all in white to watch a little and dear old Stan
said he felt like a profane heathen and crept out till they called him
back. I can believe it for her face in daylight was like nothing
earthly.'[11] The next day the Brighton to Rottingdean omnibus,
which normally circled the green several times, with Scribbets
playing his horn, suspended its service. Phil and Margaret carried
the ashes to a grave that had been lined with roses and moss – they
wanted his family to take him to his final rest. Ruskin had sent

forget-me-nots, Watts a laurel wreath. Georgie stood at the head of the grave with her eyes closed; then she knelt, and was left to be alone with her husband for the last time.

It was the beginning of a long series of disasters. By the end of the year, Georgie had decided to leave the Grange and move entirely to Rottingdean, where there were no uncomfortable memories. She arranged to keep the garden studio at the Grange, but in December 1898 she left her home of thirty years. 'The pain of leaving the Grange is great,' she told Mary Gladstone Drew. Like Rudyard and Stan, she believed that the painful path was the one to choose, and, despite the trauma of the move, 'I do not doubt that it is right and best for me to go.'[12] Nevertheless, she was so overwhelmed by losing her home that, when Trix became ill, she was not able to help Alice at all.

In India, Trix had pursued her mother's interest in spiritualism much further. She had experimented not only with table-turning and with crystal balls, but also with more troubling aspects of the occult, including 'withdrawing her spirit from her body'. Years later she described how,

withdrawing one day, in spirit, from her bodily shell, she found to her horror, when she had wished to return, so to speak, inside herself, that powerful occult forces barred her way: which had kept her painfully suspended in the cosmos for many years . . . when she described this experience . . . she did so (though the details of her voyage into space seemed vague, not to say incomprehensible) with a total and sincere conviction . . .[13]

It was her immersion in the occult that her father and brother blamed for the crisis that now descended.

In December 1898 Trix had some sort of psychotic breakdown. Various diagnoses have been suggested in retrospect – schizophrenia, manic depression – and there is, of course, no way of knowing which is correct. The symptoms were distressing: they ranged from mutism to hyper-manic states in which she did not stop talking, mostly nonsense. She refused all food, and at one point appears to have been nearly catatonic. At first she was treated by a man described by one of Rudyard's biographers as a 'quack', who taught at the Camberwell School of Arts and Crafts and believed that diet and massage would solve the problem.[14] Given his workplace, it is likely that Georgie initially recommended him.

Within weeks the acknowledgement that Trix had a serious mental illness could no longer be avoided, and she was sent to a private hospital in London, where she was force fed – although the doctor assured Jack that they had not had to use 'much' force. The problem for the family was twofold. First was money. The place she was in cost nearly 16 guineas a week, or well over £800 a year – an unsustainable sum for an army officer or a retired civil servant. A private asylum would cost only half of that; the drawback was that for Trix to be placed there she would have to be certified as insane, and her husband and her parents all baulked at that. The more serious problem was Alice. She felt she could look after Trix – that she was the only one who could. Trix reinforced this by responding savagely every time she saw Fleming – sometimes with violence. For the moment Fleming prevailed and she stayed in London under the care of her doctor.*

Rudyard did not appear to feel himself intimately involved with his sister's problems. There is no indication now or later that he offered to help financially – it is perfectly clear, in fact, that no such offer was made, as paying for Trix's medical care was her husband's main problem for years after. Instead, in February 1899 Rudyard decided to return to America for the first time since he had left Vermont so precipitately three years before. He had never sold his house there, and it is possible that he was returning to see if things had calmed down enough for the family to move back.

As usual, the whole family travelled together. Shortly after their arrival in New York, the papers announced that Beatty, always one to embrace trouble, was to bring an action for $50,000 against Rudyard, for malicious persecution, false arrest and defamation of character. No such action was ever brought, and it was unlikely that it ever could have been brought, but the threat kept the feud

---

* At one point Trix was treated by George Savage, who as well as being the superintendent of Bethlem, the lunatic asylum, was also Virginia Woolf's doctor in 1904, when she had a breakdown following her father's death. Savage was liked by the families of his patients, as he diagnosed things like 'neurasthenia' and 'loss of nerve force', rather than insanity.

going, and kept Rudyard uncomfortably in the spotlight. Two weeks later, however, more important things were ensuring that Beatty became the least of the Kiplings' worries. A scrappy, scrawled note to Lockwood de Forest, from the Hotel Grenoble, where the family was staying, is the first evidence of a crisis: 'Dear Lock, Could you come up and see us, as soon as possible on receipt of this as we are in somewhat of a difficulty and naturally turn to you. Ever, Rud.'[15] This may have been a reference to the fact that the children had arrived in America with whooping cough, although Carrie was taking it calmly enough: 'we are comfortable even luxurious and hot pipes and bath rooms make it easier than it might be'.[16] Things moved quickly. A desperate note from Alice to Georgie was the first the family heard of real trouble: 'Dearest Georgie, I have just got a cablegram from New York, "Rud ill inflammation lung". She [Carrie] wouldn't have wired if he wasn't very ill I am sure. No address sent and I can do nothing. Your loving, Alice.' Then, scrawled across the bottom, a return to days when they were closer, and a sign of Alice's frantic anxiety: 'Tell sisters.'[17] It was a rare moment when family solidarity was assumed.

Rudyard had developed pneumonia, and was not responding well to treatment – for several weeks he lay delirious,* and it appeared impossible that he could survive. His fame was such that two dozen reporters camped in the hotel virtually day and night, waiting for bulletins.† Carrie was coping, as she always did, until Josephine developed pneumonia too. She could not look after both of them, and, as Rudyard was decidedly the iller, she asked Meta de Forest if she could take Josephine and nurse her at her home.

Agnes offered to go and stay with Alice, but by now the cry for her sisters was past and Alice wanted nobody except Trix and Lockwood – she could 'fight [her] dreadful anxiety best alone'.[18] Lockwood went to London to get Trix from the hospital, and the three of them sat together waiting for news. For weeks they waited

---

* In true writerly fashion, almost his first reaction on recovering was to get a stenographer and dictate what he could remember of his delirium.

† The degree of Rudyard's fame is unimaginable for a writer today. One indication of its extent is a postcard in the Unversity of Sussex's collection addressed, 'To Kipling, at England'. The Post Office had scribbled on it 'Try Burwash, Sussex', and, with no delay at all, it was delivered.

– Rudyard was a little worse, he might survive the night, he had survived the night. Then the crushing blow. Josephine, 'the apple of her father's eye – the delight of his heart'[19] – Josephine all at once got worse. Carrie visited two or three times a day, when she could be spared from Rudyard's side, and Dr James Conland, their friend and doctor from Vermont, went to stay with the de Forests, so someone Josephine knew would be with her. Suddenly, on 6 March, without her mother or her family near her, Josephine died. She was six years old. Rudyard was fighting for his life, and knew nothing. The entire responsibility for his health, and for her surviving children, ill themselves, and for Josephine's funeral, fell to Carrie.

Carrie was stoic – 'it must be done and so I am doing it' – and she

never lost her nerve for a moment and had in mind all the thousand and one matters which covered her husband's life and great fame and her children's welfare. She has eaten meals at regular times and done everything which intelligence could dictate to keep up her strength and spirits. I have never seen such a remarkable exhibition of pure nerve.[20]

As always with Carrie, however, even when she was rising to a crisis in a way no one could fault, she was prickly and difficult and just plain odd. She had called in Frank Doubleday, Rudyard's American publisher, to help her deal with the press and the various business matters that could not be postponed. Now she asked him to write to Alec Watt, Rudyard's agent, in England, who in turn was to write to Rudyard's parents. Watt relayed the letter's contents:

Mrs. Kipling has asked me to write to you and tell you . . . the history of these last terrible ten days. She would like to have you realize that she can never go back to this time of distress to discuss the matter or attempt to tell you what she has gone through. She has asked me to give you all the details which are essential, so that you may communicate them to Mr. and Mrs. Kipling.[21]

Carrie did not find the time – or have the desire – to write to her parents-in-law at all, although three days after she had instructed someone else to write to her in-laws she herself wrote to Georgie. The letter is distracted and disjointed, flicking madly between what is happening in New York and what needs to be done in Rottingdean – could Georgie pay the gardener, and Elsie and John are better, although 'They feel such a small family only 2 and so young . . . Love us hard we are in sad need of all you can give us.'[22] She never felt able to say this to Lockwood and Alice.

They themselves were suffering. Not only was Rudyard hovering on the edge of death, Trix, now at the Gables, was as ill as she had been in December. Alice told Georgie:

My poor Trix is with me, very very far from being herself. The mutism which was first so trying has changed to almost constant talk – and oh – my dear – nearly all nonsense. There are times in every day when she is her own bright self and then she suddenly changes and drifts away into a world of her own – always a sad one – into which I cannot follow her. If only I could keep her with me – but her husband is coming tomorrow to take her away . . . Oh, my Georgie my heart is bursting full – both my dear children so smitten – Did I tell you how I have been haunted by visions of the sunshine pouring into the empty rooms at the Elms . . .[23]

By the middle of March it was decided that they could find the money for Lockwood to go to New York. (It is interesting that Carrie did not feel the need to offer financial help, any more than Rudyard had earlier for Trix.) Sally Norton, who had gone to New York to support Carrie, reported on his arrival:

he looks as well and cheery as if he had not anxiety of late! Oh! That blessed English temperament, so steady, so matter of fact even and capable of achieving so much and repressing so much when the time comes. I could not but think of the contrast with Carrie's temperament as I observed Mr. Kipling, Carrie so splendidly restrained and self-controlled, but vibrating with sensitiveness and bodily worn by it.[24]

By now Rudyard had improved and was well enough to be told of Josephine's death. Carrie had kept it to herself for three weeks, and then she could bear it no longer. At first he was too ill to take it in.

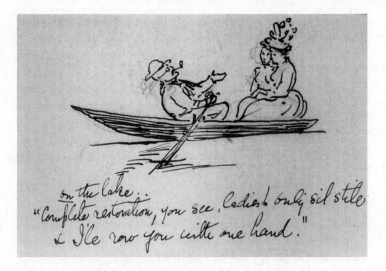

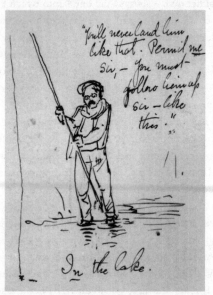

Kipling as seen by his father when recovering from pneumonia in 1899

Then, as he got stronger, the reality became stronger as well, and made it harder for him to fight off the depression that comes with near-fatal illness.

By April Kipling was well enough to be moved and he went first to New Jersey, to a hotel he and Carrie had stayed at in their Vermont days, then to friends nearby for a month, then to the Doubledays on Long Island.* It was only in June that he was well enough for the family to pack up to return to England. Their arrival back at the Elms was harder than they had expected. 'The house and garden are full of the lost child and poor Rud told his mother how he saw her when a door opened, when a space was vacant at table – coming out of every green dark corner of the garden – radiant and – heartbreaking.'[26] They could now talk about Josephine a little, even Carrie. Georgie mothered them – they went across the green to her every day, and she saw that Carrie was 'a very remarkable woman':[27] Georgie was one of the few people apart from Rudyard to see the good in her. Rudyard drew closer to Phil, who 'has a great capacity – under his half assumed triviality – for sympathy and affection. He is not the happiest of men these days. The superficial side of society which he has mainly cared to cultivate is somewhat arid and unsatisfactory diet for a continuance.'[28]

Alfred too recognized Carrie's worth, and he wrote her a moving letter: 'I can only say this, that after all you have done and passed through I hold you in a loving reverence that will last my life . . . God bless you.'[29] Others of the cousinhood showed up rather less well. After a visit to Alice in Tisbury, while Lockwood was in New York, Margaret wrote a rather formal little note of condolence, although not until nearly a month had passed. This may have triggered a dislike of the Mackail family that was to grow ever stronger, although Rudyard's love of Georgie prevented an open breach for many years. Lockwood too expressed his reservations about Mackail, and they were ones that Rudyard shared: 'I find his

---

* While at the Doubledays, Rudyard cheered up enough to print, on a toy printing set, the following 'biography' of George Putnam, whom Rudyard was suing over copyright infringements. (Rudyard later claimed this squib was not his, although Doubleday remembered it well.) 'Life of George Putnam. George Haven Putnam was born of poor but most disreputable parents. This was done in the retail department without his knowledge . . . Shortly after attaining his majority he was arrested for stealing a hymn-book from a dying Missionary. He defended his action on the ground of past labours in behalf of American copyright.'[25]

notions are on so lofty and merely academic a plane that they have
but little concern with any of the actualities of life and so don't
count.'[30]

Lockwood had reason to compare high-sounding ideas with
concern that involved practical help. Trix was once again much
worse, and had come back to Tisbury. In November Lockwood
reported that

We, our little family I mean, have been going through a pack of troubles,
– none the less grievous to be borne because they turn out to have been
mainly causeless. The brunt of the worst of it fell on me, and for a long
time I did nothing but attend to my burden. Things have cleared up at
last and we may fairly hope for peace. Meanwhile, I have lost a good deal
of my respect for the medical profession, and especially for those who
profess to know about the nerves and brain.

Also I have acquired some highly heretical notions about husbands and
their relatives. But since things seem to be turning out happily, I am
content to let my small resentments grow cold . . . I am these days a very
lonely man, I mean so far as *men* are concerned. I see only my wife and
daughter but fortunately I have some work to do.[31]

But, whatever Lockwood hoped, things were not clearing up.
At Rudyard's request, a specialist came to see Trix. He reported to
Jack Fleming that he had wanted Trix to go away with a nurse,

but to no purpose. Mrs. Kipling was on the verge of frenzy at any
suggestion of such a thing and Mr. Kipling, though ready to be firm
when he was with me, yielded before his wife's excitement at once . . .
[the nurse at Tisbury] is convinced that your wife will go on well now
with her mother, whose nervousness is less when they are quiet together
and is too familiar to your wife to have the harmful influence it would
seem, to a stranger, to be likely . . . Your wife is quite as determined not to
be separated from her mother as the latter is not to allow her to leave her.[32]

It is an interesting letter, for it makes Alice appear almost as ill as
Trix: 'frenzy', 'excitement', 'nervousness' – all these were words
that were normally applied to the mentally ill at the time, particularly to women, who were subject to what was then called hysteria.

In February 1900 Rudyard and Carrie invited Lockwood to travel to South Africa with them. (Rudyard was now forbidden to stay in England for the winters, and until the First World War he travelled regularly every year in search of sun.) Lockwood refused because '[I] could hardly leave Trix and her mother alone'.[33] Not just Trix. Not Alice with Trix. It now appeared that neither of them could be left. When the Ruddies returned from South Africa in the spring, things were no better. Carrie – who was, granted, an unsympathetic audience in matters relating to Alice – told Meta de Forest that Trix was worse again. 'It . . . is to be expected when you know nothing has been allowed to be done to cure her Mrs. K. will not have it so it is not done.'[34] And for the next two years Alice ruled, until the autumn of 1902, when it could no longer be denied that Trix was as well as she had ever been: nervy, easily excited, with, according to her doctors, 'intellectual activity, excessive in degree even for her' – but with no return of the psychotic episodes that had been so distressing four years earlier. There was at this point no further excuse for Alice, and Trix returned to Calcutta, with Alice 'low and dull in consequence'.[35]

Rudyard and Carrie were improving, too. Rudyard's health was better, although his spirits were not. At the end of Carrie's annual diary, where Rudyard was in the habit of writing a sentence to sum each year up, all he could manage in 1899 was 'I owe my life to Carrie.' A great compliment to Carrie, though five months before, in a letter to his old friend Edmonia Hill, he had indicated the value he placed on that life that Carrie had saved: 'this fool sickness of mine which had the bad taste to leave me and take my little Maiden'.[36]

Rudyard and Carrie never set foot in America again. They arranged for their old coachman, now acting as the caretaker at Naulakha, to bring them various sentimental pieces from the house, including a portrait of Josephine. Carrie sold the house and furniture to their friend Mary Cabot for $10,000 – much less than they had paid to build it. They may have welcomed the loss, just to close the American chapter altogether.

The Baldwins, when they visited Rottingdean, became part of the Kipling/Burne-Jones family life; otherwise they were very far away during these years. Alfred was concentrating on his businesses, and his parliamentary career. (Walter Long, a Unionist Cabinet minister, thought that, had he concentrated on politics with the devotion he had given his business career, Alfred could have been Chancellor of the Exchequer.) Stan was taking on more and more responsibilities from his father in both of these worlds. Cissie was pregnant for much of the time, and in 1899 their first son was born, after three daughters, which was a cause for celebration. For the most part the widening gap between the Mackails and Rudyard and Carrie was echoed with the Baldwins by Lockwood after Rudyard's return from America: 'Aunt Louie and Mr. Baldwin [*sic*] are struggling with the melancholy that seems to be settling on the latter. 'Tis very odd how piety, wealth and a loudly asserted trust in a personal deity seem to make some people apprehensive and gloomy.'[37] The distance the families had grown apart, and the traumas of the year, can be judged by the fact that there does not appear to be one surviving letter that mentions that in 1899 Fred was made president of the Methodist Conference. His parents would have been so proud to have seen their son reach such eminence; among the dozens of assorted Kiplings, Flemings, Burne-Joneses, Mackails, Poynters and Baldwins it passed completely unremarked.

Rottingdean, which had been a refuge from urban life, was being encroached upon more each day. Even when Burne-Jones was alive, modernization was creeping in. In the last years of his life he had spent some of his waning energy fighting off those who wanted to bring electricity to the village. He claimed that the electricity company would have put their 'engine' too close to North End House, and he took them to court over it. He won, and the plan was temporarily dropped. (He claimed that this gave him a taste for litigation: 'now I want to go to law again, and have actions right and left, so much have I caught the energy of the place. I want to have an action against a man here who has a vile expression on his face – and it is so injurious to my work that nothing short of heavy damages will content me.')[38] Then there was the 'Daddy Long-Legs', a sort of marine railway. Tracks were laid on concrete posts in the sea, and a small railway car ran along them from Brighton, carrying 150 people at a time to Rottingdean. Happily for Burne-Jones and the Kiplings, who were violently opposed to it, a storm damaged the tracks after only a week and the train never really ran properly after that. Not every incursion could be stopped, however: the sewer was relaid, meaning unpleasantness and disruption for everyone, and, even worse, day trippers from Brighton now began to invade the village on a regular basis – in default of the Daddy Long-Legs, by omnibus. Rudyard was particularly singled out: the driver of the omnibus, as it circled the green, pointed out his house to the curious. Others disturbed him as he fished off the pier, pestering him for autographs. (He dealt with this in an unusually practical manner. He signed a batch of autographs which he gave to the Rottingdean Rifle Club, and let it be known to anyone who wanted an autograph that they were being sold by the club to raise funds.)

Rottingdean's days as a retreat were over. In addition, Carrie and Rudyard suffered from memories of Josephine at the Elms. By the turn of the century they were looking for a new house – they ranged across the country from Sussex, through Wiltshire, to Somerset, often in Rudyard's latest toy, a motor car. Georgie went with them sometimes, valiantly, as she hated cars – his was the only one she ever went in. (And, in these early days of motoring, it is not hard to understand why. Rudyard wrote of a later car, 'She smells like a fried fish shop and spits her condenser water, boiling, over our knees.')[39]

Their relationship had become that of a mother and son. (As a grown man, Rudyard often signed his letters to Georgie 'your boy'; she acknowledged that 'They have been my very own children.')[40] It was a relationship that mothers and sons rarely have in reality – certainly not the kind Rudyard had with his own mother, or Georgie with her son. Perhaps it was in part because Carrie was equally fond of Georgie: Georgie reported that

For a long time they came to me *every* evening after dinner for an hour or two, and never once did she look at him as if to say 'let us go', much less utter the words – but left it to him always. She brought her sewing, the dear girl . . . and she worked and he and I played colerito, and we talked, and often laughed, and about 9.30 it was over. Never the shadow of a cloud came between us, nor did a thing happen that is not sweet to remember.[41]

Not something anyone could say about life with Alice.

Their one area of conflict – politics and, more precisely, the Boer War – they simply avoided as much as possible, like all the Macdonalds. War fever had swept the country, whirling everyone, including Rudyard and Carrie, into a patriotic fervour. No one was exempt. Children wore buttons showing their 'favourite' generals; they could buy a 'get the ball into the socket of the stick' game which had pictures of Boer leaders on the stick. If the ball fell into the socket, the Boer's teeth were knocked out.[42] When the town of Mafeking was relieved, in October 1900, after a nine-month siege, Britain celebrated as never before. Trains across the country blew their whistles all the way down the lines to let towns and villages know. Shops were opened in the middle of the night so that roaring crowds could buy bunting.[43] There were parades, banners, bonfires. When the news arrived at the Stock Exchange, trading was suspended as brokers and clerks sang patriotic songs together.

Georgie, however, was against British involvement in South Africa. Famously, after the news of Mafeking arrived, she hung a banner outside North End House which read, 'We have killed and also taken possession.' Rudyard had to go across the green and ensure that the enraged locals did not attempt violence. Her choice of wording for the banner is significant. The Methodist minister's daughter was never far from the surface, and to illustrate her political opposition she chose to quote 1 Kings 21, the story of Naboth's vineyard. When Naboth refuses to give his vineyard to the king, the king's wife, Jezebel, arranges for him to be killed so that the king can take over his land. The prophet Elijah warns the king, 'Thus saith the Lord, Hast thou killed and also taken possession? . . . Thus saith the Lord, In the place where dogs licked the blood of Naboth shall dogs lick thy blood . . .'

Rudyard rescued her that night and, again in Macdonald fashion, they kept silent on their differences. In December 1901 Georgie described the situation to Crom Price when

The Ruddies left for the Cape . . . this morning. He looks a great deal aged [since Josephine's death], to my eyes, but as loving as ever. O that he loved his fellow men enough to give them their own space in the world! We *never* mention the War – and he must feel that gap that this means just as much as I do – but somehow we go on caring more and more for each other, notwithstanding.[44]

The conflict remained ever present: Rudyard in South Africa was producing a newspaper for the British troops, and 'It is one of life's griefs that on this subject the heart's division divides Ruddy and Carrie from me.'[45]

The Boer War continued the work of time and distance in separating the cousins from each other. Where Rudyard and Carrie did not have the great love that they had for Georgie, they were less forgiving. Margaret and Jack Mackail worked actively against the war, Margaret collecting clothes for Boer women and children. She felt, with Georgie, 'unhappy about the war, unhappy and ashamed'.[46] It is amazing that Georgie's politics did not completely destroy the bond she had with the Kiplings, for they were extreme for her class. When the 1905 revolution took place in Russia, she wrote to Sydney Cockerell, 'I too greatly fear that in a few days we shall be told "order has been restored". If only Finland would rise now (it is possible) and the news from St Petersburgh [*sic*] spread quickly to Moscow, and Moscow imitate, *perhaps* the soldiers will "fraternize" with the people and then a great thing would be seen . . .' And when the Bolshevik Revolution began in 1917, and everyone in Britain felt that this was the beginning of the end, she was 'rejoicing about Russia, and thankful. So far things have gone wonderfully well . . . God grant them strength and devotion to the last.'[47] However, when Rudyard wrote his will in 1936 he specified that no stocks in Russian companies were ever to be bought with any of his money.

In marked contrast to Alice, who confessed to never reading a paper, and Louie, who was now a stalwart of the Conservative wives, Georgie was becoming more radical as she grew older. Partly this was because she no longer had to keep her views from her husband, who would have objected to them most vehemently; partly it was her inheritance from Morris. It was also that, for the first time, she was doing a solid piece of creative work. Soon after Burne-Jones died, she had decided to write a biography of him, as 'my share in raising a Cairn' to his memory.[48] This look back at the ideals of their youth may well have rekindled some of the excitement and hope for change they had been imbued with then.

Both Louie and Alice had ventured into print: Louie with her novels, Alice in verse published in magazines. In 1902 Alice and Trix published *Hand in Hand: Verses by a Mother and Daughter*, which was just what it said, the first half being Alice's verses to Trix, the second half Trix's to Alice, marking the end of Trix's long illness. Georgie had never been anything except Burne-Jones's helpmeet. She confessed to Norton, at the age of sixty-five, that 'Ever since I was 18 or 19 I have always greatly desired to write a novel, and have never ceased dealing in thought with a set of imaginary people.'[49] For years it was no more than this, and it was only a month before he died that she finally showed something to Burne-Jones. He admired it and encouraged her to write more. The year before he died, when perhaps she was working on this story, she was in correspondence with Cockerell about some cartoons of Burne-Jones's that had gone missing, and she added wistfully, 'How I wish I had done so much work in my life that a couple of things that size could slip out of sight and not be noticed doing it because of the abundance of others.'[50] With his death, perhaps because of the overwhelming amount Burne-Jones had done in comparison, instead of continuing with her story she put it aside and began to write about her husband. She found a fulfilment in the process that was rarely open to women: 'Never before had I undertaken a serious piece of work and carried it through; that alone is an epoch in anyone's life.'[51]

It was an epoch in her life and it was also a serious undertaking. Mackail – never one to praise anyone's writing without meaning it – told Cockerell, 'The more I see of it the more I am impressed by the genius (it is nothing less than that) which has gone to the making of it.'[52] If not genius, certainly art went into it. There was the detail to be gathered, selected and ordered to portray a long and active life, and there were also the details that had to be kept out. For example, Georgie told Norton that the break in the two volumes came when she was ill with scarlet fever before they moved to Kensington, when they left their early life behind. The break is actually after they moved to the Grange, between 1867 and 1868, during the time Burne-Jones was involved with Mary Zambaco – perhaps when Georgie left her youth behind.

In the meantime Georgie was losing a large part of her present. Rudyard and Carrie had found a house near Burwash, in Sussex, and not a moment too soon. Rudyard had apparently recovered his health, and some mental stability; now Carrie was well on the road to 'nerves' and permanent invalidism. Early in 1902 Rudyard was hopeful that Carrie was better than she had been for years, 'happier and less nervous'; but Carrie herself was less sure. She felt everything as a burden. Long gone were the days when childbirth was considered to be an illness, but Carrie had persisted even in this. Rudyard reported when she was still in the 'sick room' after the birth of their son:

The doctor and nurse are amazing. C. is naturally languorous and does not demand novels or a skirt dance on the third or fourth day; – and they don't understand it. She is 'an 'ealthy little lady' says the nurse, 'why don't she pick up like the others' . . . 'shock' they have heard of but do not understand . . . I have explained that one of the many inexplicable peculiarities of the American woman is to feel that kind of thing.[53]

A new project like a house was just the thing to keep her organizational talents busy, and her happy. Bateman's was an old iron-founder's house, built in 1634 and coming with a small amount of land. It was larger than the Elms, and they could also buy it rather than rent it. The plan was to 'electrify' the house, and turn an oast house in the grounds into a cottage for a gardener who could act as caretaker when they were away. They asked Ambo, who was now a fully fledged and not particularly successful architect, to take on the project.* Ambo had gone into practice on his own nine years earlier, but, although he had a fairly busy career, there were no particular buildings which marked him out. He designed, with Alma-Tadema (again, a friend of his father), the

---

* Although later, perhaps in a replay of the Beatty Balestier story, Rudyard wrote to a friend saying that Ambo had had nothing to do with the planning of Bateman's.[54]

balustrade outside the Athenaeum, and often did sympathetic reconstruction work. The height of his early career came when he won a design competition for a clock tower in Buenos Aires. Poynter – unusually open in his pride in his offspring – stated that 'it was the finest structure of its kind conceived since the fifteenth century'.[55] But there is no indication that it was ever built. (Perhaps if Ambo had been less honest about his shortcomings he would have gone further. His telegraphic address was 'Illiteracy, London'.)

By August 1902 the Kiplings had moved into the new house, and in the first six weeks they had had eighteen people to stay. Hugh Poynter, now nearly twenty and about to go out to Constantinople to work for Baldwin's, and Stan and Cissie were their first visitors, and then the rest of the family came in relays: Georgie with Margaret, then Ambo, then one of Fred's sons. It was a full month before Alice and Lockwood came down from Tisbury, and they coincided with Agnes, which was particularly happy, as Agnes's many chronic illnesses had now settled down to one major illness. They all feared, although they didn't say, cancer.

Georgie said that she felt that she needed to finish her memoir of Burne-Jones as soon as possible, as she didn't expect to live long – 'no one of us in this or the last generation' had had a long life.[56] It is likely that it was Agnes in particular she was thinking of. The year after her visit to Bateman's Agnes had a serious operation, possibly the removal of a tumour. Georgie went up to London to be with her, and for a while there was a rapprochement between the Kiplings and the Mackails, as Georgie kept the family informed of progress via Jack Mackail. It was not long, however, before they were back to scratching at each other. When Rudyard returned from a trip to South Africa in the spring of 1904, he told Norton that Agnes was a bit better, 'but I haven't met any of the family except the President of the Royal Academy and he was too busy with his labours among Princes ignorant of art to tell me any news'.[57] Sadly, Poynter was ever unable to express his emotions, even after his wife underwent a second operation. She needed quiet, love and attention; she got none of them from her husband. By March 1906 it was clear that Agnes was 'fading out of life'.[58] She had never recovered from her surgery three years before.

Louie came up to London and, with Georgie, took over the nursing of their sister. Edie went and spent some time in Rotting-dean; neither she nor Alice appears to have gone to see Agnes one more time, although they may have – the evidence is purely negative, no visit being mentioned in any surviving correspon-dence. Fred was now living in London, having been made honorary secretary of the Foreign Missionary Society the year before. Poynter, spurred into action, decided that the very best thing for a dying woman would be to leave the flat she had lived in for many years. He bought a house in Addison Road, Kensington, part of the new development being created on the land where Burne-Jones's friends the Prinseps had lived at Little Holland House. The eccen-tricity in moving house at such a time he explained by saying that it had a beautiful garden for Agnes to sit in when she was better. But she was never to sit in it. She now never left her room, and was for long periods unconscious. Hugh, who had met and married the daughter of the American consul-general in Constantinople, brought his wife to England to see his dying mother.

On 12 June 1906, aged only sixty-two, Agnes left the life on which she had made so little mark. After his wife's death, Poynter showed the feelings he had reserved throughout their marriage. He had not himself come from a loving home – Agnes had said, on the death of his father, 'I do not suppose Mr. Poynter's children remember a tender loving speech.' Now, Alice noted, 'He could not tell her, or by manner show dear Aggie his love for her – but he can show his grief now she is gone.'[59] Poynter said he was desolate. He frequently went round the corner to his friends the Fildeses, where he would talk to Mrs Fildes about Agnes, and how much he missed her – he who had scarcely mentioned her in life. Phil saw it plain: his uncle was

without the quality of nature which would attract friends to visit him, and melancholy and grumpy to a degree. I expect he finds little entertain-ment in life nowadays – though when Aunt Aggie was here that didn't seem to make him any cheerier! Now she's gone he behaves as though they had been the most devoted couple . . . which heaven knows they weren't![60]

16. 'The pain of parting'

Ambrose shared his parents' reticence. Georgie thought him too introverted, and wished he could display his emotions more easily. The cousins either could not show their emotions at all or they lived entirely on them. By now Ambo was growing distant from his Burne-Jones relations, and the younger Kiplings, too, were beginning to keep a distance. He married in 1907, but neither family appeared to be at his wedding, nor felt the need to discuss it among themselves. In 1905 he had taken Cherry, his fiancée, to Bateman's for a visit, and that was the last time he visited until 1907. Previously he had been a guest there up to six times a year.

The Bateman's guest book shows another separation. Phil visited once, in 1903, and then never again. Phil's career had never really caught fire, although he persisted, much to his credit. In February 1902 he had decided to go to America for a year, to try to gain commissions. Margaret said drily that 'he appears to be travelling with a quite particularly shady set of people. Most of them looked as if their only reason for going was to escape the strong arm of the law.'[1] Before he left, Georgie worried whether people would understand that he was in the USA to work, not to grace society with his presence. It was a moot point. He wangled an invitation to Long Island to meet Teddy Roosevelt, a friend of Rudyard, but was not commissioned to paint him, which had been his hope. He spent a lot of time trying (still) to sell *The Vampire*, although the friends he chose to help him were no better than the ones Margaret had noted – in January 1903 he wrote to Eliot Norton (Charles Eliot Norton's son, a contemporary of Phil) saying that the man who wanted to show the picture seemed to be in New York under an assumed name, and did Eliot think he was too dubious? After staying with the Nortons – 'interminably', according to their friend William James – he returned to England after nearly twelve months away with very little to show for his time except society portraits, in which he was beginning to specialize by default.

It was after this return that he went to Bateman's. He dismissed it as 'the little estate', and told Norton that he hadn't read Rudyard's last book, which (without reading) 'doesn't seem to be up to the mark', so it is not surprising that he was not invited again. He was no closer to the Poynter boys. He sneered at Hugh's engagement, suggesting it was 'improvident' and that, although his fiancée was 'older than himself, [she was] not *quite* so poor'.[2] This from a man who was selling his father's paintings to maintain his lifestyle. And he wasn't even in charge of that aspect of his life. In 1903 Mackail had told Cockerell that he himself was 'for most practical purposes, sole effective Trustee of Sir E. Burne-Jones's estate'.[3] In 1907 Phil took himself off to a rest home for nearly two months. It is not clear quite what was wrong with him, and he continued his rather rootless life as soon as he was back home: painting his friends, summering (and often wintering) in Europe with the beau monde, taking Georgie on short trips.

Phil strove to keep up with the social world. Alfred and Stan, seemingly without trying, were now very much of it. Business had continued to boom under their diligent care. In 1902 they brought together their multitude of companies, steel and tinplate works, forges and so on under one umbrella company. Baldwin's Ltd became at a stroke one of the largest trade organizations in the country, with capital of more than £1.1 million. Alfred was chairman, and Stan one of the eight directors, responsible for the Midland division, with more than a thousand men working for him. These two very wealthy men mixed with other very wealthy men – including Rudyard, who from time to time wrote to Alfred that he had 'a few thousands to invest' and were there any family shares going? He also asked Stan to be his trustee (together with A. P. Watt, his agent) if he and Carrie were to die while their children were minors.

Rudyard was proud of his uncle, and of his uncle's accomplishments. They thought alike about many things. While Rudyard had gone out to South Africa in 1899 to join in the Boer War effort, Alfred had continued his patronage (in the best sense of the word) of the friendly societies and lodges, paying the contributions of all West Worcestershire members who served in the war. In 1905 Alfred was made chairman of the board of the Great Western Railway. He made a great success of his tenure, among other things overseeing the inauguration of the Fishguard–Rosslare route to Ireland, which Brunel had proposed some sixty years before. The family realized that this was the peak of his career. Soon after Alfred's 'elevation' Rudyard reported that, on his way to visit Stan and Cissie at Astley Hall, which they had rented in 1902, not long after Baldwin's Ltd was consolidated,*

a guard . . . came to me on Paddington platform which was full of a seething mob of holiday makers. Said he seductively: – 'Ain't you Mr. Kipling?' 'Yes' said I 'but what is a heap more important I'm the Chairman's nephew.' 'I should say it was!' said the guard and he stood guard over our compartment to beat off agitated females and families till we left. This is a true tale.[4]

(Oliver, Stan's son, was less impressed when he discovered that his grandfather had neither a whistle to blow nor a flag to wave.)

It was perhaps this new closeness to Rudyard that led Louie to invite Trix for a visit in 1905, on her return from India. Trix continued to be deeply involved in spiritualism. She had begun to channel as a medium in India. In the 1890s she had done some automatic writing. (In this the channeller receives communications from the spirit world which she – it was mostly women who channelled – writes down, usually without knowing what they say or understanding their purport.) In 1903 Trix had read a book entitled *Human Personality and Its Survival of Bodily Death*, written by F. W. H. Myers, one of the stalwarts of the Society for Psychical Research. After this her automatic writing changed and became more frequent, and she became involved in a project which became known as the Palm Sunday scripts, although she contributed under the name of Mrs Holland, to spare her family's blushes.

The Palm Sunday scripts were cases of automatic writing by different people in different places, none of whom supposedly had any knowledge of a youthful romance between the then Prime Minister, Arthur Balfour, and a girl who had died on Palm Sunday 1875. When the different bits taken down by different people in different places were put together, they were said to be evidence

* They bought it in 1912.

that this dead woman was waiting for Balfour on the other side.★
Louie may have heard about this from Alice and, as a serious,
committed Christian, may have felt that Trix needed talking out of
her dangerous pastime. It is certainly the only time Trix was invited
to stay with Alfred and Louie, and it is seductive to think that these
two facts are related.

In 1907 the Kipling–Baldwin link strengthened still further.
Oliver Baldwin and John Kipling were both ready to be sent to
school: although John was two years older, for some reason he had
been kept at home longer. Now it was settled that they would both
go to St Aubyn's prep school in Rottingdean, where Aunt Georgie
could keep her eye on the little boys. John's career had been
mapped out by his anxious parents for years. In 1897, when he was
just a month old, Rudyard was already writing to Crom that he
was sorry there was no longer a Westward Ho! to send young John
to before he went into the Navy. John's nurse, when he was five
months old, declared that he had 'a regular soldier's chest'.[5] Rudyard
doted on his son – perhaps partly because of his lost daughter. In
1901 he had written proudly, 'I am owned by a 3-year-old of
entirely circular outline who is very kind and merciful to me.'[6]

In September 1907 Rudyard, 'grey and pinched by the pain of
parting', thought Georgie,[7] brought John down to Rottingdean
for his first term. John, in contrast, a cheerful, pragmatic boy, took
well to his new environment – 'I think all the trouble is laid on the
household he leaves.'[8] By now, Rudyard's plans for John's entry
into the Navy were already dubious: John shared his poor eyesight,
and it looked as though none of the services would take him – a
blow to the super-patriots that Rudyard and Carrie had become.
In term time John and Oliver visited Georgie at North End House
every other Sunday. Georgie claimed that John was so like his
father that she frequently called him 'Ruddy' by mistake. Rudyard
agreed: 'He let me into North End House the other day with such
a pleasant air of proprietorship as it might have been the ghost of

★ The Palm Sunday scripts are discussed at length in the *Proceedings of the Society
for Psychical Research*, vols. 21, 24, 25. In 1938 H. F. Saltmarsh published a small
book on the case, *Evidence of Personal Survival from Cross Correspondence* (London:
G. Bell & Sons, Ltd).

myself.'[9] Georgie kept a toy cupboard specially for them, which had Russian bears, men that sawed wood, a family of Russian peasants, and birds that turned and chirped when you wound them up. Oliver was less pleased when his Baldwin grandmother visited. During visits to Rottingdean, Louie would sometimes go down to the playing fields and watch the boys. Like small boys everywhere, Oliver 'would pray she did not notice me, lest I should suffer for it. Once she had been speaking to me, and the next time she appeared there were cries of "Hi, Baldwin, there's your old nurse come to see you." Followed by "I say, you fellows, Baldwin's got a nurse." '[10]

Luckily for Louie, she probably remained sublimely unaware of this humiliation for her grandson. She was still writing, although, as the power of the circulating libraries waned, and with it the three-volume novel, she was moving more to short stories. She published widely in magazines, including *Longman's*, *The Cornhill* and *The Argosy*, and in 1904 brought out *A Chaplet of Verses for Children* and *The Pedlar's Pack*, more children's stories. She was clearly working hard; the following year *From Fancy's Realm* was ready for publication – yet more stories.*

Georgie had pulled herself out of a depression she had fallen into after her own literary work was complete. *Memorials of Edward Burne-Jones* was published in 1904, and now she fussed about her friends. Janey was always ill, depressed, worried, and Georgie saw it as her job to help arrange her life, cheer her up – 'I saw Mrs. Morris and *made her laugh*.'[11] She wrote to William Rothenstein (later principal of the Royal College of Art), 'I am sorry to trouble you again, but *nothing* can be done without it that is worth doing',[12] and this could very well have been her motto for life. She was secretary of the Rottingdean Nursing Society, as well as a parish councillor. She explained her exertions to Norton: 'I cannot do anything lightly, and have no administrative power or capacity for using agents – so all I do is at the cost of what might be called unnecessary labour, but my belief is that the cost of a thing does not matter if the thing is accomplished – so I toil on . . .' She thought she might move from these local affairs to something else,

* An indication of Edie's status is that *From Fancy's Realm* had no dedication. Louie had dedicated two books to Alfred, one to Stan, one to Agnes, one to Georgie, two to friends. And none to her companion of thirty years.

but whatever it may be it is not of more importance than daily life, which I have an enduring wish to make as useful and beautiful as possible. – I muse often on the world, and hope underlies the musings . . . I never despair of the power that made us all and the love of which I feel a reflection in my own soul.[13]

The next requirement from her was very much part of daily life, or rather death. In 1907 Louie had a scare: it was thought that she might have pneumonia. (It is notable that news, good or bad, was now being received more quickly. Georgie was sent a message by Stan 'through a friend's telephone'.) Worried enquiries flooded Wilden, so much so that, when Louie recovered, instead of answering them all she asked the parish magazine to insert a note of thanks and regret that she couldn't respond personally to each one. Anxiety receded, if only for a brief interlude. At the beginning of the following year Alfred was feeling intermittently poorly, but he paid it no attention.

Early in February 1908 he went up to London, to Kensington Palace Mansions, where he and Louie had had a flat for years. There were parliamentary sittings, and a meeting of the board of directors of the GWR. On the 13th he returned from his office at Paddington station in a cab, feeling a bit faint. Louie was out paying calls. The cab driver and the porter helped him into the hall. When he had not recovered after twenty minutes, a doctor was sent for. Before he could arrive Alfred had been carried upstairs, and had died, quietly and painlessly. His last words were a request to the porter to pay the cab driver.

Five days after his death Alfred was brought back to Wilden, his home for nearly forty years. On the train from Paddington to Worcester the coffin was placed in a special carriage that had been draped in purple. When the train for Kidderminster pulled out of Worcester station, the entire station staff stood, heads bared, facing it. The mayor of Kidderminster and other local dignitaries met it, and the coffin was taken to All Saints, the church Alfred had endowed, carried by twelve men from the Wilden works. On the day of the funeral Phil and Jack Mackail came from London; Ambo stood in for Poynter, who had just had surgery on his eyes and couldn't travel. (Lockwood, too, was ill, and Rudyard, in South

Africa, could not represent him.) Fred arrived with one of his sons. All of Baldwin's Ltd multifarious interests were shut for the day, and the flag over the offices flew at half mast. Every house in Wilden had drawn its blinds. Every business closed. The street leading to the churchyard was lined with workmen standing bare-headed. A special train ran from Paddington bringing Alfred's Great Western colleagues, his fellow directors of the Metropolitan Bank and other London associates. Another from Worcester brought the local Conservative leaders and representatives of the dozens of organizations, friendly societies and charities that Alfred had patron-ized. The church could accommodate 150 at most; two thousand more stood in the churchyard. Alfred was carried, again by his men, to his grave, which ultimately was marked by a gravestone inscribed with a verse from Micah: 'What doth the Lord require of thee but to do justly and to love mercy and to walk humbly with thy God.'

Perhaps the last word on Alfred should be given to a Mr Broome, who had served as one of his fellow JPs. He told the *Kidderminster Shuttle* that

during the 50 years of uninterrupted friendship he had been privileged to enjoy with him, he had never known him to do an unkind action or say an unkind word of anyone, and he veritably believed that all that time he had never had an unkind thought of anyone. He had never met such a man nor had any of them, and they never expected to meet his like again.

Ten days after his father's death, Stan was unanimously nominated by the local Conservatives to stand as the West Worcestershire parliamentary candidate. He accepted both on his own behalf and more particularly as a duty he owed to Alfred's memory. Louie, in Rottingdean, found comfort in her son's having been chosen for her husband's sake. Georgie and Stan took care of Louie in her first grief, and then she was passed around the family: after ten weeks in Rottingdean with Georgie the two of them went to Canterbury for a month. Louie then returned to Rottingdean, where she took a house for May and June. She moved on to Bateman's, then to Stan, then back to Georgie for Christmas. Lockwood suggested

that an unfair burden was being put on Georgie – although it is
noticeable that he and Alice did not offer to share it:

Georgie and Stan: have held her up and carried her in their arms sharing
her sorrow in the most marvellous way. At a great cost for Georgie, who
I venture to think might have been a little spared, though indeed I should
be puzzled to say exactly how. As a matter of fact, Louie, tho' she has led
what they call in Staffordshire a 'caded' (that is to say – well scarcely
spoilt, – sheltered, screened, protected) life had not originally a weak
nature. She has shown it indeed and would have come through as well
without so much sacrifice on Georgie's part. But you know all of them
– bar Aggie – have a decided touch of the elegiac in their nature and are just
a little prone to what a poor but pious Yorkshire poet, Jas. Montgomery –
called 'the joy of grief' . . .[14]

In this joy of grief, other people's desires took second place.
Rudyard was roped in as literary tutor as Louie in her loss decided
to take to poetry. Lockwood noted, ''Tis the oddest thing she
should want to write poems at all, seeing that though she has many
dainty ideas – she has but little notion of how to put them and
absolutely no ear for rhythm or cadence. But it took her mind off
brooding.'[15]★ This disregard for others may have been fostered by
Louie's long separation from the world in her invalid state, by what
Lockwood called her 'caded' life, which prevented the self-
absorption of childhood from ever quite disappearing. This is
certainly what Georgie thought, and she said so bluntly: 'There is
a childlike streak in her character which is an immense help in the
great times of life, and death.'[16] There was another aspect, however,
which might also have been rooted in childhood. Louie suggested
to Stan that it would have been a 'dutiful and graceful thing' if
Alfred's grandchildren took the money he had given them over the
years – presents at Christmas, and for birthdays – and which had
been put in savings accounts, and used it to pay for a stained-glass
window to be put up in his memory.[17] (Cissie put her foot down,
and the pillaging of the accounts was stayed.) A friend of Georgie's
told a similar story. When Morris was dying, the friend took one

★ Her poems were published as *Afterglow* in 1911. Lockwood's opinion is sound.

of his treasured illuminated books to show Morris and to give them something to talk about during the visit. Morris wrote to him afterwards, when he was at Rottingdean with the Burne-Joneses, offering him £250 for it. The friend was astonished, and shared his astonishment with Georgie, who said, 'But isn't that very selfish of you? When Morris wants it much more than you do?' This appropriation of other people's possessions, the sublime indifference to what others want, may be rooted in the puritan idea of giving up what you really want for the benefit of others. But it is a stern and narrow way of looking at the world.

Margaret had picked up Georgie's way of speaking openly of her disappointment in people, including her own children. As Georgie had disparaged Phil to Rosalind Howard while he was in his teens, Margaret now wrote to her friend Gilbert Murray about her own son, Denis, then aged nine, 'I wish our Denis had a little of [your son] Denis's hardiness and manliness: school has made no difference so far, and he remains soft and silly.' Ten months later, 'How charming about your Denis. Ours is bottom.' And her opinion never changed much. Ten years later she wrote, 'Denis is back from Switzerland looking really well at last – but quite unsatisfactory in other ways.'[18]

It was not only Denis who was judged. Margaret had inherited her husband's habit of making *ex cathedra* pronouncements – nothing was followed by 'I think' or 'it seems to me'. She *knew*. A play they went to see was 'about as stupid and unreal as anything could be'. Everyone is allowed to have opinions on art, but her remarks were always followed by a condemnation of everyone who did not share her view, often with an aspersion on the caste of those who thought differently: 'everybody round us was tearfully enthusiastic: but there is nobody so easily touched at the theatre as a stock-broker . . .'[19] This quickness to sit in judgement was as strong towards herself as it was towards others. At the age of seventy she thought little enough of herself to sign a letter, 'Georgie Burne-Jones's daughter, though not worthy to be it.'[20]

This odd and difficult woman remained now only tenuously linked to the Baldwin, Poynter and Kipling parts of her family. One of the few connections was Burne-Jones's old schoolfriend Crom Price, whom all the family knew and loved. Crom had retired from Westward Ho! and had married his housekeeper when he was sixty and she thirty-two. They had a son named Edward William – for Burne-Jones and Morris – and, with the need to educate him and provide for his wife, Crom continued to tutor schoolboys into his old age. It is here that the Macdonald family can be seen at its best: Georgie kept an eye on him, and when he began to fail she helped financially; Rudyard and Carrie lent him Bateman's when they were abroad, so that he and his family could have a free holiday, with servants to look after them.★ Eventually Georgie rented, and furnished, a house in Rottingdean so that Crom could spend his last days among friends. In May 1910 he died. The only time Rudyard ever returned to Westward Ho! was for a ceremony where a tablet was put up, reading:

TO THE GLORY OF GOD AND IN LOVING MEMORY OF
CORMELL PRICE, ESQ., M.A., B.C.L., OXON.,
FOR TWENTY YEARS THE FIRST HEADMASTER OF
THE UNITED SERVICES COLLEGE, WESTWARD HO!
WHO DIED 4TH MAY, 1910, AGED SEVENTY-FOUR YEARS.

Who with toil of his Today
Brought for us Tomorrow
Kipling

For Georgie and Alice, Crom's death was a great loss – the last of the Birmingham set was gone, and they had no friends who could remember them as young girls. The year before, Fred's wife had died, but this seemed to make little or no impression on the sisters. There was no breach with their brother, but they were now very far apart in all aspects of their lives.

With Crom's passing, Rudyard had lost a father figure. It was only the beginning of a decade of much greater losses for him. The Lockwood Kiplings had now been in Tisbury for nearly twenty

★ The younger Kiplings were more closely tied to Crom than to some of their own family. When the Dunhams, Carrie's sister and her family, came to England, Carrie saw them a bit and then sent them a note at Christmas, hoping that, given that they were not at home, their Christmas was as good as could be expected. Inviting them to Bateman's to share in the family Christmas was not apparently a possibility.

years. Alice was happy – or as happy as she ever was in her later years; she rarely went out, rarely visited her sisters, was often ill with minor ailments. Her main occupation was Trix, who had arrived to stay in 1909 and only intermittently returned to her husband when he was home on leave. Trix had somehow become a semi-permanent fixture, returning to a childhood she had not had, daughter and mother living together. Alice's astringency had separated her from her neighbours, who 'held her in wholesome awe . . . She knew how to give advice in pungent form.' This was Fred, who tempered these remarks by adding that she performed 'many acts of kindness'.[21] It is, however, the formidable character and pungency of speech that remain in the mind, rather than the kindnesses, unnamed.

Lockwood felt the lack of outside friends much more than his wife and daughter appeared to: 'In my irreverent youth I used to say old people should be resigned to their shelf as long as they are comfortable and can't fall off. My shelf is all right and I can't fall off, but –'[22] That was when he had been in Tisbury only six years, and was continuing to travel a great deal. As Alice became frailer, his jaunts were more circumscribed, and 'I fear I worry Alice a good deal by complaints of the loneliness and dullness of this sepulchre. It is true we are two – but I have a fidgety craving for society.'[23] When Rudyard paid a visit in 1905, he saw that 'They grow old – a disease for which there is no remedy.'[24] Lockwood knew it too – in 1908 he admitted that 'during the last six months I have plunged five years full into old age and decrepitude, with a good deal of perfectly useless, unwarrantable, wicked & therefore uncontrollable discontent'.[25]

Lockwood tried to keep busy – he had illustrated *Kim* for Rudyard; he drew pictures for his grandchildren; he gave drawing lessons to the Wyndham children nearby. But essentially his and Alice's lives were over and they were just waiting for death, as for a train that was late. It was not long in coming. By early 1910 Alice was chronically ill. Some accounts say it was Graves' disease; some heart trouble. It is not really important what it was: at seventy-three she was failing, and could not long survive. Louie arrived to stay in November, and Rudyard came up to wait for the inevitable. On 23 November Alice died, with her Family Square about her.

Lockwood was devastated. He wrote to Editha Plowden, 'You have lost a friend who loved you, while I – but it cannot be written of.'[26] Rudyard described him as 'quietly stunned'. Unfortunately, Trix was not. She was hysterical. It is unclear how well or ill she had been during Alice's last days, but when Jack Fleming arrived, two days after Alice's death, 'Trix met me screaming.'[27] Within a month she had relapsed completely, and by the end of the year a professional nurse was necessary. Rudyard had returned to Bateman's, and Fleming left for Scotland. Lockwood thought this a bonus – 'she seems to get on better with me alone', and Fleming 'would give a brass monkey depression'.[28]

By the middle of January Trix had to be moved to a nursing home. Lockwood – exhausted with the effort of looking after her, and desperately lonely and lost without Alice – was taken in by his neighbours the Wyndhams. It was a house he loved, the Wyndhams were his friends of many years, and there, two weeks later, he simply passed out of life, gently and without troubling anyone. Rudyard and Carrie were in Switzerland. John was ill, and Lockwood's fading away was so quiet that Rudyard did not know to return in time. As soon as he received the telegram he made his second pilgrimage to Tisbury in three months. After the funeral he wrote to Georgie, 'I feel the loneliest creature on God's earth today.'[29]

The changes brought about by the deaths of Alice and Lockwood were immense. Agnes had died without any ripples being felt: everyone was sad, but everything went on pretty much as before. Alfred's death was a blow, but Louie soldiered on. With the deaths of both Kiplings, the Macdonald family was no more: that moment of critical mass when a group suddenly fragments had arrived. It is not easy to say just why this happens at a particular time, and yet it is always completely clear when it has. Three out of the five Macdonald sisters survived, but they were geographically and emotionally too far apart to keep their ever expanding families together. Now what survived were the Burne-Jones, Mackail, Kipling, Poynter and Baldwin families, which were a very different thing.

The Kipling Family Square could certainly not survive the death of two of its members. Trix's fragile mental equilibrium did not stabilize, and she was certified insane in March 1911. She was not to return to her husband for another two years. When she did and was well enough to take notice, Rudyard's actions after their parents' deaths became a way of focusing her distress.

Rudyard had acted strangely, but not in any way out of character. He had destroyed all his letters to his parents and any other documents he found at the Gables. His overwhelming sense of privacy made this a normal response for him; Trix saw it as a way of ensuring that only his reading of their family history would survive. Alice and Lockwood had both died intestate; Trix declared that Rudyard had destroyed their wills. On balance, this is unlikely – but only on balance. Alice almost certainly did die without a will – this was not at all uncommon for a woman with no money of her own. That Lockwood had no will is rather more surprising. True, he had very little money: probate had valued his estate at £1,155 6s. 1d. However, Trix had clearly been heading for another breakdown. She had spent four of the previous eleven years needing concentrated – and expensive – medical attention. What kind of father does not attempt to provide for his child who clearly cannot help herself, and who in this case is rendered even more unstable by the sight of her husband? It is difficult to believe that parents as loving, as protective, as Lockwood and Alice had been could be this careless.

As it was, Rudyard was automatically appointed administrator of the estate, and by law everything was divided in half. He invested Trix's share for her, handing over only the interest to Fleming. It is clear from his correspondence with Fleming in the following years that the thought of making over Lockwood's entire little estate for Trix's care never occurred to him. His own wealth was phenomenal: between 1911 and 1915 he asked his friend Max Aitken (later Lord Beaverbrook), only one of the several people he relied on for financial advice, to invest nearly half a million dollars for him.★ He spent more than Lockwood's entire estate on a new car.

Rudyard had a curiously ambivalent attitude to Trix. He told Louie that he could not, as she had suggested, settle on a memorial to Alice at Wilden, because anything that was done had to be done

---

★ It *was* dollars. Rudyard saw the war coming, and moved a great deal of money abroad.

on behalf of both of Alice's children and Trix was not, at that point, able to be consulted. Yet there were long months when he did not even have an address for his sister in her various nursing homes. Perhaps the memorial was a link to his past, where Trix continued to have a part to play; she had none in his present.

Rudyard's family contracted further with the First World War. John, aged seventeen, joined the Irish Guards and disappeared in the Battle of Loos, in October 1915. His body was never found. His parents, who had always hoped for a military career for their boy, never recovered from the loss of their second child. They did not complain – Carrie had written to her mother two months earlier, 'one cant let ones friends and neighbours sons be killed in order to save us and our son. There is no chance John will survive unless he is so maimed from a wound as to be unfit to fight. We know it and he does.'[30] But missing in action was even harder than death. For several years thereafter they feared that John was in a German prison (unlikely, as Kipling's son a prisoner would have been too big a propaganda coup to keep quiet), or that he had lost his memory and was wandering across the Continent, destitute and alone. They withdrew even further into themselves.

It is an indication of how far links with the family had deteriorated that Louie heard that John was missing from *The Times*. She was kept abreast of the search for him or his body by Stan. During the war Stan became the consummate politician, known as someone who could get things done in committee. In 1917 he joined the government, shedding all his business directorships to do so. This was part of the service ethic that Alfred and Louie had drilled into him, and as part of the war effort it seemed very little, although he always expected to go back to the business world when the war was over. In 1914 Stan followed his father's example during the Boer War and paid the friendly-society contributions of all servicemen in Worcestershire.* Baldwin's made a great deal of money from the war, but Stan regarded this as blood money. By 1918 he had come to the conclusion that the only way to expiate this was to give away the profits that had accrued to him during the previous four years.

* Alfred in the Boer War had paid only for his own West Worcestershire constituency. Stan broadened the base, which with conscription made this a financial obligation of thousands of pounds.

He gave about a fifth of his whole wealth (not just his income) towards the redemption of the war debt: about £120,000 of a £580,000 fortune, or, in modern terms, about £3 million out of £14 million. By 1920 he had given away another £40,000.

He was a full-time politician by now. He had had a dizzying rise, being made parliamentary private secretary to the Chancellor of the Exchequer in 1916, Junior Lord of the Treasury a month later, and Joint Financial Secretary six months after that, in June 1917. By 1918 he was sole Financial Secretary, and in 1921 he became a Cabinet minister. When Bonar Law retired in 1923, he and Curzon were the two obvious choices for the Prime Minister's job. Stan was appointed, and began the first of his three terms.★ A few days later the party met to recognize him as the Conservative leader (a position he held until 1937). After Louie made her first visit to Chequers, in 1923, when Stan was given the use of the house by Bonar Law, who didn't like the countryside, she wrote to him, 'You have inflated your mother with pride.' After he became PM there is hardly a letter from Louie that does not contain the phrase 'the Prime Minister says . . .' or '. . . does . . .' or '. . . thinks . . .'.

Stan and Rudyard remained on visiting terms for years, with the Baldwins going frequently to Bateman's, where jokes and horseplay substituted for real closeness of spirit. (Stan, a great walker, once found a notice in his room when he arrived: 'Rules for Guests: 1. No guest to walk more than 5 miles an hour. 2. No guest to walk more than two hours at a time. 3. Guests are strictly forbidden to coerce or cajole to accompany them in said walks, as the proprietors cannot be responsible for the consequences. Signed RK, CK, EK (natives).'[31] Their fundamental similarities were too great for friendship: they both needed to preach, to convert, and by the 1930s they scarcely saw anything of each other, although they had not formally fallen out. When Carrie was taken ill in Bermuda in 1930, Rudyard wrote to Elsie, 'You needn't fuss . . . Neither [Stan nor Cissie] have sent us one word of any sort. It's a family that doesn't waste on postage.'[32] Stan was no more enthusiastic: 'I am

★ He was Prime Minister in 1923–4, 1924–9 and 1935–7. The general election in December 1923 was a disaster for him, but he came back with a landslide victory in 1924, and again in 1935, when the Conservatives had a majority of 200.

not happy about [Rudyard] either and am looking forward to being with him with no sense of rush.'[33] Part of the estrangement was political. Much more was emotional. Yet the connection was never entirely severed. In 1933 a visit to Bateman's was, Stan said, 'roses all the way'.

When Oliver came back from the war, unharmed, there was general rejoicing. He went often to visit the Kiplings, and took his friend George Bambridge with him. In 1924, aged twenty-eight, Elsie married Oliver's friend. Bambridge was not a terrific catch. True, he was a young diplomat and he came from a good family – his father had been a secretary to the Duke of Edinburgh: with his family and Kipling's money, anything was possible. However, his very close friendship with Oliver came under scrutiny when in the 1920s Oliver began to live openly with another man. In addition, Oliver became a socialist in 1923 (and in 1929, briefly a Labour MP). A socialist *and* a homosexual: Kipling never spoke to him again.

Elsie and George were posted to Madrid and France. When they came to England they travelled in great style, with a chauffeur, a maid for Elsie, and a Spanish valet in elaborate livery for George. It has been suggested that the Bambridges' footmen were suspiciously good-looking. It was generally accepted by friends that this was a *mariage blanc* that suited both parties: Bambridge was kept in the style to which he aspired; Elsie got away from home. (The authorized biography of Kipling has an afterword by Elsie in which she leaves it in no doubt that she got on no better with Carrie than most did.) Bambridge resigned from the diplomatic service in 1933, aged forty, and Rudyard rented Wimpole Hall in Cambridgeshire for them.

Rudyard, a very rich man, had for thirty years been content to live in a house with half a dozen bedrooms. Elsie and George wanted more. Wimpole Hall had a mere forty-four bedrooms, as well as John Soane-designed reception rooms. It also had no mains electricity, no drainage, and no water supply. Rudyard thought it a *folie de grandeur*, although he died before he could persuade them of this. Within a year of his death they had purchased the house outright, and with Elsie's inheritance they began a buying spree to rebuild and redecorate it. Bambridge died in 1943, aged only fifty. Elsie's childhood nicknames, 'Prophet of Doom', or 'Bird of Ill Omen', which had been a family tease about her pessimism, gradually came to take over the whole of her personality. She remained at Wimpole another thirty years, interested in little except the house and preserving her father's legacy.

As controlling as Carrie was, she could not control her and her husband's ends. Rudyard died on their forty-fourth wedding anniversary, in 1936, of a burst ulcer. Carrie spent the three years remaining to her attempting to destroy, tidy and arrange everything to do with him into a form that could be interpreted only in her way after her death: 'No one', she foretold, 'does anything they promise to do after people are no longer living.'[34]* Only the Bambridges and Carrie's secretary were at her cremation.

The Poynter family had dwindled away too. During the war, Poynter had fought a rearguard action against the forces of progress at the Royal Academy: he was over eighty, and his time had passed. In November 1918 he made 'a painful scene' at a council meeting, announcing with great bitterness that, as it was clear to him that he was no longer wanted, he would resign at the general assembly scheduled to meet in ten days' time.[35] It is a sign of just how much he was not wanted that, when he made the promised resignation speech at the general assembly, no one had prepared any response to thank him for his twenty-two years' work as the Academy's president. There was small recompense when in the 1918 honours list he was made a GCVO – a Knight Grand Cross of the Royal Victorian Order – to add to the baronetcy he had collected in 1902, but it was not much for a lifetime's labours. He had not long to brood over these slights: in July 1919 he died.

In his will, he divided his quite substantial estate between his two sons, and he made it clear how little he thought of Ambo. In most ways it is a very traditional will: the assets are divided in half, with his paintings to be handed down in the male line. But a clause says that Ambo is not to receive his share if he is an undischarged bankrupt; if he is, then he is to get the income only. Hugh's inheritance has no clause like this attached to it. In any case, Ambo

* Of course, neither did Carrie. When Rudyard died, he specified in his will that everything was to go to Carrie and, after her death and Elsie's, to the Fairbridge Farm School. When Carrie died she left Bateman's and money for its upkeep to the National Trust. Elsie in her turn lived up to her mother's prophecy and left nothing at all to the Fairbridge Farm School.

did not long outlive his father. Much like Phil, he had a breakdown, attributed to 'overwork', in 1922, and in the following year he died of heart failure after an operation, only four years after Poynter. Hugh by this time had emigrated to Canada, where he worked for Baldwin's for some years, before moving on once more, to Australia, where he finally settled.

The Burne-Joneses were also spreading out across the globe. Angela Mackail had grown from the bossy little girl nicknamed A.K.B. into an overwhelmingly confident young woman. Like her mother, she had no doubts about her own opinions and her place in the world. In 1911 she met a singer, James Campbell McInnes.* McInnes was much in demand at the house parties and drawing rooms of fashionable London. Within six weeks of meeting him, and despite the fact that he was living in a relationship with a composer, Graham Peel, they married. (His father had been an engraver and an alcoholic, so Mackail thought it best if the groom's family was not mentioned in the announcement in the paper: whether it was the occupation or the drinking that bothered him most is not clear.) They had two sons, and were living quietly in London when the war began. Now McInnes's career dipped: this was not a time for entertainment. He started to drink. Despite his age – he was forty in 1914 – he obtained a commission in the Royal Flying Corps. True, he was only an equipment officer stationed at Regent's Park, but there had been no need for him to enlist at all. Denis nastily referred to Regent's Park as 'one of the most coveted funk-holes in the army'.[36] But, because of various ailments, Denis, aged twenty-two, managed to avoid conscription entirely, so he is perhaps not the most reliable source. The marriage did not survive the war. By 1917, two months after the birth of a daughter, Angela asked her parents to take her away.

Quite what had happened is open to question. There is no doubt at all that McInnes was drinking heavily. Angela said that he had attempted to rape the nursemaid. Their son Colin later claimed that he had also approached Clare, Angela's younger sister.† Stan,

* His last name was spelled thus. Their son Colin changed the spelling of his name to MacInnes later.
† Notes Colin made for a never written book include the phrases 'Tries to rape C.', 'Assault on — at Rottingdean', 'Attack on C. on cliff'.[37]

the businessman of the family, suggested the name of a lawyer who would handle divorce (most respectable firms would not touch it), and lent Angela money. Although McInnes was persuaded not to contest the divorce, there were headlines in the less reputable papers – 'Wife's Life of Horror' – and even *The Times* reported the case.

Angela and the children had moved in with her parents, and early in 1918 her little girl died of pneumonia. Angela left it to her mother and grandmother to arrange the funeral, refusing to attend herself. By this time she had already met a Tasmanian soldier, George Thirkell, and she married him shortly after her divorce became final. In 1920 she, her new husband and her boys left for Australia, where they settled for ten years, until Angela left this husband too (and her two boys), returning once more to her parents.

Phil had all this time stayed close to home. There was some talk of war work with Belgian refugees, but nothing concrete. (He was, admittedly, fifty-seven by the end of the war, but his cousin Ambo, only five years younger, served with distinction in the Navy.) By the end of the war he was ready for another rest cure. He spent six weeks in a nursing home, as he had before, and found some measure of calm. This was fortunate, because two years later, on 2 February 1920, Georgie, the great stabilizing influence on his life, died. Angela and her new family had just set sail for Australia, and the separation was more than Georgie could bear. She could not bring herself to speak of it, she wrote. By now she was extremely frail and she was contemplating leaving Rottingdean. She did not want to, but she could no longer manage, and wanted to be near her daughter, in particular. Phil felt her loss terribly: she was the one 'who would never misunderstand – and always make allowances'.[38]

He needed allowances made. He was, at nearly sixty, never going to make a name for himself, and so he dropped everyone else's. He was 'seeing' a great deal of Melba; the 'new Prime Minister . . . I have known intimately since childhood'; the PM was asking his advice on a new trustee for the National Gallery but 'it was a name so unsuitable . . . that I at once put a spoke in his wheel'. Sometimes he could not even be bothered to name-drop properly: 'I heard an amusing anecdote of the Prince of Wales yesterday – a clever repartee he made in Canada – which hasn't got into the Press yet', but he then wrote that it was too long to be told in a letter – and then left two pages blank.[39]

His income from his painting could not possibly keep him suitably, so he relied more and more on his patrimony. Rudyard noted with disgust that 'Phil (whose sudden departure for the USA at half a day's notice, you may have seen) is going to "make his fortune" by selling some more of his father's drawings to the Americans. I don't suppose that there will be more of that ancestor left "unexploited" than a high-class bacon-factory leaves of a pig.'[40] The family was roped in where necessary: Phil asked Stan to present Burne-Jones's Chaucer drawings to Cambridge (that is, purchase them, for 1,000 guineas). Stan agreed, but then Phil couldn't even take the trouble to see that they were sent off in good order:

The exact number of the drawings I cannot at the moment remember – but they are sure to be delivered as they left me . . . Of course your telephone [*sic*] asking for the exact number of the drawings – and suggesting eighty-seven – came at the busiest possible moment, when I was just going out and had no time to count them – I sent a post-card saying that eighty-seven was correct, because it was so *very* near the right number, if it wasn't actually it.[41]

Despite his very busy social life he had few friends. Gradually his mental health deteriorated. There is an undated fragment of a letter to Sydney Cockerell: 'Don't let Margaret see this. I trust you not to. I want her to think me happier than I am.'[42] Margaret was not blind: 'I can well imagine the effect Phil produces on a stranger, and he certainly doesn't sound in any more control of himself.'[43] In April 1926 he went into a rest home for another 'cure', but this time cure was no longer possible. He was there for two months, and at the end of that time Margaret 'saw him on Saturday when he knew me, but was rambling and pitiably weak . . . 4.30 His spirit left his body a few minutes ago very peacefully.'[44] What he died of is not clear. Some books say without hesitation that he committed suicide. There is no indication of this in any documents surviving, although that would be in keeping with the times. Alcoholism also suggests itself, although again there is no evidence. Certainly *The*

Times wouldn't mention either in its obituary of him (which looks as if it was written by Mackail). It did, however, perhaps hit on the truth when it said, 'He inherited . . . the artistic temperament at its full tension: but with him it was perhaps less a gift than a burden.'[45] An artistic temperament without any artistic ability could easily be a curse.

Margaret's third child, too, seemed cursed. From our perspective it is easy to see what was wrong, but in the early part of the last century it was a great mystery. Clare showed early artistic promise, although Georgie 'distrust[ed] artistic gift . . . in women'.[46] Perhaps they all did, and this led to what was obviously anorexia. Perhaps McInnes had assaulted her in some way. In any case, by 1912, at the age of sixteen, she had to leave school because she was 'over-grown and underfed'.[47] She did not improve at home, and by the end of the year her mother said she 'looks as if I ought to be sent to prison by the NSPCC'. During the next forty years Clare was diagnosed with 'poisoning', thyroid conditions, Graves' disease, a troubled aorta. She claimed in the 1950s to have had a spine fractured in the Blitz, but there is no contemporary mention of it, although Margaret's letters are a catalogue of tiny improvements and dramatic relapses. It is possible that anorexia was avoided as a diagnosis because the treatment was so extreme. Dominating the 'unsound mind' of the patient was the key. The sufferer was removed from her family, who would be too loving and sympath-etic, and 'moral control' was exerted by a 'medical attendant'.[48] Instead, for over thirty years Margaret and Clare found a modus vivendi very much like Alice and Trix before them. Clare, although often abroad for cures, or in the country for her health, or in nursing homes and hospitals, never really left home until her mother died in 1953.

Denis, on the other hand, could not wait to leave. He began his working life as a stage designer, soon moving on to start a long and modestly successful career as a popular novelist, writing nearly two dozen books over twenty-five years. There is little surviving of his thoughts in the public domain: some letters to his publisher, a few to friends. One of the few glimpses of him we get is in 1932 from Rudyard, who clearly disliked him, and even he had it at second hand:

[Trix has] seen a lot, evidently, of the Mackails and Angela. Also, of Denis Mackail, who does not as a rule visit his own people, but who came in to tea while she was there. I gather that he looks down on his own family, does not at all approve of his Papa-in-law, and generally preserves an air of aloofness towards all the world which is not *his* world. He does not bring his kids over to see their grandmother – to her no small distress – and sits about as though there were some sort of evil smell under his nose. His father (Jack Mackail) feels this a good deal . . . the notion of his having the face to look down on anyone on earth is rather too much for me.[49]

This is so sour that it is hard to take at face value. Denis's relationship to his family in his writing life must have been difficult. There was his cousin Rudyard, whose work he couldn't hope to equal, then his sister Angela took up novel-writing too. In 1932, after she returned from Australia, she published a short memoir, *Three Houses*, recalling her childhood. Thereafter, almost to her death in 1961, 'the new Thirkell' came out every year. She was the Joanna Trollope of her day – the reliable, middle-brow woman's read – and she was terrifically successful.

She and her siblings had by now completely lost all sense of connection with their mother's family. Louie had survived into Stan's second term as Prime Minister and into her eightieth year, despite her many decades of committed invalidism. Five years before her death in 1925, the 149 inhabitants of Wilden village had presented her with an illuminated address, marking her fifty years' residency: 'We, the undersigned, desire to express to you our affection and respect. We are thankful to you for your thoughtful generosity and admire the courage with which you have faced suffering and bereavement . . . We trust that you may long be spared to us, and that God's blessing may rest upon you in time and in eternity.'[50]

She was followed very quickly by Fred, who died in 1928. It was not until 1937 that Edie, the most overlooked, undervalued, member of the family – still living at Wilden House, as she had for sixty-two years – finally released her grip on life, exactly 100 years after her sister Alice had been born. With her passing went the last of the Macdonald sisters, the preacher's daughters who had travelled so far.

Afterword

Were the Macdonalds in any way remarkable? Were they worth the 300-odd pages dedicated to them above? It could be said that all they did was marry well, but that would be unfair. One married a prosperous ironmaster with whom she could have been expected to reside in bourgeois obscurity for the rest of their lives. The other three married, in the eyes of the world, a poor artist of moderate family, a poor artist of no family, and an art teacher; and they all rose to contribute greatly to their worlds. Could it be said, therefore, that the Macdonald sisters 'made' the men they married? They probably did play a part in their husbands' rise, although not the sole one. Did they 'make' their children? It is notable that the children fell broadly into two groups. Those of Edward Burne-Jones and Edward Poynter, the men who made a prominent mark in their day, were at best untouched by ambition, at worst content to live off the reputation of their fathers. The children of the businessman and the art teacher became Prime Minister and the uncrowned Poet Laureate of Empire. It is probably safe to say that nurture had as much to do with that as nature.

Edie summed up the family:

If there was a flaw common to all their characters it could be said, and doubtless was said in the broader-minded world that acknowledged their enchanting virtues, that, while they were seldom slow to bless, they were often incontinently swift to chide. Forbearance of others' conduct which they deemed below their own moral standards was not among the social graces successfully learned in chapel or at home; and as they fared abroad they found no lack of occasion for disapproval that was prone to find expression in immediate and telling form.[1]

Colin MacInnes too drew up a balance sheet of their virtues and defects.[2] On the credit side, they had 'a real, total and quite unquestioning respect for art and learning', as well as a lack of respect for money without the corresponding contempt for business that so often goes with it. They were astonishingly literary. Of the siblings, their husbands, wives, parents, children and grandchildren, half were published writers.★ Among their defects he thought that 'They had, to a man and woman, an excellent opinion of themselves' and they were all rather less tolerant than they imagined they were. 'They were not particularly loving', or rather their love 'seemed, however intense, to be rather chill and demanding'. Their standards for themselves were set high; those for others equally so.

MacInnes, himself an extraordinary writer, might as well have the last word: 'If they were inspiring people, they were also appallingly demanding. They were, in fact, the sort of family that one would perhaps rather read about than belong to.'

★ George Macdonald (pamphlets and sermons), Alice and Trix (poetry), Louie (novels and poems), Georgie and A. W. Baldwin (biography), Fred, Edie, Graham McInnes, Lance Thirkell, Oliver Baldwin and Margot Baldwin (memoirs), Lockwood (*Beast and Man in India* and journalism), Mackail (literary criticism), Phil (magazine articles), Angela Thirkell and Colin MacInnes (novels), Poynter and Stan (essays and speeches or lectures), Rudyard (no description needed).

Notes

Key to Archives

B-JP   Burne-Jones papers, Fitzwilliam Museum
BL   British Library
CC   Carpenter Collection, Library of Congress
CH   Castle Howard
GMP   Gilbert Murray papers, Bodleian Library
JLKP   John Lockwood Kipling papers, University of Sussex
McG   Rare Books and Special Collections, McGill University
NP   Norton papers, bMS Am 1088, Houghton Library, Harvard University
TGA   Tate Gallery Archive
V & A   Victoria & Albert Museum

Introduction

1. Martha Vicinus, *A Widening Sphere: Changing Roles of Victorian Women* (Bloomington: Indiana University Press, 1977), p. ix.
2. William Allingham to Henry Sutton, 31 March 1849, Queen's University, Belfast.
3. It is almost impossible to stop quoting this repellent little work. For those who can't bear to read it all, the passages cited are at pp. 135–7, 138–9 and 148–9 of John Ruskin, 'Of Queens' Gardens' in *Sesame and Lilies, Two Lectures by John Ruskin, LL.D., 1. Of Kings' Treasures; 2. Of Queens' Gardens* (Orpington: George Allen, 1887).

1. Inheritance

1. F. W. Macdonald, *As a Tale That is Told* (London: Cassell, 1919), pp. 2–3.
2. James Macdonald, *The Letters of James Macdonald, 1816–31, with Notes*

by His Grandson, F. W. Macdonald (London: Robert Culley, 1907), p. 100. James was later to publish several pamphlets: *Strictures of Methodism* (1804), *On the Catholic Question* (1815), *An Address to the Preachers on Christian Education* (1821) and *The Memoirs of Rev. Joseph Benson* (1822).

3. James Macdonald, *Letters*, pp. 132–3.
4. Ibid., pp. 48–50.
5. Ibid., pp. 102–4.
6. Ibid., p. 120.
7. Ibid., pp. 102–4.
8. Ibid., p. 56.
9. Ibid., p. 102.
10. Ibid.
11. Ibid., p. 107.
12. Edith Macdonald, *Annals of the Macdonald Family* (London: Horace Marshall & Son, 1923), pp. 13–15.
13. James Macdonald, *Letters*, pp. 178–9.

2. 'So entirely domestic': 1835–1850

1. Quoted in Asa Briggs, *Victorian Cities* (London: Penguin Books, 1990), pp. 106–7.
2. A. W. Baldwin (Earl Baldwin of Bewdley), *The Macdonald Sisters* (London: Peter Davies, 1960), pp. 18–19.
3. Ibid., p. 41.
4. Pamela Horn, *The Victorian Town Child* (Stroud: Sutton Publishing, 1977), p. 128.
5. Mrs H. R. Haweis, *The Art of Housekeeping: A Bridal Garland* (London: Samson Low, Marston, Searle & Rivington, 1889), p. 115.
6. Ibid.
7. Edith Macdonald, *Annals*, pp. 27–8.
8. Ibid., pp. 21–5.
9. F. W. Macdonald, *A Tale*, p. 58.
10. Ibid.
11. Edith Macdonald, *Annals*, p. 27.
12. Horn, *The Victorian Town Child*, p. 27.
13. R. Davis, A. R. George and G. Rupp, *A History of the Methodist Church*

in Great Britain Vol. 2 (London: Epworth Press, 1978), pp. 231–2.

14. Hannah to Fred, F. W. Macdonald, *A Tale*, p. 61.
15. Ibid., pp. 4–5.
16. A. W. Baldwin, *Macdonald Sisters*, p. 17.
17. Mrs [Isabella] Beeton, *Mrs Beeton's Book of Cookery and Household Management* (London: S. O. Beeton, 1860), pp. 1044–60.
18. A. W. Baldwin, *Macdonald Sisters*, p. 16.
19. Michael Freeman, *Railways and the Victorian Imagination* (London: Yale University Press, 1999), p. 1.
20. Cited in Davis, George and Rupp, *The Methodist Church in Great Britain Vol. 2*, p. 98.
21. Ibid., p. 110.
22. F. W. Macdonald, *A Tale*, p. 34.
23. A. W. Baldwin, *Macdonald Sisters*, p. 25.
24. Horn, *The Victorian Town Child*, p. 27.
25. F. W. Macdonald, *A Tale*, pp. 35–9.
26. Horn, *The Victorian Town Child*, p. 27.
27. F. W. Macdonald, *A Tale*, p. 17.
28. Ibid., pp. 16–17.
29. This splendid thought was promulgated by the Revd J. P. Faunthorpe, M.A., Principal of Whitelands College, in *Household Science: Readings in Necessary Knowledge for Girls and Young Women* (5th edn, London, Edward Stanford, 1889), p. 5.
30. A. W. Baldwin, *Macdonald Sisters*, pp. 5–6.
31. Edith Macdonald, *Annals*, pp. 15–16.
32. A. W. Baldwin, *Macdonald Sisters*, p. 16.
33. F. W. Macdonald, *A Tale*, p. 20.
34. Ibid., p. 18.
35. David Hempton, *The Religion of the People: Methodism and Popular Religion, c. 1750–1900* (London: Routledge, 1996), pp. 86–7.
36. Ibid., pp. 9–12.
37. A. W. Baldwin, *Macdonald Sisters*, p. 17.
38. F. W. Macdonald, *A Tale*, p. 15.
39. J. F. C. Harrison, *Early Victorian Britain, 1832–51* (Fontana: London: 1971), quoted in Freeman, *Railways and the Victorian Imagination*, p. 10.
40. F. W. Macdonald, *A Tale*, p. 334.
41. A. W. Baldwin, *Macdonald Sisters*, p. 35.
42. F. W. Macdonald, *A Tale*, pp. 5–6.

3. 'A moving tent': 1850–1853

1. F. W. Macdonald, *A Tale*, p. 21.
2. Ibid., p. 27.
3. Georgiana Burne-Jones, *Memorials of Edward Burne-Jones* (London: Macmillan, 1904), vol. 1, p. 67.
4. Ibid., pp. 55–6.
5. Ibid., p. 65.
6. Ibid., p. 66.
7. Ibid., p. 19.
8. Ibid., p. 69.
9. Ibid., p. 19.
10. Alison Winter, *Mesmerized: Powers of Mind in Victorian Britain* (Chicago: University of Chicago Press, 1998), p. 253.
11. Georgiana Burne-Jones, *Memorials*, vol. 1, p. 94.
12. A. W. Baldwin, *Macdonald Sisters*, p. 36.
13. Ibid., pp. 14–15.
14. Georgiana Burne-Jones, *Memorials*, vol. 1, p. 107.
15. Quoted in M. Harrison and B. Waters, *Burne-Jones* (London: Barrie & Jenkins, 1973), pp. 3–4.
16. Penelope Fitzgerald, *Burne-Jones* (London: Michael Joseph, 1975; rev. edn Stroud: Sutton Publishing, 1997), p. 19.
17. *The English Housekeeper, or, Manual of Domestic Management: containing advice on the conduct of household affairs, and Practical Instructions concerning the store-room, the pantry, the larder, the kitchen, the cellar, the dairy . . . The whole being intended for the use of young ladies who undertake the superintendence of their own housekeeping* (London: A. Cobbett, 3rd edn, 1842), p. 119.
18. Ibid., p. 406.
19. Beeton, *Cookery and Household Management*, p. 904.
20. The list of symptoms comes from Thomas Dormandy, *The White Death: A History of Tuberculosis* (London: Hambledon Press, 1999). My information in these two paragraphs is heavily indebted to this work.
21. Faunthorpe, *Household Science*, p. 339.
22. Ibid., pp. 42–3.
23. Winter, *Mesmerized*, p. 122.

24. Quoted in Dormandy, *The White Death*, p. 42.

25. Ibid., p. 44.

26. Georgiana Burne-Jones, *Memorials*, vol. 1, p. 87.

27. F. W. Macdonald, *A Tale*, p. 53.

28. William Allingham, *William Allingham: A Diary* (1911), ed. H. Allingham and D. Radford (London: Penguin Books, 1985), p. 208 (6 March 1872).

29. F. W. Macdonald, *A Tale*, pp. 46–8.

30. Ibid.

31. Ibid., p. 35.

32. Georgiana Burne-Jones, *Memorials*, vol. 1, pp. 89–92.

33. F. W. Macdonald, *A Tale*, pp. 39–43.

34. Ibid.

35. Burne-Jones to Cormell Price, TGA, 7926.

36. Pat Jalland, *Death in the Victorian Family* (Oxford: Oxford University Press, 1996), pp. 40–41.

37. Ibid., p. 109.

38. Ibid., pp. 40–41, 93.

39. Dormandy, *The White Death*, p. 39.

40. Cited in Jalland, *Death in the Victorian Family*, pp. 40–41.

41. Cited in Dormandy, *The White Death*, pp. 93–4.

42. Jalland, *Death in the Victorian Family*, p. 222.

4. London: 'enchanted ground': 1853–1858

1. JLKP.

2. Pamela Horn, *Pleasures and Pastimes in Victorian Britain* (Stroud: Sutton Publishing, 1999), p. 181.

3. Burne-Jones to Cormell Price, TGA, 7926.

4. Georgiana Burne-Jone, *Memorials*, vol. 1, p. 99.

5. Ibid., pp. 71–2.

6. Ibid., p. 121.

7. Ibid., p. 114.

8. Quoted in Harrison and Waters, *Burne-Jones*, p. 20.

9. D. G. Rossetti, *Letters of Dante Gabriel Rossetti*, ed. O. Doughty and J. R. Wahl (Oxford: Oxford University Press, 1965–7), vol. 1, p. 192.

10. Burne-Jones to Cormell Price, 15 June 1856, TGA, 7926.

11. Georgiana Burne-Jones, *Memorials*, vol. 1, p. 134.

12. Ibid., p. 142.

13. Ibid., pp. 134–5.

14. Ibid., pp. 142–4.

15. Ibid., p. 67.

16. Ibid., p. 44.

17. Edith Macdonald, *Annals*, p. 36.

18. F. W. Macdonald, *A Tale*, p. 48.

19. Ibid., p. 58.

20. D. G. Rossetti, *Letters of Dante Gabriel Rossetti*, vol. 1, p. 193.

21. F. W. Macdonald, *A Tale*, pp. 66–7.

22. Zuzanna Shonfield, *The Precariously Privileged: A Professional Family in Victorian London* (Oxford: Oxford University Press, 1987), pp. 47–9. I am indebted to Shonfield for the description of London in this paragraph.

23. F. W. Macdonald, *A Tale*, p. 61.

24. Ibid., p. 60.

25. Stephen Halliday, *The Great Stink of London: Sir Joseph Bazalgette and the Cleansing of the Victorian Capital* (Stroud: Sutton Publishing, 1999), pp. 32, 40–41. I am indebted to this work for much of my information in this paragraph.

26. Faunthorpe, *Household Science*, p. 321.

27. Georgiana Burne-Jones, *Memorials*, vol. 1, p. 141.

28. F. W. Macdonald, *A Tale*, pp. 69–70.

29. Georgiana Burne-Jones, *Memorials*, vol. 1, pp. 170–72.

30. Ibid., p. 187.

31. Algernon Swinburne, *The Swinburne Letters*, ed. Cecil Y. Lang (New Haven: Yale University Press, 1959–62), vol. 1, p. 14.

32. From Thomas Rooke's papers, cited in Jan Marsh, *The Pre-Raphaelite Sisterhood* (London: Quartet, 1985), p. 143.

33. Cited in George Boyce, *The Diaries of George Price Boyce*, ed. Virginia Surtees (Norwich: Real World, 1980), p. 200.

34. Georgiana Burne-Jones, *Memorials*, vol. 1, p. 147.

35. Ibid., p. 183.

36. A. W. Baldwin, *Macdonald Sisters*, p. 26.

37. Charles Carrington, *Rudyard Kipling: His Life and Work* (London: Penguin Books, 1986), p. 157.

38. KP.

39. Georgiana Burne-Jones, *Memorials*, vol. 1, pp. 189–90.

40. F. W. Macdonald, *A Tale*, pp. 34–5.

5. *Travelling in New Worlds: 1859–1862*

1. Georgiana Burne-Jones, *Memorials*, vol. 1, pp. 185–6.

2. Cited in Boyce, *Diaries*, p. 200.

3. Georgiana Burne-Jones, *Memorials*, vol. 1, p. 176.

4. Edith Macdonald, *Annals*, p. 38.

5. Georgiana Burne-Jones, *Memorials*, vol. 1, pp. 178, 180.

6. F. W. Macdonald, *A Tale*, p. 80.

7. Rossetti to Allingham, 10 May 1861, D. G. Rossetti, *Letters of Dante Gabriel Rossetti to William Allingham 1854–70*, ed. George B. Hill (London: Unwin, 1897), p. 258, and 24 January 1863, D. G. Rossetti, *Letters of Dante Gabriel Rossetti*, vol. 2, p. 474.

8. Allingham to Henry Sutton, 15 July 1849; Queen's University, Belfast.

9. Georgiana Burne-Jones, *Memorials*, vol. 1, p. 140.

10. Rossetti to Allingham, D. G. Rossetti, *Letters of Dante Gabriel Rossetti to William Allingham 1854–70*, p. 372.

11. Georgiana Burne-Jones, *Memorials*, vol. 1, pp. 194, 254.

12. John Ruskin to Charles Eliot Norton, 2 June 1861, John Ruskin, *The Correspondence of John Ruskin and Charles Eliot Norton*, ed. John Lewis Bradley and Ian Ousby (Cambridge: Cambridge University Press, 1987), pp. 63–4.

13. Boyce, *Diaries*, p. 189.

14. Georgiana Burne-Jones, *Memorials*, vol. 1, pp. 202–4.

15. Ibid., p. 204.

16. Cited in Marsh, *Pre-Raphaelite Sisterhood*, p. 176.

17. Georgiana Burne-Jones, *Memorials*, vol. 1, p. 204.

18. Ibid., p. 56.

19. Ibid., p. 204.

20. This is cited in Violet Hunt's book about Lizzie Siddal, *The Wife of Rossetti* (London: John Lane, The Bodley Head, 1932), p. 247. Violet Hunt was viciously anti-Rossetti (and therefore anti his friends, such as Burne-Jones), and all her citations need to be treated with caution. I have attempted to weed out what seem the most slanted parts of

her text, and will highlight anything not backed up by independent
sources. This particular comment, however, seems too innocuous to
worry about.

21. William Morris, *Collected Letters of William Morris*, ed. Norman Kelvin
    (Princeton: Princeton University Press, 1984), vol. 1, p. 211.

22. Ibid., p. 43.

23. Ford Madox Brown, *The Diary of Ford Madox Brown*, ed. Virginia
    Surtees (London: Yale University Press, 1981), p. xi.

24. Daphne du Maurier, ed., *The Young George du Maurier: A Selection of
    His Letters, 1860–67* (London: Peter Davies, 1951), p. 183.

25. K. Theodore Hoppen, *The Mid-Victorian Generation, 1846–1886*
    (Oxford: Clarendon Press, 1998), pp. 212–13.

26. Reported by Henry Holiday, cited in Simon Reynolds, *The Vision
    of Simeon Solomon* (Stroud: Catalpa Press, 1985), p. 4.

27. Caroline Dakers, *The Holland Park Circle: Artists and Victorian Society*
    (London: Yale University Press, 1999), p. 65.

28. Georgiana Burne-Jones, *Memorials*, vol. 1, p. 227.

29. Hunt, *The Wife of Rossetti*, p. 190.

30. Georgiana Burne-Jones, *Memorials*, vol. 1, p. 276.

31. *The English Housekeeper*, pp. 104–5.

32. Georgiana Burne-Jones, *Memorials*, vol. 1, p. 222.

33. D. G. Rossetti, *Letters of Dante Gabriel Rossetti*, vol. 2, p. 410.

34. Patricia Branca, *Silent Sisterhood: Middle Class Women in the Victorian
    Home* (London: Croom Helm, 1975), p. 63.

35. Beeton, *Cookery and Household Management*, p. 1020.

36. Ibid. The main childbirth and baby sections are on pp. 1033–44.

37. Margaret Mackail to Lady Mary Murray, 12 November 1942, GMP;
    Burne-Jones to Cormell Price, 23 February 1862, TGA, 7926.

38. Beeton, *Cookery and Household Management*, p. 1022.

39. Georgiana Burne-Jones, *Memorials*, vol. 1, pp. 230–31.

40. Hoppen, *The Mid-Victorian Generation*, p. 325.

41. Burne-Jones to Cormell Price, 23 February 1862, TGA, 7926.

42. Georgiana Burne-Jones, *Memorials*, vol. 1, pp. 235–6.

43. Ibid., p. 262.

44. Rossetti to Alexander Gilchrist, 20 April 1861, D. G. Rossetti, *Letters
    of Dante Gabriel Rossetti*, vol. 2, p. 396.

45. Georgiana Burne-Jones, *Memorials*, vol. 1, pp. 232–3.

46. Robert Southey to Charlotte Brontë, March 1837, cited in Juliet

Barker, *The Brontës* (London: Weidenfeld & Nicolson, 1994), p. 262.

47. Georgiana Burne-Jones, *Memorials*, vol. 1, p. 266.

48. February and March 1862; Daphne du Maurier, *Young George du Maurier*, p. 114.

49. Georgiana Burne-Jones, *Memorials*, vol. 1, p. 233.

6. The Industrious Apprentices: 1862–1866

1. Ruskin to Charles Eliot Norton, 2 June 1861, Ruskin, *The Correspondence of John Ruskin and Charles Eliot Norton*, pp. 63–4.

2. Georgiana Burne-Jones, *Memorials*, vol. 1, p. 245.

3. Georgiana Burne-Jones to John Ruskin, 16 December 1862, B-JP.

4. Ruskin to his father, 12 August 1862, cited in John Ruskin, *Sublime and Instructive: Letters from John Ruskin to Louisa, Marchioness of Waterford, Anna Blundon and Ellen Heaton*, ed. Virginia Surtees (London: Michael Joseph, 1972), pp. 239–40.

5. Hunt, *The Wife of Rossetti*, p. 247.

6. Janet Oppenheim, *Shattered Nerves: Doctors, Patients and Depression in Victorian England* (New York: Oxford University Press, 1991), pp. 36–7.

7. Ibid., pp. 118, 114.

8. *Kipling Journal*, vol. 179, September 1971.

9. Ankers papers, Kipling Society library.

10. The biographical information in this paragraph appears in Mahrukh Tarapor, 'John Lockwood Kipling and British Art Education in India', *Victorian Studies*, vol. 24, no. 1, autumn 1980, pp. 53–82.

11. John Maynard, 'Let Us Now Praise Famous Men' in *Kipling Journal*, vol. 139, September 1961, pp. 13–19.

12. Kay Robinson, 'Kipling in India', *McClure's Magazine*, July 1896.

13. Edward Bok, *Notes and Queries*, 24 October 1942.

14. Frances Macdonald, in 'The Father and Mother of Rudyard Kipling', *Kipling Journal*, vol. 10, September 1936.

15. Robinson, 'Kipling in India'.

16. Editha Plowden, 'Rudyard Kipling's Parents in India', in *Kipling Journal*, vol. 46, July 1938.

17. John Gross, ed., *Rudyard Kipling: The Man, His Work and His World* (London: Weidenfeld & Nicolson, 1972), p. 25.

18. Plowden, 'Rudyard Kipling's Parents in India'.

19. Algernon Swinburne to Burne-Jones, November 1864, Swinburne, *The Swinburne Letters*, vol. 1, p. 111.

20. Georgie Burne-Jones to Ruskin, 13 December 1864, B-JP, vol. 28.

21. Morris to Burne-Jones, November 1864, William Morris, *Collected Letters*, vol. 1, pp. 138–9.

22. Haweis, *The Art of Housekeeping*, p. 33.

23. Ibid., pp. 40–48.

24. Burne-Jones to Ruskin, n.d. (*c.* 1865/6), NP.

25. Horn, *Pleasures and Pastimes*, pp. 86–9.

26. Sir Charles Trevelyan, 1853, cited in Tarapor, 'John Lockwood Kipling and British Art Education in India'. All the information on art education in this paragraph comes from Mahrukh Tarapor's work.

27. *Kipling Journal*, vol. 180, December 1971.

28. Ibid., vol. 283, September 1997.

29. Georgiana Burne-Jones, *Memorials*, vol. 1, p. 290; John Gross, ed., *The Age of Kipling* (New York: Simon & Schuster, 1972), p. 21; Trix Fleming to W. G. B. Maitland, 18 March 1937, CC.

30. Gross, *The Age of Kipling*, p. 21.

31. Rudyard Kipling, *Something of Myself* (1937), ed. Robert Hampson (London: Penguin Books, 1987), p. 33.

32. Cited in Mildred Archer, 'Lockwood Kipling and Indian Decorative Arts', in *Apollo*, April 1986, pp. 264–9.

33. Gross, *The Age of Kipling*, p. 21.

34. J. J. Rivett-Carnac, *Many Memories, of Life in India, at Home, and Abroad* (Edinburgh and London: William Blackwood & Sons, 1910), p. 224.

35. Plowden, 'Rudyard Kipling's Parents in India'.

36. Maynard, 'Let Us Now Praise Famous Men'.

37. Tarapor, 'John Lockwood Kipling and British Art Education in India'. Once again I must indicate my debt to this article for much of the knowledge I have of Lockwood Kipling's Indian career. The information in this paragraph is based entirely on Mahrukh Tarapor's work, and all citations come from it.

38. Fitzgerald, *Burne-Jones*, pp. 99, 118.

39. David Bindman, ed., *The Thames and Hudson Encyclopaedia of British Art* (London: Thames and Hudson, 1985), pp. 27–8.

40. Daphne du Maurier, *Young George du Maurier*, p. 204.

41. Ibid., p. 249.
42. Ibid., p. 33.
43. Ibid., p. 138.
44. Georgiana Burne-Jones, *Memorials*, vol. 1, p. 294.
45. Philip Williamson, *Stanley Baldwin: Conservative Leadership and National Values* (Cambridge: Cambridge University Press, 1999), pp. 89–95. I am deeply indebted to this astonishing work of intellectual history, and have relied heavily on Philip Williamson's groundbreaking study, in this paragraph and elsewhere as indicated.
46. H. Montgomery Hyde, *Baldwin: The Unexpected Prime Minister* (London: Hart-Davis, MacGibbon, 1973), p. 6.
47. Georgiana Burne-Jones, *Memorials*, vol. 1, p. 294.
48. Ibid., p. 300.

7. *'Love enough to last out a long life': 1866–1871*

1. F. W. Macdonald, *A Tale*, p. 42.
2. Ibid., p. 43.
3. Ibid., p. 44.
4. Georgiana Burne-Jones to Sydney Cockerell, 22 June 1918, V & A.
5. All the information on this picture comes from Patrick Conner, 'Wedding Archaeology to Art: Poynter's Israel in Egypt' in Sarah Macready and F. H. Thompson, eds., *Influences in Victorian Art and Architecture* (London: Society of Antiquaries of London, 1985), pp. 112–20.
6. Cited in Dakers, *The Holland Park Circle*, p. 94.
7. Burne-Jones to George Howard, n.d. [1867], CH, J22/27.
8. Cited in Fitzgerald, *Burne-Jones*, p. 104.
9. Andrea Rose, *Pre-Raphaelite Portraits* (Yeovil: Oxford Illustrated Press, 1972), p. 98.
10. William Morris to unknown recipient, 1883, William Morris, *Collected Letters*, vol. 2, p. 231.
11. William Morris to Louisa Baldwin, 25 March 1875, ibid., vol. 1, p. 247.
12. Georgiana Burne-Jones, diary extracts, B-JP.
13. Simon Reynolds, *The Vision of Simeon Solomon*; BL, Add. MSS 52,708.

14. Cited in Simon Reynolds, *The Vision of Simeon Solomon*, p. 13.
15. Georgiana Burne-Jones to Rosalind Howard, 5 July 1868, CH, J22/27.
16. Jalland, *Death in the Victorian Family*, pp. 299ff.
17. Cited in Horn, *The Victorian Town Child*, p. 145.
18. Daphne du Maurier, *Young George du Maurier*, p. 20.
19. Burne-Jones to George Howard, n.d., CH, J22/27.
20. Burne-Jones to George Howard, September 1867, CH J22/27.
21. Georgiana Burne-Jones to Rosalind Howard, 5 July 1868, CH, J22/27.
22. Ibid., 5 September 1868, CH, J22/27.
23. Rossetti to Brown, 23 January 1869, D. G. Rossetti, *Letters of Dante Gabriel Rossetti*, vol. 1, p. 685.
24. Rosalind Howard's diary, 29 January 1869, CH, J23/102.
25. Ibid., 26 January 1869, CH, J23/102.
26. Ibid., 25 June 1869, CH, J23/102/15.
27. Georgiana Burne-Jones to Rosalind Howard, 27 January 1869, CH, J22/27.
28. Rosalind Howard's diary, 10 February 1869, CH, J23/102.
29. Burne-Jones to George Howard, n.d. [February/March 1869], CH, J22/27.
30. Georgiana Burne-Jones to Rosalind Howard, n.d., CH, J22/27.
31. Virginia Surtees, *The Artist and the Aristocrat: George and Rosalind Howard, Earl and Countess of Carlisle* (Salisbury: Michael Russell, 1988), pp. 75–6; Georgiana Burne-Jones to Rosalind Howard, 3 May 1904, CH, J22/27; Margaret Mackail to Gilbert Murray, 25 October 1921 and 4 November 1921, GMP.
32. Georgiana Burne-Jones to Susan Norton, 28 July 1869, NP.
33. Georgiana Burne-Jones to Rosalind Howard, 1 April 1870, CH, J22/27.
34. Burne-Jones to Charles Eliot Norton, 1869, NP.
35. Georgiana Burne-Jones, *Memorials*, vol. 2, p. 1.
36. Hoppen, *The Mid-Victorian Generation*, p. 351.
37. A. W. Baldwin, *My Father: The True Story* (London: George Allen & Unwin, 1955), p. 34.
38. Poynter to F. G. Stephens, 25 August 1875, Bodleian Library, MS Don.e.85.

39. Rosalind Howard's diary, 4 and 23 February 1869, CH, J23/102.

40. Freeman, *Railways and the Victorian Imagination*, p. 133.

41. Cited in Burne-Jones to Mary Gladstone Drew, July 1879, BL, Add. MSS 46,246.

42. Editha Plowden, cited in Andrew Lycett, *Rudyard Kipling* (London: Weidenfeld & Nicolson, 1999), p. 40.

43. Mrs A. M. Fleming, 'Some Childhood Memories of Rudyard Kipling by his Sister', in *Chambers Journal*, March 1939, pp. 168–78.

44. Cited in Lycett, *Rudyard Kipling*, p. 500.

45. Trix Fleming to Stanley Baldwin, 11 April 1945, JLKP.

46. Fleming, 'Some Childhood Memories'.

47. Trix Fleming, 'Through Judy's Eyes, 1874–7', typescript in the Macdonald papers, University of Sussex.

48. Kathryn Hughes, *The Victorian Governess* (London: Hambledon Press, 1993), pp. 69ff.

49. Charles Dickens, *Little Dorrit*, Book II, Chapter 30 (London: Penguin Books, 1985), p. 843.

50. A printed version of this poem is held in the Carpenter Collection, Library of Congress.

8. Spartan Mothers: 1872–1877

1. Georgiana Burne-Jones to Rosalind Howard, 28 September 1869, CH, J22/27.

2. *The Times*, 27 April 1870, p. 4.

3. The manuscript is in the British Library, Add. MSS 45,328.

4. William Morris to Louisa Baldwin, 22 June 1872, William Morris, *Collected Letters*, vol. 1, p. 162.

5. Ibid.

6. William Morris, *Stories in Prose, &c . . .*, Centenary edn (New York: Random House, 1944), p. 53.

7. Charles Eliot Norton's diary, 5 December 1872, NP.

8. Georgiana Burne-Jones to Rosalind Howard, 18 August 1867, CH, J22/27.

9. Cited in Marsh, *Pre-Raphaelite Sisterhood*, p. 128.

10. Georgiana Burne-Jones, *Memorials*, vol. 2, p. 111.

11. William Morris to Aglaia Coronio, 25 November 1872, William Morris, *Collected Letters*, vol. 1, p. 172.

12. Frances Horner, *Time Remembered* (London: William Heinemann, 1933), p. 6.

13. Georgiana Burne-Jones, *Memorials*, vol. 2, p. 309.

14. William Morris to Louisa Baldwin, 30 September 1871, William Morris, *Collected Letters*, vol. 1, p. 150.

15. Worcester Public Record Office, 705:1030, BA 9338, papers of Canon Cory.

16. William Morris to Aglaia Coronio, 25 November 1872, William Morris, *Collected Letters*, vol. 1, p. 172.

17. Beeton, *Cookery and Household Management*, p. 23.

18. Haweis, *The Art of Housekeeping*, pp. 38–9.

19. Georgiana Burne-Jones to Rosalind Howard, 29 August 1875, CH, J22/27.

20. William Morris to Louisa Baldwin, 6 March 1874, William Morris, *Collected Letters*, vol. 1, pp. 198–9.

21. Burne-Jones to Dante Gabriel Rossetti, two letters, n.d. [1874], B-JP, vol. 26.

22. Georgiana Burne-Jones to Mrs Armstrong, 5 May 1894, Thomas Armstrong letters, V & A.

23. Rossetti to Janey Morris, 17 November 1880, BL, Add. MSS 52,333.

24. Burne-Jones to Mary Gladstone Drew, May 1878, BL, Add. MSS 46,246.

25. BL, Add. MSS 45,346.

26. Swinburne to Burne-Jones, 1874, Swinburne, *The Swinburne Letters*, vol. 3, p. 17.

27. Burne-Jones to Louisa Baldwin, 17 November 1874, B-JP, vol. 25, no. 9.

28. Burne-Jones to Philip Burne-Jones, 29 September 1974, B-JP, vol. 25, no. 9.

29. Georgiana Burne-Jones to Rosalind Howard, 22 January 1878, CH, J22/27.

30. Burne-Jones to Charles Eliot Norton, 19 November 1875, NP.

31. Horn, *The Victorian Town Child*, p. 28.

32. Lorraine Price, 'Uncle Crom: Kipling's friendship with Crom Price', in *Kipling Journal*, vol. 269, March 1994.

33. Gross, *The Age of Kipling*, p. 8.
34. Alice Kipling to Editha Plowden, 18 November 1880, JLKP. (The date is noted on the letter thus, but there seems some confusion, as from internal evidence it is clearly written just after their arrival in Lahore.)
35. Ankers papers, Kipling Society library.
36. Alice Kipling to Editha Plowden, 18 November 1880, JLKP.
37. John Lockwood Kipling to Editha Plowden, December 1906, cited in Gross, *Rudyard Kipling*, p. 26.
38. Walter Roper-Lawrence, *The India We Served* (London: Cassell, 1928), p. 22.
39. Trix Fleming to Caroline Kipling, 29 November 1936, JLKP.
40. Oppenheim, *Shattered Nerves*, p. 111.
41. Ibid., p. 131.
42. Hoppen, *The Mid-Victorian Generation*, p. 317.
43. Georgiana Burne-Jones to Rosalind Howard, 31 July 1874 and 4 August 1874, CH, J22/27.
44. Burne-Jones to Watts, *c.* 1870s, cited in Harrison and Waters, *Burne-Jones*, p. 110.
45. Burne-Jones to Charles Eliot Norton, 21 June 1884, NP.
46. Cited in Joseph A. Kestner, *Mythology and Misogyny: The Social Discourse of 19th-Century British Classical-Subject Painting* (Madison: University of Wisconsin Press, 1989), p. 213.
47. Rudyard Kipling, *Wee Willie Winkie and Other Child Stories* (1890) (London: Penguin Books, 1988), p. 284.
48. Rudyard Kipling, *Something of Myself*, p. 42.
49. Georgiana Burne-Jones to Caroline Kipling, 21 May 1907, KP.
50. Cited in David Cecil, *Visionary and Dreamer: Two Poetic Painters, Samuel Palmer and Edward Burne-Jones* (London: Constable, 1969), p. 172.
51. This interpretation is given by Penelope Fitzgerald in *Burne-Jones*, p. 130.
52. All cited in Linda Merril, *The Peacock Room: A Cultural Biography* (New Haven: Yale University Press, 1998), pp. 275–6.
53. Walter Crane, *An Artist's Reminiscences* (London: Methuen, 1907), p. 199.

9. Faith and Works: 1877–1882

1. I am greatly indebted once more to Philip Williamson's *Stanley Baldwin* for much of the information that follows.

2. Menu card, Gross, *Rudyard Kipling*, facing p. 53; etiquette book cited in Horn, *Pleasures and Pastimes*, p. 29; advertisement in Branca, *Silent Sisterhood*, p. 67.

3. Quoted in Cecil, *Visionary and Dreamer*, p. 185.

4. Lockwood Kipling to Margaret Burne-Jones, 10 October 1885, JLKP.

5. Cited in Gross, *The Age of Kipling*, p. 23.

6. Georgiana Burne-Jones to Sydney Cockerell, 25 February 1919, V & A.

7. Georgiana Burne-Jones to Charles Eliot Norton, 4 June 1877, NP.

8. Cited in Cecil, *Visionary and Dreamer*, pp. 184–5.

9. Worcester Public Record Office, 705:1030, BA9338, papers of Canon Cory.

10. Cited in Williamson, *Stanley Baldwin*, p. 122. My information – and all quotations – in this paragraph and the next come from Williamson's book, especially pp. 106–7, 120–22, 124.

11. Worcester Public Record Office, 705:1030, BA9338, papers of Canon Cory.

12. Ibid.

13. Georgiana Burne-Jones to Charles Eliot Norton, 25 February 1905, NP.

14. Georgiana Burne-Jones to Rosalind Howard, 27 September 1871, CH, J22/27.

15. BL, Add. MSS 45,337.

16. This letter was sold at Sotheby's, and reproduced in the sale catalogue.

17. Rossetti to Janey Morris, n.d. [late January or early February 1879], D. G. Rossetti, *Dante Gabriel Rossetti and Jane Morris: Their Correspondence*, ed. John Bryson and J. C. Troxell (Oxford: Clarendon Press, 1976), p. 86.

18. Georgiana Burne-Jones to Rosalind Howard, 6 July 1879, CH, J22/27.

19. Georgiana Burne-Jones to Charles Eliot Norton, 2 July 1877 and 21 July 1875, NP.

20. B-JP.

21. Horn, *Pleasures and Pastimes*, pp. 148–9.

22. CC.

23. A. W. Baldwin, *My Father*, p. 39.

24. BL, Add. MSS 45,337.

25. Burne-Jones to George Howard, n.d., CH, J22/27.

26. William Morris to Janey Morris, 14 December 1877, William Morris, *Collected Letters*, vol. 1, p. 416.

27. *Kipling Journal*, vol. 11, December 1937.

28. Burne-Jones to George Howard, n.d., CH, J22/27.

29. Burne-Jones to Mary Gladstone Drew, April 1880, BL, Add. MSS 46,246.

30. Burne-Jones to Mary Gladstone Drew, end March 1880, BL, Add. MSS 46,246.

31. Burne-Jones to George Howard, n.d., CH, J22/27.

32. Cited in Fitzgerald, *Burne-Jones*, p. 176.

33. Burne-Jones to Mary Gladstone Drew, n.d. [*c.* 1880], BL, Add. MSS 46,246; Rossetti to Janey Morris, [7?] February 1881, D. G. Rossetti, *Dante Gabriel Rossetti and Jane Morris: Their Correspondence*, p. 173.

34. Freeman, *Railways and the Victorian Imagination*, p. 208.

35. George Eliot to Georgiana Burne-Jones, 5 May 1880, George Eliot, *The George Eliot Letters*, ed. Gordon S. Haight (London: Yale University Press, 1954–5), vol. 7, pp. 269–70.

36. Ibid., 6–7 May 1880, 16 June 1880, pp. 272, 299.

37. Georgiana Burne-Jones to Rosalind Howard, 10 May 1880, CH, J22/27.

38. Georgiana Burne-Jones to Charles Eliot Norton, 19 January 1895, NP.

39. Cited in Margot Strickland, *Angela Thirkell: Portrait of a Lady Novelist* (London: Duckworth, 1977), p. 6.

40. Georgiana Burne-Jones to Rosalind Howard, 10 November 1881, CH, J22/27.

41. Georgiana Burne-Jones to Sydney Cockerell, 5 October 1916, BL, Add. MSS 52,708.

42. Alice Kipling to Editha Plowden, 8–13 March 1882, JLKP.

43. Ibid., 28 April 1882, JLKP.

44. Ibid.

45. Lockwood Kipling to Cormell Price, 23 October 1881, cited in *Kipling Journal*, vol. 269, March 1994.

46. Alice Kipling to Editha Plowden, 18 December 1881, JLKP.
47. Ibid., 8–13 March 1882, JLKP.
48. John Lockwood Kipling to Editha Plowden, 26 July 1880, JLKP.
49. F. W. Macdonald, *A Tale*, pp. 155–6.

10. The Families Square: 1882–1884

1. Rudyard Kipling, *Something of Myself*, p. 56.
2. Mrs A. M. Fleming, 'Some Remembrances of My Brother', in *Kipling Journal*, vol. 11, December 1937.
3. Rudyard Kipling, *Something of Myself*, p. 43.
4. A. W. Baldwin, *My Father*, p. 46.
5. Georgiana Burne-Jones, *Memorials*, vol. 2, p. 9.
6. Williamson, *Stanley Baldwin*; David J. Jeremy, ed., *Dictionary of Business Biography: A Biographical Dictionary of Business Leaders Active in Britain in the Period 1860–1980* (London: Butterworth, 1984); Keith Middlemas and John Barnes, *Baldwin* (London: Weidenfeld & Nicolson, 1969).
7. Fleming, 'Some Remembrances of My Brother'.
8. Cited in Rose, *Pre-Raphaelite Portraits*, p. 30.
9. Edith Macdonald, *Annals*, p. 63.
10. Georgiana Burne-Jones, *Memorials*, vol. 2, p. 125.
11. W. Graham Robertson, *Time Was* (London: Hamish Hamilton, 1931), pp. 75–6.
12. [Alice Carr], *J. Comyns Carr: Stray Memories, by His Wife* (London: Macmillan, 1920), pp. 20–22.
13. Ibid., p. 121.
14. Burne-Jones to Val Prinsep, n.d., Pennell-Whistler Collection, Library of Congress.
15. Strickland, *Angela Thirkell*, p. 11.
16. Burne-Jones to Charles Eliot Norton, n.d., NP.
17. Georgiana Burne-Jones to Charles Eliot Norton, 7 October 1885, NP.
18. Georgiana Burne-Jones, *Memorials*, vol. 2, p. 109.
19. Burne-Jones to Mary Gladstone Drew, n.d. [1883], BL, Add. MSS 46,246.
20. Quoted in Cecil, *Visionary and Dreamer*, p. 171.

21. Burne-Jones to George Howard, 25 May 1880, CH, J22/27.

22. Hoppen, *The Mid-Victorian Generation*, p. 662.

23. Fitzgerald, *Burne-Jones*, p. 189.

24. Janey Morris to Mr Watts, n.d., BL, Add. MSS 45,353.

25. Georgiana Burne-Jones to the editor of *Commonweal*, 30 September 1865, William Morris, *Collected Letters*, vol. 2, pp. 459–60.

26. Georgiana Burne-Jones to Charles Eliot Norton, 19 January 1885, NP.

27. Ibid., 15 May 1886, NP.

28. Cecil, *Visionary and Dreamer*, p. 190.

29. Rudyard Kipling to Crom Price, 29 August 1883, Rudyard Kipling, *The Letters of Rudyard Kipling*, ed. Thomas Pinney (Iowa City: University of Iowa Press, 1990–), vol. 1, p. 42.

30. Rudyard Kipling to Edith Macdonald, 28 April 1884, Rudyard Kipling, *Letters*, vol. 1, pp. 61–2.

31. Fleming, 'Some Remembrances of My Brother'.

32. Edmonia Hill, unpublished memoir of Rudyard Kipling, Cornell University.

33. Rudyard Kipling to Edith Macdonald, [26–28 January 1884], Rudyard Kipling, *Letters*, vol. 1, p. 52.

34. Ibid.

35. Ibid., 2–7 June 1884, vol. 1, p. 65.

36. Ibid., [10–14] July [1884], p. 69.

37. Rudyard Kipling to Edmonia Hill, [7–8] July 1888, ibid., p. 241.

38. Ibid.

39. Maynard, 'Let Us Now Praise Famous Men'.

40. I am indebted for much of my information in this paragraph about Lockwood Kipling's connection with the Duke of Connaught and Bagshot Park to Mildred Archer's article, 'Lockwood Kipling and Indian Decorative Arts'.

41. J. H. McGivering, 'Kipling and Son: A Successful Partnership', *Kipling Journal*, vol. 176, December 1970.

42. Trix Fleming to Stanley Baldwin, 27 March 1945, JLKP.

43. Lockwood Kipling to Sara Norton, 27 July 1899, NP.

44. Lockwood Kipling to Margaret Burne-Jones, 10 October 1885, JLKP.

45. Trix Fleming to General Sir Ian Hamilton, cited in General Sir Ian Hamilton, *Listening for the Drums* (London: Faber, 1944), p. 209.

46. Trix Fleming to Stanley Baldwin, 27 March 1945, JLKP.

47. Trix Fleming to W. G. B. Maitland, n.d., CC.

48. Inter many alia, *Kipling Journal*, vol. 232, October 1964.

49. Rudyard Kipling, *Rudyard Kipling's Verse: Inclusive Edition* (New York: Doubleday, Doran & Co., 1938), pp. 23–4.

50. Trix Fleming to W. G. B. Maitland, 1 January 1938, CC.

51. Trix Fleming to Stanley Baldwin, 27 March 1945, JLKP.

52. Rudyard Kipling to Edith Macdonald, [26–28 January 1884], Rudyard Kipling, *Letters*, vol. 1, p. 52.

53. From a list in Kipling's hand, CC.

54. Fleming, 'Some Remembrances of My Brother'.

55. Ibid.

56. Rudyard Kipling, *Something of Myself*, p. 86.

57. Mrs A. M. Fleming, 'My Brother, Rudyard Kipling', in *Kipling Journal*, vol. 83, October 1947.

58. Rudyard Kipling to Edmonia Hill, 30 April 1888, Rudyard Kipling, *Letters*, vol. 1, p. 164.

59. Florence Macdonald, 'Some Memories of My Cousin', in *Kipling Journal*, vol. 46, July 1948.

60. Robinson, 'Kipling in India'.

61. Trix Fleming to W. G. B. Maitland, 21 January 1938, CC.

62. Rudyard Kipling to Margaret Burne-Jones, 28 November 1885–11 January 1886 [one letter], Rudyard Kipling, *Letters*, vol. 1, p. 95.

63. Ibid., 27 September 1885, p. 94.

11. Leaving Home: 1884–1888

1. Cited in Horn, *Pleasures and Pastimes*, p. 51.

2. Ibid.

3. Beeton, *Cookery and Household Management*, p. 5.

4. Shonfield, *The Precariously Privileged*, p. 117.

5. Ibid.

6. Margaret Burne-Jones to Charles Eliot Norton, 12 April 1885, NP.

7. Graham Robertson, cited in Tony Gould, *Inside Outsider: The Life and Times of Colin MacInnes* (London: Allison & Busby, 1983), p. 8.

8. Cited in Strickland, *Angela Thirkell*, p. 6.

9. Georgiana Burne-Jones to Charles Eliot Norton, 19 June 1884, NP.

10. Ibid., 7 July 1884, NP.

11. Ibid., 24 July 1885 and 7 October 1885, NP.

12. Ibid., 7 October 1885, NP.

13. Margaret Burne-Jones to Charles Eliot Norton, 12 April 1885, NP.

14. Cited in Georgiana Burne-Jones, *Memorials*, vol. 2, pp. 137–8.

15. Reported in Rudyard Kipling to Margaret Mackail, 11–14 February 1889, Rudyard Kipling, *Letters*, vol. 1, p. 289.

16. Georgiana Burne-Jones to Charles Eliot Norton, 15 May 1886, NP.

17. Ibid.

18. Ibid., 7 October 1885, NP.

19. Dakers, *The Holland Park Circle*, p. 238.

20. Faunthorpe, *Household Science*, pp. 300–304.

21. Haweis, *The Art of Housekeeping*, pp. 98–9.

22. Georgiana Burne-Jones to Sydney Cockerell, 3 August 1917, V & A.

23. As always, most of the information on Baldwin's early life in this paragraph and the next comes from Williamson, *Stanley Baldwin*.

24. Louisa Baldwin, *A Martyr to Mammon* (London: Swan Sonnenschein & Co., 1886), vol. 1, p. 58.

25. Ibid., vol. 3, p. 58.

26. Frederic L. V. Fildes, *Luke Fildes R.A.: A Victorian Painter* (London: Michael Joseph, 1968), p. 99.

27. Burne-Jones to F. G. Stephens, Bodleian Library, MS Don.e.62.

28. Georgiana Burne-Jones to Charles Eliot Norton, 24 July 1885, NP.

29. Cited in Simon Reynolds, *William Blake Richmond: An Artist's Life, 1842–1921* (Wilby: Michael Russell, 1995), p. 114.

30. Crane, *An Artist's Reminiscences*, p. 322.

31. Burne-Jones to George Howard, [November 1887], CH, J22/27.

32. Cited in *Kipling Journal*, vol. 180, December 1971, from the annual luncheon address.

33. Rudyard Kipling to Margaret Burne-Jones, [27] September 1885, Rudyard Kipling, *Letters*, vol. 1, p. 94.

34. Ibid., 3 May–24 June 1886, p. 136.

35. Rudyard Kipling to Edmonia Hill, 28 June–1 July 1888, ibid., p. 223.

36. Ibid., 4–6 July 1888, p. 231.

37. Ibid.

38. Ibid., 15 July 1888, p. 254.

39. Lockwood Kipling to Editha Plowden, 28 August 1888, JLKP.

40. Rudyard Kipling to Alexander and Edmonia Hill, [6] October 1888, Rudyard Kipling, *Letters*, vol. 1, p. 258.

41. Fleming, 'My Brother, Rudyard Kipling'.

42. Rudyard Kipling to Margaret Burne-Jones, 28 November 1885–11 January 1886 [one letter], Rudyard Kipling, *Letters*, vol. 1, p. 103.

43. Rudyard Kipling to Edith Macdonald, 2–7 June 1884, ibid., pp. 64–5.

44. Ibid., 13 July–1 August 1885, pp. 81–3.

45. Rudyard Kipling to Edmonia Hill, 9–10 July 1888, ibid., p. 243.

46. Cited in Rudyard Kipling, *Letters*, vol. 1, p. 246.

47. Rudyard Kipling to Edmonia Hill, 22 June 1888, ibid., p. 205.

48. Ibid., 5–6 June 1888, pp. 201–2.

49. Edmonia Hill, unpublished memoir of Rudyard Kipling, Cornell University.

50. Rudyard Kipling to W. C. Crofts, 18–22 February 1886, Rudyard Kipling, *Letters*, vol. 1, p. 120.

51. Rudyard Kipling to Margaret Burne-Jones, 27 September 1885, ibid., p. 93.

52. Rudyard Kipling to Professor and Mrs Alexander Hill, 6 October 1888, ibid., p. 93.

53. Rudyard Kipling to E. K. Robinson, 30 April 1886, ibid., pp. 126–7.

54. Rudyard Kipling, *Something of Myself*, p. 86.

55. Rudyard Kipling, 'Baa Baa, Black Sheep', in *Wee Willie Winkie*, p. 288.

56. Alice Kipling to Georgiana Burne-Jones, quoted in *Kipling Journal*, vol. 121, April 1987, from 'A Biographical and Critical Sketch [of Rudyard Kipling]' by Andrew Lang, reprinted from *Harper's Weekly*, n.d.

57. Rudyard Kipling to Margaret Mackail, 11–14 February 1889, Rudyard Kipling, *Letters*, vol. 1, pp. 285–8.

58. Carrington, *Rudyard Kipling*, p. 157.

59. Rudyard Kipling to Edmonia Hill, 10 September 1889, Rudyard Kipling, *Letters*, vol. 1, p. 340.

60. Cited in Carrington, *Rudyard Kipling*, p. 175.

61. Rudyard Kipling to Edmonia Hill, 13 July 1888, Rudyard Kipling, *Letters*, vol. 1, p. 252.

62. Ibid., p. 248.

12. The Cousinhood: 1888–1892

1. Georgiana Burne-Jones to Charles Eliot Norton, 5 February 1888, NP.
2. Ibid., 22 August 1888 and 2 July 1890, NP.
3. Cited in Richard Jenkyns, *The Victorians and Ancient Greece* (Oxford: Basil Blackwell, 1980), p. 295.
4. Cited in Gould, *Inside Outsider*, p. 9.
5. Georgiana Burne-Jones to Charles Eliot Norton, 9 March 1888, NP.
6. The reference may appear in the Baldwin papers, which I have not had access to.
7. Georgiana Burne-Jones to Charles Eliot Norton, January 1897, NP.
8. Burne-Jones to Frederick Leyland, 14 September 1888, Pennell–Whistler Collection, Library of Congress.
9. Branca, *Silent Sisterhood*, p. 82.
10. Georgiana Burne-Jones to Charles Eliot Norton, 10 May 1889, NP.
11. Colonel S. M. Moens, *Rottingdean: The Story of a Village*, ed. H. E. Blyth (Brighton: John Beal & Son, 1952), p. 38.
12. Ibid., p. 30.
13. Ibid., p. 13.
14. Georgiana Burne-Jones to S. C. Cockerell, 21 May 1897, BL, Add. MSS 52,708.
15. Cecil, *Visionary and Dreamer*, p. 185.
16. Haweis, *The Art of Housekeeping*, p. 49.
17. Shonfield, *The Precariously Privileged*, pp. 110–11.
18. Rudyard Kipling to Edmonia Hill, 8–16 November 1889, Rudyard Kipling, *Letters*, vol. 1, pp. 365–6.
19. Rudyard Kipling to Isabella Burton, 26 October 1887, ibid., p. 144.
20. Rudyard Kipling to Edmonia Hill, 8–16 November 1889, ibid., p. 360.
21. Ibid.
22. Ibid., pp. 360–61.
23. Ibid., 3–25 December 1889, p. 370.
24. Ibid.
25. Ibid.
26. Rudyard Kipling to Edmund Gosse, 11 November 1890, CC.

27. Kipling–Balestier–Dunham papers, University of Sussex.

28. Fleming, 'My Brother, Rudyard Kipling'.

29. Lockwood Kipling to Rudyard Kipling, 2 March 1890, JLKP.

30. Lockwood Kipling to Lockwood de Forest, 31 August 1890, NP.

31. Cited in Tarapor, 'John Lockwood Kipling and British Art Education in India', p. 77.

32. Cited in F. W. Macdonald, *A Tale*, p. 199.

33. Tarapor, 'John Lockwood Kipling and British Art Education in India', p. 77.

34. Raymond Head, 'Bagshot Park and Indian Crafts', in Macready and Thompson, *Influences in Victorian Art and Architecture*, pp. 139–49.

35. Notebook in the Macdonald papers, University of Sussex.

36. Lockwood Kipling to Maurice Macmillan, 13 April 1892, BL, Add. MSS 54,940.

37. Cited in Tarapor, 'John Lockwood Kipling and British Art Education in India', pp. 60ff.

38. This and the following, BL, Add. MSS 54,940.

39. Lockwood Kipling to Lockwood de Forest, 'Ash Wednesday' 1892, McG.

40. Ibid.

41. Rudyard Kipling to Edmonia Hill, 9–10 July 1888, Rudyard Kipling, *Letters*, vol. 1, p. 244.

42. Lockwood Kipling to Rudyard Kipling, 18 April 1890, JLKP.

43. Lockwood Kipling to Maurice Macmillan, 16 October 1892, BL, Add. MSS 54,940.

44. Lockwood Kipling to Editha Plowden, [autumn 1890], JLKP.

45. Cited in *Kipling Journal*, vol. 165, March 1968.

46. Stanley Baldwin to Joan Dickinson, 16 November 1916. I am grateful to Philip Williamson for this reference.

47. Rudyard Kipling to Margaret Burne-Jones, 28 November 1885–11 January 1886, Rudyard Kipling, *Letters*, vol. 1, pp. 109–10.

48. Georgiana Burne-Jones to Charles Eliot Norton, 29 September 1890, NP.

49. Rudyard Kipling, *Something of Myself*, p. 86.

50. Caroline Balestier to Anna Starr Balestier, [1890], Kipling–Balestier–Dunham papers, University of Sussex.

51. Edmund Gosse's description, reprinted from an essay of 1892 in *Kipling Journal*, vol. 252, December 1989.

52. Mary Cabot, unpublished memoir of Kipling in Vermont, CC.
53. Cited in Gross, *The Age of Kipling*, p. 69.
54. Undated letter from Henry James to unknown recipient, CC.
55. Lockwood Kipling to Lockwood de Forest, 'Ash Wednesday' 1892, McG.

13. Settling Down: 1892–1894

1. Angela Thirkell, *Three Houses* (Oxford: Oxford University Press, 1932), pp. 107–8.
2. Moens, *Rottingdean*, pp. 59–60.
3. Stanley Baldwin to Louisa Baldwin, 13 April 1892, cited in Williamson, *Stanley Baldwin*, p. 123.
4. John Lockwood Kipling to Editha Plowden, [autumn 1891], JLKP.
5. Ibid., 8 August 1892.
6. Rudyard Kipling to Lockwood de Forest, 1 October 1892, McG; Rudyard Kipling to Trix Fleming, 25 February 1931, KP.
7. Caroline Kipling to Anna Starr Balestier, n.d., Kipling–Balestier–Dunham papers, University of Sussex.
8. Rudyard Kipling to Edward Bok, 9 December 1897, CC.
9. Mary Cabot, unpublished memoir of Kipling in Vermont, CC.
10. Rudyard Kipling to John Cope Cornford, 5 December 1896, CC.
11. Obituary in *Kidderminster Shuttle*, 18 February 1908.
12. Jeremy, *Dictionary of Business Biography*; Williamson, *Stanley Baldwin*, p. 98.
13. Rudyard Kipling to Louisa Baldwin, 18 January 1898, KP. In the University of Sussex Kipling papers alone there are twenty-one letters of this kind, dating from 1894 to 1923.
14. Cited in Rudyard Kipling to Lockwood de Forest, 1 October 1892, McG.
15. Caroline Kipling to Meta de Forest, 5 July 1893, McG.
16. Lockwood Kipling to Lockwood de Forest, 11 August 1893, McG.
17. Rudyard Kipling to Meta de Forest, 21 August 1893, McG.
18. Lockwood Kipling to Meta de Forest, 29 August 1893, McG.
19. Caroline Kipling to Meta de Forest, 5 July 1893, McG.
20. Burne-Jones to Helen Mary Gaskell, 17 August 1893, BL, Add. MSS 54,217.

21. The bulk of his letters to her are in BL, Add. MSS 54,217. Unless otherwise cited, this is the source throughout.

22. Cutting contained in BL, Add. MSS 54,217, dated August 1894.

23. Postmarked 4 September 1894.

24. *Apollo*, November 1875, part of a special issue on Burne-Jones.

25. 16 February 1893.

26. [9 September 1893?]

27. Burne-Jones to Val Prinsep, n.d., Pennell–Whistler Collection, Library of Congress.

28. Burne-Jones to Mary Gladstone Drew, October 1893, BL, Add. MSS 46,246.

29. Ibid., [1892], BL, Add. MSS 46,246.

30. Ibid., 21 August 1893, BL, Add. MSS 46,246.

31. Alfred Lys Baldry, 'Marcus Stone', in *Art Journal*, vol. 58, 1896, p. 5.

32. *The Times*, 20 May 1885, p. 10.

33. Ibid., 22 May 1885, p. 5.

34. Ibid., 23 May 1885, p. 10.

35. Ibid., 28 May 1885, p. 4.

36. Jenkyns, *The Victorians and Ancient Greece*, pp. 306–7.

37. Rudyard Kipling to B. H. Walton, 24 November 1906, CC.

38. Cited in Alan Bell, 'Colvin vs. Poynter: The Directorship of the National Gallery, 1892–4', in *Connoisseur*, December 1975, pp. 278–83.

39. Ibid.

40. Burne-Jones to Helen Mary Gaskell, 28 April 1894, BL, Add. MSS 54,217.

41. Cited in Paula Gillett, *The Victorian Painter's World* (Gloucester: Alan Sutton, 1990), pp. 227–8.

42. Agnes Poynter to Florrie Mason, 25 June 1900, TGA, 741.

43. Burne-Jones to Mary Gladstone Drew, November 1893, BL, Add. MSS 46,246.

44. Burne-Jones to F. G. Stephens, June 1885, Bodleian Library, MS Don.e.62.

45. Margaret Mackail to Charles Eliot Norton, 20 July 1889, NP.

46. Angela Thirkell to Gilbert Murray, 23 November 1956, GMP.

47. Lockwood Kipling to Macmillan & Co., 3 January 1895, BL, Add. MSS 54,940.

48. Philip Burne-Jones to Sydney Cockerell, 20 February 1925, BL, Add. MSS 52,708.

49. Burne-Jones to Lady Simon, February 1894, B-JP, vol. 26.

50. Janey Morris to Wilfrid Scawen Blunt, 12 March 1894, B-JP.

51. Georgiana Burne-Jones, *Memorials*, vol. 2, p. 241.

14. Separations: 1895–1898

1. Mary Cabot, unpublished memoir of Kipling in Vermont, CC.

2. Caroline Kipling to Meta de Forest, [*c*. 1893], NP.

3. Ibid., 14 July 1894.

4. As related by Charles Warren Stoddard in 'Kipling and Stoddard: Days of Joyous Companionship at Naulakha', in *National Magazine*, 1895 [no other date on cutting].

5. Caroline Kipling to Meta de Forest, 15 June 1893, McG.

6. Cited in Frederic van de Water, *Rudyard Kipling's Vermont Feud* (New York: Haskell House Publishers, 1974), pp. 47–8.

7. Rudyard Kipling to Meta de Forest, 30 January 1895, NP.

8. Caroline Kipling to Meta de Forest, 14 July 1894, NP.

9. Georgiana Burne-Jones to Rosalind Howard, 28 March 1893, CH, J22/27.

10. William Morris to Georgiana Burne-Jones, 20 December 1894, William Morris, *Collected Letters*, vol. 4, pp. 242–3.

11. Burne-Jones to Mrs Watts, 17 December 1894, B-JP, vol. 26.

12. William Morris to Georgiana Burne-Jones, 14 December 1894, William Morris, *Collected Letters*, vol. 4, pp. 240–41.

13. Burne-Jones to Helen Mary Gaskell, 12 November 1894, BL, Add. MSS 54,217.

14. Ibid., 22 October 1894, BL, Add. MSS 54,217.

15. Ibid., [before April 1894], BL, Add. MSS 54,217.

16. Ibid., postmarked 19 November 1894, BL, Add. MSS 54,217.

17. Poynter to George Howard, 22 January 1901, CH, J22/57.

18. Ibid., 11 May 1896, CH, J22/57.

19. Poynter to Sir Henry Layard, 20 December 1873, BL, Add. MSS 39,004.

20. Poynter to Sir Henry Tate, 6 November 1896, TGA, 7811.2.55.

21. Rudyard Kipling to Charles Eliot Norton, 31 December 1896, NP.

22. Cited in Gillett, *The Victorian Painter's World*, p. 213.

23. Poynter to George Howard, 30 July 1904, CH, J22/57.

24. Frances Spalding, *The Tate: A History* (London: Tate Gallery Publishing, 1998), pp. 23ff.

25. Cited in Dakers, *The Holland Park Circle*, pp. 266–7.

26. Poynter to George Howard, 8 March 1896, CH, J22/57.

27. Cited in Spalding, *The Tate*, p. 23.

28. Rudyard Kipling to Charles Eliot Norton, 29 June 1896, NP.

29. Georgiana Burne-Jones to Charles Eliot Norton, 2 July 1890 and 1 September 1897, NP.

30. Burne-Jones to Helen Mary Gaskell, 25 September, 14 October and 23 October 1894, BL, Add. MSS 54,217.

31. George Calvin Carter, 'Why Kipling Did Not Become an American Citizen', reprinted in *Kipling Journal*, vol. 156, December 1965, from an article originally published in April 1931.

32. Caroline Kipling to Meta de Forest, 29 June 1896, NP.

33. Burne-Jones to Mary Gladstone Drew, n.d., BL, Add. MSS 46, 246.

34. Janey Morris to Wilfrid Scawen Blunt, 13 April 1892, William Morris, *Collected Letters*, vol. 3, p. 287.

35. William Morris to Georgiana Burne-Jones, 28 April 1896, ibid., vol. 4, p. 369.

36. Janey Morris to Wilfrid Scawen Blunt, 27 June 1896, ibid., p. 377.

37. William Morris to Georgiana Burne-Jones, 1 September 1896, ibid., p. 391.

38. William Morris to Jenny Morris, 14 September 1896, ibid., p. 391.

39. Cited in Cecil, *Visionary and Dreamer*, p. 198.

40. Georgiana Burne-Jones to Charles Eliot Norton, 1 September 1897, NP.

41. Ibid., 4 June 1877, NP.

42. Georgiana Burne-Jones to Charles Eliot Norton, 10 May 1889, NP.

43. Georgiana Burne-Jones to Rosalind Howard, 11 February 1892, CH, J22/27.

44. Cited in Jalland, *Death in the Victorian Family*, p. 52.

45. Both letters to George Howard, 3 October 1896, CH, J22/27.

46. Georgiana Burne-Jones to May Morris, 3 October 1896, BL, Add. MSS 45,346.

47. Georgiana Burne-Jones to Sydney Cockerell, 7 October 1896, BL, Add. MSS 52,772.

48. Ibid., 23 March 1897, BL, Add. MSS 52,708.

49. Wilfrid Scawen Blunt, 4 and 5 October 1896, secret memoirs, vol. 18, Fitzwilliam Museum.

50. Philip Burne-Jones to Henry James, 8 October 1903, NP.

51. Caroline Kipling to Meta de Forest, 25 June 1897, McG.

52. Caroline Kipling to Miss Lawrence, n.d., CC.

53. Rudyard Kipling to Dr James Conland, 8–17 November [?1896], CC.

54. Rudyard Kipling to Louisa Baldwin, 7 January 1897, JLKP.

55. Rudyard Kipling to Jack Mackail, 18 August 1897, KP.

56. Rudyard Kipling to Alfred Baldwin, August 1897, JLKP.

57. Georgiana Burne-Jones to Charles Eliot Norton, 11 April 1902, NP.

58. Cited in Gould, *Inside Outsider*, p. 9.

59. Georgiana Burne-Jones to Rosalind Howard, n.d., CH, J22/27; and to Charles Eliot Norton, 10 May 1889, NP.

60. Burne-Jones to Helen Mary Gaskell, 26 October 1894, BL, Add. MSS 54,217.

61. Cited in Rose, *Pre-Raphaelite Portraits*, p. 32.

62. Burne-Jones to Olive Maxse, n.d. [1890s], cited in Rose, *Pre-Raphaelite Portraits*, p. 33.

63. Burne-Jones to Helen Mary Gaskell, [January ?1893], [spring 1894], 15 November–31 December 1894, [postmarked 9 April 1894], BL, Add. MSS 54,217.

64. Ibid., 29 August 1893, BL, Add. MSS 54,217.

65. Georgiana Burne-Jones to Charles Eliot Norton, 7 October 1885, NP.

66. Burne-Jones to Helen Mary Gaskell, postmarked 23 October 1894, BL, Add. MSS 54,217.

67. Georgiana Burne-Jones, *Memorials*, vol. 2, p. 193.

68. All cited in Kestner, *Mythology and Misogyny*, p. 80.

69. Burne-Jones to Helen Mary Gaskell, [March 1895], BL, Add. MSS 54,217.

70. Burne-Jones to Susan Norton, 28 September 1896, NP.

71. Georgiana Burne-Jones to Val Prinsep, 14 January 1899, Pennell–Whistler Collection, Library of Congress.

15. 'A pack of troubles': 1898–1906

1. Rudyard Kipling to Stanley Weyman, 30 December 1895, CC.
2. Mary Cabot, unpublished memoir of Kipling in Vermont, CC.
3. Caroline Kipling to Meta de Forest, 5 December 1897, NP.
4. Rudyard Kipling to Dr James Conland, 17 December 1897, CC.
5. Colin MacInnes, *England, Half English* (London: MacGibbon & Kee, 1961), p. 115.
6. Philip Burne-Jones to Charles Eliot Norton, 15 April 1898, NP.
7. Philip Burne-Jones to Sir Isidore Spielmann, 21 December 1898, V & A.
8. Georgiana Burne-Jones to Charles Eliot Norton, 17 June 1898, NP.
9. Georgiana Burne-Jones to Sydney Cockerell, [June/July 1898], V & A.
10. Georgiana Burne-Jones to Alice Kipling, 17 March 1899, KP.
11. Rudyard Kipling to Charles Eliot Norton, 22 June 1898, NP.
12. Georgiana Burne-Jones to Mary Gladstone Drew, 16 December 1898, BL, Add. MSS 46,246.
13. MacInnes, *England, Half English*, p. 116.
14. Cited in Lycett, *Rudyard Kipling*, p. 316.
15. Rudyard Kipling to Lockwood de Forest, n.d. [February 1899], NP.
16. Caroline Kipling to Georgiana Burne-Jones, 14 February 1899, KP.
17. Alice Kipling to Georgiana Burne-Jones, 22 February 1899, KP.
18. Ibid., 1 March 1899, KP.
19. Ibid., 6 March 1899, KP.
20. A. P. Watt to John Lockwood Kipling, 14 March 1899, KP.
21. Ibid.
22. Caroline Kipling to Georgiana Burne-Jones, 17 March 1899, KP.
23. Alice Kipling to Georgiana Burne-Jones, 6 March 1899, KP.
24. Sally Norton to Charles Eliot Norton, 30 March 1899, NP.
25. Copy in CC.
26. John Lockwood Kipling to Sally Norton, 22 July 1899, JLKP.
27. Georgiana Burne-Jones to Mary Gladstone Drew, 6 July 1899, BL, Add. MSS 46,246.
28. John Lockwood Kipling to Sally Norton, 22 July 1899, JLKP.
29. Alfred Baldwin to Caroline Kipling, 6 April 1899, KP.

30. John Lockwood Kipling to Sally Norton, 5 February 1900, JLKP.
31. Ibid., 21 November 1899, NP.
32. Dr R. Gowers to Jack Fleming, 15 November 1899, Macdonald papers, University of Sussex.
33. John Lockwood Kipling to Sally Norton, 5 February 1900, JLKP.
34. Caroline Kipling to Meta de Forest, 11 May 1900, NP.
35. Ibid., 28 October 1902, NP.
36. Rudyard Kipling to Edmonia Hill, 30 July 1899, CC.
37. John Lockwood Kipling to Sally Norton, 4 July 1899, JLKP.
38. Burne-Jones to Lady Rayleigh, 29 December 1896, B-JP, vol. 26.
39. Rudyard Kipling to Barclay Walton, 23 June 1904, CC.
40. Georgiana Burne-Jones to Gilbert Murray, September 1902, GMP.
41. Georgiana Burne-Jones to Charles Eliot Norton, 19 February 1905, NP.
42. Horn, *Pleasures and Pastimes*, p. 32.
43. Ibid., p. 263.
44. Georgiana Burne-Jones to Cormell Price, 2 December 1901, NP.
45. Georgiana Burne-Jones to Charles Eliot Norton, 12 July 1901, NP.
46. Ibid.
47. Georgiana Burne-Jones to Sydney Cockerell, 26 January 1905 and 12 April 1917, V & A.
48. Georgiana Burne-Jones to Sydney Cockerell, 4 December 1902, V & A.
49. Georgiana Burne-Jones to Charles Eliot Norton, 15 December 1905, NP.
50. Georgiana Burne-Jones to Sydney Cockerell, 21 May 1897, BL, Add. MSS 52,708.
51. Georgiana Burne-Jones to Charles Eliot Norton, 28 December 1904, NP.
52. J. W. Mackail to Sydney Cockerell, 3 January 1904, BL, Add. MSS 52,734.
53. Rudyard Kipling to Sally Norton, 21 August 1897, NP.
54. *Kipling Journal*, vol. 171, September 1989, from the annual luncheon address.
55. *The Times*, 1 June 1923, p. 17.
56. Georgiana Burne-Jones to Charles Eliot Norton, 14 August 1900, NP.
57. Rudyard Kipling to Charles Eliot Norton, 2 May 1904, NP.

58. Georgiana Burne-Jones to Sydney Cockerell, 29 March 1906, BL, Add. MSS 52,708.

59. Cited in Kestner, *Mythology and Misogyny*, p. 213.

60. Philip Burne-Jones to Charles Eliot Norton, 12 January 1907, NP.

16. *'The pain of parting'*

1. Margaret Mackail to Gilbert Murray, 19 February 1902, GMP.

2. Philip Burne-Jones to Charles Eliot Norton, 9 November 1903, 9 November 1904, 2 July 1905, NP.

3. J. W. Mackail to Sydney Cockerell, 11 November 1903, BL, Add. MSS 52,734.

4. Rudyard Kipling to Alfred Baldwin, 19 August 1905, JLKP.

5. Trix Fleming to G. B. Maitland, 5 February 1938, CC.

6. Rudyard Kipling to Cope Cornford, 16 May 1901, CC.

7. Georgiana Burne-Jones to Charles Eliot Norton, 22 September 1907, NP.

8. Rudyard Kipling to Cormell Price, 5 November 1907, CC.

9. Rudyard Kipling to Charles Eliot Norton, 18 February 1908, NP.

10. Oliver Baldwin, *The Questing Beast* (London: Grayson & Grayson, 1932), pp. 23–4.

11. Georgiana Burne-Jones to Sydney Cockerell, 23 March 1906, V & A.

12. Georgiana Burne-Jones to William Rothenstein, 12 May 1907, NP.

13. Georgiana Burne-Jones to Charles Eliot Norton, 22 September 1906, NP.

14. Lockwood Kipling to Editha Plowden, 17 July 1908, JLKP.

15. Ibid.

16. Georgiana Burne-Jones to Sydney Cockerell, 22 December 1908, V & A.

17. Oliver Baldwin, *The Questing Beast*, pp. 12–13.

18. Margaret Mackail to Gilbert Murray, 19 February 1902, 25 December 1902, 1 August 1912, GMP.

19. Ibid., 19 February 1902.

20. Margaret Mackail to Sydney Cockerell, 17 March 1940, V & A.

21. F. W. Macdonald, *A Tale*, p. 333.

22. Lockwood Kipling to Sara Norton, 22 July 1899, NP.

23. Lockwood Kipling to Editha Plowden, 13 December 1905, JLKP.

24. Rudyard Kipling to Edmonia Hill, 23 October 1905, CC.

25. Lockwood Kipling to Editha Plowden, 1908, cited in Gross, *The Age of Kipling*, p. 26.

26. Ibid., 23 November 1910, JLKP.

27. Undated chronology of Trix's illness drawn up by Jack Fleming, KP.

28. Lockwood Kipling to Editha Plowden, 25 December 1910, JLKP.

29. Cited in Plowden, 'Rudyard Kipling's Parents in India'.

30. Caroline Kipling to Anna Starr Balestier, 6 August 1915, Kipling–Balestier–Dunham papers, University of Sussex.

31. Cited in *Kipling Journal*, vol. 165, March 1968.

32. Rudyard Kipling to Elsie Bambridge, 19 May 1930, KP.

33. Stanley Baldwin to Lady Milner, 9 July 1934, Violet Milner papers 33, 133/6, Bodleian Library.

34. Caroline Kipling to Anna Starr Balestier, 8 January [1909?], Kipling–Balestier–Dunham papers, University of Sussex.

35. Fildes, *Luke Fildes*, p. 214.

36. Cited in Gould, *Inside Outsider*, p. 21.

37. Ibid., pp. 17ff.

38. Philip Burne-Jones to Sydney Cockerell, 10 August 1920, BL, Add. MSS 52,708.

39. Philip Burne-Jones to Sydney Cockerell, 18 February 1923, BL, Add. MSS 52,708; to Mary Gladstone Drew, 28 May 1923, BL, Add. MSS 46,246; to Sydney Cockerell, 16 May 1925 and 21 June 1921, BL, Add. MSS 52,708.

40. Rudyard Kipling to Elsie Bambridge, 11 December 1924, KP.

41. Philip Burne-Jones to Sydney Cockerell, 3 June 1921, BL, Add. MSS 52,708.

42. Ibid., n.d, BL, Add. MSS 52,708.

43. Margaret Mackail to Sydney Cockerell, 31 March 1926, BL, Add. MSS 52,708.

44. Ibid., 21 June 1926.

45. *The Times*, 22 June 1926, p. 21.

46. Georgiana Burne-Jones to Charles Eliot Norton, 15 February 1905, NP.

47. All these comments on Clare come from Margaret Mackail's letters to Gilbert Murray, GMP.

48. Oppenheim, *Shattered Nerves*, pp. 211–13.

49. Rudyard Kipling to Elsie Bambridge, 11 October 1932, KP.
50. Edith Macdonald, *Annals*, p. 62.

Afterword

1. Edith Macdonald, *Annals*, p. 44.
2. Cited in Gould, *Inside Outsider*, p. 9.

Select Bibliography

Allingham, William, *Letters to William Allingham*, ed. H. Allingham and E. B. Williams (London: Longmans, Green & Co., 1911)

——, *Letters to Mr and Mrs Browning* (pamphlet addendum to *Letters to William Allingham*), [no publication details cited]

——, *William Allingham: A Diary* (1911), ed. H. Allingham and D. Radford (London: Penguin Books, 1985)

Altick, Richard D., *Victorian People and Ideas* (New York: Norton, 1973)

Angeli, Helen Rossetti, *Dante Gabriel Rossetti, His Friends and Enemies* (London: Hamish Hamilton, 1949)

——, *Pre-Raphaelite Twilight: The Story of Charles Augustus Howell* (London: The Richards Press, 1954)

Ankers, Arthur R., *The Pater: John Lockwood Kipling, His Life and Times, 1837–1911* (Otford, Kent: Pond View Books, 1988)

Ansell, Charles, *On the Rate of Mortality at Early Periods of Life, the Age of Marriage, the Number of Children to a Marriage, and Other Statistics of Families, in the Upper and Professional Classes* (London: National Life Assurance Society, C. & E. Layton, 1874)

Baber, C., and Boyns, T., 'Alfred Baldwin', in David J. Jeremy, ed., *Dictionary of Business Biography: A Biographical Dictionary of Business Leaders Active in Britain in the Period 1860–1980* (London, Butterworth, 1984), vol. 1, pp. 116–18

Baldwin, A. W. (Earl Baldwin of Bewdley), *My Father: The True Story* (London: George Allen & Unwin, 1955)

——, *The Macdonald Sisters* (London: Peter Davies, 1960)

Baldwin, Louisa, *A Martyr to Mammon* (London: Swan Sonnenschein & Co., 1886)

——, *Where Town and Country Meet* (London: Longmans, 1891)

——, *Richard Dare* (London: Smith, Elder, 1894)

——, *The Shadow on the Blind and Other Ghost Stories* (London: J. M. Dent, 1895)

——, *The Story of a Marriage* (London: Ward & Downey, 1895; rev. edn London: J. M. Dent, 1899)

——, *A Chaplet of Verses for Children* (London: Elkin Matthews, 1904)

——, *The Pedlar's Pack* (London: W. & R. Chambers, 1904)

——, *From Fancy's Realm* (London: W. & R. Chambers, 1905)

——, *Afterglow* (London: Methuen, 1911)

Baldwin, Monica, *I Leap Over the Wall* (London: Hamish Hamilton, 1949)

Baldwin, Oliver, *The Questing Beast* (London: Grayson & Grayson, 1932)

Baldwin, Stanley, *On England* (London: Philip Allan & Co., 1926)

——, *Our Inheritance* (London: Hodder & Stoughton, 1928)

——, 'Burne-Jones' in *This Torch of Freedom* (London: Hodder & Stoughton, 1937)

——, *Service of our Lives* (London: Hodder & Stoughton, 1937)

Balestier, Wolcott, *A Victorious Defeat* (New York: Harper & Brothers, 1886)

Balfour, Arthur, *Chapters of an Autobiography* (London: Cassell, 1930)

Balfour, Lady Frances, *Ne Obliviscaris: Dinna Forget* (London: Hodder & Stoughton, 1930)

Barr, Pat, and Desmond, Ray, *Simla: A Hill Station in British India* (London: Scolar Press, 1982)

Barringer, Tim, and Prettejohn, Elizabeth, *Frederic Leighton: Antiquity, Renaissance, Modernity* (London: Yale University Press, 1999)

Barrington, Emilie Isabel, *G. F. Watts: Reminiscences* (London: George Allen, 1905)

Bartram, Michael, *The Pre-Raphaelite Camera* (London: Weidenfeld & Nicolson, 1985)

Beckson, Karl, *London in the 1890s* (London: W. W. Norton & Co., 1992)

Beeton, Mrs [Isabella], *Mrs Beeton's Book of Cookery and Household Management* (London: S. O. Beeton, 1860)

Beeton's Penny Guides to Domestic Service (London: S. O. Beeton, n.d.)

Bell, Quentin, *Victorian Artists* (London: Routledge & Kegan Paul, 1967)

Benge-Jones, Mark, *The Viceroys of India* (London: Constable, 1982)

Beresford, G. C., *Schooldays with Kipling* (New York: G. P. Putnam's Sons, 1936)

Blackburn, Henry, *Academy Notes* (London: Chatto & Windus, 1875–84)

——, *Grosvenor Notes* (London: Chatto & Windus, 1880–89)

Blunt, Wilfrid Scawen, *Memoirs* (London: Martin Secker, 1921)

——, *My Diaries: Being a Personal Narrative of Events, 1888–1914* (London: Martin Secker, 1921)

Blyth, Henry, *Smuggler's Village: The Story of Rottingdean* (privately printed, n.d.)

Boyce, George, *The Diaries of George Price Boyce*, ed. Virginia Surtees (Norwich: Real World, 1980)

Branca, Patricia, *Silent Sisterhood: Middle Class Women in the Victorian Home* (London: Croom Helm, 1975)

Brown, Ford Madox, *The Diary of Ford Madox Brown*, ed. Virginia Surtees (London: Yale University Press, 1981)

Buck, E. J., *Simla Past and Present* (Calcutta: Thacker, Spink & Co., 1904)

Burne-Jones, Edward Coley, *Burne-Jones Talking*, ed. Mary Lago (London: John Murray, 1981)

——, *Letters to Katie* (London: British Museum Publications, 1988)

Burne-Jones, Georgiana, *Address to the Electors of Rottingdean* (privately printed, 1894)

——, *What We Have Done* (privately printed, 1896)

——, *Memorials of Edward Burne-Jones* (London: Macmillan, 1904)

Campbell, Mrs Patrick, *My Life and Some Letters* (London: Hutchinson, 1925)

[Carr, Alice], *J. Comyns Carr: Stray Memories, by His Wife* (London: Macmillan, 1920)

Carr, J. Comyns, *Some Eminent Victorians: Personal Recollections in the World of Art and Letters* (London: Duckworth, 1908)

——, *Coasting Bohemia* (London: Macmillan, 1914)

——, *Reminiscences* (London: Hutchinson, 1926)

Carrington, Charles, *Rudyard Kipling: His Life and Work* (London: Penguin Books, 1986)

Casteras, Susan P., and Denney, Colleen, eds., *The Grosvenor Gallery: A Palace of Art in Victorian England* (London: Yale University Press, 1996)

Cecil, David, *Visionary and Dreamer: Two Poetic Painters, Samuel Palmer and Edward Burne-Jones* (London: Constable, 1969)

Cobden-Sanderson, R., ed., *The Journals of T. J. Cobden-Sanderson, 1879–1922* (London: Richard Cobden-Sanderson, 1926)

Cohen, Morton N., *Rudyard Kipling to Rider Haggard: The Record of a Friendship* (London: Hutchinson, 1965)

Colvin, Sidney, *Memories and Notes of Persons and Places, 1852–1912* (London: Edward Arnold, 1921)

Cook, Edward T., *A Popular Handbook to the Tate Gallery: National Gallery of British Art* (5th edn London: Macmillan, 1898)

Cox, Gwladys, *Aunt Trix: Mrs Alice Macdonald Fleming, Some Recollections* (privately published, n.d.)

Crane, Walter, *An Artist's Reminiscences* (London: Methuen, 1907)

Curzon, William, *The Manufacturing Industries of Worcestershire* (Birmingham: W. D. Curzon, 1883)

Dakers, Caroline, *The Holland Park Circle: Artists and Victorian Society* (London: Yale University Press, 1999)

Dalziel, E. and G., *The Brothers Dalziel: A Record of Fifty Years' Work* (London: Methuen, 1910)

Davies, M., *Unorthodox London, or Phases of Religious Life in the Metropolis* (London: Tinsley Bros., 1873)

Davis, R., George, A. R., and Rupp, G., *A History of the Methodist Church in Great Britain Vol. 2* (London: Epworth Press, 1978)

Dent, Robert, *Old and New Birmingham: A History of the Town and its People* (Birmingham, Houghton & Hammond, 1880)

——, *The Making of Birmingham* (Birmingham: J. L. Allday, 1904)

Denvir, Bernard, *The Late Victorians: Art, Design and Society, 1852–1910* (London: Longman, 1986)

Dever, Carolyn, *Death and the Mother, from Dickens to Freud: Victorian Fiction and the Anxiety of Origins* (Cambridge: Cambridge University Press, 1998)

Dewey, Clive, *Anglo-Indian Attitudes: The Mind of the Indian Civil Service* (London: Hambledon Press, 1993)

Dormandy, Thomas, *The White Death: A History of Tuberculosis* (London: Hambledon Press, 1999)

Dufferin, Lady, *Our Viceregal Life in India* (London: John Murray, 1890)

Du Maurier, Daphne, ed., *The Young George du Maurier: A Selection of His Letters, 1860–67* (London: Peter Davies, 1951)

Du Maurier, George, *Trilby* (London: Osgood, McIlvaine & Co., 1895)

Dunn, Henry Treffry, *Recollections of Dante Gabriel Rossetti and His Circle* (London: Elkin Matthews, 1904)

Dunsterville, L. C., *Stalky's Reminiscences* (London: Jonathan Cape, 1928)

Eliot, George, *The George Eliot Letters*, ed. Gordon S. Haight (London: Yale University Press, 1954–5)

——, *The Journals of George Eliot*, ed. Margaret Harris and Judith Johnston (Cambridge: Cambridge University Press, 1998)

The English Housekeeper, or, Manual of Domestic Management: containing advice on the conduct of household affairs, and Practical Instructions concerning the store-room, the pantry, the larder, the kitchen, the cellar, the dairy . . . The whole being intended for the use of young ladies who undertake the superintendence of their own housekeeping (3rd edn London: A. Cobbett, 1842)

Faunthorpe, Revd J. P., M.A., *Household Science: Readings in Necessary Knowledge for Girls and Young Women* (5th edn London: Edward Stanford, 1889)

Ferguson, Rachel, *Royal Borough* (London: Jonathan Cape, 1950)

Fildes, Frederic L. V., *Luke Fildes R.A.: A Victorian Painter* (London: Michael Joseph, 1968)

Fitzgerald, Penelope, *Burne-Jones* (London: Michael Joseph, 1975; rev. edn Stroud: Sutton Publishing, 1997)

Fredeman, W. E., *Pre-Raphaelitism: A Bibliocritical Study* (Cambridge, Mass.: Harvard University Press, 1965)

Freeman, Michael, *Railways and the Victorian Imagination* (London: Yale University Press, 1999)

Gilbert, A. D., *Religion and Society in Industrial England: Church, Chapel and Social Change, 1740–1914* (London: Longman, 1976)

Gillett, Paula, *The Victorian Painter's World* (Gloucester: Alan Sutton, 1990)

Gladstone, Mary, *Mary Gladstone: Her Diaries and Letters*, ed. Lucy Masterman (London: Methuen, 1930)

Gould, Tony, *Inside Outsider: The Life and Times of Colin MacInnes* (London: Allison & Busby, 1983)

Grayson, Rupert, *Voyage Not Completed* (London: Macmillan, 1969)

Gross, John, ed., *The Age of Kipling* (New York: Simon & Schuster, 1972)

——, ed., *Rudyard Kipling: The Man, His Work and His World* (London: Weidenfeld & Nicolson, 1972)

Haight, Gordon S., *George Eliot* (Oxford: Oxford University Press, 1968)

Hake, T. G., *Memoirs of Eighty Years* (London: Richard Bantley & Son, 1892)

Hallé, C. E., *Notes from a Painter's Life* (London: John Murray, 1909)

Halliday, Stephen, *The Great Stink of London: Sir Joseph Bazalgette and the*

Cleansing of the Victorian Capital (Stroud: Sutton Publishing, 1999)

Hamilton, General Sir Ian, *Listening for the Drums* (London: Faber, 1944)

Hanford, F. E., and Evans, G. A. C., *The Story of the Grange, North End Crescent, Fulham* (London: Fulham Historical Society, 1953)

Harrison, M., and Waters, B., *Burne-Jones* (London: Barrie & Jenkins, 1973)

Haweis, Mrs H. R., *The Art of Housekeeping: A Bridal Garland* (London: Samson Low, Marston, Searle & Rivington, 1889)

Hempton, David, *The Religion of the People: Methodism and Popular Religion, c. 1750–1900* (London: Routledge, 1996)

Henderson, Philip, *William Morris: His Life, Work and Friends* (London: Thames and Hudson, 1967)

——, *Swinburne* (London: Routledge & Kegan Paul, 1974)

Henley, Dorothy, *Rosalind Howard, Countess of Carlisle* (London: Hogarth Press, 1958)

Holmes, Sir Charles, and Baker, C. H. Collins, *The Making of the National Gallery, 1824–1924* (London: [no publisher cited], 1924)

Holt, Tonie and Valmai, *My Boy Jack: The Search for Kipling's Only Son* (London: Pen and Sword Books, 1998)

Hoppen, K. Theodore, *The Mid-Victorian Generation, 1846–1886* (Oxford: Clarendon Press, 1998)

Horn, Pamela, *The Victorian Town Child* (Stroud: Sutton Publishing, 1977)

——, *Pleasures and Pastimes in Victorian Britain* (Stroud: Sutton Publishing, 1999)

Horner, Frances, *Time Remembered* (London: William Heinemann, 1933)

Houghton, Walter, E., *The Victorian Frame of Mind, 1830–1870* (New Haven: Yale University Press, 1957)

Hueffer, F. M., *Ford Madox Brown: A Record of His Life and Works* (London: Longmans, 1896)

——, *The Pre-Raphaelites* (London: Duckworth, 1907)

Hughes, Kathryn, *The Victorian Governess* (London: Hambledon Press, 1993)

——, *George Eliot: The Last Victorian* (London: Fourth Estate, 1998)

Hunt, Violet, *The Wife of Rossetti* (London: John Lane, The Bodley Head, 1932)

Hutchinson, S. C., *The History of the Royal Academy* (Chapman & Hall, 1968)

Hyde, H. Montgomery, *Baldwin: The Unexpected Prime Minister* (London: Hart-Davis, MacGibbon, 1973)

Ionides, Alexander, *Ion: A Grandfather's Tale* (Dublin: Cuala Press, 1927)

Ionides, Luke, *Memories* (Paris: Herbert Press, 1925)

Ireland, Gordon, *The Balestiers of Beechwood* (published by the author, 1948)

Jalland, Pat, *Death in the Victorian Family* (Oxford: Oxford University Press, 1996)

Jenkins, Roy, *Baldwin* (London: Collins, 1987)

Jenkyns, Richard, *The Victorians and Ancient Greece* (Oxford: Basil Blackwell, 1980)

Kestner, Joseph A., *Mythology and Misogyny: The Social Discourse of 19th-Century British Classical-Subject Painting* (Madison: University of Wisconsin Press, 1989)

Kincaid, Dennis, *British Social Life in India 1608–1937* (London: Routledge, 1938)

Kipling, Lockwood, *Beast and Man in India* (London: Macmillan, 1891)

Kipling, Rudyard, *Wee Willie Winkie and Other Child Stories* (1890) (London: Penguin Books, 1988)

——, *Something of Myself* (1937), ed. Robert Hampson (London: Penguin Books, 1987)

——, *O Beloved Kids: Rudyard Kipling's Letters to his Children*, ed. Elliot L. Gilbert (London: Weidenfeld & Nicolson, 1983)

——, *The Letters of Rudyard Kipling*, ed. Thomas Pinney (Iowa City: University of Iowa Press, 1990–)

[Kipling, Trix, writing as] Beatrice Grange, *The Heart of a Maid* (Allahabad: A. H. Wheeler & Co., 1890)

[——,] Mrs J. M. Fleming (Alice M. Kipling), *A Pinchbeck Goddess* (London: William Heinemann, 1897)

[Kipling, Trix and Alice], *Hand in Hand: Verses by a Mother and Daughter* (London: Elkin Matthews, [1902])

[Kipling, Trix and Rudyard], *Echoes, by Two Writers* (Lahore: The Civil and Military Gazette Press, [1884])

Laidlay, W. J., *The Royal Academy: Its Uses and Abuses* (London: Simpkin, Marshall & Co., 1898)

Leslie, G. D., *Inner Life of the Royal Academy. With an Account of its Schools and Exhibitions, Principally in the Reign of Queen Victoria* (London: John Murray, 1914)

Letters Addressed to A. P. Watt and his Sons, 1883–1929 (London: A. P. Watt & Son, 1929)

Liversidge, Mark, and Edwards, Catharine, *Imagining Rome: British Artists and Rome in the 19th Century* (London: Merrell Holberton, 1996)

Lycett, Andrew, *Rudyard Kipling* (London: Weidenfeld & Nicolson, 1999)

Maas, Jeremy, *Victorian Painters* (London: Barrie & Jenkins, 1969)

MacCarthy, Fiona, *William Morris: A Life for Our Time* (London: Faber, 1994)

MacDermot, E. T., *History of the Great Western Railway* (rev. edn London: C. R. Clinker, 1964)

Macdonald, Edith, *Annals of the Macdonald Family* (London: Horace Marshall & Son, 1923)

——, *Thoughts on Many Themes* (London: H. R. Altenson, [1924])

Macdonald, F. W., *As a Tale That is Told* (London: Cassell, 1919)

Macdonald, George, *An Apology for the Disuse of Alcoholic Drink* (London: [no publisher cited], 1841)

Macdonald, James, *The Letters of James Macdonald, 1816–31, with Notes by his Grandson, F. W. Macdonald* (London: Robert Culley, 1907)

MacInnes, Colin, *England, Half English* (London: MacGibbon & Kee, 1961)

McInnes, Graham, *The Road to Gundagai* (London: Hamish Hamilton, 1965)

——, *Humping My Bluey* (London: Hamish Hamilton, 1966)

——, *Finding a Father* (London: Hamish Hamilton, 1967)

——, *Goodbye Melbourne Town* (London: Hamish Hamilton, 1968)

Mackail, J. W., *Life of William Morris* (London: Longmans, 1899)

——, *William Morris and His Circle* (Oxford: Clarendon Press, 1907)

Macready, Sarah, and Thompson, F. H., eds., *Influences in Victorian Art and Architecture* (London: Society of Antiquaries of London, 1985)

Marsh, Jan, *The Pre-Raphaelite Sisterhood* (London: Quartet, 1985)

——, *Dante Gabriel Rossetti, Painter and Poet* (London: Weidenfeld & Nicolson, 1999)

Merril, Linda, *The Peacock Room: A Cultural Biography* (New Haven: Yale University Press, 1998)

Middlemas, Keith, and Barnes, John, *Baldwin* (London: Weidenfeld & Nicolson, 1969)

Millman, Richard, *Britain and the Eastern Question, 1875–1878* (Oxford: Oxford University Press, 1979)

Moens, Colonel S. M., *Rottingdean: The Story of a Village*, ed. H. E. Blyth (Brighton: John Beal & Son, 1952)

Monkhouse, W. C., *Sir Edward J. Poynter, President of the Royal Academy. His Life and Work* (London: J. S. Virtue & Co., 1897)

Morris, Jane, *Letters of Jane Morris to Wilfrid Scawen Blunt*, ed. Peter Faulkner (Exeter: University of Exeter Press, 1986)

Morris, William, *Letters of William Morris to his Family and Friends*, ed. Philip Henderson (London: Longman, 1950)

——, *Collected Letters of William Morris*, ed. Norman Kelvin (Princeton: Princeton University Press, 1984)

Norton, Charles Eliot, *Rudyard Kipling: A Biographical Sketch* (New York: Doubleday & McClure Co., 1899)

——, *Letters of C. E. Norton with Biographical Comment by His Daughter Sara Norton and M. R. de Wolfe Howe* (London: Constable, 1913)

Oppenheim, Janet, *Shattered Nerves: Doctors, Patients and Depression in Victorian England* (New York: Oxford University Press, 1991)

Orel, Harold, ed., *Rudyard Kipling: Interviews and Recollections* (London: Macmillan, 1983)

Parris, Leslie, *The Pre-Raphaelites* (London: Tate Gallery, 1994)

Ponton, Dorothy, *Rudyard Kipling at Home and at Work* (Poole: published by the author, 1953)

Poynter, Edward J., *Ten Lectures on Art* (London: Chapman & Hall, 1880)

Reader, W. J., *Professional Men: The Rise of the Professional Classes in 19th-Century England* (London: Weidenfeld & Nicolson, 1966)

Reynolds, Graham, *Victorian Painters* (rev. edn London: The Herbert Press, 1987)

Reynolds, Simon, *The Vision of Simeon Solomon* (Stroud: Catalpa Press, 1985)

——, *William Blake Richmond: An Artist's Life, 1842–1921* (Wilby: Michael Russell, 1995)

Rice, Howard C., *Rudyard Kipling in New England* (Brattleboro, Vt: The Book Cellar, 1951)

Rivett-Carnac, J. J., *Many Memories, of Life in India, at Home, and Abroad* (Edinburgh and London: William Blackwood & Sons, 1910)

Roberts, Charles, *The Radical Countess: The History of the Life of Rosalind, Countess of Carlisle* (Carlisle: Steel Brothers, 1962)

Robertson, David, *Sir Charles Eastlake and the Victorian Art World* (Guildford: Princeton University Press, 1978)

Robertson, W. Graham, *Time Was* (London: Hamish Hamilton, 1931)

Roper-Lawrence, Walter, *The India We Served* (London: Cassell, 1928)

Rose, Andrea, *Pre-Raphaelite Portraits* (Yeovil: Oxford Illustrated Press, 1972)

Rossetti, D. G., *Dante Gabriel Rossetti: His Family Letters, with a Memoir by William Michael Rossetti* (London: Ellis & Elvey, 1895)

——, *Letters of Dante Gabriel Rossetti to William Allingham 1854–70*, ed. George B. Hill (London: Unwin, 1897); reprinted from *Atlantic Monthly* LXXVII (May 1896); (June 1896); LXXVIII (July 1896, August 1896)

——, *Letters to Fanny Cornforth*, ed. Paul Franklin Baum (Baltimore: Johns Hopkins Press, 1940)

——, *Letters of Dante Gabriel Rossetti*, ed. O. Doughty and J. R. Wahl (Oxford: Oxford University Press, 1965–7)

——, *Dante Gabriel Rossetti and Jane Morris: Their Correspondence*, ed. John Bryson and J. C. Troxell (Oxford: Clarendon Press, 1976)

Rossetti, William Michael, *Ruskin, Rossetti: Pre-Raphaelitism, Papers, 1854 to 1862* (London: G. Allen, 1899)

——, *Letters, Pre-Raphaelite Diaries* (London: Hurst & Blackett, 1900)

——, ed., *Letters, Rossetti Papers, 1862–70* (London: Sands & Co., 1903)

——, *Some Reminiscences of William Michael Rossetti* (London: Brown, Langham & Co., 1906)

Rothenstein, Sir William, *Men and Memories* (London: Faber, 1931)

Rubinstein, David, *Before the Suffragettes: Women's Emancipation in the 1890s* (Brighton: Harvester Press, 1986)

Ruskin, John, *Sesame and Lilies, Two Lectures by John Ruskin, LL.D., 1. Of Kings' Treasures; 2. Of Queens' Gardens* (Orpington: George Allen, 1887)

——, *Letters from John Ruskin to Charles Eliot Norton* (Boston: Houghton Mifflin, 1905)

——, *The Diaries of John Ruskin*, sel. and ed. Joan Evans and John Howard Whitehouse (Oxford: Clarendon Press, 1958)

——, *The Letters of John Ruskin to Lord and Lady Mount-Temple*, ed. John Lewis Bradley (Columbus: Ohio State University Press, 1964)

——, *Sublime and Instructive: Letters from John Ruskin to Louisa, Marchioness of Waterford, Anna Blundon and Ellen Heaton*, ed. Virginia Surtees (London: Michael Joseph, 1972)

——, *The Correspondence of John Ruskin and Charles Eliot Norton*, ed. John Lewis Bradley and Ian Ousby (Cambridge: Cambridge University Press, 1987)

Shonfield, Zuzanna, *The Precariously Privileged: A Professional Family in Victorian London* (Oxford: Oxford University Press, 1987)

Showalter, Elaine, *Sexual Anarchy: Gender and Culture at the Fin de Siècle* (London: Bloomsbury, 1991)

Spalding, Frances, *Magnificent Dreams: Burne-Jones and the Late Victorians* (Oxford: Phaidon, 1978)

——, *The Tate: A History* (London: Tate Gallery Publishing, 1998)

Strickland, Margot, *Angela Thirkell: Portrait of a Lady Novelist* (London: Duckworth, 1977)

Surtees, Virginia, *The Artist and the Aristocrat: George and Rosalind Howard, Earl and Countess of Carlisle* (Salisbury: Michael Russell, 1988)

Swinburne, Algernon, *Letters addressed to A. C. Swinburne by Ruskin, Morris, Burne-Jones and Rossetti* (privately printed for T. J. Wise, 1919)

——, *The Swinburne Letters*, ed. Cecil Y. Lang (New Haven: Yale University Press, 1959–62)

Thirkell, Angela, *Three Houses* (Oxford: Oxford University Press, 1932)

Thompson, F. M. L., *The Rise of Respectable Society: A Social History of Victorian Britain, 1830–1900* (London: Fontana, 1988)

van de Water, Frederic, *Rudyard Kipling's Vermont Feud* (New York: Haskell House Publishers, 1974)

Vicinus, Martha, ed., *Suffer and be Still: Women in the Victorian Age* (Bloomington: Indiana University Press, 1972)

——, *A Widening Sphere: Changing Roles of Victorian Women* (Bloomington: Indiana University Press, 1977)

Walton, John K., *The English Seaside Resort, a Social History, 1750–1914* (Leicester: Leicester University Press, 1983)

Waugh, Arthur, *One Man's Road* (London: Chapman & Hall, 1931)

Weeks, John, *The Dream Weavers* (Santa Barbara: Woodbridge Press, 1980)

Wildman, Stephen, and Christian, John, *Burne-Jones: Victorian Artist-Dreamer* (New York: Metropolitan Museum of Art, 1998)

Williamson, Philip, *Stanley Baldwin: Conservative Leadership and National Values* (Cambridge: Cambridge University Press, 1999)

Wilson, Angus, *The Strange Ride of Rudyard Kipling* (London: Secker & Warburg, 1977)

Winter, Alison, *Mesmerized: Powers of Mind in Victorian Britain* (Chicago: University of Chicago Press, 1998)

Wolff, J., and Seed, J., eds., *The Culture of Capital: Art, Power and the 19th-Century Middle Class* (Manchester: Manchester University Press, 1988)

Wood, Christopher, *Victorian Panorama: Paintings of Victorian Life* (London: Faber, 1976)

——, *Olympian Dreamers: Victorian Classical Painters, 1860–1914* (London: Constable, 1983)

Young, G. H., *Stanley Baldwin* (London: Rupert Hart-Davis, 1952)

Young, Kenneth, *Baldwin* (London: Weidenfeld & Nicolson, 1976)

Index